POSITIVE APPROACHES TO OPTIMAL RELATIONSHIP DEVELOPMENT

How can we get the most out of our close relationships? Research in the area of personal relationships continues to grow, but most prior work has emphasized how to overcome negative aspects. This volume demonstrates that a good relationship is more than simply the absence of a bad relationship, and that establishing and maintaining optimal relationships entails enacting a set of processes that are distinct from merely avoiding negative or harmful behaviors. Drawing on recent relationship science to explore issues such as intimacy, attachment, passion, sacrifice, and compassionate goals, the essays in this volume emphasize the positive features that allow relationships to flourish. In doing so, they integrate several theoretical perspectives, concepts, and mechanisms that produce optimal relationships. The volume also includes a section on intensive and abbreviated interventions that have been empirically validated to be effective in promoting the positive features of close relationships.

C. Raymond Knee is Professor of Psychology and Director of Graduate Education in the Department of Psychology at the University of Houston.

Harry T. Reis is Professor of Psychology at the University of Rochester.

Advances in Personal Relationships

Christopher R. Agnew
Purdue University

John P. Caughlin
University of Illinois at Urbana-Champaign

Susan Sprecher
Illinois State University

C. Raymond Knee
University of Houston

Although scholars from a variety of disciplines have written and conversed about the importance of personal relationships for decades, the emergence of personal relationships as a field of study is relatively recent. *Advances in Personal Relationships* represents the culmination of years of multidisciplinary and interdisciplinary work on personal relationships. Sponsored by the International Association for Relationship Research, the series offers readers cutting-edge research and theory in the field. Contributing authors are internationally known scholars from a variety of disciplines, including social psychology, clinical psychology, communication, history, sociology, gerontology, and family studies. Volumes include integrative reviews, conceptual pieces, summaries of research programs, and major theoretical works. *Advances in Personal Relationships* presents first-rate scholarship that is both provocative and theoretically grounded. The theoretical and empirical work described by authors will stimulate readers and advance the field by offering new ideas and retooling old ones. The series will be of interest to upper-division undergraduate students, graduate students, researchers, and practitioners.

Other Books in the Series

Attribution, Communication Behavior, and Close Relationships
Valerie Manusov and John H. Harvey, editors

Stability and Change in Relationships
Anita L. Vangelisti, Harry T. Reis, and Mary Anne Fitzpatrick, editors

Understanding Marriage: Developments in the Study of Couple Interaction
Patricia Noller and Judith A. Feeney, editors

Growing Together: Personal Relationships across the Life Span
Frieder R. Lang and Karen L. Fingerman, editors

Communicating Social Support
Daena J. Goldsmith

Communicating Affection: Interpersonal Behavior and Social Context
Kory Floyd

Changing Relations: Achieving Intimacy in a Time of Social Transition
Robin Goodwin

Feeling Hurt in Close Relationships
Anita L. Vangelisti, editor

Romantic Relationships in Emerging Adulthood
Frank D. Fincham and Ming Cui, editors

Responding to Intimate Violence Against Women: The Role of Informal Networks
Renate Klein

Social Influences on Romantic Relationships: Beyond the Dyad
Christopher R. Agnew, editor

Positive Approaches to Optimal Relationship Development

Edited by

C. Raymond Knee
University of Houston

Harry T. Reis
University of Rochester

CAMBRIDGE
UNIVERSITY PRESS

University Printing House, Cambridge CB2 8BS, United Kingdom

Cambridge University Press is part of the University of Cambridge.

It furthers the University's mission by disseminating knowledge in the pursuit of education, learning and research at the highest international levels of excellence.

www.cambridge.org
Information on this title: www.cambridge.org/9781107102743

© Cambridge University Press 2016

First published 2016

A catalog record for this publication is available from the British Library

Library of Congress Cataloging in Publication data
Knee, C. Raymond, editor. | Reis, Harry T., editor.
Positive approaches to optimal relationship development / edited by C. Raymond Knee and Harry T. Reis.
Cambridge, United Kingdom : Cambridge University Press, 2016. | Series: Advances in personal relationships
LCCN 2015049382 | ISBN 9781107102743 (hardback)
LCSH: Intimacy (Psychology) | Interpersonal relations. | Attachment behavior.
LCC BF575.I5 P67 2016 | DDC 158.2–dc23
LC record available at http://lccn.loc.gov/2015049382

ISBN 978-1-107-10274-3 Hardback

CONTENTS

v

FIGURES AND TABLES

FIGURES

TABLE

CONTRIBUTORS

JASON F. ANDERSON, University of California, Santa Barbara

ARTHUR ARON, Stony Brook University

ZACHARY BAKER, University of Houston

STEVEN R. H. BEACH, University of Georgia

THOMAS N. BRADBURY, University of California, Los Angeles

LORNE CAMPBELL, University of Western Ontario

AMY CANEVELLO, University of North Carolina at Charlotte

NOÉMIE CARBONNEAU, Université du Quebec à Montreal

JENNIFER CROCKER, The Ohio State University

LISA C. DAY, University of Toronto

DAVID C. DE JONG, University of Rochester

FRANK D. FINCHAM, Florida State University

SHELLY L. GABLE, University of California, Santa Barbara

YUTHIKA U. GIRME, University of Auckland

BENJAMIN W. HADDEN, University of Houston

EMILY A. IMPETT, University of Toronto, Mississauga

JAMES J. KIM, University of Toronto, Mississauga

C. RAYMOND KNEE, University of Houston

JUSTIN A. LAVNER, University of Georgia

KARISA Y. LEE, University of Rochester

GARY W. LEWANDOWSKI JR., Monmouth University

ROSS MAY, Florida State University

JAMES K. MCNULTY, Florida State University

MARIO MIKULINCER, Interdisciplinary Center (IDC) Herzliya

SARAH MOROZ, University of Western Ontario

AMY MUISE, University of Toronto, Mississauga

STEPHANIE D. O'KEEFE, University of Rochester

NICKOLA C. OVERALL, University of Auckland

BRETT J. PETERS, University of Rochester

HARRY T. REIS, University of Rochester

RONALD D. ROGGE, University of Rochester

JACI L. ROLFFS, University of Rochester

PHILLIP R. SHAVER, University of California, Davis

JEFFRY A. SIMPSON, University of Minnesota

TANYA VACHARKULKSEMSUK, University of California, Berkeley

ROBERT J. VALLERAND, Université du Quebec à Montreal

XIAOMENG XU, Idaho State University

PREFACE

The inspiration for this edited volume emerged from numerous sources, including a figment of our imagination that we affectionately refer to as "Sal the Jedi Master" who specializes in relationships. Sal made an earlier appearance to us in a commentary we wrote back in 1996 (Reis & Knee, 1996). We thought then that he had left us for good, but like the *Star Wars* series, he recently returned with fresh insights. On a series of particularly challenging mountain bike rides, Sal would appear and share various pieces of wisdom about the field of close relationships and the direction in which it has been headed.

His first pearl of wisdom went something like this: "Studying the negative, hmmm? Taken you far, it has, but at what cost? There is more to relationships than avoiding their dark side. The light side of the force must be embraced and understood with equal ambition, no?"

Sal was concerned about the literature's seeming assumption that a good relationship is simply the absence of a bad relationship. Clearly we resonated to Sal's suggestion (the force was with us). As we surveyed the most popular empirical perspectives on what produces good relationships, we agreed that most of them focused on what went wrong with relationships and how to avoid those events or how to deal with them after they had already occurred.

Sal's second suggestion was equally insightful. "From the positive side of the force, theories also benefit, do they not?"

Indeed, as Sal suggested, whereas theories that emphasize the study of positive psychological approaches had once been rare and empirically limited, contemporary empirical findings and theories make a compelling case for the independence of positive and negative relationship processes. Sal had helped us to realize that approaches that focus solely on the reduction of negative relationship experiences are potentially missing out on innovative ways to enhance positive relationship experiences.

On Sal's third visit, his suggestion was more obscure. "Optimal relationships are more than simply what we typically observe to occur, no?" We scratched our heads a few times and eventually realized that Sal was getting philosophical on us.

All sorts of relationship processes have been documented and observed to occur, and research has amply documented normative patterns, but that does not mean that what is normative and typical is necessarily what is optimal. Sal had provoked us to think about not what *does* happen, but what *can* happen.

Sal's fourth and final appearance came just as we were in the initial planning stages of the volume, pondering how we could best accomplish the goals he set for us. "Remember . . . a small army of Jedi who are attuned to the positive side of the force can achieve very great things." Clearly Sal was not referring to us, but rather to the potential colleagues and Jedi Masters we could reach out to for help in this endeavor. We set out to assemble the strongest alliance of inspired relationship researchers we could find.

We hope that this volume will promote theoretical and empirical research advances on facilitating the optimal development of close relationships. Relationship science has put forth numerous empirically validated theories and mechanisms that predict the likelihood of having a satisfying relationship. This volume both complements and extends these efforts. By focusing on the development and functioning of optimal close relationships, we can provide a broader perspective on what it means to have a "good relationship." We believe that this is what people aim for when they establish and then commit to a close relationship, yet too often these goals become obscure over time and circumstances. Relationship research can re-illuminate these intentions, as the chapters in this volume illustrate. Positive approaches can also facilitate the development of empirically validated interventions for promoting optimal relationships, and even brief interventions have been shown to be effective.

Here are a few examples of what we mean: satisfying relationships are those that mutually support and fulfill basic psychological needs for autonomy, competence, and relatedness (according to self-determination theory); that promote mutual responsiveness and felt security (according to attachment theory), intimacy (as in the intimacy model), and facilitate disclosure of both positive and negative events (as with approach motives and capitalization); that are characterized by harmonious rather than obsessive passion (according to the dualistic model of passion), in which partners can authentically express and embrace their true selves (authenticity models), and enjoy satisfying sexuality. Further, optimal close relationships are self-expanding (according to self-expansion theory) and are characterized by compassionate goals rather than ego goals, and forgiveness; and satisfy partners' relationship ideals (according to the ideal standards model).

The volume is divided into three parts. Part I introduces major theoretical perspectives on promoting optimal relationships. In particular, Reis, de Jong, Lee, O'Keefe, and Peters provide a framework on intimacy that distinguishes appetitive and aversive processes, and sets up the chapters that follow. Additionally, Knee, Hadden, and Baker (this volume) emphasize mutual fulfillment of basic psychological needs, and in doing so, attempt to integrate many of the concepts and mechanisms that follow into a self-determination theory perspective. Mikulincer and Shaver (this volume) present attachment theory, one of the richest and most empirically validated theories on close relationships. Finally, rounding out the major theoretical perspectives, Xu, Lewandowski, and Aron (this volume) discuss self-expansion theory's contributions to understanding optimal relationships. Part II introduces concepts and mechanisms that have been empirically shown to promote better relationships, ranging from capitalizing on positive events to the importance of passion and sex, the benefits of compassionate goals and sacrifices, and even behavioral synchrony and rapport. Part III sums up empirical research on both intensive and abbreviated interventions that have been shown to promote better relationships.

We hope that you enjoy this integrative volume as much as we enjoyed developing it. Who knows, after reading these chapters, perhaps Sal will appear to you with fresh insights!

REFERENCE

Reis, H. T., & Knee, C. R. (1996). What we know, what we don't know, and what we need to know about relationship knowledge structures. In G. F. O. Fletcher & J. Fitness (Eds.), *Knowledge structures and interaction in close relationships: A social psychological approach*. Hillsdale, NJ: Erlbaum.

PART I

MAJOR THEORETICAL PERSPECTIVES

Promoting intimacy: strategies suggested by the appetitive side

HARRY T. REIS, DAVID C. DE JONG, KARISA Y. LEE, STEPHANIE D. O'KEEFE, AND BRETT J. PETERS

The road to intimacy is well-traveled by both basic researchers and interventionists. At the intersection of their journeys lies the possibility that theoretically grounded research can suggest useful strategies for helping couples increase the level of intimacy in their relationships. The value of better integrating these two approaches has often been noted. For example, researchers commonly observe that therapeutic applications can provide tests of the real-world relevance of theories developed in the lab (e.g., Olson, Russell, & Sprenkle, 1980; Reis, 2002). Also, basic relationship research can identify promising new possibilities for intervening with distressed couples (Bradbury, 2002). Practitioners, on the other hand, contribute to relationship research by indicating some of the more common problems and patterns that appear in their case work, and by establishing "what works" in an ecologically valid setting (Cowan & Cowan, 2002).

In the case of intimacy, interventions, both informal and formal, are plentiful. For example, premarital skills-training programs typically focus on communication skills that help partners maintain or enhance intimacy, given the high potential for conflict that marriage entails (e.g., Markman, Stanley, & Blumberg, 1994; Rogge & Rolffs, Chapter 15, this volume). More generally, most couples' therapies focus on preventing or overcoming destructive patterns of communication and interaction, both of which are closely linked to intimacy (see Lavner & Bradbury, Chapter 13, this volume, for a review). In this chapter, we propose that this emphasis addresses only one side of the relevant relationship processes, namely the aversive side. A significant body of research, described later in the chapter, indicates that appetitive processes – approach-oriented processes activated by positively valenced cues or states – also play an influential role in the life of relationships. These processes, we believe, have received insufficient attention in the

Completion of this chapter was supported by a grant from the Netherlands Institute for Advanced Study in the Humanities and Social Sciences (NIAS) to the first author.

development and application of interventions to increase intimacy. This omission seems unfortunate, because intimacy itself reflects a largely appetitive process – that is, intimacy is a desired goal that people hope to attain and are motivated to pursue. Indeed, intimacy is one of the most prized outcomes that people seek from their close relationships (Reis, 1990; Reis & Gable, 2003). That being the case, interventions that target appetitive motives and processes may be better suited toward enhancing intimacy than interventions that focus on aversive motives and processes.

The distinction between appetitive and aversive processes in relationships provides a theme that cuts across most of the chapters in this volume. Traditional approaches to research and intervention have often seemed to assume that a good relationship is simply the absence of a bad relationship. Although historically sensible – a major impetus for relationship research has been (and continues to be) the desire to alleviate this all too often toxic source of human distress – the conflation of good relating with the absence of bad relating reveals a significant gap in knowledge and treatment: Once conflict has been alleviated, how can gratifying, meaningful, and enjoyable patterns of interacting be established? "Bad may be stronger than good," as Baumeister et al. (2001) concluded in their wide-ranging review of evidence from many areas of research, including relationships, but that does not imply that the elimination of bad is sufficient to create good. The premise of this volume is that successful relating requires a separate understanding of the distinctive appetitive processes that promote successful relationships. This chapter therefore provides a general framework for the rest of this volume.

The chapter begins with a discussion of the distinction between appetitive and aversive processes, explaining why we believe that intimacy is better characterized in terms of the former than the latter. This account will set the stage for discussions of several areas of relationship research that describe processes that are largely appetitive in nature and that suggest promising possibilities for intimacy-promoting interventions. In each section, we link lines of research within the appetitive tradition to existing or potentially fruitful interventions for promoting intimacy.

IMPLICATIONS OF THE APPETITIVE–AVERSIVE DISTINCTION FOR RELATIONSHIPS

Imagine running into an old friend who asks how your romantic relationship is going. Most people would begin their reply with a single adjective, located somewhere along a roughly univariate continuum ranging from awful to amazing. Phenomenologically, the characterization of affective ratings along a single dimension is effortless, familiar, and natural, which is probably one reason why it appears often in research. For example, the classic Osgood semantic differential model posits that people appraise most entities along three dimensions, the primary one of which is evaluation, ranging from bad to good (the other two dimensions are potency and activity; Osgood, Suci, & Tannenbaum, 1957). This primacy may reflect the impact of evolutionary forces, which have shaped the human brain to rapidly and efficiently evaluate whether a newly encountered stimulus is hostile or hospitable (Cacioppo & Gardner, 1999; Hunt & Campbell, 1997).

Although the single-dimension approach may be a useful heuristic for quickly summarizing one's assessment of an entity, considerable evidence now indicates that the underlying processes are better represented by a bivariate approach. That is, across diverse conceptual domains, researchers have found support for a two-dimensional model – one dimension denoting the presence or absence of unfavorable attributes, and the other representing the presence or absence of favorable attributes (which Gable & Reis, 2001, referred to as the *aversive* and *appetitive systems*, respectively). For example:

- Cacioppo, Gardner, and Berntson (1997) proposed with supportive evidence that the positive and negative aspects of an attitude object are assessed via independent mechanisms, the results of which are then combined to yield an overall attitude.
- In affect research, the causes and mechanisms underlying positive affects (e.g., elation, enthusiasm) have been distinguished from the causes and mechanisms underlying negative affects (e.g., sadness, fear, anger; Carver, Sutton, & Scheier, 2000; Watson & Tellegen, 1985).
- Several theoretical models of motivation and self-regulation distinguish processes designed to reduce the discrepancy between the self and desired outcomes from those that are intended to increase the discrepancy between the self and non-desired outcomes. Carver (1996) and Elliot (2006) referred to these as approach and avoidance motives, respectively, whereas Higgins (2011) described these motives as promotion and prevention orientations. In Gray's (1987) theoretical model, these tendencies are the products of functionally independent neurobiological mechanisms – the behavioral activation and behavioral inhibition systems.
- Most models of personality structure differentiate sensitivities to real or potential rewards (positives) and punishments or threats (negatives). In the well-known Big 5 model, extraversion and neuroticism are conceptualized in this way.
- Coping skills can be categorized according to whether they involve movement toward or away from stressful or disturbing events (Moos & Holahan, 2003).

Although these diverse constructs describe distinct behavioral domains, their conceptual parallels suggest the existence of an underlying common core, a notion that some of the aforementioned theorists have advanced. These theorists were treading a well-worn path: William James (1890), for example, commented that "present pleasures are tremendous reinforcers, and present pains tremendous inhibitors of whatever action leads to them," thus positing pleasure and pain as basic but distinct "springs of action" (both quotes, pp. 549–550). Similar ideas were offered by Freud and Pavlov, among others. Gable, Reis, and Elliot (2003) took a more empirical tack to this question, factor-analyzing measures from the domains noted earlier, to determine whether a pair of latent variables, representing separate appetitive and aversive factors, would emerge. They did – in several data sets spanning varied constructs, measures, and samples, a two-factor solution corresponding to the appetitive–aversive distinction provided a better fit to the data than several conceptually plausible alternative models.

In the domain of intimacy and relationships, however, the appetitive-aversive distinction has not gained much traction, although the idea has not been entirely ignored either. For example, consistent with the domain-specificity idea advanced earlier, Fiori and Consedine (2013) found that among first-year college students, more frequent positive social exchanges predicted better emotional well-being on positive dimensions (e.g., life satisfaction), whereas more negative social exchanges predicted poorer emotional well-being on negative dimensions (e.g., depressed mood). Newsom, Rook, Nishishiba, Sorkin, and Mahan (2005) found a similar pattern of results in a large national sample of older adults (see also Finch, Okun, Barrera, Zautra, & Reich, 1989). In a somewhat different vein, Fincham and Linfield (1997) developed a measure designed to separately assess positive and negative feelings toward a spouse, finding that each of these predicted a unique pattern of behaviors and attributions. This work has been extended by several researchers, who demonstrated that two-factor solutions (positive and negative) better modeled their data than a single-factor solution (bad-good), and that these factors uniquely predicted distinct outcomes (e.g., Mattson, Paldino, & Johnson, 2007; Mattson, Rogge, Johnson, Davidson, & Fincham, 2013). For example, in one study of romantic couples, positive appraisals, but not negative appraisals, predicted sexual satisfaction, whereas negative appraisals, but not positive appraisals, predicted hostile conflict (Mattson et al., 2013). In another study, women's relationship maintenance behaviors were related to both positive and negative appraisals, but men's relationship maintenance behaviors were related only to positive appraisals (Malinen, Tolvanen, & Rönkä, 2012).

The idea that positive and negative features of close relationships represent separable dimensions underlies recent interest in ambivalent relationships. That is, beyond being bad or good, relationships may also be ambivalent – that is, high in both good and bad qualities – or indifferent – that is, low in both good and bad qualities. In a series of studies, Uchino, Holt-Lunstad, and their colleagues have shown that ambivalent relationships have undesirable effects on health and well-being, compared to both positive (supportive) or negative (hostile) relationships (e.g., Uchino, Holt-Lunstad, Uno, & Flinders, 2001; Uchino et al., 2012; see Holt-Lunstad & Uchino, 2015, for a review). Ambivalence, as these researchers conceptualize it, may be similar to Gottman's (1993) description of volatile couples, for whom frequent conflict is tempered by recurrent expressions of affection (although in Gottman's work their balance of positive to negative is thought to be largely salutary).

It may seem surprising to some readers that the differentiation of positives and negatives is not more fully established in relationship research. After all, as mentioned earlier and as Fincham, May, and Beach (this volume) explain, it is a logical fallacy to assume that the absence of a negative indicates the presence of a positive. A person's leg may not be broken, but that does not mean that he or she is capable of running a mile at a fast pace. At present, there are few interventions for couples that directly target the advancement of positive relationship features. The good news, however, is that basic research in relationship science has generated theory and evidence concerning several relationship processes that are primarily appetitive in their operation. We next discuss six such examples, including possible implications for application.

RESPONSIVENESS

Partner responsiveness is key to the development of intimacy. Relationships deepen when people feel that their partners have been responsive to their "opening up" – that is, when they have revealed important, central aspects of the self, their partners have shown understanding, validation, and caring (Reis & Patrick, 1996; Reis & Shaver, 1988). Thus, whereas earlier models of intimacy development emphasized self-disclosure, it is now recognized that self-disclosure is relevant only insofar as it establishes the possibility for partners to display (or not to display) responsiveness.

Both self-disclosure and responsiveness may take myriad forms, spanning verbal, nonverbal, and behavior expressions. For example, one might reveal an important personal loss by speaking to a friend, by crying silently, or by staying home all day in one's pajamas; similarly, a partner might be responsive by saying, "I'm so sorry," by hugging the person, or by coming over and keeping the stay-at-home person company. Self-disclosure of self-relevant material, such as values, personal feelings, and private facts (Pronin, Fleming, & Steffel, 2008), is a necessary stage-setting part of this process but it also makes the discloser vulnerable to the responder. Interdependence theorists refer to this as a diagnostic situation, because the discloser can infer the extent to which the responder prioritizes being supportive of her needs and concerns from the listener's choice to be responsive or not (Murray, Holmes, & Collins, 2006; Simpson, 2007).

Numerous studies have shown that supportive partner responses to self-disclosure promote the development and maintenance of intimacy and closeness (e.g., Canevello & Crocker, 2010; Laurenceau & Barrett, 1998; Laurenceau, Barrett, & Rovine, 2005; Reis, 2006). On the part of the discloser, responsiveness signals the partner's understanding and concern, which normatively enhances the willingness to engage in further self-disclosure, to trust the partner's goodwill, and to commit to the relationship. Responsiveness also benefits the listener, in the manner of mutual cyclical growth, a concept that will be discussed in the next section. The discloser's commitment engenders a greater willingness to be responsive when the original listener self-discloses, effectively reversing roles and promoting intimacy from both partners' perspectives. Further adding to this cyclical buildup of closeness and connection, serving in the role of listener helps fulfill belongingness needs when the discloser accepts support (Hackenbracht & Gasper, 2013).

Given that self-disclosure and responsiveness foster relationship flourishing, it might be asked, to what extent is this an appetitive process? Traditional conceptualizations of this process emphasize relatively aversive contexts. For example, responsiveness is most often studied in two substantive contexts, conflict resolution and social support. Conflict resolution refers to the manner in which partners resolve differences of preference or opinion, or find ways to overcome actions and events that threaten their relationship. Social support refers to helping a partner cope with stressful or adverse life events. Both cases, in other words, concern the avoidance or amelioration of undesirable circumstances, which should be understood conceptually in terms of aversive processes.

Responsiveness has an appetitive side, which, although less well understood, also contributes to relationship intimacy. One such example concerns the role of a partner's responsive support in promoting progress toward personal goals and aspirations. Research on the Michelangelo Phenomenon indicates that a partner's responsive support of personal goals – termed behavioral affirmation in that work – facilitates movement toward those goals as well as relationship well-being (Drigotas, Rusbult, Wieselquist, & Whitton, 1999). This kind of support can also promote relationship development, as shown by Fitzsimons and Fishbach (2010), who found that people tend to feel closer to others who are instrumental in helping them attain desired goals (in that work, feeling closer is considered a motivated cognition that facilitates goal pursuit). A close other's success in pursuing personal goals may also produce vicarious satisfaction for partners (Beach et al., 1998; McCulloch, Fitzsimons, Chua, & Albarracin, 2011).

Another example of the appetitive side of responsiveness comes from attachment theory. Bowlby (1969) proposed that when the attachment system is dormant, other behavioral systems, such as affiliation, exploration, and sexuality, may become behaviorally salient. In other words, in terms of the appetitive-aversive distinction, when the aversive system is quiet, the influence of the appetitive system is more evident. Responsive support, experienced either in a partner's current availability or in mental representations of secure relationships, allows people to engage in these positive relationships processes. For example, secure individuals tend to socialize more enjoyably and more intimately, even with others who are not attachment figures (Bartholomew, 1990; Schwartz, Lindley, & Buboltz, 2007; Tidwell, Reis, & Shaver, 1996), and are more likely to enjoy sexuality as part of a healthy intimate relationship (J. Feeney & Noller, 2004; Mikulincer & Shaver, 2007). Responsive support and attachment security have also been linked to exploration in the achievement domain and in intrinsically interesting laboratory tasks (e.g., Elliot & Reis, 2003; B. Feeney & Thrush, 2010), although existing studies have not directly examined exploration in more relational terms. Presumably, exploration in relationships would involve openness and receptivity to novel relational experiences, a predominance of approach as opposed to avoidance motives, and an emphasis on thriving as opposed to maintaining safety (B. Feeney & Collins, 2015). Future research is needed here.

Many interventions target communication skills that are designed to enhance responsiveness (see Lavner & Bradbury, Chapter 13, this volume, for a review), although most of these seem oriented toward precluding, minimizing, or ameliorating conflict. An important possibility for the future will be to integrate a more appetitive approach to responsiveness in conjunction with these existing methods, perhaps by emphasizing the manner in which virtuous cycles can be initiated and maintained.

INTERDEPENDENCE THEORY AND MUTUAL CYCLICAL GROWTH

Interdependence theory describes the processes by which interacting partners influence each other's outcomes. Intimate relationships are always interdependent, of course, so the theory provides a useful model for explaining how each partner's actions influence the other's thoughts, feelings, and behavior. In its most popular application, interdependence theory is used to describe partners' reactions to conflicts of interest – situations in which one partner's personal needs, preferences, or goals directly contradict those of the other (Rusbult & Van Lange, 1996). Such situations are thought to be diagnostic of the state of a relationship, because they demonstrate how partners take each other's wishes and needs into account in deciding how to resolve these conflicts (Murray et al., 2006). Less well-known are the ways in which interdependence theory applies to more appetitive circumstances.

Rusbult and colleagues' (e.g., Rusbult, Olsen, Davis, & Hannon, 2001) model of mutual cyclical growth illustrates how increasing interdependence can promote the development of intimacy. Although intimacy is not explicitly discussed in most papers on interdependence theory, research indicates that relatively high levels of interdependence are necessary to develop and maintain intimacy (Baker & McNulty, 2013). Mutual cyclical growth is a dyadic process in which each partner's perception of the other's pro-relational behavior (behavior enacted to benefit the relationship) fosters his or her own pro-relational behavior, thereby increasing the overall level of relationship-enhancing behaviors present, in the manner of a virtuous cycle. For example, imagine that Ashley feels gratitude about Chris's kindness to her. These feelings should strengthen her trust in Chris and her commitment to their relationship, both factors that would increase her tendency to behave in a kindly manner toward Chris. Chris, perceiving Ashley's goodwill, should experience comparable gains in trust and commitment, which would increase his kindly inclination toward Ashley, and so on.

Virtuous cycles are less well-established in relationship science than vicious cycles, their less benevolent counterpart: for example, the pattern of escalating negativity known as negative affect reciprocity, in which partners respond to each other's disagreeable behavior with additional negativity. This pattern is one of the best predictors of divorce and breakup (Gottman, Coan, Carrere, & Swanson, 1998). Alternatively, virtuous cycles, in which positive behaviors are reciprocated, are less well-known, but they may nonetheless be influential in cultivating relationship well-being. Wieselquist, Rusbult, Foster, and Agnew (1999) demonstrated one such cycle in the context of commitment: Commitment inspires relationship-enhancing behaviors such as accommodation and sacrifice, which are interpreted by partners as signs of goodwill, thus inspiring trust and commitment, and the partner's own willingness to enact relationship-enhancing behaviors. It follows that this sequence would also enhance intimacy, in that the vulnerability inherent in intimacy requires trusting in a partner's well-meaning intentions toward oneself.

Recent research on gratitude provides another example of this process in an appetitive context. Expressing gratitude conveys trust to a partner, inasmuch as it acknowledges awareness of his or her benevolence (Emmons, 2004). Feeling and expressing gratitude toward one's romantic partner has been linked to higher communal strength and satisfaction in romantic relationships (e.g., Algoe, Fredrickson, & Gable, 2013; Lambert, Clarke, Durtschi, Fincham, & Graham, 2010). Additionally, when people feel appreciated by their partners they report showing more appreciation and being more responsive in return (Gordon, Impett, Kogan, Oveis, & Keltner, 2012). These effects persist, such that expressed gratitude is associated with increased next-day relationship satisfaction and feelings of connectedness in both partners (Algoe, Gable, & Maisel, 2010). It is easy to make sense of these findings in terms of mutual cyclical growth: expressions of gratitude prompt feelings of appreciation and commitment, which enhance one's willingness to enact relationship-enhancing behaviors toward a partner, which, when enacted, are likely to foster expressions of gratitude by one's partner, and so on. Altogether, this process indicates how expressions of gratitude may benefit both the provider and recipient of appreciative feelings.

The idea of mutual cyclical growth has broad shoulders: It applies to most behaviors that are beneficial to relationships and in which one partners' enactment is likely to foster feelings in the recipient that encourage him or her to behave similarly. Although the concept has not gained widespread recognition in relationship research or interventions, it may be seen as a particularly striking example of how a focus on appetitive processes may trigger potentially valuable new research directions for relationship science.

SELF-EXPANSION

The self-expansion model of motivation and cognition in close relationships (see Xu, Lewandowski, & Aron, this volume) proposes that people have a fundamental motivation to expand the self, in the sense of enhancing their self-efficacy by increasing their resources, perspectives, and identities. One way that people expand the self is by forming close relationships in which they "include others in the self." As romantic partners grow increasingly close, they incorporate certain aspects of their partners into their own sense of self, thus experientially gaining access to the others' resources, perspectives, and identities. In this sense, the self-expansion model can be considered the prototype of an appetitive process: Individuals improve themselves (i.e., move toward a desired state) in the context of deepening a close relationship.

Beginning a new relationship provides ample opportunity for self-expansion, as partners learn about each other and engage in new experiences together. However, as relationships progress and partners become accustomed to each other, opportunities for self-expansion within the relationship may dwindle, and the couple must find new ways to fulfill self-expansion needs and avoid the well-documented decline of relationship satisfaction over time (see Bradbury, Fincham, & Beach, 2000, for a review). Maintaining and promoting intimacy is one of the primary hurdles that long-term relationships face. Whereas many theories tend to focus on overcoming problems and reducing conflict (aversive relationship processes), self-expansion describes an intrinsically appetitive process. The model theorizes that if individuals can successfully meet the challenge of fulfilling their need to self-expand through activities that are associated with the partner, they and their relationships will benefit (see Xu, Lewandowski, & Aron, this volume, for a review). Self-expansion can be fostered in long-term relationships through (a) jointly engaging in shared novel and challenging activities, and/or (b) supporting each other's independent self-expansion (Aron, Lewandowski, Mashek, & Aron, 2013).

Shared self-expanding activities

In the first test of the hypothesis that shared self-expanding activities increase relationship quality, Reissman, Aron, and Bergen (1993) found that married couples who participated in 90 minutes of shared exciting activities per week experienced greater subsequent relationship satisfaction than couples who engaged in pleasant joint activities or couples assigned to a no-activity control condition. Aron, Norman, Aron, McKenna, and Heyman (2000) replicated this association in two surveys and three laboratory experiments, and further established that the association between shared self-expanding activities and relationship quality can be considered causal.

Consistent with the idea that self-expansion is an appetitive process, several researchers have documented the role of positive affect as a mediating mechanism of the shared-novel-and-challenging-activities effect in ongoing relationships (e.g., Graham, 2008; Strong & Aron, 2006). For example, in a 1-week experience sampling study, couples whose daily reports included shared activities that were high in "activation" (operationalized as feeling alert, involved, active, and excited) experienced greater relationship quality (Graham, 2008). Importantly, this association was mediated by positive affect, such that when self-expanding activities were shared with one's partner, a mental association between the partner and the positive affect was formed, reinforcing a sense of closeness and intimacy.

Self-expansion theory provides a useful perspective on closeness and intimacy in long-term relationships. In a longitudinal study, Tsapelas, Aron, and Orbuch (2009) found that current boredom was positively correlated with a decrease in relationship satisfaction 9 years in the future, and that this effect was mediated by closeness. Other studies have shown that experiencing self-expansion was positively associated with passionate, but not companionate, love (Sheets, 2014) and with long-term intense love (O'Leary, Acevedo, Aron, Huddy, & Mashek, 2012). These demonstrated effects have led interventionists to design marital enhancement programs along the lines of self-expansion theory. For example, Carson, Carson, Gil, and Baucom (2007) tested the benefits of a mindfulness-based marital intervention program, involving meditation, novel partner adaptations of yoga poses, mindful touch activities, and dyadic eye-gazing exercises. Mediation analyses revealed that the significant improvements in relationship quality produced by the program were attributable to the couple's sense of having engaged in novel and exciting activities together.

Partner support for individual self-expansion

Partner support for individual self-expansion may also enhance relationship quality, if people associate their partners with the positive affect inherent in personally acquiring novel resources, skills, or knowledge. For example, Fivecoat, Tomlinson, Aron, and Caprariello (2015) showed that relationship satisfaction increased among long-term partners who received active (rather than passive) partner support for an individual self-expansion opportunity, such as learning a new hobby. For people in shorter-term relationships, there was little or no effect of active versus passive partner support for self-expansion. Similarly, Gordon and Baucom (2009) found that high levels of individual self-expansion were strongly related to both partners' positive affectivity, which in turn helped to increase relationship satisfaction. These findings highlight the possibility that providing active partner support for individual self-expansion opportunities may be influential for promoting and maintaining intimacy in long-term relationships.

The research reviewed here points to an effective, yet simple, way in which people can promote intimacy, reduce boredom in their lives, generate positive affect, and increase relationship satisfaction. Self-expansion thus provides a prototype for designing practical, appetitively oriented applications that can be utilized by anyone, do not require intensive therapy, and rapidly generate positive feelings.

Fun in relationships

One of the major reasons why people choose to deepen certain relationships and not others is that they experience those relationships as fun. This can be seen, for example, in statements like "I just enjoy spending time with her" and "he makes me laugh," or, alternatively, in statements commonly heard when relationships dissolve, such as "we don't have fun anymore." Here we distinguish fun from self-expanding activities, discussed in the prior section, because there are many kinds of shared activities that are enjoyable that may not be self-expanding; for example, watching TV together, going to a favorite restaurant, or taking a walk in the park.

Fun might be considered a quintessentially appetitive process. Although little research has directly examined shared fun and its impact on relationship development and maintenance, several existing lines of research provide relevant insights. For example, Crawford, Houts, Huston, and George (2002) demonstrated that marital satisfaction was associated with a greater tendency to engage in shared, as opposed to independent, leisure activities. This association may be stronger when both spouses enjoy the activity itself (as opposed to participating so as to spend time with their partner; Crawford, 2009). Moreover, the drop in shared recreation that typically accompanies the birth of a first child has been linked to corresponding decreases in marital satisfaction during this transition (Claxton & Perry-Jenkins, 2008). Other studies, reviewed in the prior section on self-expansion, have found that experimentally induced increases in shared mild-to-exciting activities (e.g., hiking, seeing a play or concert) but not low-arousal pleasant activities (e.g., visiting friends, eating out) led to increases in marital satisfaction (Reissman et al., 1993).

Humor also relates to the development of intimacy and closeness. Both men and women rate "a good sense of humor" as a highly desired mate characteristic (e.g., Buss, 1988; Sprecher & Regan, 2002), and other studies show that marital satisfaction is higher among individuals who believe their partner has a good sense of humor (Rust & Goldstein, 1989; Ziv & Gadish, 1989). Humor may also help couples reduce tension and defuse conflict, promoting constructive conflict resolution. For example, more satisfied couples use humor more often than dissatisfied couples during conflict discussions (e.g., Carstensen, Gottman, & Levenson, 1995), and in one study humor use was associated with lesser distress and greater perceived resolution of the conflict (Campbell, Martin, & Ward, 2008). Although rarely studied outside of marriage, the benefits of humor for relationship development may not be limited to romantic couples. In one counterexample, Fraley and Aron (2004) found that a shared-fun laboratory task that involved drawing Dr. Seuss illustrations increased feelings of closeness between same-sex strangers.

These two examples suggest that having fun together may represent a particularly influential appetitive factor drawing people to close relationships. There are good theoretical reasons why this may be the case. Sharing an experience with another person tends to amplify the affective quality of that experience, both generally (Boothby, Clark, & Bargh, 2014; Rimé, 2009) and in the specific instance of fun (Reis, O'Keefe, & Lane, under review). Fredrickson's (1998) "broaden and build" model of positive affect proposes that positive emotions benefit individuals by strengthening their interpersonal bonds, a principle consistent with the idea that inclusion and acceptance satisfy the evolutionarily significant "need to belong" (Leary & Baumeister, 2000). Even more generally, a fundamental tenet of behaviorism is that rewards experienced consistently in the presence of a stimulus will come to be associated with that stimulus, which in this case would be a relationship partner. This linkage may be particularly potent in the case of high-arousal rewards. Excitation transfer theory posits that arousal will be attributed to any salient environmental factor – for example, the partner with whom an activity is shared (Zillmann, 1983). Of course, as such rewards diminish, relationships may become stagnant (Aron et al., 2000; Berscheid & Ammazzalorso, 2001).

In sum, focus on the role of appetitive processes in relationship development calls attention to the positive reasons why people seek out others and remain connected to them. The pleasure inherent in many types of social activity is surely prominent among these reasons and we therefore suggest that intervention research might consider how the fun with which most romantic relationships begin might be maintained. One possibility is reminiscent of Harvey and Omarzu's (2006) concept of "minding" the relationship, which proposes that couples prioritize their interaction with each other, rather than the many other demands of modern life. Although this practice seems unlikely to overcome significant relationship distress, it may well be that working to preserve the affective experiences that brought a couple together in the first place can forestall a certain level of deterioration.

CAPITALIZING ON POSITIVE EVENTS

Imagine you just found out that you received your dream job and have a strong desire to share this news with your best friend. This news is exciting on a personal level but could potentially be even more rewarding if your friend responds enthusiastically. Much relationship research has examined how partners respond to accounts of misfortune and stress: Are they empathic and supportive? But what about responses to reports of good news? The act of relating a personal positive event to a relationship partner with the hope of eliciting a caring response is termed *capitalization* (Gable, Reis, Impett, & Asher, 2004; Langston, 1994; see also Gable & Anderson, this volume). When this process unfolds successfully, intimacy and closeness may be enhanced; on the other hand, when the other seems distant or disinterested, intimacy and closeness may suffer (Gable et al., 2004; Gable & Reis, 2010).

People desire to share positive news with close others – indeed, Argyle and Henderson (1984) identified this as the most important rule of friendship. Responses to these disclosures may be more variable. Following Rusbult, Zembrodt, and Gunn's (1982) analysis of responses to a partner's disagreeable behavior, Gable et al. (2004) characterized responders' feedback to capitalization attempts along two dimensions, active-passive and constructive-destructive, resulting in four distinct response-types: (a) active-constructive; (b) passive-constructive; (c) active-destructive; and (d) passive-destructive. *Active-constructive* support occurs when a responder is excited, enthusiastic, and engaged with the positive event. Behaviorally, an active-constructive responder will elaborate on the implications and benefits of the shared event, while communicating a genuine attempt to appreciate the event's significance to the discloser. *Passive-constructive* responses convey a nominally positive attitude toward the event, but – unlike an active response – without elaboration or engagement with the partner's joy. *Passive-destructive* responses signal disinterest in the event, such as by changing the subject or focusing on the self (i.e., the responder) instead of the discloser. Finally, in *active-destructive* support, the responder may appear engaged in the conversation but expresses a negative assessment of the event, such as by emphasizing potential downsides or trivializing its importance.

Research has demonstrated that active-constructive responses to capitalization attempts are associated with satisfaction, closeness, and intimacy in romantic relationships (e.g., Gable, Gonzaga, & Strachman, 2006; Gable et al., 2004; Lambert et al., 2012; Woods et al., 2014). Gable and Reis (2010) theorize that a capitalization attempt gives partners an opportunity to show their concern for the well-being of the other. Whereas research usually investigates such demonstrations of concern in the context of ameliorating harm, positive events also provide relevant evidence – after all, instead of sharing the joy, partners might just as well feel threatened, jealous, or apathetic. In fact, in one set of studies, partner responses to reports of good news were stronger predictors of relationship longevity than partner responses in discussions of conflictual issues and stressful life events (Gable, Gosnell, Maisel, & Strachman, 2012).

It is thought that these benefits to intimacy occur because capitalization motivates partners to broaden and build their relationships (Fredrickson & Branigan, 2005). Research by Reis et al. (2010) supported this proposal, showing that when partners were perceived to respond enthusiastically, capitalizers acted more prosocially toward them on the following day. However, responses to a capitalization attempt will promote relationship well-being only to the extent that the capitalizer *perceives* the response to be engaging and enthusiastic. To be sure, such perceptions are facilitated by actual, enthusiastic responses (Reis & Clark, 2013), but a growing literature also suggests other influences; for example, individual differences that bias people to see their partners as more or less responsive (Shallcross, Howland, Bemis, Simpson, & Frazier, 2011), general patterns of enjoyable socializing (Shorey & Lakey, 2011), and one's own intentions to be responsive to the capitalizer (Lemay & Clark, 2008).

It bears mention that disclosing good news and *perceiving* an engaged, constructive, and enthusiastic partner is also associated with individual well-being: that is, higher levels of emotional well-being and open-mindedness, as well as lower levels of negative affect and loneliness (Gable et al., 2004; MacGregor, Fitzsimons, & Holmes, 2013; MacGregor & Holmes, 2011; Maisel & Gable, 2009; Reis et al., 2010; Smith & Reis, 2012). Some of the underlying mechanisms thought to be driving these benefits are that responding to good news serves to maximize the event's perceived value and memorability (Gable et al., 2004; Reis et al., 2010). Also, supporting a partner's attempts to capitalize may be infectious, begetting subsequent capitalization attempts by one's partner (Rimé, 2009; Rimé, Mesquita, Boca, & Philippot, 1991) and fostering a virtuous cycle that may help enhance and maintain intimacy.

Capitalizing on capitalization research

Given consistent findings that enthusiastic support for personal positive news promotes relationship well-being, researchers have begun to develop and test interventions based on this principle. In one study, Woods et al. (2014) assigned couples randomly to an intervention condition or a joint-activity control condition. Couples in the intervention condition listened to an audio-guided PowerPoint presentation that provided an in-depth explanation of the value of disclosing positive events in addition to tips about how to respond in an active-constructive manner. After the presentation, they were given handouts providing additional examples and engaged in a brief practice session. Couples in the joint-activity control condition went through a similar intervention except that the topic was how to discuss television with each other. (This control condition was used to rule out the possibility that working on communication skills or jointly engaging in an enjoyable activity would be responsible for any observed benefits of the training.)

Over the course of a month, dyads who engaged in the active-constructive responding intervention reported receiving more appreciation from their partners and higher relationship satisfaction relative to dyads in the joint activity control group. These results suggest that active-constructive responding is a skill that can be easily and rapidly acquired and utilized. Of course, further research is needed to replicate these results, consider its durability over time, and examine its boundary conditions (e.g., for which types of individuals and couples might it be most effective). Of particular interest will be the viability of this intervention with distressed couples, inasmuch as treatments for relationship dysfunction invariably emphasize improvement in managing conflicts rather than finding ways for partners to experience more sources of shared pleasure.

PROMOTING INTIMACY THROUGH SEX

Although researchers recognize that sex and intimacy can occur in the absence of each other, and that their underlying motivational systems are distinct (Birnbaum, 2010), in relational life, sex and intimacy are often intertwined. For example, sexual desire is often central to initial attraction, first sex often designates the deepening of a relationship, and pleasurable sex may powerfully bond partners and help maintain relationships (for a review, see Sprecher, Cate, Christopher, & Perlman, 2006). Less obvious are the processes by which sex may foster intimacy. In this section we discuss several possibilities that are suggested by considering sexual activity as an example of an appetitive process.

Affective consequences of sexual activity

Mutually satisfying sex brings with it a range of positive feelings: pleasure, joy, excitement, love, contentment, and tenderness. According to Fredrickson's (1998) *broaden-and-build* theory, events that trigger positive affect motivate further approach and broader engagement with the source of that affect, fostering creativity, exploration, and integration (see also Carver et al., 2000). In the context of relationships, good sex may encourage partners to broaden their engagement with each other, such as by nurturing a communal orientation toward the other and by increasing one's willingness to risk vulnerability by intimate self-disclosure and being emotionally open and receptive to the other. These ideas are supported by several diary studies demonstrating that couples whose sex is motivated by approach goals, such as pleasure or enhanced intimacy, rather than avoidance goals, such as to not disappoint one's partner, experienced greater relationship satisfaction and stability over time. In these studies, the effect of goals on relationship outcomes was mediated by positive affects surrounding sexual activity (Impett, Peplau, & Gable, 2005; Muise, Impett, & Desmarais, 2013; see Muise, Kim, McNulty, & Impett, this volume, for a review).

Good sex may also offset the effects of negativity in relationships. For example, in two separate diary studies, Little, McNulty, and Russell (2010) found that frequent and satisfying sex buffered the harmful effects of attachment insecurity on relationship satisfaction. More generally, other studies have shown that dissatisfying or disappointing sex, or sex engaged in begrudgingly, can reduce closeness and foster resentment (Augin & Heiman, 2004). In other words, the appetitive pull of the pleasures and positive feelings of good sex may mitigate the impact of aversive factors that might otherwise impede the unfolding of intimacy.

Oxytocin

One mechanism by which the pleasures of sex may enhance intimacy is through activation of the oxytocinergic system. Though growing evidence suggests that the relational implications of oxytocin may depend on contextual and individual differences (Bartz, Zaki, Bolger, & Ochsner, 2011), it is clear that oxytocin plays a role in fostering pair bonding between adult romantic partners (Young & Wang, 2004). Genital stimulation, sexual arousal, sex, and orgasm trigger the release of oxytocin in both men and women. In turn, oxytocin is associated with a host of behaviors and interpersonal processes that promote intimacy. For example, higher levels of oxytocin are associated with increased frequency and duration of eye contact and hugs, as well as feelings of trust, security, contentment, and well-being. Oxytocin also facilitates interpersonal processes that contribute to intimacy: enhanced feelings of support from one's partner; improved memory regarding the romantic partner; and enhanced perspective taking, empathy, and accurate identification of emotions (for review, see Campbell, 2010; MacDonald & MacDonald, 2010).

Sex as adult playtime

Surprisingly absent from research into couples' sex lives are investigations that either conceptualize sex as *play* or examine playfulness in sex. Studied extensively outside of the sexual domain, play has been defined as sustained and intrinsically motivated voluntary engagement in an activity (Garvey, 1977). In contrast to goal-driven behavior, play is self-reinforcing, exploratory, and improvisational. Across mammals, play functions as an adaptive means of learning, confronting challenges, and developing social skills and physical competence, in a context in which levels of positive emotions and enjoyable engagement are higher than levels of tension and conflict (Panksepp, 1998). In romantic relationships, play, like fun (discussed earlier), fosters positive interactions and emotions, builds affectionate bonds, and lessens the impact of stressors related to relationship conflict, parenting, and careers (Vanderbleek, Robinson, Casado-Kehoe, & Young, 2011).

Romantic play tends to be spontaneous and idiosyncratic to couples and may include private nicknames, shared fantasies and jokes, role-playing, games, and roughhousing (Betcher, 1981). Couples who approach sex in a playful manner may create optimal conditions for the development of intimacy and trust. Because play entails sustained and enjoyable engagement, it is likely to facilitate sexual arousal and attention to positive and sexually arousing stimuli and interactions (de Jong, 2009). Furthermore, because play is inherently involving, sexual playfulness may heighten engagement with one's partner and sexual stimulation while shutting out distraction, self-consciousness, and worries. Thus, sexual playfulness may enhance sexual pleasure, facilitate orgasm, and increase positive affect, and in doing so, foster intimacy.

A playful approach to sex may foster an openness that trickles over to other areas of the relationship. When playful sex involves novelty and challenge, it can be considered self-expanding (Xu, Lewandoski, & Aron, this volume). During playful sex, partners can try on new personas, express aspects of the self that they would not normally feel comfortable exposing, or reveal and act out previously hidden desires and fantasies. In turn, partners have the opportunity to be responsive to aspects of the self that are revealed, potentially setting the stage for the development of intimacy.

Sex, self-disclosure, and responsiveness

Sexual desire motivates people to seek sexual gratification and contact with each other. However, coitus is rarely the only goal. People also want to experience great sex, or at least good sex, which often involves experiencing and giving pleasure, trying new things, exploring positions and dynamics, and acting out fantasies. However, because sexual activity is intrinsically inter-dependent, these things are only possible if partners clearly communicate their desires and needs, either verbally or nonverbally, and doing so entails revealing deeply personal aspects of the self that are typically shared with very few people (MacNeil & Byers, 2009). Thus, the drive toward sexual pleasure brings with it the need to reveal core aspects of the self and the risk of painful rejection or humiliation.

Research demonstrates that higher sexual self-disclosure is associated with greater sexual satisfaction, because such self-disclosures promote a partner's understanding of one's likes and dislikes (e.g., MacNeil & Byers, 2005). In other words, when people make themselves vulnerable to each other in this way, they create an opportunity for their partners to demonstrate responsiveness in the sexual arena. Such responsiveness, in turn, makes it possible for people to feel sexually understood and valued by their partners (de Jong & Reis, 2014). Thus, by revealing, recognizing, and accepting aspects of their sexual selves, couples enact a sexually specific form of the intimacy process (Reis & Shaver, 1988) that may generalize to their broader relationship. Though only speculative, this possibility warrants future investigation.

CONCLUSION

Why do people establish close relationships? Although theorists have offered numerous answers to this question, a layperson's answer would likely mention the following factors: because they bring pleasure and offer opportunities for sharing in life's important activities, personal growth, and meaningful connections. It seems unlikely that spontaneous answers to this question would mention many of the factors that dominate the literature – for example, resolving disagreements in a constructive manner, forgiving a partner for infidelity or bad behavior, or staying committed through adversity. In this light, it seems striking that many, if not most, contemporary interventions target the aversive rather than the appetitive aspects of relationships. It would seem that these interventions, successful as they may be, aim to eliminate distress rather than to foster a thriving, happy, optimal relationship.

We do not dispute extensive evidence, mentioned in passing earlier, that indicates that "bad is stronger than good" (Baumeister et al., 2001). Nor do we dispute the fact that distressing relationships are the cause of significant personal, familial, and societal problems. What we do suggest, however, is that the presence of good is something more than the absence of bad. In other words, establishing and maintaining optimal relationships entails enacting a set of processes that are distinct from merely avoiding harmful behaviors. If relationship researchers are to fulfill the twin goals of creating an accurate, insightful empirical literature and of designing interventions that help people fashion the kind of relationship life that they seek, it will be necessary to consider appetitive processes and interactions as something distinct from the relatively more aversive processes and interactions that have dominated past theorizing and research.

One benefit of appraising relationship processes from the appetitive side is that it will direct researcher attention to what people want from their relationships, and how they might attain it, rather than focusing on what couples should avoid. Goal-striving is a relatively recent addition to the relationships literature, and much of this work is based on the premise that pursuing many of life's most important personal goals requires coordination between close relationship partners (Fitzsimons & Finkel, 2011). Most of the examples in this chapter describe social coordination of this sort; for example, the added value provided by shared fun or capitalization, and the synchronization of behavior intrinsic to responsiveness or good sex. It may be that appetitive processes can only be successful in close relationships when both partners contribute in an engaged, constructive, and well-coordinated way to their individual and shared pursuits. In contrast, it seems relatively easier for either partner to independently harm relationships; for example, by having an affair or being inconsiderate or argumentative. In this way, appetitive processes may better highlight the fundamentally interdependent processes involved in creating and maintaining optimal relationships.

This review was intended neither as a complete theoretical model of appetitive relationship processes nor as a comprehensive outline of possible interventions. Rather, we hope that this review has provided a menu of sorts that samples promising candidates from among the many options that an appetitive approach to relationships offers. As at any good restaurant, a menu is intended to whet one's appetite, but the proof is in what the chef delivers to the table. A great menu begins with sound conceptual understanding of how ingredients mix together, a goal toward which researchers and students alike may find the ideas expressed herein illuminating. We hope that this chapter serves up a plateful of inspiration for relationship chef-theorists who wish to satisfy the palate of those who seek to develop optimal relationships.

REFERENCES

Algoe, S. B., Fredrickson, B. L., & Gable, S. L. (2013). The social functions of the emotion of gratitude via expression. *Emotion*, 13(4), 605–609.

Algoe, S., Gable, S., & Maisel, N. (2010). Everyday gratitude in romantic relationships. *Personal Relationships*, 17, 217–233.

Argyle, M., & Henderson, M. (1984). The rules of friendship. *Journal of Social and Personal Relationships*, 1, 211–237.

Aron, A., Lewandowski Jr, G. W., Mashek, D., & Aron, E. N. (2013). The self-expansion model of motivation and cognition in close relationships. In J. A. Simpson & L. Campbell (Eds.), *The Oxford handbook of close relationships* (pp. 90–115). New York: Oxford University Press.

Aron, A., Norman, C. C., Aron, E. N., McKenna, C., & Heyman, R. E. (2000). Couples' shared participation in novel and arousing activities and experienced relationship quality. *Journal of Personality and Social Psychology*, 78(2), 273–284.

Augin, S., & Heiman, J. R. (2004). Sexual dysfunction from a relationship perspective. In J. H. Harvey, A. Wenzel, & S. Sprecher (Eds.), *The handbook of sexuality in close relationships* (pp. 477–517). Mahwah, NJ: Lawrence Erlbaum Associates.

Baker, L. R., & McNulty, J. K. (2013). When low self-esteem encourages behaviors that risk rejection to increase interdependence: The role of relational self-construal. *Journal of Personality and Social Psychology*, 104(6), 995–1018.

Bartholomew, K. (1990). Avoidance of intimacy: An attachment perspective. *Journal of Social and Personal Relationships*, 7, 147–178.

Bartz, J. A., Zaki, J., Bolger, N., & Ochsner, K. N. (2011). Social effects of oxytocin in humans: Context and person matter. *Trends in Cognitive Sciences*, 15, 301–309.

Baumeister, R. F., Bratslavsky, E., Finkenauer, C., & Vohs, K. D. (2001). Bad is stronger than good. *Review of General Psychology*, 5 (4), 323–370.

Beach, S. R. H., Tesser, A., Fincham, F. D., Jones, D. J., Johnson, D., & Whitaker, D. J. (1998). Pleasure and pain in doing well, together: An investigation of performance-related affect in close relationships. *Journal of Personality and Social Psychology*, 74, 923–938.

Berscheid, E., & Ammazzalorso, H. (2001). Emotional experience in close relationships. In G. J. O. Fletcher & M. S. Clark (Eds.), *Blackwell handbook of social psychology* (Vol. 2, pp. 308–330). Oxford, UK: Blackwell.

Betcher, R. W. (1981). Intimate play and marital adaptation. *Psychiatry: Journal for the Study of Interpersonal Processes*, 44, 13–33.

Birnbaum, G. E. (2010). Bound to interact: The divergent goals and complex interplay of attachment and sex within romantic relationships. *Journal of Social and Personal Relationships*, 27, 245–252.

Boothby, E. J., Clark, M. S., & Bargh, J. A. (2014). Shared experiences are amplified. *Psychological Science*, 25(12), 2209–2216.

Bowlby, J. (1969). *Attachment and loss: Vol. 1. Attachment* (2nd ed.). New York: Basic Books.

Bradbury, T. N. (2002). Research on relationships as a prelude to action. *Journal of Social and Personal Relationships*, 19, 235–263.

Bradbury, T. N., Fincham, F. D., & Beach, S. R. (2000). Research on the nature and determinants of marital satisfaction: A decade in review. *Journal of Marriage and Family*, 62(4), 964–980.

Buss, D. M. (1988). Love acts: The evolutionary biology of love. In R. J. Sternberg & M. L. Barnes (Eds.), *The psychology of love* (pp. 100–118). New Haven, CT: Yale University Press.

Cacioppo, J. T., & Gardner, W. L. (1999). Emotions. *Annual Review of Psychology*, 50, 191–214.

Cacioppo, J. T., Gardner, W. L., & Berntson, G. G. (1997). Beyond bipolar conceptua-lizations and measures: The case of attitudes and evaluative space. *Personality and Social Psychology Review*, 1(1), 3–25.

Campbell, A. (2010). Oxytocin and human social behavior. *Personality and Social Psychology Review*, 14, 281–295.

Campbell, L., Martin, R. A., & Ward, J. R. (2008). An observational study of humor use while resolving conflict in dating couples. *Personal Relationships*, 15(1), 41–55.

Canevello, A., & Crocker, J. (2010). Creating good relationships: Responsiveness, relationship quality, and interpersonal goals. *Journal of Personality and Social Psychology*, 99, 78–106.

Carson, J. W., Carson, K. M., Gil, K. M., & Baucom, D. H. (2007). Self-expansion as a mediator of relationship improvements in a mindfulness intervention. *Journal of Marital and Family Therapy*, 33(4), 517–528.

Carstensen, L. L., Gottman, J. M., & Levenson, R. W. (1995). Emotional behavior in long-term marriage. *Psychology and Aging*, 10(1), 140–149.

Carver, C. S. (1996). Emergent integration in contemporary personality psychology. *Journal of Research in Personality*, 30(3), 319–334.

Carver, C. S., Sutton, S. K., & Scheier, M. F. (2000). Action, emotion, and personality: Emerging conceptual integration. *Personality and Social Psychology Bulletin*, 26, 741.

Claxton, A., & Perry-Jenkins, M. (2008). No fun anymore: Leisure and marital quality across the transition to parenthood. *Journal of Marriage and Family*, 70(1), 28–43.

Cowan, P. A., & Cowan, C. P. (2002). Interventions as tests of family systems theories: Marital and family relationships in children's development, and psychopathology. *Development and Psychopathology*, 14, 731–760.

Crawford, D. W. (2009). Leisure activities. In H. T. Reis & S. Sprecher (Eds.), *The encyclopedia of human relationships*. Thousand Oaks, CA: Sage.

Crawford, D. W., Houts, R. M., Huston, T. L., & George, L. J. (2002). Compatibility, leisure, and satisfaction in marital relationships. *Journal of Marriage and Family*, 64(2), 433–449.

de Jong, D. C. (2009). The role of attention in sexual arousal: Implications for treatment of sexual dysfunction. *Journal of Sex Research*, 46, 237–248.

de Jong, D. C., & Reis, H. T. (2014). Sexual kindred spirits: Actual and overperceived similarity, complementarity, and partner accuracy in heterosexual couples. *Personality and Social Psychology Bulletin*, 40, 1316–1329.

Drigotas, S. M., Rusbult, C. E., Wieselquist, J., & Whitton, S. W. (1999). Close partner as sculptor of the ideal self: Behavioral affirmation and the Michelangelo phenom-enon. *Journal of Personality and Social Psychology*, 77, 293–323.

Elliot, A. J. (2006). The hierarchical model of approach-avoidance motivation. *Motivation and Emotion*, 30(2), 111–116.

Elliot, A. J., & Reis, H. T. (2003). Attachment and exploration in adulthood. *Journal of Personality and Social Psychology*, 85, 317–331.

Emmons, R.A. (2004). The psychology of gratitude: An introduction. In R.A. Emmons & M.E. McCullough (Eds.), *The psychology of gratitude* (pp. 3–16). New York: Oxford University Press.

Feeney, B. C., & Collins, N. L. (2015). A new look at social support: A theoretical perspective on thriving through relationships. *Personality and Social Psychology Review*, 19, 113–147

Feeney, B. C., & Thrush, R. L. (2010). Relationship influences on exploration in adulthood: The characteristics and function of a secure base. *Journal of Personality and Social Psychology*, 98, 57–76.

Feeney, J. A., & Noller, P. (2004). Attachment and sexuality in close relationships. In J. H. Harvey, A. Wenzel, & S. Sprecher (Eds.), *Handbook of sexuality in close relationships* (pp. 183–201). Mahwah, NJ: Lawrence Erlbaum Associates.

Finch, J. F., Okun, M. A., Barrera, M., Zautra, A. J., & Reich, J. W. (1989). Positive and negative social ties among older adults: Measurement models and the prediction of psychological distress and well-being. *American Journal of Community Psychology*, 17(5), 585–605.

Fincham, F. D., & Linfield, K. J. (1997). A new look at marital quality: Can spouses feel positive and negative about their marriage? *Journal of Family Psychology*, 4, 489–502.

Fiori, K. L., & Consedine, N. S. (2013). Positive and negative social exchanges and mental health across the transition to college: Loneliness as a mediator. *Journal of Social and Personal Relationships*, 30(7), 920–941.

Fitzsimons, G. M., & Finkel, E. J. (2011). The effects of self-regulation on social relationships. In K. D. Vohs & R. F. Baumeister (Eds.), *Handbook of self-regulation: Research, theory, and applications* (vol. 2, pp. 407–421). New York: Guilford Press.

Fitzsimons, G. M., & Fishbach, A. (2010). Shifting closeness: Interpersonal effects of personal goal progress. *Journal of Personality and Social Psychology*, 98(4), 535–549.

Fivecoat, H. C., Tomlinson, J. M., Aron, A., & Caprariello, P. A. (2015). Partner support for individual self-expansion opportunities: effects on relationship satisfaction in long-term couples. *Journal of Social and Personal Relationships*, 32, 368–385.

Fraley, B., & Aron, A. (2004). The effect of a shared humorous experience on closeness in initial encounters. *Personal Relationships*, 11(1), 61–78.

Fredrickson, B. L. (1998). What good are positive emotions? *Review of General Psychology*, 2, 300–319.

Fredrickson, B. L., & Branigan, C. (2005). Positive emotions broaden the scope of attention and thought-action repertoires. *Cognition & Emotion*, 19(3), 313–332.

Gable, S. L., Gonzaga, G. C., & Strachman, A. (2006). Will you be there for me when things go right? Supportive responses to positive event disclosures. *Journal of Personality and Social Psychology*, 91(5), 904–917.

Gable, S. L., Gosnell, C. L., Maisel, N. C., & Strachman, A. (2012). Safely testing the alarm: Close others' responses to personal positive events. *Journal of Personality and Social Psychology*, 103(6), 963–981.

Gable, S. L. & Reis, H. T. (2001). Appetitive and aversive social interaction. In J. H. Harvey & A. E. Wenzel (Eds.), *Close romantic relationship maintenance and enhancement* (pp. 169–194). Mahwah, NJ: Erlbaum.

Gable, S. L. & Reis, H. T. (2010). Good news! Capitalizing on positive events in an interpersonal context. In M. P. Zanna (Ed.), *Advances in experimental social psychology* (vol. 42, pp. 195–257). San Diego, CA: Elsevier Academic Press.

Gable, S. L., Reis, H. T., & Elliot, A. J. (2003). Evidence for bivariate systems: An empirical test of appetition and aversion across domains. *Journal of Research in Personality*, 37, 349–372.

Garvey, C. (1977). *Play: The developing child*. Cambridge, MA: Harvard University Press.

Gordon, A. M., Impett, E. A., Kogan, A., Oveis, C., & Keltner, D. (2012). To have and to hold: Gratitude promotes relationship maintenance in intimate bonds. *Journal of Personality and Social Psychology*, 103, 257–274.

Gordon, C. L., & Baucom, D. H. (2009). Examining the individual within marriage: Personal strengths and relationship satisfaction. *Personal Relationships*, 16(3), 421–435.

Gottman, J. M. (1993). The roles of conflict engagement, escalation, and avoidance in marital interaction: A longitudinal view of five types of couples. *Journal of Consulting and Clinical Psychology*, 61, 6–15.

Gottman, J. M., Coan, J., Carrere, S., & Swanson, C. (1998). Predicting marital happiness and stability from newlywed interactions. *Journal of Marriage and the Family*, 60, 5–22.

Graham, J. M. (2008). Self-expansion and flow in couples' momentary experiences: An experience sampling study. *Journal of Personality and Social Psychology*, 95(3), 679–694.

Gray, J. A. (1987). *The psychology of fear and stress* (2ⁿᵈ ed.). Cambridge, UK: Cambridge University Press.

Hackenbracht, J., & Gasper, K. (2013). I'm all ears: The need to belong motivates listening to emotional disclosure. *Journal of Experimental Social Psychology*, 49(5), 915–921.

Harvey, J. H., & Omarzu, J. (2006). *Minding the close relationship: A theory of relationship enhancement*. New York: Cambridge University Press.

Higgins, E. T. (2011). *Beyond pleasure and pain: How motivation works*. New York: Oxford University Press.

Holt-Lunstad, J., & Uchino, B. (2015). Social ambivalence and disease (SAD): A theoretical model aimed at understanding of the health implications of ambivalent social relationships. Unpublished manuscript, Brigham Young University.

Hunt, P. S., & Campbell, B. A. (1997). Autonomic and behavioral correlates of appetitive conditioning in rats. *Behavioral Neuroscience*, 111(3), 494–502.

Impett, E. A., Peplau, L. A., & Gable, S. L. (2005). Approach and avoidance sexual motives: Implications for personal and interpersonal well-being. *Personal Relationships*, 12, 465–482.

James, W. (1890). *The principles of psychology*. New York: H. Holt and Company.

Lambert, N. M., Clarke, M. S., Durtschi, J. A., Fincham, F. D., & Graham, S. M. (2010). Benefits of expressing gratitude for the expresser: An examination of gratitude's contribution to perceived communal strength. *Psychological Science*, 21, 574–580.

Langston, C. A. (1994). Capitalizing on and coping with daily-life events: Expressive responses to positive events. *Journal of Personality and Social Psychology*, 67(6), 1112–1125.

Laurenceau, J. P., Barrett, L. F., & Rovine, M. J. (2005). The interpersonal process model of intimacy in marriage: A daily-diary and multilevel modeling approach. *Journal of Family Psychology*, 19, 314–323.

Leary, M. R., & Baumeister, R. F. (2000). The nature and function of self-esteem: Sociometer theory. In M. P. Zanna (Ed.), *Advances in Experimental Social Psychology* (vol, 32, pp. 1–62). San Diego, CA: Academic Press.

Little, K. C., McNulty, J. K., & Russell, V. M. (2010). Sex buffers intimates against the negative implications of attachment insecurity. *Personality and Social Psychology Bulletin*, 36, 484–498.

MacDonald, K., & MacDonald, T. M. (2010). The peptide that binds: A systematic review of oxytocin and its prosocial effects in humans. *Harvard Review of Psychiatry*, 18, 1–21.

MacGregor, J. C., Fitzsimons, G. M., & Holmes, J. G. (2013). Perceiving low self-esteem in close others impedes capitalization and undermines the relationship. *Personal Relationships*, 20(4), 690–705.

MacGregor, J. C., & Holmes, J. G. (2011). Rain on my parade: Perceiving low self-esteem in close others hinders positive self-disclosure. *Social Psychological and Personality Science*, 2, 523–530.

MacNeil, S., & Byers, E. S. (2005). Dyadic assessment of sexual self-disclosure and sexual satisfaction in heterosexual dating couples. *Journal of Social and Personal Relationships*, 22(2), 169–181.

MacNeil, S., & Byers, E. (2009). Role of sexual self-disclosure in the sexual satisfaction of long-term heterosexual couples. *Journal of Sex Research*, 46, 3–14.

Maisel, N. C., & Gable, S. L. (2009). The paradox of received support: The importance of responsiveness. *Psychological Science*, 20, 928–932.

Malinen, K., Tolvanen, A., & Rönkä, A. (2012). Accentuating the positive, eliminating the negative? Relationship maintenance as a predictor of two-dimensional relationship quality. *Family Relations*, 61(5), 784–797.

Markman, H. J., Stanley, S., & Blumberg, S. (1994). *Fighting for your marriage: Positive steps for preventing divorce and preserving a lasting love*. San Francisco, CA: Jossey-Bass.

Mattson, R. E., Paldino, D., & Johnson, M. D. (2007). The increased construct validity and clinical utility of assessing relationship quality using separate positive and negative dimensions. *Psychological Assessment*, 19(1), 146.

Mattson, R. E., Rogge, R. D., Johnson, M. D., Davidson, E. K., & Fincham, F. D. (2013). The positive and negative semantic dimensions of relationship satisfaction. *Personal Relationships*, 20(2), 328–355.

Mikulincer, M., & Shaver, P. R. (2007). A behavioral systems perspective on the psychodynamics of attachment and sexuality. In D. Diamond, S. J. Blatt, & J. D. Lichtenberg (Eds.), *Attachment and sexuality* (pp. 51–78). New York: Analytic Press.

Moos, R. H., & Holahan, C. J. (2003). Dispositional and contextual perspectives on coping: Toward an integrative framework. *Journal of Clinical Psychology*, 59, 1387–1403.

Muise, A., Impett, E. A., & Desmarais, S. (2013). Getting it on versus getting it over with: Sexual motivation, desire, and satisfaction in intimate bonds. *Personality and Social Psychology Bulletin*, 39, 1320–1332.

Murray, S. L., Holmes, J. G., & Collins, N. L. (2006). Optimizing assurance: The risk regulation system in relationships. *Psychological Bulletin*, 132, 641–666.

Newsom, J. T., Rook, K. S., Nishishiba, M., Sorkin, D. H., & Mahan, T. L. (2005). Understanding the relative importance of positive and negative social exchanges: Examining specific domains and appraisals. *The Journals of Gerontology Series B: Psychological Sciences and Social Sciences*, 60(6), P304–P312.

O'Leary, K. D., Acevedo, B. P., Aron, A., Huddy, L., & Mashek, D. (2012). Is long-term love more than a rare phenomenon? If so, what are its correlates? *Social Psychological and Personality Science*, 3(2), 241–249.

Olson, D. H., Russell, C. S., & Sprenkle, D. H. (1980). Marital and family therapy: A decade review. *Journal of Marriage and the Family*, 42, 973–993.

Osgood, C. E., Suci, G. J., & Tannenbaum, P. H. (1957). *The measurement of meaning*. Urbana, IL: University of Illinois Press.

Panksepp, J. (1998). *Affective neuroscience: The foundations of human and animal emotions*. New York: Oxford University Press.

Pronin, E., Fleming, J. J., & Steffel, M. (2008). Value revelations: Disclosure is in the eye of the beholder. *Journal of Personality and Social Psychology*, 95(4), 795–809.

Reis, H. T. (1990). The role of intimacy in interpersonal relations. *Journal of Social and Clinical Psychology*, 9, 15–30.

Reis, H. T. (2002). Action matters, but relationship science is basic. *Journal of Social and Personal Relationships*, 19, 601–611.

Reis, H. T. (2006). Implications of attachment theory for research on intimacy. In M. Mikulincer & G. S. Goodman (Eds.), *Dynamics of romantic love: Attachment, caregiving, and sex* (pp. 383–403). New York: Guilford Press.

Reis, H. T., & Clark, M. S. (2013). Responsiveness. In J. A. Simpson & L. Campbell (Eds.), *The Oxford handbook of close relationships* (pp. 400–423). New York: Oxford University Press.

Reis, H. T., & Gable, S. L. (2003). Toward a positive psychology of relationships. In C. L. Keyes & J. Haidt (Eds.), *Flourishing: The positive person and the good life* (pp. 129–159). Washington, D.C.: APA Press.

Reis, H. T., O'Keefe, S., & Lane, R. D. (under review). Fun is more fun when others are involved. Manuscript under review.

Reis, H. T., & Patrick, B. C. (1996). Attachment and intimacy: Component processes. In A. Kruglanski & E. T. Higgins (Eds.), *Social psychology: Handbook of basic principles* (pp. 523–563). New York: Guilford.

Reis, H. T., & Shaver, P. (1988). Intimacy as an interpersonal process. In S. Duck (Ed.), *Handbook of personal relationships* (pp. 367–389). Chichester: John Wiley and Sons, Ltd.

Reis, H. T., Smith, S. M., Carmichael, C. L., Caprariello, P. A., Tsai, F. F., Rodrigues, A., & Maniaci, M. R. (2010). Are you happy for me? How sharing positive events with others provides personal and interpersonal benefits. *Journal of Personality and Social Psychology*, 99, 311–329.

Reissman, C., Aron, A., & Bergen, M. R. (1993). Shared activities and marital satisfaction: Causal direction and self-expansion versus boredom. *Journal of Social and Personal Relationships*, 1, 243–254.

Rimé, B. (2009). Emotion elicits the social sharing of emotion: Theory and empirical review. *Emotion Review*, 1(1), 60–85.

Rimé, B., Mesquita, B., Boca, S., & Philippot, P. (1991). Beyond the emotional event: Six studies on the social sharing of emotion. *Cognition & Emotion*, 5(5–6), 435–465.

Rusbult, C. E., Olsen, N., Davis, J. L., Hannon, P. A. (2001). Commitment and relationship maintenance mechanisms. In J. H. Harvey & A. Wenzel (Eds.), *Close romantic relationships: Maintenance and enhancement* (pp. 87–113). Mahwah, NJ: Erlbaum.

Rusbult, C. E. & Van Lange, P. A. M. (1996). Interdependence processes. In E. T. Higgins & A. Kruglanski (Eds.), *Social psychology: Handbook of basic mechanisms and processes* (pp. 564–596). New York: Guilford.

Rusbult, C. E., Zembrodt, I. M., & Gunn, L. K. (1982). Exit, voice, loyalty, and neglect: Responses to dissatisfaction in romantic involvements. *Journal of Personality and Social Psychology*, 43(6), 1230–1242.

Rust, J., & Goldstein, J. (1989). Humor in marital adjustment. *Humor-International Journal of Humor Research*, 2(3), 217–224.

Schwartz, J. P., Lindley, L. D., & Buboltz Jr, W. C. (2007). Adult attachment orientations: Relation to affiliation motivation. *Counselling Psychology Quarterly*, 20(3), 253–265.

Shallcross, S. L., Howland, M., Bemis, J., Simpson, J. A., & Frazier, P. (2011). Not "capitalizing" on social capitalization interactions: The role of attachment insecurity. *Journal of Family Psychology*, 25, 77–85.

Sheets, V. L. (2014). Passion for life: Self-expansion and passionate love across the life span. *Journal of Social and Personal Relationships*, 31(7), 958–974.

Shorey, R. C., & Lakey, B. (2011). Perceived and capitalization support are substantially similar: Implications for social support theory. *Personality and Social Psychology Bulletin*, 37, 1068–1079.

Simpson, J. A. (2007). Foundations of interpersonal trust. In A. W. Kruglanski & E. T. Higgins (Eds.), *Social psychology: Handbook of basic principles* (2nd ed., pp. 587–607). New York: Guilford Press.

Smith, S. M., & Reis, H. T. (2012). Perceived responses to capitalization attempts are influenced by self-esteem and relationship threat. *Personal Relationships*, 19, 367–385.

Sprecher, S., Cate, R. M., Christopher, F. S., & Perlman, D. (2006). Sexuality in close relationships. In A. Vangelisti & D. Perlman (Eds.), *The Cambridge handbook of personal relationships* (pp. 463–482). New York: Cambridge University Press.

Sprecher, S., & Regan, P. C. (2002). Liking some things (in some people) more than others: Partner preferences in romantic relationships and friendships. *Journal of Social and Personal Relationships*, 19(4), 463–481.

Strong, G., & Aron, A. (2006). The effect of shared participation in novel and challenging activities on experienced relationship quality: Is it mediated by high positive affect? In K. D. Vohs & E. J. Finkel (Eds.), *Self and relationships: Connecting intrapersonal and interpersonal processes* (pp. 342–359). New York: Guilford Press.

Tidwell, M. O., Reis, H. T., & Shaver, P. R. (1996). Attachment, attractiveness, and social interaction: A diary study. *Journal of Personality and Social Psychology*, 71, 729–745.

Tsapelas, I., Aron, A., & Orbuch, T. (2009). Marital boredom now predicts less satisfaction 9 years later. *Psychological Science*, 20(5), 543–545.

Uchino, B. N., Cawthon, R. M., Smith, T. W., Light, K. C., McKenzie, J., Carlisle, M., . . . & Bowen, K. (2012). Social relationships and health: Is feeling positive, negative, or both (ambivalent) about your social ties related to telomeres? *Health Psychology*, 31(6), 789–796.

Uchino, B. N., Holt-Lunstad, J., Uno, D., & Flinders, J. B. (2001). Heterogeneity in the social networks of young and older adults: Prediction of mental health and cardiovascular reactivity during acute stress. *Journal of Behavioral Medicine*, 24(4), 361–382.

Vanderbleek, L., Robinson, E. H., Casado-Kehoe, M., & Young, M. E. (2011). The relationship between play and couple satisfaction and stability. *The Family Journal*, 19, 132–139.

Watson, D., & Tellegen, A. (1985). Toward a consensual structure of mood. *Psychological Bulletin*, 98, 291–235.

Wieselquist, J., Rusbult, C. E., Foster, C. A., & Agnew, C. R. (1999). Commitment, pro-relationship behavior, and trust in close relationships. *Journal of Personality and Social Psychology*, 77, 942–966.

Woods, S., Lambert, N., Brown, P., Fincham, F., & May, R. (2014). "I'm so excited for you!" How an enthusiastic responding intervention enhances close relationships. *Journal of Social and Personal Relationships*, 32, 24–40.

Young, L. J., & Wang, Z. (2004). The neurobiology of pair bonding. *Nature Neuroscience, 7*, 1048–1054.

Zillmann, D. (1983). Transfer of excitation in emotional behavior. In J. T. Cacioppo & R. E. Petty (Eds.), *Social psychophysiology: A sourcebook* (pp. 215–240). New York: Guilford Press.

Ziv, A., & Gadish, O. (1989). Humor and marital satisfaction. *Journal of Social Psychology, 129*(6), 759–768.

2

Optimal relationships as mutual fulfillment of self-determination theory's basic psychological needs

C. RAYMOND KNEE, BENJAMIN W. HADDEN, AND ZACHARY BAKER

> It isn't normal to know what we want. It is a rare and difficult psychological achievement.
> – Abraham Maslow

As Abraham Maslow suggests, it can be difficult to know what one wants, but perhaps even more challenging and important to know what one *needs*. Further, the additional challenge of being responsive to one's partner's needs places us at the very crux of what cultivating optimal relationships involves. Knowing one's own and one's partner's needs and managing the dynamic to facilitate mutual fulfillment of those needs, on an ongoing basis, is one of the pivotal challenges for relationship partners. In this chapter, we present a motivational perspective on the development of optimal relationships. Self-determination theory (SDT; Deci & Ryan, 1985, 2000, 2008) is a theory of motivation that incorporates developmental and situational influences on optimal individual psychological health and well-being. Although it originally emphasized individual well-being, it can also be viewed as a theory of optimal relationship development and functioning (Deci & Ryan, 2014; Knee, Hadden, Porter, & Rodriguez, 2013; La Guardia & Patrick, 2008).

In this chapter, we examine how SDT's concept of basic psychological needs, and the interpersonal processes and mechanisms that stem from mutual need fulfillment, offer a novel and integrative perspective on optimal relationship development. We first present SDT's perspective on basic psychological needs. We then discuss how need fulfillment facilitates true-self involvement and self-determined relationship motivation, along with their downstream relationship benefits. Finally, we offer an integration of SDT with several major theoretical perspectives, concepts, and mechanisms on optimal close relationships to illustrate the utility and explanatory power of this framework.

WHAT DOES SELF-DETERMINATION MEAN?

According to SDT (Deci & Ryan, 1985, 2000, 2008), being self-determined means that one's actions are relatively autonomous, freely chosen, and fully endorsed by the individual rather than coerced or pressured by external forces or internal expectations. This definition of autonomy emphasizes authenticity of choices and behaviors that are congruent with one's needs; a mindful, reflective awareness of those needs; and the capacity of one's social environment to support them. The "self" in SDT thus refers to those aspects of a person's identity that have been more fully internalized and adopted and endorsed by the person. This is sometimes referred to as "core self," "true self," or "integrated self" in the literature. Hereon, we will use the term *true self* to mean the SDT definition of self. It should be noted that SDT's use of the terms "autonomy" and "self-determination" does not suggest independence strivings (Murray, 1938), detachment (Steinberg & Silverberg, 1986), or independence from others (Markus, Kitayama, & Heiman, 1996). These other uses of autonomy have been characterized elsewhere as "reactive autonomy" and distinguished from SDT's notion of reflective autonomy in several ways (Koestner & Losier, 1996). For example, reflective autonomy predicted more positive thoughts on a daily basis as well as better mood regulation, more intimate and pleasurable interactions with peers, and more openness to expert advice, compared to reactive autonomy. Fundamentally, SDT's construct of autonomy reflects an integration of the behavior with one's true self.

Within close relationships, self-determination refers to endorsing one's own involvement in the relationship fully, at the true-self level rather than feeling coerced, obligated, guilty, or not knowing why one is involved in the relationship (Knee, Lonsbary, Canevello, & Patrick, 2005). Before we can discuss SDT and close relationships, we first turn to basic psychological needs and the motivation continuum. Fulfillment of basic needs promotes self-determined motivation and true-self involvement, and these are what allow optimal relationship development and more effective relationship mechanisms and processes.

Basic psychological need fulfillment

In SDT, needs specify innate psychological nutriments that are essential for ongoing psychological growth, integrity, and well-being (Deci & Ryan, 2000). According to SDT, optimal psychological health and well-being emerge from the satisfaction of basic psychological needs for autonomy, competence, and relatedness. Need for autonomy reflects the need to feel that one's behavior is personally endorsed and initiated, reflecting one's true self. In a close relationship, this means being autonomously motivated to be involved in the relationship, being present and engaged with a partner volitionally, and feeling free to express who one truly is, without avoiding, or concealing core aspects of oneself from that person.

Need for competence reflects the need to feel competent and effective at what one does. A broad literature has supported the importance of ongoing feelings of competence for optimal functioning and well-being (Bandura, 1977; Carver & Scheier, 1990; White, 1959). In a close relationship, this means feeling capable and effective when with the partner, having the ability to effectively express one's thoughts and needs, and feeling capable of negotiating challenges when they arise. Competence in close relationships is conceptually similar to relationship efficacy (Fincham, Harold, & Gano-Phillips, 2000; Lopez, Morua, & Rice, 2007).

Need for relatedness reflects the need to experience a sense of belonging, attachment, and intimacy with others (Deci & Ryan, 2000). Baumeister and Leary (1995) referred to this as the need to belong, and they reviewed extensive evidence on belongingness as a vital human motivation. Need for relatedness also derives from perspectives on intimacy and closeness (Reis & Patrick, 1996). For example, Reis and Patrick (1996) defined intimacy in terms of reciprocal responsiveness to feeling understood, validated, and cared for, and experiencing these ingredients of intimacy results in optimal psychological and relationship functioning.

Fulfillment of relatedness needs might seem most obviously important to optimal close relationships, given that it embodies intimacy, closeness, and connection. Indeed, of the three needs, relatedness fulfillment is the strongest predictor of relationship quality indicators such as satisfaction, closeness, and commitment, although autonomy and competence play significant unique roles in predicting these indicators as well (Patrick, Knee, Canevello, & Lonsbary, 2007). It is also important to note that needs for autonomy and relatedness, as defined by SDT, are complementary. Experiencing autonomy allows one to connect and relate authentically and meaningfully with close others and is associated with more positive and honest social interactions (Hodgins, Koestner, & Duncan, 1996; Koestner & Losier, 1996).

Support of these basic psychological needs facilitates development of self-determined motivation. Individuals' caregivers, romantic partners, teachers, friends, families, and larger social ties may provide ongoing support for these needs to varying degrees. These social supports, and individuals' negotiation among them for psychological need fulfillment, come to define the degree of self-determined motivation for activities and determine where one's behavior falls along the motivation continuum. Empirical support for this process comes from studies indicating that, for example, people are more securely attached to, and more likely to emotionally rely on, those who meet their needs for autonomy, competence, and relatedness (La Guardia, Ryan, Couchman, & Deci, 2000; Ryan, La Guardia, Solky-Butzel, Chirkov, & Kim, 2005), and that fulfillment of these psychological needs predicts general well-being (Reis, Sheldon, Gable, Roscoe, & Ryan, 2000; Sheldon, Ryan, & Reis, 1996), and relational well-being (Patrick et al., 2007). Additionally, individuals' perceptions that their friends support their autonomy strivings predict greater overall need satisfaction and positive relationship quality (Deci, La Guardia, Moller, Scheiner, & Ryan, 2006). Further, both partners' levels of need fulfillment uniquely predict one's own relationship functioning and well-being, attesting to the mutuality of need fulfillment (Patrick et al., 2007).

For romantic relationships more specifically, this psychological need fulfillment perspective suggests that optimal close relationships involve more than simply feeling satisfied. Relational well-being is thought to emerge when the relationship dynamic supports the basic needs of both partners, promoting autonomous motivation for being in the relationship, which in turn facilitates how the couple approaches and manages threats, disagreements, and conflicts, and promotes understanding, non-defensiveness, and partner support (Blais, Sabourin, Boucher, & Vallerand, 1990; Hadden, Rodriguez, Knee, & Porter, in press; Knee et al., 2005; Patrick et al., 2007).

The continuum of self-determined motivation

Fulfillment of basic psychological needs for autonomy, competence, and relatedness promotes self-determined motivation. A key principle of SDT is that not all enacted behaviors are regulated by the true self. Behaviors can be placed along a regulation continuum from those that are almost entirely *not* regulated by the true self to those that are almost entirely determined by the true self. The distinction at the various levels concerns the degree to which the regulated behavior has become integrated into one's sense of identity. At the far end of the continuum, behaviors lack intention. These are behaviors for which people do not know why they do them – they just go through the motions. For example, perhaps a person does not know why he or she is in the relationship, and there is no longer anything motivating him or her to remain in the relationship. At the next step, behaviors that are engaged because of threats, rewards, and demands are externally regulated. For example, perhaps one is in the relationship because important others have said how proud they are of one's relationship and one would not want to disappoint them. Behaviors that are enacted out of internal pressures and expectations are one step more internalized within the true self because the expectations are now largely "in one's head," but the origin of regulation still remains outside of the true self. These "introjected" behaviors are enacted out of guilt or to satisfy ego-related concerns about one's image, popularity, or worth. For example, perhaps the person would feel guilty and lose self-respect if he or she were not in the relationship, or perhaps he or she is in the relationship because it validates his or her sense of self-worth.

Behaviors become more reflective and expressive of true self to the degree that they involve valuing and accepting the behavior as being important to one's identity. For example, perhaps a person is in the relationship because it allows him or her to fulfill chosen life goals and experiences. Behaviors can be further integrated into one's true self when they resonate with higher order or overarching identities. For example, perhaps being in this relationship allows the person to experience who they are and also to become the person they truly want to be. Finally, behaviors can be regulated by the true self in the fullest, most unobtrusive sense when the motivation for them is intrinsic, meaning that they are simply enjoyable and enacted for only the spontaneous positive feelings that are not separable from the behavior itself. For example, perhaps one is in the relationship because of the stimulating, exciting moments and experiences that he or she has with the partner. One's motivation for being in the relationship would then be intrinsically motivated and fully self-determined.

Thus, according to SDT, not all forms of motivation for one's activities, including one's relationships, are equal (Deci & Ryan, 2008). They vary in terms of how much they involve one's true self and identity. Further, those pursuits that are more fully self-aware, self-expressive, and true-self-involved come with a number of advantages (Hodgins & Knee, 2002; Sheldon, Ryan, Deci, & Kasser, 2004), and this includes one's investment in one's relationships (Deci & Ryan, 2014; Knee et al., 2013).

Self-determined motivation and close relationships

Self-determined motivation has been operationalized at various levels of abstraction from general disposition (such as trait autonomy) to situational, domain-specific levels (such as relationship autonomy) to event-specific levels (autonomy with regard to a particular task), and these levels can influence each other in predicting behavior (Vallerand, 1997). A growing body of research suggests that self-determined motivation, at multiple levels, is important for understanding the development and maintenance of optimal relationships, fostering positive outcomes for both oneself and one's partner (for review, see Deci & Ryan, 2014; Knee et al., 2013). For instance, in one of the first investigations of relationship-specific autonomy (commonly referred to as relationship autonomy), Blais et al. (1990) assessed couples' reasons for being in the relationship, their perceptions of agreement on a variety of issues, and their satisfaction in the relationship. Path analyses supported a model in which relative autonomy toward the relationship predicted perceived agreement, which in turn predicted relationship satisfaction for both men and women. Relationship motivation is also important at task levels of specificity. Gaine and La Guardia (2009) examined motivation toward specific relationship activities such as physical intimacy, self-disclosure, and social support. Results showed that motivation for specific relationship activities uniquely predicted relationship well-being beyond reasons for being in one's relationship, which together accounted for 80 percent of the variance in relationship well-being.

To date, research has suggested two potential mechanisms between self-determined motivation and optimal relationship development. First, research has linked both trait-level autonomy and relationship-specific autonomy with more flexible, less defensive approaches to the relationship. This can be reflected in an openness and acceptance of differences, whether those differences come in the form of the qualities one seeks in an ideal partner or one's current partner's different perceptions and expectations of the relationship. For example, when one is dispositionally oriented toward autonomy, conflicts and differences in perspective become opportunities for learning and development rather than threats to one's self-concept. Knee et al. (2002) examined perceptions of current partners and ideal partners, and then videotaped couples during a semi-structured interview designed to emphasize differences in how partners view the relationship. Results showed that although people generally tended to prefer an ideal partner who was highly similar to themselves, this tendency was weaker when oriented toward autonomy. These more autonomously motivated individuals were more accepting of potential partner differences. Further, an autonomous orientation was associated with more relationship-maintaining coping strategies and less negative emotion and more positive behaviors as determined by trained coders, whereas a less self-determined orientation was associated with more denial (Knee et al., 2002).

Relationship-specific autonomy is also associated with less defensive responses to relationship conflict. Knee et al. (2005) studied understanding and defensive coping responses to reported, daily experienced, and laboratory-induced conflicts in romantic relationships. First, diary data showed that trait autonomy predicted relationship autonomy, which in turn predicted relative satisfaction after disagreements. Second, trait autonomy predicted relationship autonomy, which was associated with less defensive and more understanding responses to conflict. Finally, one's partner's relationship autonomy uniquely predicted reported and observed behavior during conflict. Autonomous reasons for being in the relationship (of both self and partner) predicted both reported and observed responses to conflict and feelings of satisfaction. In other words, not only is one's own autonomy for being in a relationship associated with more understanding, less defensiveness, and higher satisfaction, but having one's partner autonomously motivated also contributes to one's own more positive relationship outcomes.

Additionally, evidence points to the causal role of autonomy in fostering open, non-defensive interactions. For example, Niemiec and Deci (2012) studied zero-acquaintance individuals whose task was to build a relationship.

Participants were primed with autonomy (relative to two other conditions) using a scrambled sentence task and engaged in a self-disclosure task designed to increase intimacy. Results showed that autonomously primed individuals felt more satisfaction with the relationship, more positive affect, more relatedness need satisfaction, and greater well-being, and displayed greater behavioral closeness. We suggest that primed autonomy reduced people's anxiety and defensiveness toward the interaction and allowed them to openly express themselves and be open to each other, seeing the discussion as an opportunity to learn about their task-partner and build a relationship.

The second mechanism by which self-determined motivations may facilitate optimal relationships is via pro-partner orientations. Specifically, according to the relationship motivation model (RMT; Deci & Ryan, 2014; Knee et al., 2013), self-determined motivations promote interest in partners' perspectives and well-being, as well as the energy and desire to empathize with close others. In all, such an orientation should promote attention to and care for one's partner's needs, resulting in behaviors such as support provision and sacrifice that foster relationship development. For instance, research has experimentally primed autonomy and examined its impact on dyadic interactions. For example, Weinstein, Hodgins, and Ryan (2010) primed autonomy and then dyad members were videotaped as they jointly performed two tasks requiring creative thinking and persistence. Ratings of the interactions showed that dyads primed with autonomy were more emotionally and cognitively attuned to one another, and more empathic with and encouraging of each other, thus indicating more care for one's partner's needs and perspectives. Further, the dyads primed with autonomy were more engaged with the tasks, performed the tasks more effectively, and reported more closeness.

Relationship-specific autonomy is also associated with more support of partners (Hadden et al., 2015). Hadden et al. examined whether relationship autonomy is associated with reports of general, daily, and partner-reported support provision that is attentive to partner's needs. Relationship autonomy predicted being available to help one's partner, being encouraging partner's independent goal pursuits, and being emotionally responsive. Additionally, relationship autonomy was associated with less intrusiveness, suggesting that higher relationship autonomy is not simply associated with hypervigilance and being overbearing, but rather attention to the partner's needs. Relationship autonomy also predicted one's partner's receipt of support for autonomy, competence, and relatedness.

Finally, evidence also points to the benefits of task-specific motivation for caregiving. For instance, people feel more gracious toward a hypothetical helper if they think that he or she was motivated to help for self-determined reasons (Weinstein, DeHaan, & Ryan, 2010). Within close relationships, specifically, self-determined motivation for sacrificing for romantic partners is associated with higher reports of relationship quality by both the one who sacrificed and his or her partner (Patrick, 2007). We interpret these findings as suggesting that recipients of caregiving perceive that those with self-determined motivations to help genuinely care for the recipient, bolstering gratitude and relationship quality.

In sum, need fulfillment and self-determined motivation can be supported or thwarted at various levels – at the level of the individual, the situation or context of the relationship, and the unique interaction dynamic between the particular people in the particular context. At all levels, fulfillment of one's needs and self-determined motivations promote optimal relationships by reducing defensiveness and fostering pro-partner orientations. Further, the benefits of self-determined motivations extend to both oneself and one's partner, promoting gratitude and relationship quality. Thus, relationship development is optimal when partners' needs are mutually fulfilled, promoting intrinsic motivation to be in the relationship, and allowing both partners' true selves to be expressed, responded to, and openly experienced in the fullest sense. The degree to which this need-fulfilled, intrinsically motivated, true-self-engaged dynamic emerges mutually, over time, is what influences how partners negotiate relationship challenges and threats, as well as how the relationship grows and flourishes.

INTEGRATING SDT WITH OTHER MAJOR PERSPECTIVES IN THIS VOLUME

Self-determination theory's perspective on mutual basic need fulfillment, self-determined motivation for one's endeavors, and true-self involvement can be integrated with a number of major relationship theories, concepts, and mechanisms that have been shown to promote satisfying, lasting, close relationships. We begin with a comparison and integration of SDT with three major theoretical perspectives discussed in the beginning section of this volume.

Interpersonal process model of intimacy

The interpersonal process model of intimacy (Reis & Patrick, 1996; Reis & Shaver, 1988) explains the development of intimacy as the result of interactional processes. Importantly, this model includes components that capture the temporal nature of intimacy and the specific dyadic ingredients that either facilitate or inhibit self-disclosure, responsiveness, and intimacy between partners. According to the model, the intimacy process is initiated when one reveals personally relevant information to one's partner. In turn, the degree to which one's partner is responsive to self-disclosure, such that the partner feels understood, validated, and cared for, will result in stronger feelings of intimacy in an ongoing reciprocal cycle (Laurenceau, Rivera,

Schaffer, & Pietromonaco, 2004). Further, responsiveness can take on various nonverbal, verbal, and behavioral expressions (see Reis, de Jong, Lee, O'Keefe, & Peters, Chapter 1, this volume).

The intimacy process can be integrated within the SDT framework. Specifically, the mechanism described by the interpersonal process model of intimacy is fundamentally a process through which one feels that one's needs for autonomy, competence, and relatedness are being met by one's partner (and mutually). For example, research has found that emotional disclosure is more important than factual disclosure (Morton, 1978; Reis & Patrick, 1996), presumably because emotional disclosure allows "for the most core aspects of the self to be known, understood, and validated by another" (Laurenceau et al., 2004, p. 63). This process closely resembles the fulfillment of autonomy as one feels able to express one's true self and in turn feels more competent through validation and more related by feeling understood by one's partner (Uysal, Lin, & Knee, 2010).

Additionally, the SDT framework can utilize the two-component model proposed by the interpersonal process model of intimacy. That is, feelings of need fulfillment arise from both self-disclosure and responsiveness of one's partner, and both are critical to developing intimacy. The act of revealing personally relevant information increases feelings of autonomy to the extent that one is able express one's true self freely and openly. As suggested by Uysal et al. (2010), not disclosing personally relevant information results in lower autonomy because it prevents the authentic revealing of one's true self that is inherent in feeling autonomous. Further, Uysal, Lin, Knee, and Bush (2012) found that self-concealment in romantic relationships, defined as actively hiding negative personally relevant information from one's partner, predicted lower well-being because of lower need fulfillment at both between- and within-person levels.

Need fulfillment might also facilitate the second part of the intimacy process. That is, responsiveness may be important because it provides the sense that one's partner fulfills one's basic psychological needs. Specifically, responsiveness from partners following self-disclosure might increase intimacy to the extent that the response supports psychological needs. As conceptualized (e.g., Laurenceau et al., 2004; Reis & Patrick, 1996), this notion is somewhat implicit in the definition of responsiveness. In essence, self-disclosure allows one to receive autonomy support as partners express understanding of one's values, feelings, and desires. Further, at this stage in the process, one's partner can provide competence support in the form of validating certain qualities. Finally, responsiveness includes a component of caring, which reflects the need for relatedness and connection.

In sum, SDT suggests that self-disclosure itself provides a sense of need fulfillment to the extent that the disclosure emerges from the true self. Furthermore, a responsive partner is crucial for the development of intimacy specifically when, or even because, the response provides support for basic psychological needs.

Self-expansion theory

Self-expansion theory (Aron & Aron, 1996; see also Xu, Lewandowski, & Aron, Chapter 4, this volume) contends that people are motivated to expand their resources, perspectives, and characteristics by including close others within the self-concept. The theory emphasizes that satisfying romantic relationships are those in which partners engage in novel and challenging activities to satisfy this fundamental desire to grow and expand. Sometimes, as a relationship progresses, fewer opportunities to engage in exciting experiences are available, at which point self-expansion is thwarted and feelings of boredom and dissatisfaction can emerge (Aron, Norman, Aron, McKenna, & Heyman, 2000). Self-expansion theory posits that individuals assimilate the traits and characteristics of the partner into their self-concept, as a natural ongoing process of developing a close and intimate relationship. Indeed, several experiments have found that people allocate resources to a close other as they would to themselves instead of as they would to a stranger, and tend to process information about close others as if it is about themselves (e.g., Aron, Aron, Tudor, & Nelson, 1991).

In relation to SDT, a few points can be noted. First, activities that support basic needs for autonomy, competence, and relatedness are likely to also facilitate true-self development and expansion. For example, SDT emphasizes that optimally challenging tasks best support one's need for competence. That is, if an activity is too easy or too difficult, people lose interest either from boredom or capitulation (Deci & Ryan, 2000). Thus, some activities might expand the self-concept more readily than others. Activities that undermine one's autonomy, thwart one's competence by being too easy or too challenging, or hinder rather than facilitate relatedness would likely result in less true-self expansion. For example, a task that one is forced to do under controlling conditions might not be as self-expanding as one that is fun, challenging, and supportive of one's autonomy.

Second, self-expansion and the sense of closeness that derives from including another within one's self-concept seem to reflect SDT's need for relatedness. Self-expansion theory does not directly address needs for autonomy and competence other than suggesting that challenging, novel activities promote self-expansion, which may facilitate a sense of competence. Third, not all motivations for relating and expanding one's self-concept are equal. Seeking closeness from a partner to acquire resources (e.g., fame, approval from others, monetary gains) is a less self-determined form of motivation than seeking closeness to learn new perspectives and grow with one's partner. Whereas self-expansion theory suggests that both motivations satisfy the desire for self-expansion, SDT predicts that self-determined motivations are of greater benefit than less self-determined motivations.

Recent work has specifically tested the notion that not all forms of inclusion of other into one's self-concept are equally beneficial. Weinstein, Rodriguez, Knee, and Kumashiro (2015) examined whether individual differences in self-determined motivation moderate the effects of increasing self-other overlap on partner outcomes. Across studies, as self-determined individuals reported greater self-other overlap, their partners reported receiving more positive motivational support as well as enhanced well-being and relationship outcomes. On the other hand, when individuals were lower in self-determination, as operationalized in several ways, their partners reported either no or negative consequences from having greater self-other overlap. Further research on more versus less self-determined self-other overlap is needed.

Attachment theory

One of the most widely investigated theories on close relationships is attachment theory (see Mikulincer & Shaver, Chapter 3, this volume, for review), which considers felt security a key factor in the development of harmonious, stable relationships. Attachment theory (Bowlby, 1969) incorporates situational, individual, and interactional influences on the development of felt security in relation to close others. Its concept of working models explains how past relational experiences become incorporated into the person cognitively and emotionally, and in turn, guide and influence relationship experiences. Additionally, its conception of both attachment and caregiving systems helps to explain how self-focus inhibits responsiveness and sensitivity to one's partner (Collins & Ford, 2010; Feeney & Collins, 2014). Whereas attachment theory traditionally relies on felt security and feelings of responsiveness and relatedness in accounting for different attachment orientations, recent work suggests that felt security emerges from interpersonal support that promotes opportunities for growth and exploration (Feeney & Collins, 2014). Specifically, in addition to providing a "safe haven" for romantic partners, in which one is responsive during stressful times, romantic partners can promote security by providing a "secure base," in which they help partners to flourish and explore by, first, being available if their partner needs help, but also by encouraging partners to pursue personal goals and not interfering with such goal pursuits (Feeney & Collins, 2014).

Although secure base support and psychological need support arise from two distinct theoretical backgrounds, there appears to be considerable overlap between the constructs. First, both SDT and attachment theory emphasize the partner's role in promoting growth and development (Deci & Ryan, 2014; Knee et al., 2013). Further, central to both perspectives is the notion that partners can encourage growth by supporting feelings of connectedness while not being overbearing or intrusive. That is, individuals should be available for romantic partners should they seek help, but optimal growth comes when individuals also simultaneously provide autonomy support by not interfering and undermining the partner's confidence (Feeney & Collins, 2014). In this sense, SDT posits that all three basic psychological needs likely determine levels of felt security and qualities of attachment to close others. Indeed, research has shown that people are more securely attached to those who support and fulfill their basic psychological needs for autonomy, competence, and relatedness (La Guardia et al., 2000). Specifically, La Guardia and her colleagues examined the attachment security and need fulfillment of individuals across multiple close relationship partners and found that the degree of need fulfillment with each particular close other predicted significant variance in attachment security across the range of close others. Further, whereas relatedness was the strongest predictor, autonomy and competence fulfillment uniquely predicted variance in attachment security beyond it. Thus, there is evidence that those relationships with close others that are experienced as fulfilling autonomy, competence, and relatedness needs result in felt security, as SDT would suggest.

Need satisfaction has been associated with secure attachment, but alternatively, attachment anxiety can also lead to situations in which one's needs are not fulfilled. For example, Slotter and Finkel (2009) investigated attachment anxiety and need fulfillment as predictors of commitment. In two studies, they found an interaction between attachment anxiety and fulfillment of autonomy and relatedness needs in predicting commitment. Whether attachment anxiety was primed experimentally or assessed as a trait, elevated attachment anxiety led individuals to remain committed to the relationship even when needs for relatedness and autonomy were relatively unfulfilled. In contrast, experiencing elevated attachment security led individuals to adjust their level of commitment in accord with the level of need fulfillment. Thus, attachment security predicts level of commitment primarily when people are also experiencing fulfillment of psychological needs within the relationship.

In sum, researchers have recently begun to discuss the conceptual similarities (Feeney & Collins, 2014; Hadden et al., 2015; Knee et al., 2013). Both attachment and self-determination theories emphasize the importance of partner's support of one's growth, exploration, and connection. Attachment conceptualizes this as safe haven and secure base support, in which partners make themselves available in times of stress, and encourage partners' independent exploration. SDT, meanwhile, suggests that partners can promote a sense of relatedness, while also supporting partners' sense of competence and autonomy by allowing them to freely express themselves. Interestingly, these approaches both appear to suggest that support processes that promote optimal relationships involve providing a sense of connection while encouraging partners to be who they truly are. Despite the conceptual similarities, the link between need fulfillment and secure base support deserves to be more fully explored.

INTEGRATING SDT WITH MECHANISMS THAT PROMOTE BETTER RELATIONSHIPS

In addition to major theoretical perspectives, this volume (Section 2) also includes chapters describing a number of concepts and mechanisms that promote better relationships. We preview some of these processes here and explain how they might be integrated within the SDT perspective on optimal relationship development.

Dyadic regulation

Overall, Girme, and Simpson (Chapter 7, this volume) outline the many benefits of receiving support for one's relationships, including resilience, growth, reduced distress, bolstered self-esteem, and promotion of physical and psychological health. At the same time, providing support can also be costly (Bolger, Zuckerman, & Kessler, 2000). Visible support behaviors can increase levels of anxiety and depressive symptoms, reduce self-efficacy, and make receivers think they are unable to achieve goals. The authors suggest that this occurs via increased salience of stressors, which suggests to recipients that they are unable to cope by themselves and therefore feel indebted to partners. This fits well with the thwarting of SDT's needs for competence and autonomy. Signals that one is unable to cope may reflect an undermining of competence and the guilty indebtedness may reflect a lack of feeling autonomous. Indeed, invisible support may be more effective because it does not thwart one's needs for autonomy and competence, but also increases many positives such as fewer depressive symptoms and anxiety, more self-efficacy, positive perceptions of one's capability, and greater success in goal attainment.

While visible support seems to have long-term costs and invisible support reaps long-term gains, there are likely to be short-term gains that arise from visible support, which may come from increased fulfillment of one's need for relatedness. As these different types of support may satisfy different needs, the type of support provided should ideally meet the needs of support recipients. Specifically, when partners are truly unable to cope with their situation, the reassurance of visible support and its accompanying satisfaction of the need for relatedness may best serve recipients, whereas in other cases the situation should be best resolved by invisible support and the fulfillment of competence and autonomy that accompany it.

Additionally, we feel that individuals who are more autonomously motivated to be in their relationship will be more inclined to give the appropriate kind of support because they are more aware of and attentive to their partner's needs (Hadden et al., 2015).

The type of relationship motivation a provider possesses seems particularly relevant for those who are high in attachment avoidance or anxiety. When autonomously motivated, one is likely to provide more clear and consistent support, depending on what the recipient needs. Overall et al. (Chapter 7, this volume) suggest that this is exactly what highly anxious partners need as these recipients are less inclined to be soothed immediately by support but do benefit as these behaviors build up over time, generating positive perceptions. Similarly, avoidant support recipients might benefit from such autonomously motivated support because it is more likely to match what they feel they want and need from the partner.

Pro-relationship behaviors

Pro-relationship motivation has been defined as the motivation behind behavioral preferences that are driven by the desire to benefit one's partner or relationship despite the fact that the behavior conflicts with one's first immediate impulse to serve one's own preferences (Finkel & Rusbult, 2008). Pro-relationship behaviors include accommodation, sacrifice, and forgiveness, in which one forgoes immediate personal interest in favor of what will help the partner or relationship. While pro-relationship behaviors obviously can benefit relationships, it has also been shown that people's goals for sacrificing can affect their own well-being as well as that of their partner (Day & Impett, Chapter 10, this volume). For example, people high in communal motivation to meet their partner's needs experience sacrifices as more rewarding compared to those lower in communal motivation because they feel more authentic and true to themselves when they do so (Kogan et al., 2010). Further, when people experience greater authenticity while sacrificing, they in turn have better well-being and better relationships (Impett, Javam, Le, Asyabi-Eshghi, & Kogan, 2013). These findings dovetail with SDT's motivation perspective on pro-relationship behaviors. The different motivations for engaging in pro-relationship behaviors may have measurable consequences for both the actors and their partners. For example, choosing to do what is best for the relationship can occur because one authentically wishes to do what is best for it or, alternatively, because one feels obligated and like a "bad partner" if one does not do it. In the latter, the motivation behind the behavior is ego-involved, introjected, and guilt-driven, executed out of concerns for one's self-regard rather than genuine concern and interest in one's partner or relationship. Indeed, relationship autonomy has been associated with pro-relationship behavior in the form of caring for one's partner more and supporting him or her (Hadden et al., 2015). In three studies, relationship autonomy was associated with more supportiveness both in the form of secure base support and basic psychological need support.

Research has also shown that how one communicates about sacrifices is important. For example, when people try to conceal their feelings about a sacrifice from their partner, both partners' emotional experiences and feelings about the relationship are worsened (Impett et al., 2013). This is consistent with research showing that self-concealment from one's partner undermines fulfillment of autonomy, competence, and relatedness, which in turn are associated with poorer relationship well-being, and that this occurs at both between-person and within-person levels (Uysal et al., 2012).

Another prosocial behavior that has received increasing attention is forgiveness. Research on the benefits and occasional detriments of forgiveness in relationships is moving toward the notion that there are better and worse ways to forgive (Fincham, May, & Beach, Chapter 14, this volume). SDT would suggest that it could be easier to forgive a partner when autonomously motivated to be in the relationship. Having basic needs fulfilled facilitates openness to and acceptance of otherwise ego-threatening experiences (Hodgins & Knee, 2002). In fact, Hodgins et al. (2010) experimentally primed autonomous motivation and examined physiological indicators of threat and performance on an impromptu interview task. Across verbal, nonverbal, and physiological indicators, autonomously primed participants displayed less cardiovascular threat and gave better speeches, and this was mediated by interview threat response. It seems likely that autonomous motivation may likewise elevate one's threshold for interpersonal threats, including responses to transgressions by one's partner. To the extent that transgressions are less interpreted as self-threats when autonomously motivated, forgiving those transgressions may be facilitated. Additionally, part of forgiving transgressions involves processing the emotions effectively. Autonomous motivation has been examined in relation to expression of emotion following exposure to traumatic events using an expressive-writing paradigm. Experimentally primed autonomous motivation facilitated more effective written expression and regulation, leading to more positive emotional, physical, and cognitive outcomes over time (Weinstein & Hodgins, 2009). When negative emotions are processed more completely and integrated with our experience rather than avoided or defended against, forgiveness may be more likely to follow (Hodgins & Knee, 2002).

Compassionate and self-image goals

Optimal relationships can also be characterized in terms of partners having more compassionate and fewer self-image goals (Crocker & Canevello, 2008;

Crocker & Canevello, Chapter 11, this volume). Self-image goals are said to be motivated by the "egosystem" and are defined by a focus on developing or maintaining a desired image for oneself or others. Compassionate goals, on the other hand, are said to be motivated by the "ecosystem" and are defined by a desire to support others for their own sake, rather than for attaining a benefit for oneself. Compassionate goals have largely been linked to positive relationship outcomes such as perceived support given to roommates and friends (Crocker & Canevello, 2008), responsiveness to one's roommate (Canevello & Crocker, 2010), and relationship satisfaction over time (Hadden, Smith, & Knee, 2014), whereas self-image goals generally show the reverse pattern. In what is sometimes discussed as a paradox, self-image goals tend to lead to more distant, less supportive relationships for that person. That is, although those higher in self-image goals are concerned with obtaining benefits for themselves, negative feedback loops can emerge in which the support they receive from others declines over time (Crocker & Canevello, 2008).

SDT suggests that self-image goals arise from a lack of need fulfillment, which is crucial to the development of a coherent, integrated sense of self (Deci & Ryan, 2000). That is, when basic needs for autonomy, competence, and relatedness are not met consistently, one will evaluate one's self-worth according to others' outcomes or expectations (Hodgins & Knee, 2002; Ryan, Deci, & Grolnick, 1995). In other words, a lack of need fulfillment is theorized to lead people to base their feelings of self-worth upon convincing themselves and others that they match a particular self-image rather than experiencing a more genuine and stable sense of self-worth. Additionally, when one's relationship fulfills basic psychological needs, a more stable, true self emerges and one can truly value caring for one's partner and relationship without being overly focused on one's own agenda and outcomes.

The more general literature on intrinsic and extrinsic goals also supports the benefits of compassionate relative to self-image goals. For example, people who place relatively strong emphasis on extrinsic goals, such as fame, popularity, and wealth tend to have poorer well-being (Kasser & Ryan, 1993, 1996). Additional research found that both the relative valuing of extrinsic aspirations and pursuing those goals for more extrinsic reasons independently contributed to poorer well-being (Sheldon et al., 2004). Finally, there is evidence that thwarted need satisfaction is linked to having more extrinsic goals. For example, Kasser, Ryan, Zax, and Sameroff (1995) found that adolescents who placed higher importance on attaining wealth had been raised in environments that were less supportive of autonomy and relatedness. Thus, although compassionate and self-image goals are not the same as intrinsic and extrinsic goals, there is some support that suggests that their origins and processes may indeed be similar.

Ideal standards

The Ideal Standards Model (Campbell & Moroz, Chapter 9, this volume) states that people possess images of their ideal partner and relationship and that partners are evaluated against these ideals in determining one's satisfaction and other relationship outcomes. The model emphasizes the importance of perceiving that a partner meets one's ideal standards and that one also feels that one meets his or her partner's ideal standards. An SDT perspective on the ideal standards model would suggest at least two points. First, it is possible that not all ideals are equally important for optimal relationship development. Ideals that are based more closely on fulfillment of autonomy, competence, and relatedness likely have a larger impact on relationship well-being compared to ideals that are not. Second, the extent to which people evaluate their partners and relationships against these ideals, or rather the importance of falling short of these ideals, may vary with their motivation for being in the relationship, and the degree to which their needs are being met.

With regard to the first point, Rodriguez, Hadden, and Knee (2015) examined whether some attributes of the ideal standards model better reflected needs for autonomy, competence, and relatedness compared to other attributes. They defined extrinsic attributes as relatively observable and valued for their role in gaining attention, popularity, fame, and physical attraction. In contrast, intrinsic attributes were defined as less observable, and valued for their inherent benefit in developing the relationship. Results showed that satisfaction of intrinsic ideals more strongly predicted relationship quality than satisfaction of extrinsic ideals. Thus, meeting intrinsic ideals, such as being warm, compassionate, and honest was found to be more strongly associated with satisfaction in relationships than relatively more extrinsic ideals such as being attractive or having resources. Further, an interaction revealed that when intrinsic ideals are met, extrinsic ideals become less relevant for relationship quality. In this way, extrinsic ideals appear to be compensatory in that they become more relevant to satisfaction when intrinsic ideals are less fulfilled.

Turning to the second point – that the relevance of a partner falling short of one's ideals may be more or less relevant depending on one's motivation for being in the relationship – we know of only indirect evidence thus far. As mentioned earlier, Knee et al. (2002) examined autonomy orientation in relation to self-perceptions, partner ideals and perceptions of one's partner. People generally tend to see a lot of themselves in their ideal partner. However, autonomous motivation was associated with a weaker tendency to view an ideal partner as a function of one's view of self. One way to interpret this finding is that when autonomously motivated, one is less concerned about partners matching an ideal standard, in this case, their view of themselves.

This would be consistent with autonomous motivation reducing otherwise threatening experiences (Hodgins et al., 2010), reducing the tendency to evaluate others, and facilitating appreciation of others' differences (Legault & Amiot, 2014).

Harmonious and obsessive passion

SDT's perspective on optimal relationship development shares a great deal with Vallerand and Carbonneau's (Chapter 8, this volume) Dualistic Model of Passion, which distinguishes between obsessive and harmonious passion, the processes that lead to each form of passion, and the outcomes that they each engender. Obsessive passion in relationships is said to result from incomplete internalization of one's relationship into one's identity. Thus, obsessive passion develops when one is in the relationship for the "wrong reasons" or for extrinsic motivations such as popularity, guilt, possessions, and so forth. Harmonious passion, on the other hand, develops when one has more fully internalized one's relationship into one's identity and one fully endorses one's investment in the relationship such that it expresses one's true self. Harmonious passion for relationships has been linked to more positive indicators of relationship quality whereas obsessive passion for relationships has been linked to love and commitment, but not with experiencing more intimacy and satisfaction (Ratelle, Carbonneau, Vallerand, & Mageau, 2013). In this way, obsessive passion reminds us of relationship-contingent self-esteem, which as we discussed above, can sometimes keep one feeling committed to (and dependent on) a relationship, even without the positive experiences that result in greater satisfaction and intimacy (Knee, Canevello, Bush, & Cook, 2008).

Harmonious passion, and its downstream benefits, is akin to relationship autonomy in several ways. First, harmonious passion is more likely to emerge when basic needs for autonomy, competence, and relatedness are fulfilled, and one has more fully integrated one's relationship into one's true self. In this way, harmonious passion is what results from one's relationship being integrated with one's true self in the presence of psychological need fulfillment. Second, harmonious passion, like relationship autonomy, is associated with engaging in fewer damaging behaviors during relationship conflict, and this has been found in cross-sectional and event-contingent designs (Carbonneau & Vallerand, 2013). Finally, harmonious passion has been shown to lead to more positive relationship outcomes as well as fewer negative relationship outcomes, as has relationship autonomy. In this way, harmonious passion benefits from both appetitive and aversive mechanisms for optimal relationship development, whereas obsessive passion largely only relates to more aversive pathways and outcomes.

Positive sex

Good sex can be a powerful mechanism for enhancing romantic relationships (Muise, Kim, McNulty, & Impett, Chapter 6, this volume). An SDT perspective would suggest that good sex is sex that is autonomously motivated, competence-affirming, and fulfills the need for relatedness and intimacy. There is evidence to support this. For example, Jenkins (2003) found that more self-determined reasons for engaging in sex related to more need-fulfilling sexual encounters as well as personal and relational benefits. Similarly, among women, sex driven by more internal motivations (i.e., intimacy) predicted greater sexual autonomy, which in turn predicted greater sexual satisfaction, whereas sex motivated by more external factors was associated with less autonomy as well as more inhibition and dissatisfaction (Sanchez, Moss-Racusin, Phelan, & Crocker, 2011).

Smith (2007) found that general feelings of autonomy and competence in the domain of sex relate to feeling autonomous, competent, and related within the context of sexual interactions. Further, autonomy, competence, and relatedness in sexual experiences all uniquely predicted satisfaction and relaxation in the context of the experience. Brunell and Webster (2013) furthered this research by examining how motivation for sexual experiences related to sexual need fulfillment as well as relationship quality and psychological well-being. Across three studies, more self-determined motivation predicted greater relationship quality and psychological well-being, which were mediated by higher levels of need satisfaction both at the global level (general feelings) and more proximally (following the acts of physical intimacy).

In sum, it seems that it's not simply that sex is good or that good sex is even better. Rather, an SDT perspective suggests that when sex is mutually endorsed by partners' true selves, and when it leads to the fulfillment of needs to feel autonomous, competent, and related, it has especially positive impacts for the relationship as well as for partners' individual psychological well-being.

Synchrony and rapport

Behavioral synchrony is the spontaneous emergence of coordinated movements between two or more people (Vacharkulksemsuk, Chapter 12, this volume), and this core concept extends to emotional, cognitive, and physiological synchrony as well. Behavioral coordination along with mutual attentiveness and positivity are essential components of rapport (Tickle-Degnen & Rosenthal, 1990). Considerable research has linked synchrony with positive social relationships, and behavioral synchrony in particular has been shown to be a significant factor beyond self-reported feelings of positivity. We find

Vacharkulksemsuk's Superconductor Theory of Relationships intriguing in its use of the superconductor metaphor to represent synchronous relationships. During "relational superconductivity," interaction partners sync up with behavioral, emotional, or even cognitive and physiological convergence. When partners of a relational superconductor are together, they operate without losing energy, and perhaps even give and gain more energy to themselves and others around them.

This superconductive relational state reminds us of the state of being autonomously motivated during activities. At the purest level, when autonomously motivated, one engages in an activity out of interest and pleasure with no reward other than the spontaneous feelings of enjoyment that are inseparable from the activity itself. The experiential state that accompanies this form of motivation has been described as flow (Csikszentmihalyi, 1997), and is also characterized as effortless involvement and immersion in a pleasurable activity. If one considers close relationships to be potential semiconductors when they are optimally synchronous, then we would expect autonomous motivation to play a key role in that experience. Also, research has shown that autonomous motivation moderates the well-known ego-depletion effect (Muraven & Baumeister, 2000), whereby engaging in a cognitively demanding task reduces performance on a later task (e.g., Moller, Deci, & Ryan, 2006). When autonomously motivated, not only is one's ego less depleted, one's energy and vitality can actually increase (Ryan & Deci, 2008). For example, when autonomously motivated in a relationship, interacting with one's partner would not be depleting, but rather precisely the opposite.

The concept of synchrony could also have implications for fulfillment of psychological needs. SDT suggests that optimal relationship development emerges when, over time, partners' needs for autonomy, competence, and relatedness are mutually negotiated, fulfilled, and supported by the social environment. It occurs to us that mutual need fulfillment might parallel emotional, cognitive, and behavioral synchrony in a kind of relational synchrony. Relationships flourish when partners feel in tune with fulfilling each other's needs emotionally, cognitively, and behaviorally. In fact, mutual need fulfillment could be characterized as one form of synchronous convergence that fluctuates over time. Research is needed on the behavioral manifestations of mutual need fulfillment in close relationships.

CONCLUSION

Maximizing appetitive motives and minimizing aversive motives for one's relationships are both important and necessary for optimal relationship development (Reis et al., Chapter 1, this volume). Although we have emphasized SDT's perspective on appetitive processes and mechanisms such as mutual fulfillment of psychological needs, SDT also fully accounts for aversive processes and mechanisms. Recent research supports the notion that having unfulfilled needs is not equivalent to having them actively thwarted, and vice versa, not having them thwarted is not equivalent to having them fulfilled (Costa, Ntoumanis, & Bartholomew, 2015; Sheldon & Shuler, 2011). Whereas most relationship theories and research focus largely on minimizing aversive processes and outcomes, we have discussed how SDT pays unique attention to maximizing and promoting appetitive, positive processes and outcomes.

The other chapters in this volume have suggested numerous concepts, models, and theories that predict better relationship functioning and quality. As we have shown, many of these can be viewed through the lens of SDT and its motivational perspective on optimal relationships as mutual fulfillment of basic psychological needs. In this way, SDT provides an integrative perspective that elaborates and defines optimal development and true-self investment in one's close relationships. According to SDT, relationships that facilitate both partners' feelings of autonomy, competence, and relatedness, and those in which partners are engaged for relatively more integrated and intrinsic reasons, will be more likely to yield open, flexible, authentic, non-defensive intimate behaviors and stances. From the SDT perspective, investing one's true self in one's relationship means engaging one's relationship in the most immersive and genuine sense, and in a way that promotes openness and authentic understanding rather than avoidance and defensiveness. When needs for autonomy, competence, and relatedness are successfully negotiated, autonomous motivation for the relationship thrives, making it more likely that the relationship will grow and flourish.

REFERENCES

Aron, A., & Aron, E. N. (1996). Self and self-expansion in relationships. In G. O. Fletcher and J. Fitness (Eds.), *Knowledge structures in close relationships: A social psychological approach*, (pp. 325–344). Hillsdale, NJ: Lawrence Erlbaum Assoc.

Aron, A., Aron, E. N., Tudor, M., & Nelson, G. (1991). Close relationships as including other in the self. *Journal of Personality and Social Psychology*, 60, 241–253. doi:10.1037/0022-3514.60.2.241

Aron, A., Norman, C., Aron, E., McKenna, C., & Heyman, R. (2000). Couples' shared participation in novel and arousing activities and experienced relationship quality. *Journal of Personality and Social Psychology*, 78, 273–284. doi:10.1037/0022-3514.78.2.273

Bandura, A. (1977). Self-efficacy: Toward a unifying theory of behavioral change. *Psychological Review*, 84, 191–215. doi:10.1037/0033-295X.84.2.191

Baumeister, R. F., & Leary, M. R. (1995). The need to belong: desire for interpersonal attachments as a fundamental human motivation. *Psychological Bulletin*, 117, 497–529.

Blais, M. R., Sabourin, S., Boucher, C., & Vallerand, R. (1990). Toward a motivational model of couple happiness. *Journal of Personality and Social Psychology*, 59, 1021–1031.

Bolger, N., Zuckerman, A., & Kessler, R. C. (2000). Invisible support and adjustment to stress. *Journal of Personality and Social Psychology*, 79, 953–961.

Bowlby, J. (1969). *Attachment and loss: Volume 1: Attachment*. New York, NY: Basic Books.

Brunell, A. B., & Webster, G. D. (2013). Self-determination and sexual experience in dating relationships. *Personality and Social Psychology Bulletin*, 39, 970–987.

Canevello, A., & Crocker, J. (2010). Creating good relationships: Responsiveness, relationship quality, and interpersonal goals. *Journal of Personality and Social Psychology*, 99, 78–106. doi:10.1037/a0018186

Carbonneau, N., & Vallerand, R. J. (2013). On the role of harmonious and obsessive romantic passion in conflict behavior. *Motivation and Emotion*, 37, 743–757.

Carver, C. S., & Scheier, M. F. (1990). Origins and functions of positive and negative affect: A control-process view. *Psychological Review*, 97, 19–35.

Collins, N. L., & Ford, M. B. (2010). Responding to the needs of others: The caregiving behavioral system in intimate relationships. *Journal of Social and Personal Relationships*, 27, 235–244. doi:10.1177/0265407509360907

Costa, S., Ntoumanis, N., & Bartholomew, K. J. (2015). Predicting the brighter and darker sides of interpersonal relationships: Does psychological need thwarting matter? *Motivation and Emotion*, 39, 11–24.

Csikszentmihályi, M. (1997). *Finding flow. The psychology of engagement with everyday life*. New York: Basic Books.

Crocker, J., & Canevello, A. (2008). Creating and undermining social support in communal relationships: The role of compassionate and self-image goals. *Journal of Personality and Social Psychology*, 95, 555–575. doi:10.1177/0265407509360907

Deci, E. L., La Guardia, J. G., Moller, A. C., Scheiner, M. J., & Ryan, R. M. (2006). On the benefits of giving as well as receiving autonomy support: Mutuality in close friendships. *Personality and Social Psychology Bulletin*, 32, 313–327. doi:10.1177/0146167205282148

Deci, E. L., & Ryan, R. M. (1985). *Intrinsic motivation and self-determination in human behavior*. New York: Plenum.

Deci, E. L., & Ryan, R. M. (2000). The "what" and "why" of goal pursuits: Human needs and the self-determination of behavior. *Psychological Inquiry*, 11, 227–268.

Deci, E. L., & Ryan, R. M. (2008). A macrotheory of human motivation, development and health. *Canadian Psychology*, 49, 182–185. doi:10.1037/a0012801

Deci, E. L., & Ryan, R. M. (2014). Autonomy and need satisfaction in close relationships: Relationships motivation theory. In N. Weinstein (Ed.), *Human motivation and interpersonal relationships: Theory, research, and applications* (pp. 53–73). New York: Springer.

Feeney, B. C., & Collins, N. L. (2014). A new look at social support: A theoretical perspective on thriving through relationships. *Personality and Social Psychology Review*, doi:10.1177/1088868314544222

Fincham, F. D., Harold, G., & Gano-Phillips, S. (2000). The longitudinal relation between attributions and marital satisfaction: Direction of effects and role of efficacy expectations. *Journal of Family Psychology*, 14, 267–285.

Finkel, E. J., & Rusbult, C. E. (2008). Prorelationship motivation: An interdependence theory analysis of situations with conflicting interests. In J. Y. Shah, & W. L. Gardner (Eds.), *Handbook of motivation science* (pp. 547–560). New York: Guilford.

Gaine, G. S., & La Guardia, J. G. (2009). The unique contributions of motivations to maintain a relationship and motivations toward relational activities to relationship well-being. *Motivation and Emotion*, 33, 184–202. doi:10.1007/s11031-009-9120-x

Hadden, B. W., Rodriguez, L. M., Knee, C. R., & Porter, B. W. (2015). Relationship autonomy and support provision in romantic relationships. *Motivation and Emotion*, 39(3), 359–373.

Hadden, B. W., Smith, C. V., & Knee, C. R. (2014). The way I make you feel: How relatedness and compassionate goals promote partner's satisfaction. *The Journal of Positive Psychology*, 9, 155–162.

Hodgins, H. S., & Knee, C. R. (2002). The integrating self and conscious experience. In E. L. Deci, E. L., & R. M. Ryan (Eds.), *Handbook of self-determination research* (pp. 87–100). Rochester, NY: University of Rochester Press.

Hodgins, H. S., Koestner, R., & Duncan, N. (1996). On the compatibility of autonomy and relatedness. *Personality and Social Psychology Bulletin*, 22, 227–237. doi:10.1177/0146167296223001

Hodgins, H. S., Weibust, K. S., Weinstein, N., Shiffman, S., Miller, A., Coombs, G., & Adair, K. C. (2010). The cost of self-protection: Threat response and performance as a function of autonomous and controlled motivations. *Personality and Social Psychology Bulletin*, 36, 1101–1114. doi:10.1177/0146167210375618

Impett, E. A., Le, B. M., Asyabi-Eshghi, B., Day, L. C., & Kogan, A. (2013). To give or not to give? Sacrificing for avoidance goals is not costly for the highly interdependent. *Social Psychological and Personality Science*, 4, 649–657. doi:10.1177/1948550612474673

Jenkins, S. S. (2003). Gender and self-determination in sexual motivation (Doctoral dissertation, University of Rochester, 2004). *Dissertation Abstracts International*, 64, 6330.

Kasser, T., & Ryan, R. M. (1993). A dark side of the American dream: Correlates of financial success as a central life aspiration. *Journal of Personality and Social Psychology*, 65, 410–422. doi:10.1037/0022-3514.65.2.410

Kasser, T., & Ryan, R. M. (1996). Further examining the American dream: Differential correlates of intrinsic and extrinsic goals. *Personality and Social Psychology Bulletin*, 22, 280–287. doi:10.1177/0146167296223006

Kasser, T., Ryan, R. M., Zax, M., & Sameroff, A. J. (1995). The relations of maternal and social environments to late adolescents' materialistic and prosocial values. *Developmental Psychology*, 31, 907–914.

Knee, C. R., Canevello, A., Bush, A. L., & Cook, A. (2008). Relationship-contingent self-esteem and the ups and downs of romantic relationships. *Journal of Personality and Social Psychology*, 95, 608–627. doi:10.1037/0022-3514.95.3.608

Knee, C.R., Hadden, B. W., Porter, B., & Rodriguez, L. M. (2013). Self-determination theory and romantic relationship processes. *Personality and Social Psychology Review*, 17, 307–324.

Knee, C. R., Lonsbary, C., Canevello, A., & Patrick, H. (2005). Self-determination and conflict in romantic relationships. *Journal of Personality and Social Psychology*, 89, 997–1009.

Knee, C. R., Patrick, H., Vietor, N. A., Nanayakkara, A., & Neighbors, C. (2002). Self-determination as growth motivation in romantic relationships. *Personality and Social Psychology Bulletin*, 28, 609–619.

Koestner, R., & Losier, G, F. (1996). Distinguishing reactive versus reflective autonomy. *Journal of Personality*, 64, 465–494. doi:10.1111/j.1467-6494.1996.tb00518.x

Kogan, A., Impett, E. A., Oveis, C., Hui, B., Gordon, A. M., & Keltner, D. (2010) When giving feels good: The intrinsic benefits of sacrifice in romantic relationships for the communally motivated. *Psychological Science,* 21, 1918–1924. doi:10.1177/09567610388815

La Guardia, J. G., & Patrick, H. (2008). Self-determination theory as a fundamental theory of close relationships. *Canadian Psychology,* 49, 201–209. doi:10.1037/a0012760

La Guardia, J. G., Ryan, R. M., Couchman, C. E., & Deci, E. L. (2000). Within-person variation in security of attachment: A self-determination theory perspective on attachment, need fulfillment, and well-being. *Journal of Personality and Social Psychology,* 79, 367–384. doi:10.1037/0022–3514.79.3.367

Laurenceau, J-P., Rivera, L. M., Schaffer, A., & Pietromonaco, P. R. (2004). Intimacy as an interpersonal process: Current status and future directions. In D. Mashek & A. Aron (Eds.), *Handbook of closeness and intimacy* (pp. 61–78). Mahwah, NJ: Lawrence Erlbaum.

Legault, L., & Amiot, C. E. (2014). The role of autonomy in intergroup processes: Toward an integration of self-determination theory and intergroup approaches. In N. Weinstein (Ed.), *Human motivation and interpersonal relationships: Theory, research, and applications* (pp. 159–190). New York: Springer.

Lopez, F. G., Morua, W., & Rice, K. G. (2007). Factor structure, stability, and predictive validity of college students' relationship self-efficacy beliefs. *Measurement and Evaluation in Counseling and Development,* 40, 80–96.

Markus, H. R., Kitayama, S., & Heiman, R. J. (1996). Culture and "basic" psychological principles. In E. T. Higgins & A. W. Kruglanski (Eds.), *Social psychology: Handbook of basic principles* (pp. 857–913). New York: Guilford.

Morton, T. L. (1978). Intimacy and reciprocity of exchange: A comparison of spouses and strangers. *Journal of Personality and Social Psychology,* 36, 72–81.

Muraven, M. & Baumeister, R. F. (2000). Self-regulation and depletion of limited resources: Does self-control resemble a muscle? *Psychological Bulletin,* 126(2), 247–259.

Murray, H. A. (1938). *Explorations in personality.* Oxford: Oxford University Press.

Niemiec, C. P., & Deci, E. L. (2012). *The effects of provision and deprivation of autonomy on interaction quality between strangers.* Unpublished manuscript, University of Rochester, Rochester, New York.

Patrick, H. (2007). *Pro-relationship behaviors and self-determination: Why you do it matters as much as doing it at all.* Paper presented at the Third International Conference on Self-Determination Theory, Toronto, ON, Canada.

Patrick, H., Knee, C. R., Canevello, A., & Lonsbary, C. (2007). The role of need fulfillment in relationship functioning and well-being: A self-determination theory perspective. *Journal of Personality and Social Psychology,* 92, 434–457. doi:10.1037/0022–3514.92.3.434

Ratelle, C. F., Carbonneau, N., Vallerand, R. J., & Mageau, G. A. (2013). Passion in the romantic sphere: A look at relational outcomes. *Motivation and Emotion,* 37, 106–120.

Reis, H. T., & Patrick, B. C. (1996). Attachment and intimacy: Component processes. In E. Higgins & A. W. Kruglanski (Eds.), *Social psychology: Handbook of basic principles* (pp. 523–563). New York, NY: Guilford Press.

Reis, H. T., & Shaver, P. (1988). Intimacy as an interpersonal process. In S. Duck (Ed.), *Handbook of personal relationships* (pp. 367–389). Chichester, England: Wiley.

Reis, H. T., Sheldon, K. M., Gable, S. L., Roscoe, J., & Ryan, R. M. (2000). Daily well-being: The role of autonomy, competence, and relatedness. *Personality and Social Psychology Bulletin*, 26, 419–435. doi:10.1177/0146167200266002

Rodriguez, L. M., Hadden, B. W., & Knee, C. R. (2015). Not all ideals are equal: Intrinsic and extrinsic ideals in relationships. *Personal Relationships*, 22, 138–152.

Ryan, R. M., & Deci, E. L. (2008). From ego-depletion to vitality: Theory and findings concerning the facilitation of energy available to the self. *Social and Personality Psychology Compass*, 2, 702–717.

Ryan, R. M., Deci, E. L., & Grolnick, W. S. (1995). Autonomy, relatedness, and the self: Their relation to development and psychopathology. In D. Cicchetti & D. J. Cohen (Eds.), *Developmental psychopathology: Theory and methods*. (Vol. 1, pp. 618–655). New York: Wiley.

Ryan, R. M., La Guardia, J. G., Solky-Butzel, J., Chirkov, V., & Kim, Y. (2005). On the interpersonal regulation of emotions: Emotional reliance across gender, relationships, and cultures. *Personal Relationships*, 12, 145–163. doi:10.1111/j.1350-4126.2005.00106.x

Sanchez, D. T., Moss-Racusin, C. A., Phelan, J. E., & Crocker, J. (2011). Relationship contingency and sexual motivation in women: Implications for sexual satisfaction. *Archives of Sexual Behavior*, 40, 99–110.

Sheldon, K. M., Ryan, R., & Reis, H. T. (1996). What makes for a good day? Competence and autonomy in the day and in the person. *Personality and Social Psychology Bulletin*, 22, 1270–1279. doi:10.1177/01461672962212007

Sheldon, K. M., Ryan, R. M., Deci, E. L., & Kasser, T. (2004). The independent effects of goal contents and motives on well-being: It's both what you pursue and why you pursue it. *Personality and Social Psychology Bulletin*, 30, 475–486. doi:10.1177/0146167203261883

Slotter, E. B., & Finkel, E. J. (2009). The strange case of sustained dedication to an unfulfilling relationship: Predicting commitment and breakup from attachment anxiety and need fulfillment within relationships. *Personality and Social Psychology Bulletin*, 35, 85–100. doi:10.1177/0146167208325244

Smith, C. V. (2007). In pursuit of "good sex": Self-Determination and the sexual experience. *Journal of Social and Personal Relationships*, 24, 69–85.

Steinberg, L., & Silverberg, S. B. (1986). The vicissitudes of autonomy in early adolescence. *Child Development*, 57(4) 841–851.

Tickle-Degnen, L., & Rosenthal, R. (1990). The nature of rapport and its nonverbal correlates. *Psychological Inquiry*, 1, 285–293.

Uysal, A., Lin, H., & Knee, C.R. (2010). The role of need satisfaction in self-concealment and well-being. *Personality and Social Psychology Bulletin*, 36, 187–199.

Uysal, A., Lin, H.L., Knee, C. R., & Bush, A. (2012). The association between self-concealment from one's partner and relationship well-being. *Personality and Social Psychology Bulletin*, 38, 39–51.

Vallerand, R. J. (1997). Toward a hierarchical model of intrinsic and extrinsic motivation. In M. P. Zanna (Ed.), *Advances in experimental social psychology*. (Vol. 29, pp. 271–360). San Diego: Academic Press.

Weinstein, N., DeHaan, Cody R., & Ryan, R. M. (2010). Attributed motivation and the recipient experience: Perceptions of other, self, and the helping relationship. *Motivation and Emotion*, 34, 418–431.

Weinstein, N., & Hodgins, H. S. (2009). The moderating role of autonomy and control on the benefits of written emotion expression. *Personality and Social Psychology Bulletin*, 35, 351–364.

Weinstein, N., Hodgins, H. S., & Ryan, R. M. (2010). Autonomy and control in dyads: Effects on interaction quality and joint creative performance. *Personality and Social Psychology Bulletin*, 36, 1603–1617.

Weinstein, N., Rodriguez, L. M., Knee, C. R., & Kumashiro, M. (2015). *Self-determined self-other overlap: Impacts on partners' perceptions of support and well-being in close relationships*. Manuscript submitted for publication.

White, R. W. (1959). Motivation reconsidered: The concept of competence. *Psychological Review*, 66, 297–333.

3

Attachment theory as a framework for the promotion of optimal relationships

MARIO MIKULINCER AND PHILLIP R. SHAVER

In his exposition of attachment theory, John Bowlby (1973, 1980, 1982, 1988) proposed that interactions with loving, caring, and supportive relationship partners and the resulting sense of attachment security (confidence that one is socially valued and that others will be available and helpful when needed) are building blocks of mental health and social adjustment. Adult attachment researchers have found that a person's sense of attachment security is related to the development of positive character traits and moral virtues and provides a solid foundation for harmonious and stable relationships (see Mikulincer & Shaver, 2007a, for a comprehensive review). Because of its emphasis on mature, intimate, supportive, and mutually satisfying close relationships, attachment theory provides a valuable conceptual framework for the study of optimal relationship development.

In this chapter, we first present a brief overview of attachment theory and our model of attachment processes in adulthood (Mikulincer & Shaver, 2007a), an extension of Bowlby's theory that is now supported by 25 years of research by personality and social psychologists. Next, we focus on the anchoring of attachment security in expectations concerning relationship partners' sensitivity and responsiveness (expectations organized within a secure-base script), and review research findings showing that the sense of security is associated with positive appraisals of self and others and with social adjustment. We then review studies of dating and marital relationships showing that dispositional and experimentally induced feelings of security can transform otherwise destructive reactions to relationship partners' undesirable, hurtful behavior, improve a person's handling of interpersonal conflict, foster empathy and support for a partner in need, and promote positive relational emotions.

ATTACHMENT THEORY: BASIC CONCEPTS

Bowlby (1982) proposed that human infants are born with an innate psychobiological system (the *attachment behavioral system*) that motivates them to seek proximity to supportive others (*attachment figures*) as a means of protecting them from physical and psychological threats and promoting affect regulation, well-being, and healthy autonomy. Bowlby (1973) also described important individual differences in attachment-system functioning that develop as a consequence of attachment figures' reactions to a person's natural bids for proximity and support. Interactions with attachment figures who are available and responsive in times of need contribute to the optimal functioning of the attachment behavioral system, create positive working models of self and others, and promote an enduring sense of safety and security. When a person's attachment figures are not reliably available and supportive, however, this sense of security is not attained, doubts about one's lovability and others' motives and intentions arise, and affect-regulation strategies other than confident proximity seeking are adopted (strategies termed *secondary attachment strategies*, characterized by *anxiety* or defensive *avoidance*).

When studying individual differences in attachment-system functioning in adults, attachment researchers have focused on attachment orientations or styles – patterns of relational expectations, emotions, and behaviors that result from internalizing a particular history of attachment experiences (Shaver & Mikulincer, 2002). To date, it is well agreed that attachment styles can be located in a two-dimensional space defined by roughly orthogonal factors which we call attachment-related anxiety and avoidance (Brennan, Clark, & Shaver, 1998; Fraley & Waller, 1998). The avoidance dimension reflects the extent to which a person distrusts relationship partners' good will and defensively strives to maintain behavioral and emotional independence and distance. The anxiety dimension reflects the extent to which a person worries that a partner will not be available in times of need, partly because of the person's self-doubts about his or her worthiness. People who score low on both dimensions are relatively secure with respect to attachment. A person's location in the two-dimensional space can be measured with reliable and valid self-report scales (e.g., Brennan et al., 1998) and is associated in theoretically predictable ways with relationship quality and psychological adjustment (see Mikulincer & Shaver, 2007a, for a review).

Although attachment orientations are initially formed during childhood, in relationships with parents and other early caregivers (Cassidy & Shaver, 2008), Bowlby (1988) believed that important interactions with relationship partners beyond childhood can alter a person's working models and change his or her habitual attachment orientation. Moreover, although a person's attachment style is often conceptualized as a single global orientation toward relationships (which can be measured as such and has been shown to have reliable, predictable correlates), it is an emergent property of a complex network of cognitive and affective processes, which include many episodic, context-relative, and relationship-specific memories and schemas (Bowlby,

1988; Mikulincer & Shaver, 2003). Many studies indicate that a person's attachment orientation can change depending on context and recent experiences (Mikulincer & Shaver, 2007b), making it possible to study the causal effects of an experimentally primed sense of security within the confines of a social psychological laboratory or to examine the long-term effects of real-life security-enhancing interpersonal contexts.

We (Mikulincer & Shaver, 2007a) have proposed that people's location in the two-dimensional anxiety-by-avoidance space reflects both their sense of attachment security and the way they deal with threats and stressors. People who score low on the two insecurity dimensions are generally secure, hold positive working models of self and others, and tend to employ constructive and effective affect-regulation strategies. Those who score high on either attachment anxiety or avoidance suffer from attachment insecurities, worries about self-worth, or distrust of others' goodwill and responsiveness in times of need. Moreover, insecure people tend to use secondary attachment strategies that we, following Cassidy and Kobak (1988), characterize as attachment-system "hyperactivation" or "deactivation" when coping with threats, frustrations, rejections, and losses. People who score high on attachment anxiety rely on hyperactivating strategies – energetic attempts to achieve support and love combined with lack of confidence that these resources will be provided and with feelings of anger and despair when they are not provided (Cassidy & Kobak, 1988). In contrast, people who score high on attachment-related avoidance tend to use deactivating strategies, trying not to seek proximity to others when threatened, denying vulnerability and needs for other people, and avoiding closeness and interdependence in relationships.

Bowlby (1988) summarized many of the adaptive benefits of a well-functioning attachment system. First, interactions with a security-enhancing relationship partner reaffirm the value of closeness and increase relationship satisfaction. Second, successful bids for proximity and support teach a person how to down-regulate negative emotions and help him or her maintain emotional balance and resilience in the face of stress (Bowlby, 1973, 1980). Third, attachment security is a foundation for developing personal skills and competencies, because a child or adult who feels adequately protected has more courage and conflict-free attentional resources to engage in free play, curious investigation of objects and environments, and affiliative relationships with peers. In the next section, we review some of the evidence for these beneficial correlates and effects of attachment security.

MENTAL REPRESENTATIONS OF ATTACHMENT SECURITY

According to our model of adult attachment-system functioning (Mikulincer & Shaver, 2003, 2007a), appraisal of the availability and supportiveness of an attachment figure in times of need automatically activates mental representations of attachment security. These representations include both declarative and procedural knowledge organized around a relational proto-type or "secure-base script" (Waters & Waters, 2006), which contains some-thing like the following if-then propositions: "If I encounter an obstacle and/or become distressed, I can approach a significant other for help; he or she is likely to be available and supportive; I will experience relief and comfort as a result of proximity to this person; I can then return to other activities". Having many experiences that contribute to the construction of this script makes it easier for a person to confront stressful situations with optimistic expectations, which in turn helps the person maintain relative calm and optimistic hope while coping with problems.

There is evidence for the psychological reality of the secure-base script in young adults. For example, Mikulincer, Shaver, Sapir-Lavid, and Avihou-Kanza (2009) found that people who score lower on self-report scales tapping attachment anxiety or avoidance (i.e., more secure participants) were more likely than those who scored higher to include elements of the secure-base script (e.g., support seeking, support provision, distress relief) when writing about projective-test pictures of a troubled person. Moreover, the two kinds of insecurity – anxiety and avoidance – were associated with different types of gaps in the script. People who scored relatively high on the anxiety scale tended to omit or deemphasize the final step in the script (relief and return to other activities), whereas those who scored relatively high on the avoidance scale tended to omit the part about seeking and benefitting from others' support. That is, anxious participants more often wrote about an injured protagonist who was seeking support and not achieving relief, whereas avoidant participants more often wrote about a person achieving relief with-out seeking or receiving support.

Attachment-figure availability also fosters what we, following Fredrickson (2001), call a "broaden and build" cycle of attachment security, which increases a person's resilience and expands his or her perspectives, coping flexibility, and skills and capabilities. The most immediate psycholo-gical effect of attachment-figure availability is effective management of distress and restoration of emotional equanimity. According to attachment theory, interactions with available and supportive attachment figures, by imparting a pervasive sense of safety, assuage distress and elicit positive emotions such as relief, satisfaction, and gratitude. Secure people can, there-fore, remain relatively unperturbed in times of stress and experience longer periods of positive affect, which in turn contribute to their sustained emo-tional well-being and mental health.

Experiences of attachment-figure availability also contribute to a reser-voir of beneficial cognitive representations, which play a central role in maintaining emotional stability and personal adjustment. During positive interactions with sensitive and available attachment figures, individuals learn that distress is manageable, external obstacles can be overcome, and the course and outcome of most threatening events are at least partially controllable. Adult attachment studies provide extensive evidence that secure individuals, as identified by self-report measures, appraise a wide variety of stressful events in less threatening terms than insecure people (either anxious or avoidant) and hold more optimistic expectations about their ability to cope with stressors (e.g., Berant, Mikulincer, & Florian, 2001; Mikulincer & Florian, 1995; Radecki-Bush, Farrell, & Bush, 1993).

In addition, during interactions with supportive attachment figures, individuals learn about others' potential sensitivity, responsiveness, and goodwill. They also learn to view themselves as active, strong, and competent because they can effectively mobilize a partner's support and overcome threats that activate attachment behavior. Moreover, they perceive themselves as valuable, lovable, and special, thanks to being valued, loved, and regarded as special by caring attachment figures. Research has consistently shown that such positive mental representations of self and others are characteristic of secure persons (e.g., Baldwin, Fehr, Keedian, Seidel, & Thomson, 1993; Collins, 1996; Collins & Read, 1990; Cooper, Shaver, & Collins, 1998; Mickelson, Kessler, & Shaver, 1997; Mikulincer, 1995).

On the whole, research consistently indicates that the sense of attachment security contributes to positive mental representations of others, a stable sense of self-efficacy and self-esteem, and constructive ways of coping, which in turn facilitate emotional stability even under stressful conditions. Indeed, measures of dispositional attachment security are consistently associated with higher scores on measures of mental health and lower scores on measures of emotional maladies such as anxiety and depression (see Mikulincer & Shaver, 2007a, for a review).

Extending the findings reviewed so far to the realm of close relationships, one can predict that people who are secure with respect to attachment will interact with relationship partners in a confident and open fashion without being hampered by anxieties and defenses aimed at protecting a fragile sense of self-worth. Moreover, it seems likely that they can devote mental resources that otherwise would be employed in self-focused defenses to prosocial, other-focused thoughts and activities that contribute to relationship harmony and stability. In the following section, we review evidence concerning the positive changes that chronic and short-term experimental activation of mental representations of attachment security produce in relational cognitions and behavior.

ATTACHMENT SECURITY AND THE PROMOTION OF OPTIMAL RELATIONSHIPS

In the original studies of adult attachment in couple relationships, Hazan and Shaver (1987) provided evidence for an association between attachment security (measured with a 3-category measure) and the way a person construes experiences of romantic love. They found that people who classified themselves as secure with respect to attachment were more likely to report that their love relationships were friendly, warm, trusting, and supportive than insecure individuals. Findings also indicated that secure people were more likely to emphasize intimacy as a core feature of their relationships and to believe in the existence of romantic love and the possibility of maintaining intense love over the long course of a relationship. Subsequent studies have replicated and extended these initial findings, indicating that dispositionally secure individuals are more confident than their less secure counterparts about being able to establish a successful love relationship (e.g., Pietromonaco & Carnelley, 1994).

Following more than 25 years of adult attachment research, there is extensive and consistent evidence that these positive beliefs about romantic love are generally fulfilled in the quality of secure individuals' dating and marital relationships. Hundreds of studies have found that secure people report higher levels of relationship satisfaction and adjustment than insecure people (either anxious or avoidant) and maintain more stable romantic relationships (reviewed by Mikulincer, Florian, Cowan, & Cowan, 2002). This pattern has been consistently observed in cross-sectional and prospective studies of both dating and married couples, and it has not been explained by other personality factors that have been measured, such as self-esteem and the "Big Five" personality traits (e.g., Noftle & Shaver, 2006).

Attachment security seems to inhibit or preclude destructive relational behaviors, foster prosocial behavior, and contribute to a pervasive positive relational climate. We are especially interested here in three sources of relational distress – a partner's negative relational behaviors, interpersonal conflicts with a partner, and a partner's need for support – which provide opportunities for a secure partner to relieve a partner's distress, restore relational harmony, and transform what might have been destructive interactions into opportunities for personal and relational growth. We are also interested in examining whether attachment security facilitates capitalization on positive relational experiences and promotes positive relational emotions.

Responses to a partner's negative behaviors

Explicit or implicit signs of a partner's disapproval, criticism, rejection, or betrayal can evoke intense hurt feelings, arouse hostility toward a partner, and even ruin a relationship (Shaver, Mikulincer, Lavy, & Cassidy, 2009). However, attachment security can buffer these negative reactions, thereby protecting a relationship from these potentially destructive experiences. Secure individuals are generally resilient in the face of stress, which can help them cope constructively with a partner's negative behaviors. Moreover, they can activate comforting mental representations of relationship partners who have provided love and care in the past (e.g., Mikulincer, Gillath, & Shaver, 2002), which can help them maintain emotional balance when temporarily thrown for a loop by a partner's actions or comments. Secure individuals can mobilize caring qualities within themselves – qualities modeled on those of their supportive attachment figures – as well as memories (conscious and unconscious) of being loved and valued (Mikulincer & Shaver, 2004). These cognitive-affective mental representations provide genuine comfort and help a person remain relatively unperturbed by the possibility of rejection or even the possibility of betrayal.

There is extensive evidence that secure people, as compared to insecure ones, tend to react to actual or imagined partner disapproval, criticism, rejection, or betrayal with less intense negative emotions (e.g., Besser & Priel, 2010; Carnelley, Israel, & Brennan, 2007; Dewitte, De Houwer, Goubert, & Buysse, 2010). Dewitte et al. (2010) also found that attachment security was related to weaker cortisol responses and less withdrawal behaviors to signs of partner's rejection. Attachment security is also associated with less intense emotional and cognitive reactions to real or imagined cases of a partner's infidelity. More secure people tend to report lower levels of jealousy, suspicion, and worries about relationship exclusivity as compared to less secure people and to experience lower levels of fear, guilt, shame, sadness, inferiority, and anger (e.g., Donovan & Emmers-Sommer, 2012; Guerrero, 1998; Marazziti et al., 2010; Radecki-Bush et al., 1993; Wang, King, & Debernardi, 2012).

Attachment studies also show that more secure people tend to respond to signs of interpersonal rejection by adopting more approach-oriented goals (Park, 2010). For example, more secure people are more likely to talk openly with their partner about the partner's negative behavior, to attribute this behavior to temporary causes, and to work with him or her toward relationship improvement (e.g., Collins, 1996; Gaines et al., 1997; Scharfe & Bartholomew, 1995). Perunovic and Holmes (2008) also found that more secure participants reported greater inhibition of negative impulses following a partner's hurtful behavior and were more likely to engage in relationship-enhancing behavior even under time pressure. Perunovic and Holmes (2008) suggested that because of greater practice in down-regulating their negative emotions, secure people tend to accommodate relatively automatically.

There is extensive evidence that attachment security is positively associated with forgiveness – one of the most effective accommodation responses for reestablishing relational harmony following a partner's negative behavior (e.g., Ashy, Mercurio, & Malley-Morrison, 2010; Burnette, Taylor, Worthington, & Forsyth, 2007; Lawler-Row, Younger, Piferi, & Jones, 2006; Martin, Vosvick, & Riggs, 2012). Moreover, secure attachment is associated with less negative and less derogative appraisals of a partner's apologies for hurtful behavior (Brandau-Brown, Bello, & Ragsdale, 2010). In a study of feelings and thoughts associated with forgiving an offending partner, Mikulincer, Shaver, and Slav (2006) found that more secure people were less inclined to report feelings of vulnerability or humiliation and a sense of relationship deterioration when forgiving a partner.

Research also indicates that the attachment-forgiveness link is evident in studies of dating and married couples. For example, Kachadourian, Fincham, and Davila (2004) found that secure people were more likely than insecure ones to forgive their spouses. In a daily diary study of fluctuations in the tendency to forgive a dating partner, Mikulincer, Shaver, and Slav (2006) found that attachment security predicted higher levels of forgiveness across 21 consecutive days. Moreover, whereas secure people were more likely to forgive their spouse on days when they perceived more positive spousal behavior, anxious or avoidant people reported little forgiveness even on days when they perceived their spouse to be available, attentive, and supportive.

Beyond these associations between dispositional measures of attachment and forgiveness, there is increasing evidence that a state-like sense of security can alter the tendency to forgive a hurtful partner. For example, Hannon, Rusbult, Finkel, and Kamashiro (2010) found that a betraying partner's provision of a sense of security to the injured partner (by genuinely expressing interest in being responsive to the victim's needs) promoted forgiveness and restoration of relational harmony. Karremans and Aarts (2007) found that subliminal security priming (with the name of a loving other) elicited more forgiving responses than neutral priming to interpersonal transgressions.

Using an experimental priming procedure, Cassidy, Shaver, Mikulincer, and Lavy (2009) provided further evidence of the positive effects of contextual activation of the sense of attachment security on cognitive and emotional reactions to hurtful experiences in close relationships. Participants reported on their attachment orientations and wrote a description of an incident in which a close relationship partner criticized, disapproved, rejected, or ostracized them. They then completed a computerized task in which they were repeatedly exposed subliminally (for 22 milliseconds) to either a security-enhancing prime word (love, secure, affection) or a neutral prime (lamp, staple, building). Immediately after the priming trials, participants were asked to think again about the hurtful event they had described and to rate how they would react to such an event if it happened in the future – for example, how rejected they would feel and how they would feel about themselves.

In the neutral priming condition, avoidant attachment was associated with more defensive/hostile reactions and attachment anxiety was associated with more intense feelings of rejection, more crying, and more negative emotions. These correlational findings were dramatically reduced in size (most approached zero) in the security-priming condition. In other words, security priming reduced the tendency of avoidant people to rely on cool hostility or denial and the tendency of anxious people to react histrionically to a partner's hurtful behaviors. Overall, research findings indicate that (a) people who are dispositionally secure can deal constructively with hurtful relational events, and (b) contextual activation of the sense of security can soften the maladaptive responses of dispositionally insecure people.

Responses to relationship conflicts

According to attachment theory (Mikulincer & Shaver, 2007a), the sense of attachment security can improve a person's handling of interpersonal conflicts. Secure people's positive representations of self and others can sustain positive beliefs about conflicts and conflict resolution, as well as open communication and collaborative negotiation during conflicts. These positive working models can also allow for the implementation of effective conflict-resolution strategies, such as compromising and integrating one's own and a partner's needs. In this way, secure individuals can often transform relational conflicts into opportunities for greater relationship depth, harmony, satisfaction, and stability.

Adult attachment studies support this line of reasoning. For example, researchers have found that lower scores on attachment anxiety and avoidance scales are associated with appraising relational conflicts in less threatening terms, feeling more self-efficacious in handling conflict, relying more often on compromise and integrative conflict-management strategies, and fewer cases of conflict escalation and leaving a conflict unresolved (e.g., Cann, Norman, Welbourne, & Calhoun, 2008; Creasey & Hesson-McInnis, 2001; Dominique & Mollen, 2009). In addition, people who score as more secure are more likely to express affection toward a relationship partner during conflicts and are less likely to use coercive or withdrawal strategies or to engage in verbal or physical aggression during conflicts (e.g., Heene, Buysse, & Van Oost, 2005; La Valley & Guerrero, 2012; Wood et al., 2012).

Secure people's effective conflict management skills have also been noted in physiological reactions during conflictual interactions. For example, Powers, Pietromonaco, Gunlicks, and Sayer (2006) found that lower scores on attachment anxiety and avoidance scales were associated with lower levels of salivary cortisol (an index of physiological reactivity or stress) after a 15-minute discussion of an unresolved conflict with a dating partner. In addition, Lawler-Row, Hyatt-Edwards, Wuensch, and Karremans (2011) interviewed young adults about a conflict with a parent and found that attachment security in relation to parents predicted lower heart rate and blood pressure during the interview. Similarly, Beijersbergen, Bakermans-Kranenburg, van IJzendoorn, and Juffer (2008) found that secure adolescents had lower heart rate during a conflictual interaction with their mothers, compared with insecure adolescents. These differences have also been observed in a study assessing disputants' speech during real-life business-related negotiations (Nelson, Albeck-Solomon, & Ben-Ari, 2011).

Secure people's reliance on effective conflict-management strategies is also evident in observational studies of couples' discussions of unresolved conflicts. For example, more secure attachment is associated with less distress and more skillful communication tactics while discussing a major disagreement with a dating partner (e.g., Creasey & Ladd, 2004, 2005; J. Feeney, 1998; Simpson, Rholes, & Phillips, 1996). Similarly, individuals categorized as secure based on either self-report or interview measures have been coded as displaying more positive affect during conflict discussions, more attentiveness to their partner's statements, and less relationship-destructive behavior than those classified as insecure (e.g., Alexandrov, Cowan, & Cowan, 2005; Bouthillier et al., 2002; Paley et al., 1999).

In a longitudinal study of 78 individuals who have been studied intensively from infancy into their mid-20s, Simpson, Collins, Tran, and Haydon (2007) found evidence for a double-mediation model explaining associations between infant-mother attachment security in the Strange Situation assessment procedure and actual expressions of negative affect during conflict discussions with a romantic partner 20 years later (rated by observers). Specifically, participants classified as securely attached at 12 months of age were rated by their teachers as more socially competent during early elementary school, and this social competence forecasted their having more secure relationships with close friends at age 16, which in turn predicted less negative affect in conflict discussions with their romantic partners. That is, a trajectory of security from infancy to young adulthood underlies more adaptive methods of conflict resolution. Using the same sample, Salvatore et al. (2011) found that attachment security in infancy predicted better conflict recovery during a 4-minute "cool down" task following a discussion of a relationship problem with a romantic partner during young adulthood.

In a 1-year prospective study of married couples, Sullivan, Pasch, Johnson, and Bradbury (2010) highlighted the positive role that a partner's responsiveness can play in conflict management. Married couples were observed as newlyweds and again 1 year later while engaged in conflict-management interactions and support discussions. Initially, higher levels of partner responsiveness during the support discussion predicted 1-year decreases in negative emotion during conflict conversations. It therefore seems that partner responsiveness and support are key elements in managing conflictual interactions with a romantic partner.

Studies have also found that attachment security can mitigate the negative consequences of conflict discussions. For example, Simpson et al. (1996) found that more securely attached people reported less decline in love and commitment after discussing a major relationship problem with a dating partner. Gallo and Smith (2001) also found that more secure wives reacted to a conflict discussion with less negative appraisals of their husbands. In a diary study of daily conflicts within dating couples, Campbell, Simpson, Boldry, and Kashy (2005) found that more secure participants reported less conflictual interactions across 14 consecutive days. They also reacted to days of intense conflict with a smaller decline in relationship satisfaction and a more optimistic view of the relationship's future.

Responses to a distressed partner

Attachment theorists (e.g., Kunce & Shaver, 1994; Mikulincer & Shaver, 2007a; Shaver & Hazan, 1988) have hypothesized that attachment security is an important prerequisite for effectively providing support to a needy relationship partner. A person who is dispositionally secure is likely to have experienced and benefited earlier in life from effective care provided by sensitive and responsive attachment figures. This means that secure adults have memories and models of generous and empathic caregivers when they themselves occupy the caregiving role. Moreover, secure individuals' comfort with intimacy and interdependence allow them to respond favorably when a relationship partner is vulnerable or in need of support. Moreover, secure people's positive working models of others (as well-intentioned and kind-hearted; Hazan & Shaver, 1987) make it easier for them to perceive their relationship partner as deserving sympathy and support, whereas their positive self-representations allow them to feel confident that they can deal with their partner's needs or distress without being overwhelmed by their own needs and feelings.

Several studies have shown that, as compared with insecure people, secure people are more likely to provide support to a needy partner and be sensitive to his or her needs, and are less likely to adopt a controlling or compulsive caregiving orientation (e.g., J. Feeney, 1996; Kunce & Shaver, 1994; Millings & Walsh, 2009; Millings, Walsh, Hepper, & O'Brian, 2013). Davila and Kashy (2009) replicated these findings in a 14-day diary study, and found that self-reports of attachment security were associated with more sensitive and responsive provision of support to a needy partner throughout the 14-day period.

Attachment orientations are also associated with care provision among adult spouses of cancer survivors. For example, Kim and Carver (2007) found that more secure attachment (as assessed by self-report scales) was associated with more frequent provision of emotional support to a spouse with cancer. Attachment security was also associated with autonomous motives for providing care to a spouse with cancer, such as accepting the need for caregiving, loving, and respecting the care recipient (Kim, Carver, Deci, & Kasser, 2008). In addition, Braun et al. (2012) found that more secure attachment was associated with more responsive and sensitive caregiving to a spouse with cancer. Similar findings were observed in a longitudinal study of spousal caregiving in late life (Morse, Shaffer, Williamson, Dooley, & Schulz, 2012). There is also evidence that more secure caregivers of cancer patients experienced lower levels of personal distress (e.g., Askari, Madgaonkar, & Rowell, 2012; Kuscu et al., 2009; Rodin et al., 2007).

In an assessment of relationship-specific attachment orientations, Sprecher and Fehr (2011) found that more secure attachment in a specific relationship predicted more compassionate love. Along the same lines, Bartz and Lydon (2008) investigated attachment-related variation in adherence to communal norms in close relationships. Participants were randomly assigned to think about a secure, avoidant, or anxious relationship, and visualized scenarios involving the receipt or provision of support and care. Those primed with a secure relationship followed a communal script, and reported comfort with their own provision of support without expecting tit-for-tat reciprocation. In contrast, participants primed with an avoidant relationship used tit-for-tat norms and reported distress when their partner received support without expecting to reciprocate.

Similar findings have been obtained in laboratory studies of actual caregiving behavior. In the first such study, Simpson et al. (1992) videotaped dating couples while the female partner waited to endure a stressful task and judges then rated the male partners' caregiving behavior. Whereas secure men recognized their partner's worries and provided greater support as their partner showed higher levels of distress, men who scored high on avoidance provided less support as their partner's distress increased. Using a similar experimental paradigm, Simpson, Rholes, Orina, and Grich (2002) exposed male members of couples to a stressful procedure and found that more secure female partners provided more support to their needy partner.

In another observational study, Collins and Feeney (2000) videotaped dating couples while one partner disclosed a personal problem to the other (the "caregiver"). More secure caregivers were coded (by independent judges) as more supportive during the interaction regardless of whether a partner's needs were clearly expressed or not. In two subsequent laboratory experiments, B. Feeney and Collins (2001) and Collins, Ford, Guichard, and B. Feeney (2005) brought dating couples to the lab and informed one member of the couple (the "careseeker") that he or she would perform a stressful task – preparing and delivering a speech that would be videotaped.

The other member of the couple (the "caregiver") was led to believe that his or her partner was either extremely nervous (high need condition) or not at all nervous (low need condition) about the speech task, and was given the opportunity to write a private note to the partner. In both studies, the note served as a behavioral measure of caregiving and was rated for the degree of support it conveyed. More secure people wrote more emotionally suppor-tive notes in both high and low need conditions, and provided more instrumental support in the high than in the low need condition, precisely when the partner most needed support. Moreover, they reported more empathic feelings toward their partner and were more willing to switch tasks with the partner.

In a recent study, Monin, Feeney, and Schulz (2012) examined attachment-related variations in appraisals and emotional reactions to a romantic partner's expressions of distress. Participants were unobtrusively observed while their dating partner was exposed to an experimental stressor. More secure attachment was related to the expression of more positive affect toward the anxious partner and more effective caregiving (as judged by external observers). Positive interpretations of partner anxiety mediated the association between secure attachment and more effective caregiving.

The positive effects of attachment security on caregiving behavior toward a romantic partner have also been observed when a partner is exploring new career opportunities or personal plans. In two observational studies of married couples interacting in a videotaped exploration activity (e.g., discussion of one partner's personal goals), B. Feeney and Thrush (2010) and B. Feeney, Collins, van Vleet, and Tomlinson (2013) found that more secure people were more likely to provide emotional and instrumental support for a partner's exploration. Importantly, secure people's provision of support improved the partner's actual exploratory behavior (as judged by external observers).

Although all of these findings confirm an attachment-caregiving link in couple relationships, the studies have all been based on dispositional measures of attachment and therefore cannot inform us fully about the causal effects of attachment security. In order to fill this gap in the evidence, Mikulincer, Shaver, Sahdra, and Bar-On (2013) conducted a study, in both the United States and Israel, to see if experimentally augmented security would improve care provision to a romantic partner who was asked to discuss a personal problem. A second goal of the study was to examine the extent to which security priming would overcome barriers to responsive caregiving induced by mental depletion or fatigue. Dating couples came to the laboratory and were informed that they would be video-recorded during an interaction in which one of them (whom we regarded as the "care-seeker") disclosed a personal problem to the other (the "caregiver"). Care-seekers chose and wrote about any personal problem they were willing to discuss (except ones that involved conflict with the partner). And at the same time, caregivers were taken to another room where they performed a Stroop color-naming task in which we manipulated mental depletion and were subliminally exposed to either the names of security providers or the names of unfamiliar people. Following these manipulations, couple members were videotaped while they talked about the problem that the care-seeker wished to discuss, and then independent judges, viewing the video-recordings, coded participants' responsiveness to their disclosing partner.

Experimentally induced attachment security was associated with greater responsiveness to the disclosing partner. Moreover, security priming overrode the detrimental effects of mental depletion and of dispositional avoidance on responsiveness, and it counteracted the tendency of anxious caregivers to be less responsive following experimentally induced mental depletion. These effects were unexplained by the alternative variable, relationship satisfaction. Overall, the findings emphasize that attachment security facilitates effective support provision, and that an experimental enhancement of security can counteract dispositional barriers (insecure attachment orientations) and situational barriers (mental depletion) to responsive and sensitive caregiving.

Following up these findings, Mikulincer, Shaver, Bar-On, and Sahdra (2014) conducted two studies extending the investigation to another barrier to caregiving (self-esteem threat) and to the provision of secure-base support for a partner's exploration. In the first study, participants were randomly assigned to one of four conditions based on self-worth threat and security priming manipulations, and external observers rated their responsiveness to a dating partner who was disclosing a personal problem. In the second study, participants were randomly assigned to one of four conditions based on mental depletion and security priming manipulations, and external observers rated their responsiveness to a dating romantic partner who was exploring personal goals.

The findings of these studies indicate that priming mental representations of security providers (as compared to neutral priming) caused people to be more responsive to their romantic partner when the partner was either disclosing a personal problem or exploring personal goals. Moreover, security priming was found to override the detrimental effects of mental depletion on the provision of secure-base support to a romantic partner who was exploring his or her personal goals. However, such priming failed to buffer the detrimental effects of a self-worth threat on the provision of safe haven support to a distressed partner. Perhaps a self-worth threat activates negative self-representations (a proxy for anxious attachment), thereby augmenting self-focused doubts and concerns that distract caregivers from attending to a partner's needs. That is, self-worth threats might act on the same psychological mechanism acted on by security priming but in the opposite direction – augmenting rather than reducing self-focused doubts and concerns.

Positive relational emotions

Development of an optimal relationship also depends on the extent to which partners experience and express respect, admiration, and gratitude to each other and the extent to which they are able to create a climate of appreciation and friendship instead of criticism and contempt (Markman, Stanley, & Blumberg, 1994). These expressions increase a partner's sense of love and lovability, deepen mutual trust, and promote what Wieselquist, Rusbult, Foster, and Agnew (1999) called "mutual growth cycles" in relationships. In these cycles, one partner's trust increases his or her dependence on the relationship, commitment to the relationship, and pro-relationship behaviors, which in turn increases the other partner's trust, dependence, commitment, and pro-relationship behaviors, thereby heightening both partners' involvement and satisfaction.

There is accumulating evidence that secure people's positive working models of others contribute to expressions of respect, admiration, and gratitude toward a romantic partner (e.g., Beck & Clark, 2010; Frei & Shaver, 2002; Mikulincer et al., 2006). In a diary study, Mikulincer et al. (2006) explored these issues in the context of marital relationships and found that attachment security predicted higher levels of daily gratitude toward a spouse across 21 consecutive days. In addition, Nguyen and Munch (2011) found that more secure people were more positive about the desirability of giving a gift to their romantic partner.

Another interpersonal process that has positive implications for relationship satisfaction is what Gable and her colleagues call relationship capitalization, "the process of informing another person about the occurrence of a personal positive event and thereby deriving additional benefit from it" (Gable, Reis, Impett, & Asher, 2004, p. 228). In a series of correlational, experimental, and diary studies, Sofer-Roth (2008) found that attachment security facilitates such a capitalization process: More secure participants were more likely to express happiness and joy in response to a partner' disclosure of a positive event and less likely to express envy and criticism. In another study of video-recorded interactions, Shallcross, Howland, Bemis, Simpson, and Frazier (2011) found that more secure participants were rated by external observers as more responsive to a partner's disclosure of a positive event in his or her life. There is also evidence that secure people, as compared with avoidant ones, report more positive feelings toward a romantic partner after outperforming the partner or being outperformed by him or her on a cognitive task (Scinta & Gable, 2005).

CONCLUDING REMARKS

In the present chapter we have shown, in brief, how attachment theory characterizes and explains the development of optimal close relationships. Future research should attempt to examine the interplay of attachment security and other behavioral systems (e.g., exploration, sex, caregiving) in promoting optimal relationships. Research should also examine in greater depth the ways in which attachment security may protect a person and a couple from stressful life circumstances and traumatic events. Longitudinal research should examine trajectories of attachment security and relationship quality across the various stages of a relationship and at different life periods.

Another focus of new research should be methods of improving couple relationships based on attachment research. The many recent studies of security priming effects indicate that interventions can be successful, but most of the priming interventions have been very short-term, leaving open many questions about how they could be extended in time, with greater continuing effects. In addition, there are new therapeutic programs that attempt to incorporate Bowlby's (1988) theory for treating distressed couples (e.g., Johnson's 2003 emotionally focused couple therapy). These interventions explicitly recognize the trauma induced by rejection, separation, and loss and the impact these experiences have on couple functioning; the self-fulfilling nature of working models; and the likely therapeutic effects of interventions that focus on developing secure emotional connections. Moreover, they underscore the importance of the therapist as a provider of a secure base for the exploration and revision of maladaptive working models and relational patterns. For example, Johnson (2003) wrote that the updating of working models is the primary focus of couple therapy. Further studies should examine more systematically the specific attachment-related processes that contribute to the improvement of couple functioning within couple counseling and therapy. Researchers should also attempt to extend insights they coin from attachment-based therapeutic studies to the promotion of optimal relationships in the general population.

REFERENCES

Alexandrov, E. O., Cowan, P. A., & Cowan, C. P. (2005). Couple attachment and the quality of marital relationships: Method and concept in the validation of the new couple attachment interview and coding system. *Attachment and Human Development*, 7, 123–152.

Ashy, M., Mercurio, A. E., & Malley-Morrison, K. (2010). Apology, forgiveness and reconciliation: An ecological world-view framework. *Individual Differences Research*, 8, 17–26.

Askari, A., Madgaonkar, J. S., & Rowell, R. K. (2012). Current psycho-pathological issues among partners of cancer patients. *Journal of Psychosocial Research, 7*, 77–85.

Baldwin, M. W., Fehr, B., Keedian, E., Seidel, M., & Thomson, D. W. (1993). An exploration of the relational schemata underlying attachment styles: Self-report and lexical decision approaches. *Personality and Social Psychology Bulletin, 19*, 746–754.

Bartz, J. A., & Lydon, J. E. (2008). Relationship-specific attachment, risk regulation, and communal norm adherence in close relationships. *Journal of Experimental Social Psychology, 44*, 655–663.

Beck, L. A., & Clark, M. S. (2010). Looking a gift horse in the mouth as a defense against increasing intimacy. *Journal of Experimental Social Psychology, 46*, 676–679.

Beijersbergen, M. D., Bakermans-Kranenburg, M. J., van IJzendoorn, M. H., & Juffer, F. (2008). Stress regulation in adolescents: Physiological reactivity during the Adult Attachment Interview and conflict interaction. *Child Development, 79*, 1707–1720.

Berant, E., Mikulincer, M., & Florian, V. (2001). The association of mothers' attachment style and their psychological reactions to the diagnosis of their infant's congenital heart disease. *Journal of Social and Clinical Psychology, 20*, 208–232.

Besser, A., & Priel, B. (2010). Grandiose narcissism versus vulnerable narcissism in threatening situations: Emotional reactions to achievement failure and interpersonal rejection. *Journal of Social and Clinical Psychology, 29*, 874–902.

Bouthillier, D., Julien, D., Dube, M., Belanger, I., & Hamelin, M. (2002). Predictive validity of adult attachment measures in relation to emotion regulation behaviors in marital interactions. *Journal of Adult Development, 9*, 291–305.

Bowlby, J. (1973). *Attachment and loss: Vol. 2. Separation: Anxiety and anger*. New York: Basic Books.

Bowlby, J. (1980). *Attachment and loss: Vol. 3. Sadness and depression*. New York: Basic Books.

Bowlby, J. (1982). *Attachment and loss: Vol. 1. Attachment* (2nd ed.). New York: Basic Books. (Original ed. 1969)

Bowlby, J. (1988). *A secure base: Clinical applications of attachment theory*. London: Routledge.

Brandau-Brown, F. E., Bello, R. S., & Ragsdale, J. D. (2010). Attachment style and tolerance for ambiguity effects on relational repair message interpretation among remarrieds. *Marriage & Family Review, 46*, 389–399.

Braun, M., Hales, S., Gilad, L., Mikulincer, M., Rydall, A., & Rodin, G. (2012). Caregiving styles and attachment orientations in couples facing advanced cancer. *Psycho-Oncology, 21*, 935–943.

Brennan, K. A., Clark, C. L., & Shaver, P. R. (1998). Self-report measurement of adult attachment: An integrative overview. In J. A. Simpson & W. S. Rholes (Eds.), *Attachment theory and close relationships* (pp. 46–76). New York: Guilford Press.

Burnette, J. L., Taylor, K., Worthington, E. L., Jr., & Forsyth, D. R. (2007). Attachment working models and trait forgivingness: The mediating role of angry rumination. *Personality and Individual Differences, 42*, 1585–1596.

Campbell, L., Simpson, J. A., Boldry, J., & Kashy, D. A. (2005). Perceptions of conflict and support in romantic relationships: The role of attachment anxiety. *Journal of Personality and Social Psychology, 88*, 510–531.

Cann, A., Norman, M. A., Welbourne, J., & Calhoun, L. G. (2008). Attachment styles, conflict styles, and humor styles: Interrelationships and associations with relationship satisfaction. *European Journal of Personality, 22*, 131–146.

Carnelley, K. B., Israel, S., & Brennan, K. (2007). The role of attachment in influencing reactions to manipulated feedback from romantic partners. *European Journal of Social Psychology*, 37, 968–986.

Cassidy, J., & Kobak, R. R. (1988). Avoidance and its relationship with other defensive processes. In J. Belsky & T. Nezworski (Eds.), *Clinical implications of attachment* (pp. 300–323). Hillsdale, NJ: Erlbaum.

Cassidy, J., & Shaver, P. R. (Eds.) (2008). *Handbook of attachment: Theory, research, and clinical applications* (2nd ed.). New York: Guilford Press.

Cassidy, J., Shaver, P. R., Mikulincer, M., & Lavy, S. (2009). Experimentally induced security influences responses to psychological pain. *Journal of Social and Clinical Psychology*, 28, 463–478.

Collins, N. L. (1996). Working models of attachment: Implications for explanation, emotion, and behavior. *Journal of Personality and Social Psychology*, 71, 810–832.

Collins, N. L., & Feeney, B. C. (2000). A safe haven: An attachment theory perspective on support-seeking and caregiving in intimate relationships. *Journal of Personality and Social Psychology*, 78, 1053–1073.

Collins, N. L., Ford, M. B., Guichard, A. C., & Feeney, B. C. (2005). *Responding to need in intimate relationships: The role of attachment security*. Unpublished manuscript, University of California, Santa Barbara.

Collins, N. L., & Read, S. J. (1990). Adult attachment, working models, and relationship quality in dating couples. *Journal of Personality and Social Psychology*, 58, 644–663.

Cooper, M. L., Shaver, P. R., & Collins, N. L. (1998). Attachment styles, emotion regulation, and adjustment in adolescence. *Journal of Personality and Social Psychology*, 74, 1380–1397.

Creasey, G., & Hesson-McInnis, M. (2001). Affective responses, cognitive appraisals, and conflict tactics in late adolescent romantic relationships: Associations with attachment orientations. *Journal of Counseling Psychology*, 48, 85–96.

Creasey, G., & Ladd, A. (2004). Negative mood regulation expectancies and conflict behaviors in late adolescent college student romantic relationships: The moderating role of generalized attachment representations. *Journal of Research on Adolescence*, 14, 235–255.

Creasey, G., & Ladd, A. (2005). Generalized and specific attachment representations: Unique and interactive roles in predicting conflict behaviors in close relationships. *Personality and Social Psychology Bulletin*, 31, 1026–1038.

Davila, J., & Kashy, D. (2009). Secure base processes in couples: Daily associations between support experiences and attachment security. *Journal of Family Psychology*, 23, 76–88.

Dewitte, M., De Houwer, J., Goubert, L., & Buysse, A. (2010). A multi-modal approach to the study of attachment-related distress. *Biological Psychology*, 85, 149–162.

Dominique, R., & Mollen, D. (2009). Attachment and conflict communication in adult romantic relationships. *Journal of Social and Personal Relationships*, 26, 678–696.

Donovan, S., & Emmers-Sommer, T. M. (2012). Attachment style and gender as predictors of communicative responses to infidelity. *Marriage & Family Review*, 48, 125–149.

Feeney, B. C., & Collins, N. L. (2001). Predictors of caregiving in adult intimate relationships: An attachment theoretical perspective. *Journal of Personality and Social Psychology*, 80, 972–994.

Feeney, B. C., & Thrush, R. L. (2010). Relationship influences on exploration in adulthood: The characteristics and function of a secure base. *Journal of Personality and Social Psychology*, 98, 57–76.

Feeney, B. C., Collins, N. L., van Vleet, M., & Tomlinson, J. M. (2013). Motivations for providing a secure base: Links with attachment orientation and secure base support behavior. *Attachment & Human Development*, 15, 261–280.

Feeney, J. A. (1996). Attachment, caregiving, and marital satisfaction. *Personal Relationships*, 3, 401–416.

Feeney, J. A. (1998). Adult attachment and relationship-centered anxiety: Responses to physical and emotional distancing. In J. A. Simpson & W. S. Rholes (Eds.), *Attachment theory and close relationships* (pp. 189–219). New York: Guilford Press.

Fraley, R. C., & Waller, N. G. (1998). Adult attachment patterns: A test of the typological model. In J. A. Simpson & W. S. Rholes (Eds.), *Attachment theory and close relationships* (pp. 77–114). New York: Guilford Press.

Fredrickson, B. L. (2001). The role of positive emotions in positive psychology: The broaden-and-build theory of positive emotions. *American Psychologist*, 56, 218–226.

Frei, J. R., & Shaver, P. R. (2002). Respect in close relationships: Prototype definition, self-report assessment, and initial correlates. *Personal Relationships*, 9, 121–139.

Gable, S. L., Reis, H. T., Impett, E. A., & Asher, E. R. (2004). What do you do when things go right? The intrapersonal and interpersonal benefits of sharing positive events. *Journal of Personality and Social Psychology*, 87, 228–241.

Gaines, S. O., Jr., Reis, H. T., Summers, S., Rusbult, C. E., Cox, C. L., Wexler, M. O., Marelich, W. D., & Kurland, G. J. (1997). Impact of attachment style on reactions to accommodative dilemmas in close relationships. *Personal Relationships*, 4, 93–113.

Gallo, L. C., & Smith, T. W. (2001). Attachment style in marriage: Adjustment and responses to interaction. *Journal of Social and Personal Relationships*, 18, 263–289.

Guerrero, L. K. (1998). Attachment-style differences in the experience and expression of romantic jealousy. *Personal Relationships*, 5, 273–291.

Hannon, P. A., Rusbult, C. E., Finkel, E. J., & Kumashiro, M. A. (2010). In the wake of betrayal: Perpetrator amends, victim forgiveness, and the resolution of betrayal incidents. *Personal Relationships*, 17, 253–278.

Hazan, C., & Shaver, P. R. (1987). Romantic love conceptualized as an attachment process. *Journal of Personality and Social Psychology*, 52, 511–524.

Heene, E. L. D., Buysse, A., & Van Oost, P. (2005). Indirect pathways between depressive symptoms and marital distress: The role of conflict communication, attributions, and attachment style. *Family Process*, 44, 413–440.

Johnson, S. M. (2003). Attachment theory: A guide for couple therapy. In S. M. Johnson, & V. E. Whiffen (Eds.), *Attachment processes in couple and family therapy* (pp. 103–123). New York: Guilford Press.

Kachadourian, L. K., Fincham, F., & Davila, J. (2004). The tendency to forgive in dating and married couples: The role of attachment and relationship satisfaction. *Personal Relationships*, 11, 373–393.

Karremans, J. C., & Aarts, H. (2007). The role of automaticity in the inclination to forgive close others. *Journal of Experimental Social Psychology*, 43, 902–917.

Kim, Y., & Carver, C. S. (2007). Frequency and difficulty in caregiving among spouses of individuals with cancer: Effects of adult attachment and gender. *Psycho-Oncology*, 16, 714–728.

Kim, Y., Carver, C. S., Deci, E. L., & Kasser, T. (2008). Adult attachment and psychological well-being in cancer caregivers: The meditational role of spouses motives for caregiving. *Health Psychology*, 27, S144–S154.

Kunce, L. J., & Shaver, P. R. (1994). An attachment-theoretical approach to caregiving in romantic relationships. In K. Bartholomew & D. Perlman (Eds.), *Advances in personal relationships* (Vol. 5, pp. 205–237). London, England: Kingsley.

Kuscu, M. K., Dural, U., Onen, P., Yaşa, Y., Yayla, M., Basaran, G., Turhal, S., & Bekiroğlu, N. (2009). The association between individual attachment patterns, the perceived social support, and the psychological well-being of Turkish informal caregivers. *Psycho-Oncology*, 18, 927–935.

La Valley, A. G., & Guerrero, L. K. (2012). Perceptions of conflict behavior and relational satisfaction in adult parent–child relationships: A dyadic analysis from an attachment perspective. *Communication Research*, 39, 48–78.

Lawler-Row, K. A., Hyatt-Edwards, L., Wuensch, K. L., & Karremans, J. C. (2011). Forgiveness and health: The role of attachment. *Personal Relationships*, 18, 170–183

Lawler-Row, K. A., Younger, J. W., Piferi, R. L., & Jones, W. H. (2006). The role of adult attachment style in forgiveness following an interpersonal offense. *Journal of Counseling and Development*, 84, 493–502.

Marazziti, D., Consoli, G., Albanese, F., Laquidara, E., Baroni, S., & Dell'Osso, M. C. (2010). Romantic attachment and subtypes/dimensions of jealousy. *Clinical Practice and Epidemiology in Mental Health*, 6, 53–58.

Markman, H. J., Stanley, S., & Blumberg, S. L. (1994). *Fighting for your marriage: Positive steps for preventing divorce and preserving a lasting love*. San Francisco, CA: Jossey-Bass.

Martin, L. A., Vosvick, M., & Riggs, S. A. (2012). Attachment, forgiveness, and physical health quality of life in HIV + adults. *AIDS Care*, 24, 1333–1340.

Mickelson, K. D., Kessler, R. C., & Shaver, P. R. (1997). Adult attachment in a nationally representative sample. *Journal of Personality and Social Psychology*, 73, 1092–1106.

Mikulincer, M. (1995). Attachment style and the mental representation of the self. *Journal of Personality and Social Psychology*, 69, 1203–1215.

Mikulincer, M., & Florian, V. (1995). Appraisal of and coping with a real-life stressful situation: The contribution of attachment styles. *Personality and Social Psychology Bulletin*, 21, 406–414.

Mikulincer, M., Florian, V., Cowan, P. A., & Cowan, C. P. (2002). Attachment security in couple relationships: A systemic model and its implications for family dynamics. *Family Process*, 41, 405–434.

Mikulincer, M., Gillath, O., & Shaver, P. R. (2002). Activation of the attachment system in adulthood: Threat-related primes increase the accessibility of mental representations of attachment figures. *Journal of Personality and Social Psychology*, 83, 881–895.

Mikulincer, M., & Shaver, P. R. (2003). The attachment behavioral system in adulthood: Activation, psychodynamics, and interpersonal processes. In M. P. Zanna (Ed.), *Advances in experimental social psychology* (Vol. 35, pp. 53–152). San Diego, CA: Academic Press.

Mikulincer, M., & Shaver, P. R. (2004). Security-based self-representations in adulthood: Contents and processes. In W. S. Rholes & J. A. Simpson (Eds.), *Adult attachment: Theory, research, and clinical implications* (pp. 159–195). New York: Guilford Press.

Mikulincer, M., & Shaver, P. R. (2007a). *Attachment in adulthood: Structure, dynamics, and change.* New York: Guilford Press.

Mikulincer, M., & Shaver, P. R. (2007b). Boosting attachment security to promote mental health, prosocial values, and inter-group tolerance. *Psychological Inquiry*, 18, 139–156.

Mikulincer, M., Shaver, P. R., Bar-On, N., & Sahdra, B. K. (2014). Security enhancement, self-esteem threat, and mental depletion affect provision of a safe haven and secure base to a romantic partner. *Journal of Social and Personal Relationships*, 31, 630–650.

Mikulincer, M., Shaver, P. R., Sahdra, B. K., & Bar-On, N. (2013). Can security-enhancing interventions overcome psychological barriers to responsiveness in couple relationships? *Attachment and Human Development*, 15, 246–260.

Mikulincer, M., Shaver, P. R., Sapir-Lavid, Y., & Avihou-Kanza, N. (2009). What's inside the minds of securely and insecurely attached people? The secure-base script and its associations with attachment-style dimensions. *Journal of Personality and Social Psychology*, 97, 615–633.

Mikulincer, M., Shaver, P. R., & Slav, K. (2006). Attachment, mental representations of others, and gratitude and forgiveness in romantic relationships. In M. Mikulincer & G. S. Goodman (Eds.), *Dynamics of romantic love: Attachment, caregiving, and sex* (pp. 190–215). New York: Guilford Press.

Millings, A., & Walsh, J. (2009). A dyadic exploration of attachment and caregiving in long-term couples. *Personal Relationships*, 16, 437–453.

Millings, A., Walsh, J., Hepper, E., & O'Brien, M. (2013). Good partner, good parent: Responsiveness mediates the link between romantic attachment and parenting style. *Personality and Social Psychology Bulletin*, 39, 170–180.

Monin, J. K., Feeney, B. C., & Schulz, R. (2012). Attachment orientation and reactions to anxiety expression in close relationships. *Personal Relationships*, 19, 535–550.

Morse, J. Q., Shaffer, D. R., Williamson, G. M., Dooley, W. K., & Schulz, R. (2012). Models of self and others and their relation to positive and negative caregiving responses. *Psychology and Aging*, 27, 211–218.

Nelson, N., Albeck-Solomon, R., & Ben-Ari, R. (2011). Are your disputants insecure and does it matter? Attachment and disputants' speech during mediation. *Negotiation Journal*, 27, 45–68.

Nguyen, H. P., & Munch, J. M. (2011). Romantic gift giving as chore or pleasure: The effects of attachment orientations on gift giving perceptions. *Journal of Business Research*, 64, 113–118.

Noftle, E. E., & Shaver, P. R. (2006). Attachment dimensions and the big five personality traits: Associations and comparative ability to predict relationship quality. *Journal of Research in Personality*, 40, 179–208.

Paley, B., Cox, M. J., Burchinal, M. R., & Payne, C. (1999). Attachment and marital functioning: Comparison of spouses with continuous-secure, earned-secure, dismissing, and preoccupied attachment stances. *Journal of Family Psychology*, 13, 580–597.

Park, L. E. (2010). Responses to self-threat: Linking self and relational constructs with approach and avoidance motivation. *Social and Personality Psychology Compass*, 4, 201–221.

Perunovic, M., & Holmes, J. G. (2008). Automatic accommodation: The role of personality. *Personal Relationships*, 15, 57–70.

Pietromonaco, P. R., & Carnelley, K. B. (1994). Gender and working models of attachment: Consequences for perceptions of self and romantic relationships. *Personal Relationships*, 1, 63–82

Powers, S. I., Pietromonaco, P. R., Gunlicks, M., & Sayer, A. (2006). Dating couples' attachment styles and patterns of cortisol reactivity and recovery in response to a relationship conflict. *Journal of Personality and Social Psychology*, 90, 613–628.

Radecki-Bush, C., Farrell, A. D., & Bush, J. P. (1993). Predicting jealous responses: The influence of adult attachment and depression on threat appraisal. *Journal of Social and Personal Relationships*, 10, 569–588.

Rodin, G., Walsh, A., Zimmermann, C., Gagliese, L., Jones, J., Shepherd, F. A., & Mikulincer, M. (2007). The contribution of attachment security and social support to depressive symptoms in patients with metastatic cancer. *Psycho-Oncology*, 16, 1080–1091.

Salvatore, J. E., Kuo, S. I., Steele, R. D., Simpson, J. A., & Collins, W. A. (2011). Recovering from conflict in romantic relationships: A developmental perspective. *Psychological Science*, 22, 376–383.

Scharfe, E., & Bartholomew, K. (1995). Accommodation and attachment representations in young couples. *Journal of Social and Personal Relationships*, 12, 389–401.

Scinta, A., & Gable, S. L. (2005). Performance comparisons and attachment: An investigation of competitive responses in close relationships. *Personal Relationships*, 12, 357–372.

Shallcross, S. L., Howland, M., Bemis, J., Simpson, J. A., and Frazier, P. (2011). Not "capitalizing" on social capitalization interactions: The role of attachment insecurity. *Journal of Family Psychology*, 25, 77–85.

Shaver, P. R., & Hazan, C. (1988). A biased overview of the study of love. *Journal of Social and Personal Relationships*, 5, 473–501.

Shaver, P. R., & Mikulincer, M. (2002). Attachment-related psychodynamics. *Attachment and Human Development*, 4, 133–161.

Shaver, P. R., Mikulincer, M., Lavy, S., & Cassidy, J. (2009). Understanding and altering hurt feelings: An attachment-theoretical perspective on the generation and regulation of emotions. In A. Vangelisti (Ed.), *Feeling hurt in close relationships* (pp. 92–121). New York: Cambridge University Press.

Simpson, J. A., Collins, W. A., Tran, S., & Haydon, K. C. (2007). Attachment and the experience and expression of emotions in adult romantic relationships: A developmental perspective. *Journal of Personality and Social Psychology*, 92, 355–367.

Simpson, J. A., Rholes, W. S., & Nelligan, J. S. (1992). Support seeking and support giving within couples in an anxiety-provoking situation: The role of attachment styles. *Journal of Personality and Social Psychology*, 62, 434–446.

Simpson, J. A., Rholes, W. S., Orina, M., & Grich, J. (2002). Working models of attachment, support giving, and support seeking in a stressful situation. *Personality and Social Psychology Bulletin*, 28, 598–608.

Simpson, J. A., Rholes, W. S., & Phillips, D. (1996). Conflict in close relationships: An attachment perspective. *Journal of Personality and Social Psychology*, 71, 899–914.

Sofer-Roth, S. (2008). *Adult attachment and the nature of responses to a romantic partner's expression of personal happiness.* Unpublished doctoral dissertation, Bar-Ilan University, Ramat Gan, Israel.

Sprecher, S., & Fehr, B. (2011). Dispositional attachment and relationship-specific attachment as predictors of compassionate love for a partner. *Journal of Social and Personal Relationships*, 28, 558–574.

Sullivan, K. T., Pasch, L. A., Johnson, M. D., & Bradbury, T. N. (2010). Social support, problem solving, and the longitudinal course of newlywed marriage. *Journal of Personality and Social Psychology*, 98, 631–644.

Wang, C. D., King, M. L., & Debernardi, N. R. (2012), Adult attachment, cognitive appraisal, and university students' reactions to romantic infidelity. *Journal of College Counseling*, 15, 101–116.

Waters, H. S., & Waters, E. (2006). The attachment working models concept: Among other things, we build script-like representations of secure base experiences. *Attachment and Human Development*, 8, 185–198.

Wieselquist, J., Rusbult, C. E., Foster, C. A., & Agnew, C. R. (1999). Commitment, pro-relationship behavior, and trust in close relationships. *Journal of Personality and Social Psychology*, 77, 942–966.

Wood, N. D., Werner-Wilson, R. J., Parker, T. S., & Perry, M. S. (2012). Exploring the impact of attachment anxiety and avoidance on the perception of couple conflict. *Contemporary Family Therapy*, 34, 416–428.

4

The self-expansion model and optimal relationship development

XIAOMENG XU, GARY W. LEWANDOWSKI JR.,
AND ARTHUR ARON

In this chapter, we focus on the potential practical applications to optimal relationship development based on thinking and research from the self-expansion model, how its application could help move couples from being dissatisfied and bored with each other, to happy and passionate with each other. We begin with a basic description of the model and a brief review of some fundamental supporting research including some recent new directions relevant to this chapter's theme. We then proceed to sections that explore general implications of the model for relationships and, specific ways that one can make use of such implications for optimizing self-expansion in relationships (notably shared novel and challenging activities). We then consider (for the first time) applied implications of a new research direction – how individual (non-relational) self-expansion can benefit relationship development. Finally, we conclude with some possible future directions.

THE SELF-EXPANSION MODEL

In this section we elucidate the basic model itself, the foundation of the applications we will be discussing, including briefly reviewing some of the basic research support, and noting emerging directions, all emphasizing the aspects most relevant to optimal relationship development.

The model

The self-expansion model (Aron & Aron, 1986; for a recent review, see Aron, Lewandowski, Mashek, & Aron, 2013) was developed to address theoretical and applied questions about basic processes underlying experiences and behaviors in the context of close relationships (and since, extended to other contexts). The model has two key principles:

The authors would like to thank Stephanie Kaplan and Sierra Kauer for their assistance in the preparation of this chapter.

1. ***Motivational principle:*** People seek to expand their potential efficacy, to increase their ability to accomplish goals. That is, a fundamental human motive is posited to be what other scholars have previously described as exploration, effectance, self-improvement, curiosity, competence, or a broadening of one's perspective. Further, given this motivation's importance, experiencing novelty, interest, and/or challenge (or even experiences typically associated with rapid expansion, such as exciting experiences involving novelty and challenge) should be particularly rewarding.

2. ***Inclusion-of-other-in-the-self principle:*** One way in which people seek to expand the self is through close relationships, because in a close relationship the other's resources, perspectives, and identities are experienced, to some extent, as one's own.

Each of these basic principles has had considerable research support; a thorough review of this evidence can be found in Aron et al. (2013). As the focus of the present chapter is on application to creating optimal relationships, we will here only briefly review a few example studies that provide support for each of these principles in the context of relationships.

Research support for the motivational principle

Implications of this principle have been tested in a wide variety of relationship contexts. In terms of initial attraction, almost any relationship is likely to provide some degree of self-expansion. When relationship formation is uncertain, consistent with the standard similarity-attraction effect, the self-expansion model suggests that perceived similarity is most desirable (because similarity serves as an indication that a relationship – and thus expansion of the self by including the other in the self–is likely to develop). However, the self-expansion model also suggests that when relationship development is more certain, differences can be particularly desirable as a relationship with a person who has, for example, different interests, offers even greater opportunities for expansion through including that person in the self. Aron, Steele, Kashdan, and Perez (2006) tested this possibility in the context of same-sex friendships and perceived similarities/differences in interests. As predicted, when the likelihood of forming a relationship was unknown, participants preferred similarity. However, when participants were led to believe a relationship was likely, participants (especially men in this experiment) preferred dissimilarity.

In another experiment, Wright, McLaughlin-Volpe, and Brody (2004) tested the idea that differences would be especially important in directing attraction when the desire for self-expansion was high. Wright et al. manipulated the intensity of participants' self-expansion motive by providing bogus feedback from a supposed personality measure (either your current life is overstimulating or your life is dull and boring). Then, in what participants were led to believe was an unrelated part of the study, the participants selected from a list of other students with whom they would most like to work on a joint task. As predicted, participants in the high self-expansion motive condition selected more potential partners who were dissimilar (in this study, with names that indicated a different ethnicity than their own) than did participants in the low self-expansion motive condition.

Another line of research investigated expansion of the self when falling in love (Aron, Paris, & Aron, 1995). Participants across two studies completed standard measures of self-esteem, self-efficacy, and spontaneous self-concept (open-ended response to "Who are you today?") every 2 weeks over a 10-week period. In one study they indicated every 2 weeks if they fell in love and completed a love scale. In the other study a less obvious procedure was used such that at each testing they completed a check list of "significant life events" that occurred in the past 2 weeks; buried in this list was an item asking whether they had "fallen in love." In both studies, and on each self-measure, those who fell in love showed significantly greater self-concept increases (including increased number of responses to the "Who are you today?" question) from before to after falling in love when compared both to other time periods when they did not fall in love and compared to other participants who did not report the experience of falling in love. That is, falling in love appears to literally expand the self.

Yet another major line of research relevant to the self-expansion model's notion that falling in love is associated with self-expansion, and especially the greatly anticipated (and highly rewarding) self-expansion from a relationship with this person, has focused on the neural correlates of early stage romantic love. This hypothesized self-expansion (and especially the perceived very substantial opportunity for self-expansion as a relationship is created) in early stage, intense romantic love is hypothesized to represent a powerful motivational state that is represented in the brain by activation of the dopamine reward system. Several functional Magnetic Resonance Imaging (fMRI) studies have consistently demonstrated greater activation in this brain system when viewing a facial photo of (or even being subliminally shown the name of) a person with whom one has recently fallen in love versus various familiar others (for a review, see Acevedo & Aron, 2014).

These findings have been replicated cross culturally (e.g., Xu et al., 2011); for people who are still intensely in love with someone who has rejected them (Fisher, Brown, Aron, Strong, & Mashek, 2010); for those claiming to be intensely in love with someone to whom they have been married for more than 20 years (Acevedo, Aron, Fisher, & Brown, 2012); and across genders and sexual orientation (Zeki & Romaya, 2010). Further, recent research suggests that this activation resulting from intense romantic love is sufficient to offset pain response (Younger, Aron, Parke, Chatterjee, & Mackey, 2010), and to undermine craving for tobacco (e.g., Xu, Aron, Westmaas, Wang, & Sweet, 2014; Xu, Floyd, Westmaas, & Aron, 2010; Xu et al., 2012) and presumably other addictive substances. In sum, the consistent patterns of brain systems activated across these studies of intense love support the self-expansion model's implication that passionate love is a motivational state involving high levels of expected reward (in contrast to other models that were not supported such as that passionate love is a unique emotional state – as opposed to a motivational state – or that it is primarily rooted in sexual desire).

The most extensive body of research to date on self-expansion's motivational principle has focused on shared self-expanding activities. When a relationship is initially developing, experienced high levels of self-expansion through rapidly including the partner in the self are almost inevitable. Yet over time, as the partner becomes familiar, the rate of self-expansion typically slows down. However, the model hypothesizes that at this point, a sense of self-expansion can be re-invigorated by engaging together (so that the relationship is associated with the experience) in highly novel and challenging activities that generate the kind of excited engagement typically experienced with high levels of self-expansion. Such activities can be anything that is new and engaging, from an activity like sailing or skiing that the couple has never done before, or attending a class together on something they'd both like to learn about, or going out to an event type that is new to them, perhaps a county fair for some, or a comedy show for others. There are now quite a few studies focused on various aspects of, and providing consistent support for, this hypothesis (see sections below on The Benefits of Self-Expansion and Optimizing Relationships through Shared Self-Expansion).

Finally, a direct indication of self-expansion's role in relationships is the findings of greater relationship quality associated with higher scores on a measure of relationship self-expansion, the Self-Expansion Questionnaire (SEQ; Aron & Lewandowski, 2002). Example items include "How much does your partner help to expand your sense of the kind of person you are?" "How much does your partner increase your ability to accomplish new things?" and "How much do you see your partner as a way to expand your own capabilities?"

Some relevant recent developments related to the motivational principle

In addition to the main relevant lines of work over the last 30 years or so, there are many extensions, including five particularly important recent ones relevant to the current chapter. First, several experiments have demonstrated personal benefits of individual self-expansion (e.g., Mattingly & Lewandowski, 2013a; Mattingly & Lewandowski, 2014a), personal benefits that are likely to improve any relationship that person is in. Second, a recent experiment (Fivecoat, Tomlinson, Aron, & Caprariello, 2014) has shown that, after the early relationship stage, receiving active support from one's partner for an individual self-expansion opportunity caused significant increases in relationship satisfaction. Third, some recent studies (e.g., Lewandowski & Ackerman, 2006; VanderDrift, Lewandowski, & Agnew, 2011) have found effects of relationship-associated self-expansion minimizing interest in potential alternative partners. Fourth, several studies (e.g., Lewandowski & Bizzoco, 2007; Mason, Law, Bryan, Portley, & Sbarra, 2012) have demonstrated that relationship self-expansion moderates effects of dissolution, such that those with high levels of relationship self-expansion suffer most from the loss, but those who have low levels of relationship self-expansion (or whose relationships were restrictive of self-expansion) can benefit from the loss. Finally, there has recently been a significant extension/elaboration of core principles, the two-dimensional model (Mattingly, Lewandowski, & McIntyre, 2014), which proposes and demonstrates that relationships can produce self-change along two dimensions, direction (increase vs. decrease in content) and valence (positivity vs. negativity of content).

Research support for the inclusion-of-other-in-the-self principle

We now turn briefly to the aspect of the model that has received the most research attention. Although most of the applied relationship implications of the self-expansion model are based directly on the motivational principle, generally a central part of the operation or effects involves the inclusion principle. Thus, a basic grasp of the operation of the inclusion principle is important for understanding almost any application of the model to improving relationships. The basic idea underlying inclusion-of-other-in-the-self is that in a close relationship the content of the cognitive structure of the self literally overlaps and shares elements with the content of one's cognitive structure of one's close other's self (Aron, Aron, Tudor, & Nelson 1991). This has been shown particularly directly with the "me-not-me response-time procedure" in which individuals rate themselves and a close other on various traits (e.g., Aron et al., 1991, Study 3). Later, participants view each trait and indicate whether or not it is true of them. The greater closeness between self and other, the slower one is in responding to traits on which the self and other differ. Other studies have shown, for example, that closeness predicts difficulty distinguishing memories relevant to self and other (Mashek, Aron, & Boncimino, 2003), greater spontaneous sharing of resources with the others (e.g., Aron et al., 1991, Study 1), and more overlapping neural areas when hearing the names of the self and the other (Aron, Whitfield, & Lichty, 2007). Indeed, a pictorial self-report measure of perceived overlap of self and other, the Inclusion of Other in the Self Scale (IOS Scale; Aron, Aron, &

Smollan, 1992), has been used successfully in literally hundreds of studies to date.

There are also some recent developments regarding the inclusion principle with important potential practical implications: First, studies have shown that it is possible to have too much inclusion (e.g., Mashek, Le, Israel, & Aron, 2011). Another line of work, using a version of the me-not-me response time approach, has shown that to some extent we include in the self those to whom we are attracted but have not yet formed a relationship (Slotter & Gardner, 2009). Finally, perceiving one's partner as being satisfied leads to perceiving one's partner as including me in his or her self, which in turn leads to me including my partner in myself (Tomlinson & Aron, 2013). Although the applied implications of these recent findings have only been minimally explored, and we will not further elaborate on them in this chapter, we believe they each do suggest important considerations in developing optimal relationship interventions of all kinds.

THE BENEFITS OF SELF-EXPANSION

Self-expansion is a fundamental human motivation with links to positive affect, and one of the most intense forms of self-expansion is passionate love (whether in new or long-term relationships), where individuals are able to significantly and deeply increase their self-concept and resources (material, social, informational etc.). It is unsurprising then that, as noted earlier, neuroimaging research has found that intense passionate love activates the mesolimbic dopaminergic system of the brain, which is strongly associated with reward, motivation, and learning (e.g., Acevedo et al., 2012; Aron et al., 2005; Xu et al., 2011). Self-expansion is also related to flow (a mental state characterized by full immersion, energized focus, and enjoyment of an activity) and is similarly also often characterized by energetic focus and high positive affect (Graham, 2008).

In addition to being rewarding and intrinsically motivating, self-expansion leads to growth in the self-concept that is associated with increased feelings of self-efficacy (e.g., Mattingly & Lewandowski, 2013a). Although self-concept growth and increased self-efficacy may occur commonly in the context of forming a romantic relationship, relationships are certainly not the only source of this kind of self-expansion. For example, self-expansion can occur at the individual level by engaging in novel and challenging tasks or reading new and exciting facts (Mattingly & Lewandowski, 2013b). Self-expansion effects, whatever their source, also seem likely to provide many benefits to a romantic relationship. Self-related motives, such as self-expansion, help to protect social well-being, to facilitate affiliation, social interactions, and relationship initiation, development, and maintenance (Leary, 2007). Self-expansion functions primarily as an approach motivation

(Mattingly, McIntyre, & Lewandowski, 2012), and approach goals (e.g., focusing on pursuit of positive experiences in the relationship such as fun and growth) are associated with increased relationship satisfaction both on a daily level and over time. This increase in satisfaction is due in part to approach goals facilitating partner's being more responsive to each other's needs (Impett et al., 2010). Further, as self-expansion functions in part as approach motivation, it leads to increases in self-efficacy and increased effort and persistence (Mattingly, Lewandowski, & Carson, 2011; Mattingly & Lewandowski, 2013a; Mattingly & Lewandowski, 2013b), which may facilitate willingness to work on improving the relationship. For example, self-expansion predicts how frequently couples engage in relationship maintaining behaviors (e.g., communal orientation) such as sharing problems and trying to help one another, using humor / playful talk, and being physically affectionate (Ledbetter, 2013). This increased effort on working to maintain the relationship may reflect a link between self-expansion and growth beliefs – that relationships are not either destined or not, but obstacles in the relationship can be overcome and both partners can work to make the relationship stronger (Knee & Canevello, 2006).

Self-expansion is also associated with public displays of strong communal relationship orientation such as increased inclusion of other in the self on Facebook via tagging one's partner in status updates, appearing together in photographs, and listing similar interests (Carpenter & Spottswood, 2013).

Because the nature of self-expansion involves approach motivation/ goals and includes factors such as novelty, interest, and challenge, self-expansion may be especially important for the maintenance of long-term relationships. For example, approach goals facilitate sexual desire and help buffer against declines in sexual desire over time, a potential problem for long-term relationships (Impett, Strachman, Finkel, & Gable, 2008). Self-expansion may also be a strong predictor of long-term romantic love. In a study utilizing a random sample of 274 U.S. married individuals, 40 percent of those married over 10 years reported still being "very intensely in love," and this was moderately to strongly correlated with engaging in shared novel and challenging activities (O'Leary, Acevedo, Aron, Huddy, & Mashek, 2012).

Self-expansion may help with the maintenance of strong positive regard for the partner as it is linked with both admiration and adoration (Schindler, Paech, & Löwenbrück, 2014) and the partner acts as a source of reward in these passionate love relationships (Cacioppo, Grafton, & Bianchi-Demicheli, 2012).

Self-expansion may also allow us to better understand and harmoniously interact with our partners. Neuroimaging research suggests that in addition to reward, motivation, and learning systems, self-expansion may tap into common neural networks for representations of the self and other that are important in interpersonal awareness (Decety & Sommerville, 2003). The closeness and intimacy involved in self-expansion may also be associated with greater empathy (Chen, Chen, Lin, Chou, & Decety, 2010) and activation of the mirror neuron system, which is involved in simulation and understanding of the actions and intentions of others (Ortigue & Bianchi-Demicheli, 2008). Finally, as self-expansion also allows us to incorporate our partners' successes as part of our selves, it may be protective in that we are able to celebrate positive events with a partner without suffering the costs to self-esteem that are linked to social comparison (Gable & Reis, 2010; Gardner, Gabriel, & Hochschild, 2002).

OPTIMIZING RELATIONSHIPS THROUGH SHARED SELF-EXPANSION

Engaging in exciting activities with relationship partners is one method for optimizing self-expansion. In a 10-week couple's intervention study, Reissman, Aron, and Bergen (1993) followed 53 married dyads who were randomly assigned to one of three interventions: exciting activities, pleasant activities, or no-special activities. The activities were for 1.5 hours per week for 10 weeks and relationship satisfaction was measured pre- and post-intervention. The researchers found that post-intervention relationship satisfaction was significantly greater in the exciting-activities group than either the pleasant-activities or the no-activities control groups. This strongly suggests that it is not just spending time together that improves relationship satisfaction, but rather engaging together (so that excitement is linked to the relationship) in exciting activities associated with self-expansion. It is important to note that excitement is a subjective experience of positive exhilaration and the level of excitement one feels towards an activity or event is highly individualized. That is, while one person may highly anticipate the new episode of a television show and find it exciting, another may find watching TV boring. Similarly, someone may find riding roller coasters exciting, whereas another person may find the experience too overwhelming to be enjoyable.

Indeed, in the Reissman et al. study, before being assigned to conditions, members of each couple individually rated a long list of couple activities for how exciting or pleasant each would be to do with one's partner. Those couples assigned to the exciting condition were given a uniquely constructed list consisting of activities each couple member had rated as highly exciting (but not highly pleasant), and those assigned to the pleasant activities were given a list of activities both had rated as highly pleasant (but not highly exciting). Thus, an activity like hiking was part of the activities list for ten of the couples in the exciting condition, but for only two of the couples in the pleasant condition. Correspondingly, going out for a meal together was in the list for ten pleasant condition couples, but only four exciting condition couples. Both pleasant and exciting activities included physical activities as well as non-physical activities. It is important to note while physiological arousal may be present during exciting, novel, and challenging activities, arousal is distinct from self-expansion and the beneficial aspects of shared self-expanding activities can occur even without physiological arousal, such as when couples take a class together where they learn something new (Lewandowski & Aron, 2004).

Another intervention study, with 100 couples, found that those who engaged in exciting activities (deemed exciting by both members of the couple) for at least 90 minutes per week (compared to a wait-list control group) reported higher levels of romantic-relationship excitement, relationship satisfaction, and positive affect at the end of the 4-week intervention. Importantly, those who engaged in the exciting-activities intervention continued to show higher scores on these measures even 4-month post-intervention, suggesting that the benefits of self-expansion may not be quickly fleeting (Coulter & Malouff, 2013).

Even very brief (e.g., 7 minutes) shared novel, challenging, and exciting activities can lead to increases in relationship quality, with the association mediated by how exciting (vs. boring) the relationship is perceived to be. That is, when we engage in exciting activities with our partners, we tend to view both our partners and relationships as exciting (Aron, Norman, Aron, McKenna, & Heyman, 2000). This idea of associated self-expansion excitement bears out in other types of couples interventions. For example, mindfulness interventions can improve relationship satisfaction and reduce relationship distress (Carson, Carson, Gil, & Baucom, 2004), with a large part of relationship improvements attributable to the couples' sense that they were participating in exciting self-expansion together (Carson, Carson, Gil, & Baucom, 2007). That is, couples' subjective sense that the mindfulness intervention they were engaging in was exciting mediated the treatment's effect on relationship satisfaction (Carson et al., 2007). This intervention included many opportunities for excitement and self-expansion, including learning new couple yoga posture exercises and engaging in joint meditation, which allowed couples to attend to and discover new and interesting aspects of their experiences. Further, self-expansion (e.g., through self-disclosure) increases feelings of closeness and passionate love towards one's partner and can also facilitate social interaction such as becoming closer friends with other couples (Slatcher, 2010; Welker et al., 2014).

On the flip side, insufficient self-expansion (e.g., insufficient novelty, interest, or excitement) is related to feeling that the relationship is boring, which is then associated with negative affect (Harasymchuk & Fehr, 2010). Therefore, relationship boredom can have negative consequences. One longitudinal study found that among married couples, marital boredom predicted especially strong declines in marital satisfaction 9 years later (Tsapelas, Aron, & Orbuch, 2009). The boredom measure in that study was an item that also emphasized shared exciting activities: "During the past month, how often did you feel that your marriage was in a rut (or getting into a rut), that you do the same thing all the time and rarely get to do exciting things together as a couple?" Insufficient self-expansion is also associated with susceptibility to infidelity; it becomes more motivating to find another relationship that can provide sufficient self-expansion (Lewandowski & Ackerman, 2006; VanderDrift et al., 2011).

Self-expansion and attenuating relationship boredom might be especially important in long-term relationships as couples try to maintain closeness, commitment, and relationship satisfaction. Partners who engage in self-expansion together can optimize the experience by seeking out high-peak experiences (e.g., those including high positive affect) as these are more likely to have lasting effects (Graham, 2008). As passion for an activity is associated with quality of interpersonal relationships experienced within the context of that activity (Philippe, Vallerand, Houlfort, Lavigne, & Donahue, 2010), partners should ideally engage in activities together that both are passionate about. Partners should also seek to have a high ratio of positive to negative emotions in their relationship as this is associated with increased self-other overlap and complex understanding of the other (Waugh & Fredrickson, 2006).

Although we argue that self-expansion is a fundamental human motive, individual differences can affect desire for, and effects of, self-expansion. For example, individuals high in attachment anxiety (the desire for greater closeness and intimacy in relationships compared to secure and avoidant counterparts) are particularly motivated to engage in self-expansion and may have a particularly malleable self-concept (Slotter & Gardner, 2012). Similarly, individuals high in approach motivation (typified by an increased likelihood to take action and move towards something desired) are especially attracted to those who offer many expansion opportunities and unattracted to those who offer few expansion opportunities (Mattingly et al., 2012). Thus, engaging in self-expanding activities with a partner may be especially impactful for those high on approach motivation or attachment anxiety.

Although engaging in self-expanding activities together is one way to enhance a relationship, each partner may also pursue self-expansion individually (e.g., via hobbies, spiritual experiences, etc.). Partner responsiveness and support in these situations can be important. Fivecoat et al. (2014) found that among long-term couples, partner's active (rather than passive) support for an individual's opportunity for self-expansion increased relationship satisfaction.

We are also more likely to seek to self-expand with partners who are instrumental to goals that are highly motivating for us (e.g., something we are struggling with but want to achieve; Fitzsimons & Fishbach, 2010). Thus, it may be especially useful to the relationship to engage in self-expanding activities together that move at least one partner towards their desired goals, and/or to provide responsive support for those goals. This process of helping a partner move towards goals and their ideal self also directly provides individual and relationship benefits. The Michelangelo Phenomenon (Rusbult, Finkel, & Kumashiro, 2009) encapsulates this process wherein couples support and help to "sculpt" each other towards each person's own desired ideal self.

Individuals should avoid being unresponsive and unsupportive of partners' highly motivating goals, as this may prompt the partner to seek validation and opportunities to self-expand elsewhere. Individuals should also avoid self-expanding at the expense of a partner (e.g., pressuring the partner to join in an activity that the individual finds to be self-expanding but the partner does not enjoy). Although there may be a motivation to continuously self-expand and include others' resources into the self, this should not be done too quickly and without regard for the desires of the partner, but should instead be accomplished in an equitable and synergistic manner that is comfortable and beneficial for all members of the relationship (Burris, Rempel, Munteanu, & Therrien, 2013).

Self-expansion within the context of a romantic relationship is related to self-other overlap and intertwined communal selves. Although this can have very positive effects for the individual (e.g., increased satisfaction) and the relationship (e.g., increased closeness and commitment), self-other overlap also produces unique problems should the relationship dissolve. If the relationship had been an important source of self-expansion, after a breakup individuals may experience contraction of the self-concept (Lewandowski, Aron, Bassis, & Kunak, 2006), emotional distress (Slotter, Gardner, & Finkel, 2010), and breakup-related grief (Boelen & van den Hout, 2010). These negative consequences may be heightened in those high on attachment anxiety, whose sense of self may be especially susceptible to change and confusion post breakup (Slotter & Gardner, 2012).

These negative consequences of relationship dissolution may be attenuated if individuals engage in self-concept recovery and successfully redefine their sense of self (Mason et al., 2012). Individuals may also exert efforts to maintain desirable self-concept attributes that they gained in their former relationship and retain those attributes (and self-concept clarity) in the long run (Slotter, Emery, & Luchies, 2014). Finally, ending a relationship that provided little in the way of self-expansion is associated with growth in the self-concept via rediscovery of the self, positive emotions following the breakup, and less loss of the self (Lewandowski, & Bizzoco, 2007).

The self-expansion literature offers many insights for optimizing our romantic relationships (whether they are currently troubled or satisfying). Overall, research indicates that self-expansion is important in maintaining and strengthening the relationship and decreasing the likelihood of boredom and infidelity. It is important to remember, however, that individual differences such as attachment style and approach motivation can influence how likely self-expansion is to benefit the relationship, and what constitutes self-expansion will differ from person to person. Thus it is important for each member of the couple to responsively and actively support each others' self-expansion attempts while ensuring that each member is experiencing sufficient (but not excessive) self-expansion.

IMPLICATIONS FOR RELATIONSHIPS OF NON-RELATIONAL SELF-EXPANSION

The most basic assertion of the self-expansion model is that individuals possess a fundamental motivation to add to their self-concept and grow who they are as a person. As discussed, individuals experience self-expansion in their close relationships largely through inclusion of others in the self (Aron & Aron, 1986; Aron et al., 2013), and through engaging in self-expanding activities with their partner (Aron et al., 2000).

Although the research on the model emphasizes how individuals self-expand through close relationships (Aron & Aron, 1986; Aron et al., 2013), the basic model is about self-expansion as a basic motivation for individuals to increase their knowledge and abilities. Thus, appropriate experiences and activities would be expected to be sought that broaden an individual's sense of self not just through relationships but in all kinds of contexts, including non-relational self-expansion (Mattingly & Lewandowski, 2014a). Recent research supports this by demonstrating that self-expansion also occurs within individuals (e.g., Mattingly & Lewandowski, 2013a). Parallel to relational self-expansion, non-relational expansion arises from an individual's need to "broaden her/his horizons" or add to their sense of self by adding new perspectives, developing new skills, acquiring new identities, and enhancing capabilities (Aron & Aron, 1986; Aron et al., 2013).

In the first test of non-relational self-expansion, researchers conducted a series of six experimental studies to determine if the types of self-expanding activities that benefit relationships would also benefit individuals in a non-relational context (Mattingly & Lewandowski, 2013a). As the self-expansion model would predict, those who engaged in a novel, interesting, and challenging task (i.e., carried items with chopsticks) reported greater expansion than those who carried items by hand. A potential complication with most research on shared or relational self-expansion is that the activities couples engaged in were physical and potentially arousing in addition to being novel, interesting, and challenging (e.g., Aron et al., 2000). However, research subsequently showed that novelty/challenge and arousal are distinct experiences that influence relationships differently, with novelty/challenge being the important beneficial aspect of shared activities in established relationships (Lewandowski & Aron, 2004).

To similarly address the possibility that excitement or arousal was responsible for creating a sense of self-expansion in individuals, Mattingly and Lewandowski (2013a, Study 2) created an expanding activity (reading new and interesting facts) that is almost completely devoid of excitement. Again, consistent with the self-expansion model's predictions in relationships, reading new and interesting facts led to greater awareness, perspectives, knowledge, learning new things and increased sense of the ability to accomplish new things, compared to those who read mundane facts.

Like relational self-expansion, the model suggests that non-relational self-expansion should also result in an enhanced self-concept, increased self-efficacy, and greater effort (Aron et al., 2013). Across three studies, research has confirmed that non-relational self-expansion increases the size of the individual's self-concept (Mattingly & Lewandowski, 2014b). According to the self-expansion model, these increases in the self-concept provide benefits to the individual, such as greater self-efficacy. To test this, researchers examined the association between increased self-concept size and greater self-efficacy in a series of four studies (Mattingly & Lewandowski, 2013b). A series of several studies, using a variety of manipulations and measures, found that a fuller self-concept was associated with greater self-efficacy. If an individual feels more capable and more likely to experience success, it should increase the amount of effort expended. Again, across several studies, researchers confirmed that those who had engaged in novel, interesting, and challenging (i.e., self-expanding) tasks exerted more effort on physical and cognitive tasks (Mattingly & Lewandowski, 2013a).

Non-relational self-expansion's potential benefits for relationships

Importantly, the research on non-relational self-expansion establishes that new, challenging, and interesting activities can produce self-expansion, which produces a series of benefits (increased self-concept, efficacy, and effort). Though non-relational self-expansion occurs outside of the relationship and is not directly associated with the romantic partner, it is likely that each of these can provide benefits for the individual's relationship.

Understanding non-relational self-expansion is important because although many couples spend much of their day-to-day lives together, some of their time is spent apart. During time apart, each individual has the opportunity to experience self-expansion in a variety of ways, such as via business travel to a new city, taking a class at the gym, or tackling a challenging and interesting project at work. In each case, though not physically present for those experiences, the other partner should still garner the benefits and self-expansion. This is particularly true if the partners are highly included in the self (Aron et al., 1992). In highly included relationships where each partner's sense of self overlaps with each other, the partner's experiences and newly acquired perspectives and skills are felt as one's own. As a result, both partners should get to experience the feeling of self-growth that ultimately benefits the relationship. Thus, a partner who continually improves his or her own self-concept also has more positive qualities to provide the partner.

An individual's self-expansion experiences should also directly benefit the relationship by leading an individual to put forth more effort (Mattingly & Lewandowski, 2013a) and feel more confident in their ability to succeed in future tasks (Mattingly & Lewandowski, 2013b). In this case the increased effort that an individual is willing to put forth following self-expansion can be put directly into the relationship. For example, after experiencing self-expansion from finishing reading a new book, an individual may feel a greater willingness to work through and discuss a problem within the relationship.

A greater willingness to put forth effort is beneficial, because research on married couples shows that individuals who put more effort into their marriages, or premarital cohabitation relationships, report more satisfaction and higher levels of relationship stability (Shafer, Jensen, & Larson, 2014). Similarly, individual self-expansion leads to greater self-efficacy, a construct that positively correlates with relationship satisfaction (Roggero, Vacirca, Mauri, & Ciairano, 2012). Furthermore, greater self-efficacy also attenuated the negative effects of stress on the relationship, perhaps because the individual felt more capable of dealing with relationship difficulties. Of course some may argue that putting more effort into individual or non-relational self-expanding activities may mean that the person has less time and interest for the relationship. Though this is possible, it is likely largely a matter of degree. It is certainly possible for a person to experience self-expansion both within and outside the relationship at the same time. Provided that non-relational self-expansion does not occur at the expense of relational self-expansion it is unlikely to harm the relationship.

Though not empirically tested, it is likely that the two-dimensional model of self-change from relationships could also operate at the individual level (Mattingly, Lewandowski, & McIntyre, 2014). That is, through their own independent actions, individuals could gain or lose either positive or negative traits. In particular gaining positive (self-expansion) and losing negative (self-pruning) traits should enhance an individual's value as a relationship partner. For example, a person who learns yoga and begins to practice meditation to help reduce stress and quit smoking may become a better partner within the relationship, thus allowing the relationship to function at a higher level. Interestingly, self-expansion may facilitate these behaviors; for example, some research shows a link between self-expansion and smoking abstinence/cessation (Xu et al., 2010) and, as noted briefly earlier, neural attenuation of cigarette cue-reactivity (Xu et al., 2012; Xu et al., 2014).

In each of these cases, for an individual's non-relational self-expansion experiences to benefit the relationship, it would seem that a high degree of inclusion of other in the self should be present in the relationship. This way, if your highly included partner learns to play the guitar and recently went on a business trip to Italy, you can benefit from her self-expansion by gaining new knowledge and perspectives about Italy and enjoying her new guitar skills. A high degree of inclusion also minimizes the risk that either individual's non-relational self-expansion will come at the expense of the relationship.

In contemporary industrial cultures, a large portion of at least one member of a couple's time apart is spent at work. We know that daily job satisfaction is positively correlated with daily relationship satisfaction and that this association is especially strong for those with greater integration of their work and family roles (Ilies, Wilson, & Wagner, 2009). We also know that increased job satisfaction is important because negative experiences and work-related stress may "spillover" into a relationship, undermining quality and optimal functioning (Neff & Karney, 2004). In fact, on days when couples experienced greater stress at work than usual, they were less likely to view the relationship positively and were more likely to engage in negative behaviors toward their partner (Buck & Neff, 2012).

Spillover can also happen when the employee's partner perceives conflicts between work and family life as well as when the partner expresses negative attitudes toward the employee's work (Green, Bull Schaefer, MacDermid, & Weiss, 2011). In fact, employees who had partners with negative perceptions were more likely to look for another job and had lower levels of career resilience, or the ability to grow or "bounce back" from negative experiences or setbacks.

Much like how self-expansion helps improve relationship satisfaction (Aron et al., 2000), it also benefits individuals in the workplace (McIntyre, Mattingly, Lewandowski, & Simpson, 2014). Employees who reported greater self-expansion from their job, also felt a greater sense of satisfaction and commitment toward their job. Given the negative implications of "spillover" on relationships, though indirect, self-expansion's ability to improve job satisfaction is an important way to ensure optimal relationship functioning.

FUTURE DIRECTIONS

As noted at the outset, most work building on the self-expansion model has focused on theoretical questions about basic relationship processes (and more recently also basic processes in other domains, such as individual self-expansion and intergroup relations). In this chapter, we have tried to pull together self-expansion's main practical, real-world implications for optimizing close relationships, notably including a consideration of the implications for relationships of the relatively recent lines of work emphasizing individual self-expansion. However, in this process of examining the various applied relationship implications of the model, we are reminded of the many other unexplored opportunities to "expand" the model's applied side in this context.

Some future directions of this kind include simply testing some of the findings from experiments and short-term interventions using a more clinical-trial approach and with long-term follow-up, such as was done so nicely recently for the first time, by Coulter and Malouff (2013) in the context of shared self-expanding activities. For example, it would be exciting to test the very promising findings of the Slatcher (2010), two-couple closeness procedure outside of the lab and past short-term effects. Even in the central theme of shared self-expanding activities, more could be done in terms of longer-term follow up, larger samples permitting tests of potential moderators, and expanding to cross-cultural and cross-social class contexts. More generally, some of the implications of basic research that we considered here could be tested directly for their real-world applications, such as the two-dimensional model; effects of individual and relationship-based self-expansion on health, mental-health, and addictions; how individual and couple-level self-expansion experiences may reciprocally interact over time; more attention to considering and testing applied implications of the model's inclusion principle; and considering potential costs and limitations of expanding processes.

Yet another valuable future direction might be studies examining the extent to which self-expansion processes partially mediate effects of various existing couple interventions and activities, such as marital enrichment programs (or even marital counseling) or joint church attendance. These programs may be helpful to couples as they focus on improving communication, solving conflicts, and also strengthening closeness and bonding between couples, which can include encouraging self-expansion (e.g., rediscovering passion, promoting self-disclosure and inclusion-of-other-in-the-self, and engaging in exciting and novel experiences such as a weekend retreat). To the extent self-expansion does partially mediate the effects of any such programs, it would suggest strengthening the aspects of the intervention that have a self-expanding quality. Finally, it seems valuable to consider all of the potential self-expansion-related benefits that have been studied only in the context of romantic/marital relationships, for their generalization to other relationship contexts, such as friendship and family, work-place, or school interpersonal relations. Self-expansion in the context of other relationships can not only strengthen those relationships (offering additional sources of life satisfaction and meaning) but also provide the couple with further domains for self-expanding. That is, when my friendships and work relationships are especially exciting, novel, interesting, etc., I have new things to share with my partner, new people I can introduce my partner to, and new contexts that they can interact with and learn more about me and my perspectives.

CONCLUSION

In the 30 years or so since the initial conceptualization of the self-expansion model, work built on it has grown to include vast amounts of research across multiple disciplines and perspectives. Although self-expansion began with a focus on romantic relationships, we now have a broader understanding of the importance of self-expansion and associated factors (e.g., novelty, challenge) across many domains including at the individual level. It is clear that research and thinking inspired by the model is progressing along many different avenues. This includes work that will help us understand more fully the fundamental components of self-expansion and in what contexts they are necessary to produce an effect. Essentially, there is much work to be done in terms of exploring the many ways in which self-expansion operates at the individual, dyadic, and group levels, as well as the implications of these different modes of operation for what kinds of things people can do for more formal interventions that will be most effective, for whom, and under what circumstances. Applied self-expansion research is also burgeoning, with future areas such as mental and physical health, workplace contexts, group dynamics with reducing prejudice, and of course the optimization of close relationships including romantic relationships.

Although the self-expansion model has come a long way since it was first proposed in 1986, there is still much to learn and many more advances to be made. From the state of the current literature, it is clear that the next few decades will likely be an exciting time for both basic and applied self-expansion researchers, as well as for all the people we are hoping will benefit from everything this work will uncover. In the meantime, we hope the findings and implications from what has already been done that we have discussed in this chapter can be applied now to help move many people's relationships to greater happiness and passion.

REFERENCES

Acevedo, B., & Aron A. (2014). Romantic love, pair-bonding, and the dopaminergic reward system. In M. Mikulincer & P.R. Shaver (Eds.), *Nature and development of social connections: From brain to group* (pp. 55–69). Washington, DC: American Psychological Association.

Acevedo, B.P., Aron, A., Fisher, H.E., & Brown, L.L. (2012). Neural correlates of long-term intense romantic love. *Social Cognitive and Affective Neuroscience*, 7, 145–159. doi:10.1093/scan/nsq092

Aron, A., & Aron, E. (1986). *Love and the expansion of self: Understanding attraction and satisfaction*. New York: Hemisphere.

Aron, A., Aron E. N., & Smollan, D. (1992). Inclusion of other in the self scale and the structure of interpersonal closeness. *Journal of Personality and Social Psychology*, 63, 596–612. doi:10.1037/0022-3514.63.4.596

Aron, A., Aron, E.N., Tudor, M., & Nelson, G. (1991). Close relationships as including other in the self. *Journal of Personality and Social Psychology*, 60, 241–253. doi:10.1037/0022-3514.60.2.241

Aron, A., Fisher, H., Mashek, D.J., Strong, G., Li, H., & Brown, L.L. (2005). Reward, motivation, and emotion systems associated with early stage intense romantic love. *Journal of Neurophysiology*, 94, 327–337. doi:10.1152/jn.00838.2004

Aron, A., & Lewandowski, G.W., Jr. (2002). Interpersonal attraction, psychology of. In N.J. Smelser & P.B. Baltes (Eds.), *International encyclopedia of the social and behavioral sciences* (pp. 7860–7862). Oxford: Pergamon.

Aron, A., Lewandowski, G.W., Jr., Mashek, D., & Aron, E.N. (2013). The self-expansion model of motivation and cognition in close relationships. In J.A. Simpson & L. Campbell (Eds.), *The Oxford handbook of close relationships* (pp. 90–115). New York: Oxford University Press.

Aron, A., Norman, C., Aron, E., McKenna, C., & Heyman, R. (2000). Couples' shared participation in novel and arousing activities and experienced relationship quality. *Journal of Personality and Social Psychology*, 78, 273–284. doi:10.1037//0022–3514.78.2.273

Aron, A., Paris, M., & Aron, E.N. (1995). Falling in love: Prospective studies of self-concept change. *Journal of Personality and Social Psychology*, 69, 1102–1112. doi:10.1037/0022-3514.69.6.1102

Aron, A., Steele, J.L., Kashdan, T.B., & Perez, M. (2006). When similars do not attract: Tests of a prediction from the self-expansion model. *Personal Relationships*, 13, 387–396. doi:10.1111/j.1475–6811.2006.00125.x

Aron, A., Whitfield, S., & Lichty, W. (2007). Whole brain correlations: Examining similarity across conditions of overall patterns of neural activation in fMRI. In S. Sawilowsky (Ed.), *Real data analysis* (pp. 365–369). Charlotte, NC: American Educational Research Association / Information Age Publishing.

Boelen, P.A., & van den Hout, M.A. (2010). Inclusion of other in the self and breakup-related grief following relationship dissolution. *Journal of Loss and Trauma*, 15, 534–547. doi:10.1080/15325024.2010.519274

Buck, A. A., & Neff, L. A. (2012). Stress spillover in early marriage: The role of self-regulatory depletion. *Journal of Family Psychology*, 26(5), 698–708. doi:10.1037/a0029260

Burris, C.T., Rempel, J.K., Munteanu, A.R., & Therrien, P.A. (2013). More, more more: The dark side of self-expansion motivation. *Personality and Social Psychology Bulletin*, 39, 578–595. doi:10.1177/0146167213479134

Cacioppo, S., Grafton, S.T., & Bianchi-Demicheli, F. (2012). The speed of passionate love, as a subliminal prime: A high-density electrical neuroimaging study. *NeuroQuantology*, 10, 715–724.

Carpenter, C.J., & Spottswood, E.L. (2013). Exploring romantic relationships on social networking sites using the self-expansion model. *Computers in Human Behavior*, 29, 1531–1537. doi:10.1016/j.chb.2013.01.021

Carson, J., Carson, K.M., Gil, K.M., & Baucom, D.H. (2004). Mindfulness-based relationship enhancement. *Behavior Therapy*, 35, 471–494. doi:10.1016/S0005-7894(04)80028-5

Carson, J.W., Carson, K.M., Gil, K.M., & Baucom, D.H. (2007). Self-expansion as a mediator of relationship improvements in a mindfulness intervention. *Journal of Marital and Family Therapy*, 33, 517–528. doi:10.1111/j.1752–0606.2007.00035.x

Chen, Y., Chen, C., Lin, C., Chou, K., & Decety, J. (2010). Love hurts: An fMRI study. *NeuroImage*, 51, 923–929. doi:10.1016/j.neuroimage.2010.02.047

Coulter, K., & Malouff, J.M. (2013). Effects of an intervention designed to enhance romantic relationship excitement: A randomized-control trial. *Couple and Family Psychology: Research and Practice*, 2, 34–44. doi:10.1037/a0031719.

Decety, J., & Sommerville, J.A. (2003). Shared representations between self and other: A social cognitive neuroscience view. *TRENDS in Cognitive Science*, 7, 527–533. doi:10.1016/j.tics.2003.10.004

Fisher, H.E., Brown, L.L., Aron, A., Strong, G., & Mashek, D. (2010). Reward, addiction, and emotion regulation systems associated with rejection in love. *Journal of Neurophysiology*, 104, 51–60. doi:10.1152/jn.00784.2009

Fitzsimons, G.M., & Fishbach, A. (2010). Shifting closeness: Interpersonal effects of personal goal progress. *Journal of Personality and Social Psychology*, 98, 535–549. doi:10.1037/a0018581

Fivecoat, H.C., Tomlinson, J.M., Aron, A., & Caprariello, P.A. (2014). Partner support for individual self-expansion opportunities: Effects on relationship satisfaction in long-term couples. *Journal of Social and Personal Relationships*, 1–18. doi:10.1177/0265407514533767

Gable, S.L., & Reis, H.T. (2010). Good news! Capitalizing on positive events in an interpersonal context. In M.P. Zanna (Ed.), *Advances in Experimental Social Psychology* (Vol. 42, pp. 195–257). San Diego, CA: Elsevier Academic Press.

Gardner, W.L., Gabriel, S., & Hochschild, L. (2002). When you and I are "we," you are not threatening: The role of self-expansion in social comparison. *Journal of Personality and Social Psychology*, 82, 239–251. doi:10.1037/0022–3514.82.2.239

Graham, J.M. (2008). Self-expansion and flow in couples' momentary experiences: An experience sampling study. *Journal of Personality and Social Psychology*, 95, 679–694. doi:10.1037/0022–3514.95.3.679

Green, S. G., Bull Schaefer, R. A., MacDermid, S. M., & Weiss, H. M. (2011). Partner reactions to work-to-family conflict: Cognitive appraisal and indirect crossover in couples. *Journal of Management*, 37(3), 744–769. doi:10.1177/0149206309349307

Harasymchuck, C., & Fehr, B. (2010). A script analysis of relationship boredom: Causes, feelings, and coping strategies. *Journal of Social and Clinical Psychology*, 29, 988–1019. doi:10.1521/jscp.2010.29.9.988

Ilies, R., Wilson, K. S., & Wagner, D. T. (2009). The spillover of daily job satisfaction onto employees' family lives: The facilitating role of work-family integration. *Academy of Management Journal*, 52(1), 87–102. doi:10.5465/AMJ.2009.36461938

Impett, E.A., Gordon, A.M., Kogan, A., Oveis, C., Gable, S.L., & Keltner, D. (2010). Moving toward more perfect unions: Daily and long-term consequences of approach and avoidance goals in romantic relationships. *Journal of Personality and Social Psychology*, 99, 948–963. doi:10.1037/a0020271

Impett, E.A., Strachman, A., Finkel, E.J., & Gable, S.L. (2008). Maintaining sexual desire in intimate relationships: The importance of approach goals. *Journal of Personality and Social Psychology*, 94, 808–823. doi:10.1037/0022-3514.94.5.808

Knee, C.R., & Canevello, A. (2006). Implicit theories of relationships and coping in romantic relationships. In K.D. Vohs & E.J. Finkel (Eds.), *Self and relationships: Connecting intrapersonal and interpersonal processes* (pp. 160–176). New York, NY: Guilford Press.

Leary, M.R. (2007). Motivational and emotional aspects of the self. *Annual Review of Psychology*, 58, 317–344. doi:10.1146/annurev.psych.58.110405.085658

Ledbetter, A.M. (2013). Relational maintenance and inclusion of other in the self: Measure development and dyadic test of a self-expansion theory approach. *Southern Communication Journal*, 78, 289–310. doi:10.1080/1041794X.2013.815265

Lewandowski, G.W., Jr., & Ackerman, R.A. (2006). Something's missing: Need fulfillment and self-expansion as predictors of susceptibility to infidelity. *The Journal of Social Psychology*, 146, 389–403. doi:10.3200/SOCP.146.4.389–403

Lewandowski, G.W., Jr., & Aron, A., (2002). *The Self-expansion Scale: Construction and validation*. Paper presented at the Third Annual Meeting of the Society of Personality and Social Psychology, Savannah, GA.

Lewandowski, G.W., Jr., Aron, A., Bassis, S., & Kunak, J. (2006). Losing a self-expanding relationship: Implications for the self-concept. *Personal Relationships*, 13, 317–331. doi:10.1111/j.1475–6811.2006.00120.x

Lewandowski, G. W., Jr., & Bizzoco, N. (2007). Addition through subtraction: Growth following the dissolution of a low quality relationship. *The Journal of Positive Psychology*, 2, 40–54. doi:10.1080/17439760601069234

Mashek, D., Aron, A., & Boncimino, M. (2003). Confusions of self with close others. *Personality and Social Psychology Bulletin*, 29, 382–392. doi:10.1177/0146167202250220

Mashek, D., Le, B., Israel, K., & Aron, A. (2011). Wanting less closeness in romantic relationships. *Basic and Applied Social Psychology*, 33, 333–345. doi:10.1080/01973533.2011.614164

Mason, A.E., Law, R.W., Bryan, A.E., Portley, R.M., & Sbarra, D.A. (2012). Facing a breakup: Electromyographic responses moderate self-concept recovery following a romantic separation. *Personal Relationships*, 19, 551–568. doi:10.1111/j.1475-6811.2010.01343.x

Mattingly, B.A., & Lewandowski, G.W., Jr. (2013a). An expanded self is a more capable self: The association between self-concept size and self-efficacy. *Self and Identity*, 12, 621–634. doi:10.1080/15298868.2012.718863

Mattingly, B.A., & Lewandowski, G.W., Jr. (2013b). The power of one: Benefits of individual self-expansion. *The Journal of Positive Psychology*, 8, 12–22. doi:10.1080/17439760.2012.746999

Mattingly, B.A., & Lewandowski, G.W., Jr. (2014a). Broadening horizons: Self-expansion in relational and nonrelational contexts. *Social and Personality Psychology Compass*, 8, 30–40. doi:10.1111/spc3.12080

Mattingly, B.A., & Lewandowski, G.W., Jr. (2014b). Expanding the self brick by brick: Non-relational self-expansion and self-concept size. *Social Psychological and Personality Science*, 5, 483–489. doi:10.1177/1948550613503886

Mattingly, B.A, Lewandowski, G.W., Jr., & Carson, R.E.A. (2011). *Solving the unsolvable: The effects of self-expansion on generating solutions to impossible problems*. Poster presented at the 12th Annual Society for Personality and Social Psychology Conference, San Antonio, TX.

Mattingly, B.A., Lewandowski, G.W., Jr., & McIntyre, K.P. (2014). You make me a better/worse person: A two-dimensional model of relationship self-change. *Personal Relationships*, 21, 176–190. doi:10.1111/pere.12025

Mattingly, B.A., McIntyre, K.P., & Lewandowski, G.W., Jr. (2012). Approach motivation and the expansion of self in close relationships. *Personal Relationships*, 19, 113–127. doi:10.1111/j.1475-6811.2010.01343.x

McIntyre, K. P., Mattingly, B. A., Lewandowski, G. W., Jr., & Simpson, A. (2014). Workplace self-expansion: Implications for job satisfaction, commitment, self-concept clarity and self-esteem among the employed and unemployed. *Basic and Applied Social Psychology*, 36, 59–69. doi:10.1080/01973533.2013.856788

Neff, L. A., & Karney, B. R. (2004). How does context affect intimate relationships? Linking external stress and cognitive processes within marriage. *Personality and Social Psychology Bulletin*, 30, 134–148. doi:10.1177/0146167203255984

O'Leary, K.D., Acevedo, B.P., Aron, A., Huddy, L., & Mashek, D. (2012). Is long-term love more than a rare phenomenon? If so, what are its correlates? *Social Psychological and Personality Science*, 3, 241–249. doi:10.1177/1948550611417015

Ortigue, S., & Bianchi-Demicheli, F. (2008). Why is your spouse so predictable? Connecting mirror neuron system and self-expansion model of love. *Medical Hypotheses*, 71, 941–944. doi:10.1016/j.mehy.2008.07.016

Philippe, F.L., Vallerand, R.J., Houlfort, N., Lavigne, G.L., & Donahue, E.G. (2010). Passion for an activity and quality of interpersonal relationships: The mediating role of emotions. *Journal of Personality and Social Psychology*, 98, 917–932. doi:10.1037/a0018017

Reissman, C., Aron, A., & Bergen, M.R. (1993). Shared activities and martial satisfaction: Causal direction and self-expansion versus boredom. *Journal of Social and Personal Relationships*, 10, 243–254. doi:10.1177/026540759301000205

Roggero, A., Vacirca, M., Mauri, A., & Ciairano, S. (2012). The transition to cohabitation: The mediating role of self-efficacy between stress management and couple satisfaction. In M. Vassar (Ed.), *Psychology of life satisfaction* (pp. 147–171). Hauppauge, NY: Nova Science Publishers.

Rusbult, C.E., Finkel, E.J., & Kumashiro, M. (2009). The Michelangelo Phenomenon. *Current Directions in Psychological Science*, 18, 305–309.

Schindler, I., Paech, J., & Löwenbrück, F. (2014). Linking admiration and adoration to self-expansion: Different ways to enhance one's potential. *Cognition and Emotion*. Epub ahead of print. doi:10.1080/02699931.2014.903230

Shafer, K., Jensen, T. M., & Larson, J. H. (2014). Relationship effort, satisfaction, and stability: Differences across union type. *Journal of Marital and Family Therapy*, 40(2), 212–232. doi:10.1111/jmft.12007

Slatcher, R.B. (2010). When Harry and Sally met Dick and Jane: Creating closeness between couples. *Personal Relationships*, 17, 279–297. doi:10.1111/j.1475-6811.2010.01276.x

Slotter, E.B., Emery, L.F., & Luchies, L.B. (2014). Me after you: Partner influence and individual effort predict rejection of self-aspects and self-concept clarity after relationship dissolution. *Personality and Social Psychology Bulletin*, 40, 831–844. doi:10.1177/0146167214528992

Slotter, E.B., & Gardner, W.L. (2009). Where do you end and I begin? Evidence for anticipatory, motivated self–other integration between relationship partners. *Journal of Personality and Social Psychology*, 96, 1137–1151. doi:10.1037/a0013882

Slotter, E.B., & Gardner, W.L. (2012). How needing you changes me: The influence of attachment anxiety on self-concept malleability in romantic relationships. *Self and Identity*, 11, 386–408. doi:10.1080/15298868.2011.591538

Slotter, E.B., Gardner, W.L., & Finkel, E.J. (2010). Who am I without you? The influence of romantic breakup on the self-concept. *Personality and Social Psychology Bulletin*, 36, 147–160. doi:10.1177/0146167209352250

Tomlinson, J. M., & Aron, A. (2013). The path to closeness: A mediational model for overcoming the risks of increasing closeness. *Journal of Social and Personal Relationships*, 30(6), 805–812.

Tsapelas, I., Aron, A., & Orbuch, T. (2009). Marital boredom now predicts less satisfaction 9 years later. *Psychological Science*, 20, 543–545. doi:10.1111/j.1467-9280.2009.02332.x

VanderDrift, L. E., Lewandowski, G. W., Jr., & Agnew, C. R. (2011). Reduced self-expansion in current romance and interest in relationship alternatives. *Journal of Social and Personal Relationships*, 28, 356–373. doi:10.1177/0265407510382321

Waugh, C.E., & Fredrickson, B.L. (2006). Nice to know you: Positive emotions, self-other overlap, and complex understanding in the formation of a new relationship. *Journal of Positive Psychology*, 1, 93–106. doi:10.1080/17439760500510569

Welker, K.M., Baker, L., Padilla, A., Holmes, H., Aron, A., & Slatcher, R.B. (2014). Effects of self-disclosure and responsiveness between couples on passionate love within couples. *Personal Relationships*, 21, 692–708. doi:10.1111/pere.12058

Wright, S.C., McLaughlin-Volpe, T., & Brody, S.M. (2004, January). Seeking and finding an expanded "me" outside my ingroup: Outgroup friends and self change, Presentation at the Society for Personality and Social Psychology conference, Austin, TX.

Xu, X., Aron, A., Brown, L., Cao, G., Feng, T., & Weng, X. (2011). Reward and motivation systems: A brain mapping study of early-stage intense romantic love in Chinese participants. *Human Brain Mapping*, 32, 249–257. doi:10.1002/hbm.21017

Xu, X., Aron, A., Westmaas, J.L., Wang, J., & Sweet, L.H. (2014). An fMRI study of nicotine-deprived smokers' reactivity to smoking cues during novel/exciting activity. *PLoS ONE*, 9(4), e94598. doi:10.1371/journal.pone.0094598

Xu, X., Floyd, A.H.L., Westmaas, J. L., & Aron, A. (2010). Self-expansion and smoking abstinence. *Addictive Behaviors*, 35, 295–301. doi:10.1016/j.addbeh.2009.10.019

Xu, X., Wang, J., Lei, W., Aron, A., Westmaas, L., & Weng, X (2012). Intense passionate love attenuates cigarette cue-reactivity in nicotine-deprived smokers: An fMRI study. *PLoS ONE*, 7(7), e42235. doi:10.1371/journal.pone.0042235

Younger, J., Aron, A., Parke, S., Chatterjee, N., & Mackey, S. (2010). Viewing pictures of a romantic partner reduces experimental pain: Involvement of neural reward systems. *PLoS ONE*, 5, 1–7. doi:10.1371/journal.pone.0013309

Zeki, S., & Romaya, J. P. (2010). The brain reaction to viewing faces of opposite- and same sex romantic partners. *PLoS ONE*, 5(12), e15802. doi:10.1371/journal.pone.0015802

PART II

CONCEPTS AND MECHANISMS

5

Capitalization: the good news about close relationships

SHELLY L. GABLE AND JASON F. ANDERSON

A version of the American proverb – *a shared trouble is trouble halved* – can be found in many languages and cultures. Inherent in this folk wisdom is that people turn to others when bad things happen to them and doing so is beneficial. Psychologists have spent a great deal of effort on theoretical and empirical examinations aimed at understanding how turning to others in times of stress affects the individual. These processes are often referred to collectively as social support in the literature and research in this area has yielded great payoffs in terms of knowledge of how and when social support benefits the individual experiencing the stressor (e.g., Bolger & Eckenrode, 1991; Cohen, Doyle, Skoner, Rabin, & Gwaltney, 1997; Cunningham & Barbee, 2000; Harlow & Cantor, 1995; Lakey & Cassady, 1990; Uchino, Cacioppo, & Keicolt-Glaser, 1996).

Recognizing the inherently dyadic nature of social support, many researchers have also examined the role that social support plays in close relationship formation, maintenance, and dissolution (Collins & Feeney, 2000; Fincham & Bradbury, 1990; Simpson et al., 2002). This literature has similarly yielded valuable insights into the role that partners' support for stressors plays in relationship quality and stability (e.g., Gleason et al., 2003; Kane et al., 2012; Pasch & Bradbury, 1998). However, recent theoretical work has provided a compelling case for examining support processes outside of the stress and coping context and expanding models of support beyond stress buffering roles (e.g., Feeney & Collins, 2014; Finch et al., 1999). For example, Lakey and Orechek (2011) have argued that supportive interactions regarding everyday exchanges are primary sources of personal and relationship health. Further, research has consistently demonstrated that close others' support for personal goals facilitates attainment as well as relationship quality (e.g.,

This work was supported by the National Science Foundation under Grant No. BCS 1050875 awarded to the first author. Any opinions, findings, and conclusions or recommendations expressed in this material are those of the author(s) and do not necessarily reflect the views of the National Science Foundation.

Feeney 2004). In short, there is ample evidence that the context of coping with stress and negative events offers, at best, a limited view of factors that build (or degrade) close relationships and the role relationships play in personal well-being. Moreover, it is doubtful that such a limited view of relationships can provide comprehensive insights into optimal relationship development. In the remainder of this chapter, we describe the theoretical basis and empirical evidence in support of the centrality of capitalization – the process of turning to others when *good* things happen.

MANAGING POSITIVE EVENTS

Positive events play an important role in personal and interpersonal well-being, independent of the effect of negative events. For example, everyday positive event occurrences are inversely related to depressive symptoms (Zautra et al., 2000) and positively related to self-esteem, perceived control, and subjective well-being (Diener, Suh, Lucas, & Smith, 1999; Gable, Reis, & Elliot, 2000; Nezlek & Gable, 2001;). In addition, although taking advantage of and making the most of positive events traditionally has not been viewed as a form of coping, recent research suggests that people do not just take positive events in stride – they "cope" with them; and this coping has important implications for health and well-being. For example, when people systematically take note of the positive aspects of their lives (referred to in the literature as "counting one's blessings"), they experience increases in well-being across several markers (Emmons & McCullough, 2003); and savoring positive experiences by reminiscing about positive events is also associated with greater well-being (Bryant et al., 2005; Jose, Lim, & Bryant, 2012). Most important for the current review is the finding that one thing people regularly do is tell others about the occurrence of their positive events and that the sharing of the event has consequences beyond the event itself (e.g., Langston, 1994). Thus, there is good evidence that there is something to the Swedish proverb which mirrors the idiom with which we opened this chapter, *A shared joy is doubled.*[1]

Langston (1994) found that when people shared the news of a positive event with others (capitalized), celebrated, or marked the event, they reported more positive emotions than they did when they did not share or mark their positive events in some way. In our early work on the topic we replicated and extended Langston's findings (Gable et al., 2004; Gable, Gonzaga, & Strachman, 2006; Gable & Maisel, 2009). Specifically, in several large daily experience studies of naturally occurring everyday events we asked people to report on the best thing that happened to them each day and what, if anything,

---

[1] Like the proverb regarding sharing troubles, versions of this Swedish proverb are also found in many languages and cultures.

they did about it (Gable et al., 2004). The majority of the time (between 70 and 80 percent of the time), people told at least one other person about the best thing that happened to them during the day. Of course, events that are important to individuals are more likely to be capitalized on; however, capitalizing on moderately pleasant events is also common (the correlation between event importance and sharing with another person averaged around .19 in these studies). More importantly, this research has shown that *capitalizing* is an appropriate label because the processes multiply one positive moment into many benefits for the individual (see also Reis et al., 2010). Specifically, diary studies have found that on days that people shared their positive event with others, on average, they reported more positive affect and satisfaction with life than on days they did not share their positive event. These effects were above and beyond the reported (and objective) importance of the event (Gable et al., 2004) and the occurrence of other positive and negative events during the day.

Recent work from our and other laboratories has replicated the earlier findings that sharing positive events with others is linked to personal well-being and positive emotions (e.g., Reis et al., 2010). For example, in a series of lab and field studies, Lambert et al. (2013) also found that sharing positive experiences was associated with increased positive affect. Most notably, in one study, participants were randomly assigned to keep a journal of positive experiences and share them with a partner twice a week and were compared to participants who were instructed to just keep a journal of positive experi-ences or keep a journal of class learnings and shared them twice a week with a partner (Lambert et al., 2013; Study 4). The results showed that those in the sharing-their-positive-experiences condition reported greater happiness, positive affect, and life satisfaction than those in the other two conditions. Although much of the work has not focused on the context of the sharing of events in general, there is an emerging literature on the particular benefits of sharing events that happen on the job. For example, Remus and Keeney (2011) found that people who shared a positive event that occurred at work with a spouse when they got home from work showed increases in job satisfaction above and beyond the work event itself. Similarly, Hurst (2010) found that capitalizing on positive events at work was associated with increases in positive affect and job satisfaction. In short, many studies have shown that capitalizing on positive events is associated with important outcomes for the individual. These studies have used experimental, daily experience, and cross-sectional methods.

CAPITALIZATION: A DYADIC PROCESS

At the core, responsive capitalization interactions are those that are effec-tive in upregulating positive emotions. Historically, the study of emotion regulation has focused largely on negative emotion and has often been studied as an intrapersonal process such as suppressing the expression of emotions (Gross, 2013). However, researchers have more recently begun to explore both positive emotions and emotion regulation as an interpersonal experience (Bryant et al., 2005; Rimé, 2009). Although interpersonal emotion regulation research is in its empirical infancy, Zaki and Williams (2013) define it as the pursuit of a goal to regulate emotions in the live presence of others. In addition to the regulation of the emotional experience itself, expressing emotions to others can also help individuals maintain feelings of authenticity, as their subjective experience matches their outward expression. Indeed, habitual emotional suppression is associated with a host of negative outcomes, and feelings of inauthenticity mediate these effects (English & John, 2013). Recently in their work on emotionships, Cheung, Gardner, and Anderson (2015) hypothesized that some individuals in one's social network are more effective at regulating particular emotions, relative to other people in the social network. Initial empirical support for their hypotheses showed that social partners who are nominated as being sought out for effective regulation of particular emotions (e.g., down-regulating sadness, upregulating joy) vary in terms of their cognitive accessibility and closeness as a function of the participant's present emotional state. Moreover, participants were quite able to nominate effective emotionship partners for a wide array of emotions, both positive and negative emotions.

The findings that sharing positive event occurrences with others is beneficial to the individual is also consistent with Bryant's (2003) work that people's tendency to "cope with" or enhance their positive moment is associated with a wide variety of positive outcomes. In the case of capitalizing by sharing with others, however, a critical component of the process is the response of the other person. Our early work showed that 97 percent of the time that people capitalized, they did so with a close other (friend, romantic partner, family member), while only 3 percent of the time did they report sharing the event with a non-close other, such as an acquaintance or stranger (Gable et al., 2004; Study 4). These findings indicated that capitalization attempts were likely only part of the process because capitalization is an interpersonal or relationship-based process. Accordingly, much of the more recent work has focused on the response that the capitalizer (discloser) received from the person with whom they shared the event. Moreover, this dyadic perspective predicts that the effects of capitalization on the discloser are moderated by the response they receive from the person with whom they shared the event. In addition, the dyadic perspective on capitalization predicts that capitalization processes influence the relationship between the capitalizer and the responder.

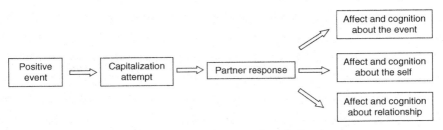

FIGURE 5.1   General model of positive events and capitalization.

Figure 5.1 shows the indirect effects that a positive event can have through capitalization.[2] The process begins with an event and a capitalization attempt. The person with whom the event is shared, the interaction partner, then influences the discloser's thoughts and feelings regarding the event, the self, and his or her relationship with the responder. This is because the response to a positive event disclosure conveys valuable pieces of information to the person disclosing the positive event. First, it reflects the responder's assessment of the event itself, such as the event's importance and significance. The response also conveys the implications the event has for the discloser and thus his or her views of the self. Finally, but likely equally impactful, the response indicates the degree to which an interaction partner takes an interest in and derives pleasure from the discloser's personal well-being and growth and therefore influences thoughts and feelings about the relationship partner.

Critical in this process, then, is the reaction to the capitalization attempt, and understanding which characteristics of responses to a capitalization attempt influence the discloser is important. When a positive event is shared, the person with whom it is shared can respond in several different ways. Similar to Rusbult and colleagues' work on responses to a partner's negative behavior (e.g., Rusbult, Zembrolt, & Gunn, 1982), responses to positive event disclosures can also vary on at least two important dimensions, as shown in Figure 5.2. Responses vary on a continuum from active to passive. That is, the responder can show interest, attention, or involvement when the event is shared (active), or the responder can be reserved, distracted, or detached in his or her reply (passive). Responses also vary on a continuum from constructive to destructive. Specifically, the responder can be positive and supportive or he or she can be negative and unsupportive. These two dimensions are independent and thus yield four different prototypical responses: active-constructive, passive-constructive, active-destructive, and passive-destructive (Gable et al., 2004).

[2] Although Figure 5.1 focuses on and illustrates the indirect effects that events have on outcomes through the capitalization response, there are also direct effects that the event can have on these outcomes. They are left out of the figure for simplicity.

	Constructive	Destructive
Active	… my partner reacts to my good fortune enthusiastically"	… he/she points out the potential problems or down sides of the good event"
Passive	… my partner says little but I know he/she is happy for me"	… sometimes I get the impression that he/she doesn't care much"

FIGURE 5.2 Sample items from the perceived responses to capitalization attempts (PRCA; Gable et al., 2004), shown in terms of the conceptual model of the two dimensions that underlie responses to capitalization attempts. PRCA items begin with the stem, "When I tell my partner about something good that happened to me".

Responses to capitalization attempts that are active-constructive are those in which the listener conveys excitement, enthusiasm, and interest in the event. The active-constructive responder asks questions about the event to obtain more details, remarks on the importance of the event for the discloser in particular, and elaborates on the implications and possible positive outcomes that could come from the event. Active-constructive responders often display joy, interest, and pride during the interaction. Responses to capitalization attempts that are passive-constructive are those in which the responder says little about the event but is generally positive and pleasant. The passive-constructive responder conveys a positive attitude toward the event through a pleasant but short or quiet exchange. The passive-constructive response differs from the active-constructive response primarily in the responder's level of involvement with limited or no questions about the event or elaboration on the event's implications and meaning for the discloser. Responses to capitalization attempts that are active-destructive are those in which the responder is involved and focused; however, the views provided are ambivalent or negative in valence. The active-destructive responder often points out or highlights negative implications of the event, questions the positivity of the event, and generally minimizes the event's significance and broader implications. Responses to capitalization attempts that are passive-destructive are those in which the disclosure of the event is barely acknowledged or not responded to at all. The passive-destructive responder can either change the topic of conversation to something completely different than the disclosed event or instead simply begin talking about something that happened to him or her.

The following example illustrates four different ways of responding to a capitalization attempt. Imagine that Rich calls his sister Mary to share the good news that after trying for a while he and his wife just found out they were pregnant. An active-constructive response from Mary would be: "That is fantastic news! I know you both will be great parents. You've been talking about babies for years. How is she feeling? I can't wait to greet the newest member of our family." A passive-constructive response would be "That is nice news." An active-destructive response from Mary would be "Wow that is going to put an end to your care-free life style. Kids are such a financial strain – I hope you have a big saving account. You have never really been good at taking care of things; remember that pet hamster you had as a kid, Mom always had to feed it. Are you sure you two are ready for the responsibility of being parents?" Finally, Mary could give a passive-destructive response when Rich shares his news like "Did you remember to call Dad for his birthday yesterday" or "Wait until I tell you what happened to me at the office today!"

RESPONSES TO CAPITALIZATION ATTEMPTS

Several studies have focused on understanding how the response of the person with whom the event is shared affects perceptions of the event, the thoughts and feelings of the discloser, and the relationship between the discloser and the responder (see Figure 5.1). These studies, which have employed multiple methods, have shown that only active-constructive responses were positively associated with good outcomes; active-destructive, passive-destructive, and passive-constructive were all negatively associated with interpersonal and intrapersonal good outcomes (e.g., Gable et al., 2004, 2006; Lambert et al., 2013; Reis et al., 2010). For example, regarding intrapersonal outcomes, daily experience studies showed that receiving active-constructive responses from others in response to capitalization attempts was associated with increases in positive affect, self-esteem, and subjective well-being. Moreover, receiving passive or destructive responses, at best, was associated with diminished or no benefits from the positive event, and at worst was predictive of decreases in positive affect and well-being from baseline (Gable et al., 2004; Reis et al., 2010). It is important to note that these effects were above and beyond the importance of the event itself in the eyes of the discloser, so they cannot be explained by the likelihood that responders react more enthusiastically to bigger events.

Similarly, Demir and Davidson (2013) found that participants who perceived their friends to be active and constructive responders in general also reported greater happiness than those whose friends tended to respond to their capitalization attempts in a passive or destructive manner. Altermatt (2011) found that sharing positive events with peers in middle school predicted more positive school attitudes. Again though, the response of the other person matters. In another study (an observational study of 4th and 6th graders who outperformed a friend), Altermatt and Ivers (2011) found that when their friends reacted in an engaged manner, the children had increases in positive affect after the discussion.

Monfort and colleagues (2014) were able to more closely examine the capitalization process as it unfolded in a laboratory study and thus separately examined reactions to the positive event, sharing the event, and responses to that sharing. One member of a romantic couple received positive feedback regarding his or her performance on a computer task and then shared their success with the partner via text message. The partner then responded to that news. They found that positive affect and happy facial expressions increased in particular when participants received constructive and active responses from their partners. In addition, the partners also reported more positive affect themselves when they provided supportive responses.

In addition to the associations with well-being and self-esteem observed in these studies, several studies have also shown that capitalization responses influence thoughts and feelings about the event itself. In one study, people showed better recall of events that they shared and for which they received active-constructive responses than they did for events they shared and for which they received passive or destructive responses or did not share at all (Gable et al., 2004). Using an experimental method, Reis and colleagues (2010) conducted a series of studies in which they randomly assigned participants to receive an active-constructive or a passive-constructive response from trained experimenters when discussing a positive event. They found that participants who received an active-constructive response (compared to those who received a passive-constructive response) felt better after the discussion and increased their ratings of the event importance; and the increase in importance ratings remained at a later follow-up (Reis et al., 2010). Taken together, this work clearly demonstrates that receiving positive reactions from others is beneficial for the individual disclosing the event and enhances the appraisal of the shared event.

In addition to outcomes related solely to the discloser, research has also found strong evidence that active-constructive, and not passive or destructive responses to capitalization attempts have a positive impact on close relationships. Several studies of close relationship outcomes have assessed how social networks or a particular relationship partner typically responds. These studies often use a measure called the Perceived Responses to Capitalization Attempts (PRCA) that assesses interaction partners' (friend, romantic partner, average of the social network) typical response to one's capitalization attempts. The measure contains items tapping each of the four types of responses that can happen when telling someone about something good that has happened. Example items from the PRCA are listed in Figure 5.2. The measure has demonstrated good reliability and criterion-related validity (Pagani, Donato, & Iafrate, 2013). In addition, the factor structure is consistent with the four theoretically derived types of responses (Pagani et al., 2013). Several studies of dating and married couples using the PRCA have found that perceptions that one's partner typically responds in an active-constructive manner are associated with greater relationship satisfaction, trust, and intimacy, daily relationship satisfaction, positive activities, and fewer daily conflicts. However, reporting that one's partner typically responds in a passive-constructive, active-destructive, or passive-destructive manner was consistently negatively correlated with these outcomes (for a review, see Gable & Reis, 2010). The results have been largely identical across males and females. Extending this in a longitudinal study, Logan and Cobb (2013) followed individuals in romantic relationships for over 1 year. They found that perceptions of supportive capitalization responses were predictive of relationship satisfaction, independent of reports of how supportive partners were for negative events. In this study, there was also evidence that capitalization support was particularly important early on in relationships. However, in cross-sectional data, Shorey and Lakey (2011) found that perceived availability of support from family and friends for future negative events was more consistently correlated with concurrent measures of affect conflict than perceptions of typical capitalization responses from family and friends.

Results from studies using data that rely on perceptions of typical responses are also consistent with studies that assess the quality of responses in particular interactions. Daily experience studies have found that a partner's active-constructive reactions to specific positive event disclosures predict increases in relationship satisfaction and passive or destructive responses predict decreases in relationship satisfaction (Gosnell & Gable, 2013). In addition, active-constructive responses (and not passive or destructive responses) from social network members are associated with increase in belongingness and feelings of social connection on a daily basis (Gable, Gosnell, Maisel, & Strachman, 2012). Similarly, behavioral observation studies have shown that active-constructive responses to positive event disclosures in the laboratory were associated with better relationship quality across a variety of measures concurrently and down the road. Moreover, active-constructive responding, self-reported and observed, was the only significant (negative) predictor of break-up (Gable et al., 2006). In experimental work, Reis and colleagues (2010) demonstrated that participants who were randomly assigned to receive an active-constructive response from a confederate reported more liking for and felt closer to the confederate (concurrently and 1 week later) than those assigned to receive the passive-constructive response; and they felt more trusting of confederates if they received an active-constructive response than if they were assigned to the condition in which

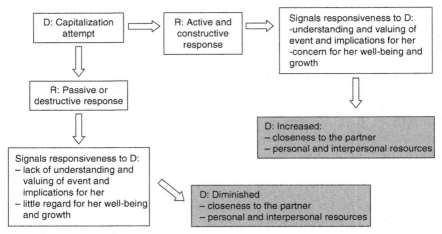

FIGURE 5.3 Proposed consequences of responsive and unresponsive reactions to capitalization attempts.

they simply had a fun interaction doing a humorous joint activity. Finally, in an intervention study (Woods, Lambert, Brown, Fincham, & May 2015), participants who were randomly assigned to receive training in providing active–constructive responses to their study partners showed increases in perceptions of a greater amount of gratitude from their study partner and perceived their study partner as having greater relationship satisfaction.

Overall, empirical studies support the model that active-constructive and not passive or destructive responses to capitalization attempts are associated with enhanced significance of the event itself, increases in personal resources, and increase in interpersonal resources. As seen in Figure 5.3, active and constructive responses signal two important messages to the discloser. First, the active constructive response signals that the responder understands the discloser and values his or her abilities, talents, motivation, or even luck associated with the positive event. Second, the active-constructive response conveys caring for the well-being of the discloser. Passive or destructive responses signal a lack of understanding, valuing, and concern for the discloser. The combination of understanding, validation, and caring has been called responsiveness to the self (Reis, Clark, & Holmes, 2004) and has been identified by several theories (e.g., attachment theory, communal relationships theory) as a central tenet of satisfying intimate relationships (Lemay, Clark, & Feeney, 2007; Murray, Holmes, & Collins, 2006). Moreover, in the research on capitalization, responsiveness to the self has emerged as a consistent mediator of the interpersonal and intrapersonal outcomes associated with capitalization (e.g., Gable et al., 2006; Maisel & Gable, 2009; Maisel,

Gable, & Strachman, 2008). Thus, it seems that responsiveness to the self accounts for the action in active-constructive responding.

CAPITALIZATION AND PERSONAL
AND INTERPERSONAL RESOURCES

One reason that capitalization responses may be associated with personal and interpersonal resources is because they may moderate how people react to the negative events or stressors in their lives. We already know that positive emotions play a significant role in the stress response (e.g., Tugade & Fredrickson, 2004), which is consistent with Fredrickson's (1998) broaden-and-build theory of positive emotions. For example, previous research has found that positive emotions lead to increases in broad-minded coping (Fredrickson & Joiner, 2002), where broad-minded coping has been defined as active and engaged approaches to coping with stressors (Burns et al., 2008). However, distinct from the effect that positive emotions have on coping, we suggest that responses of others to positive event disclosures affect stress buffering processes. Specifically, akin to resource models of coping (e.g., Hobfoll, 2001), supportive responses to capitalization attempts contribute to resources that buffer the impact of stressors, and unsupportive processes detract from these resources. A demonstration of concern for one's well-being and growth in good times may bolster perceptions that one has others available more broadly, including when the proverbial rain does fall. That is, experiences with active-constructive responding should directly impact what researchers have referred to as perceived availability of support. The perception that others will be there for us when we need them is very strongly associated with positive health and well-being outcomes (for review, see Holt-Lunstad and Uchino, 2015; Lakey & Cassady, 1990).

Although *believing* that others will be available in bad times is beneficial, the associations among enacted support, perceived support, and well-being are mixed (e.g., Kaul & Lakey, 2003; Lakey et al., 2002). There is little consistent evidence that people's perception of the availability of support is systematically or strongly related to the actual enacted support they receive in times of stress. Moreover, several studies show that actual support transactions are not associated with better adjustment; or worse, they are negatively correlated with well-being (e.g., Barbee et al., 1998; Bolger, Zuckerman, & Kessler, 2000; Coyne, Wortman, & Lehman, 1988). One possible reason that receiving social support may have neutral or detrimental effects is that it may be a signal to the recipient that he or she is unable to cope with the stressor, which can be a blow to self-efficacy, control, and self-esteem (e.g., Fisher, Nadler, & Whitcher-Alagna, 1982). Moreover, because it is a *close* other that is often a primary support provider, the perception of indebtedness and a diminished sense of self-worth in the eyes of the other (even if this is completely imagined) may be especially problematic (e.g., Shrout, Herman, & Bolger, 2006). For example, Murray and colleagues have demonstrated that feeling inferior to one's romantic partner is associated with less commitment, relationship satisfaction, and love for the partner (e.g., Murray, Holmes, & Griffin, 2000; Murray, Holmes, & Collins, 2006). These costs may offset any tangible or emotional benefits of a partner's assistance in times of stress.

In addition, the actual receipt of support from others may draw more attention to the problem, thereby validating or enhancing the stress reaction to the situation (e.g., Bolger et al., 2000). Finally, actual support received may not be very skilled and consequently be unhelpful (Dunkel-Schetter & Bennett, 1990; Rini et al., 2006). In fact, as Rini and colleagues (2006) discussed and empirically validated, several criteria need to be met in order for a particular support transaction to be effective, including complex processes such as matching to the recipient's needs in terms of scope and proportionality, and delivering the support with little apparent effort or difficulty. Gable and colleagues (2012) found evidence consistent with these findings in a daily experience study. Participants perceived their partners' responses to negative event disclosures as less understanding, validating, and caring (i.e., responsive) than their responses to positive event disclosures. Reflecting the reality of this difficulty in providing support, Gosnell (2014) found that people are often worried that their responses to their partners' event disclosure will be effective in terms of their supportiveness. This concern is especially heightened in the context of providing support for negative event disclosures. Moreover, Gable and colleagues (2012) found that intentions to provide responsive support were less likely to be perceived as such during negative event interactions compared to positive event interactions.

It is likely that these risks and costs are a major source of the disconnect between people's perceptions of the availability of support in times of need and the support they actually receive (Kaul & Lakey, 2003). So, where do perceptions of available support come from? It is possible that one way to contribute to the perceived availability of support is to provide support in a context that has fewer risks and associated costs.[3] The inherent drawbacks of enacted support (even effective support) during stressful times may limit their contribution to one's overall perceived availability of support, or worse, reduce it. Our prior research is consistent with this idea. Capitalization

---

[3] One example of diminished risk comes from Bolger and colleagues (2000) who found that *invisible support* (support which goes unnoticed by the distressed recipient) was more effective at reducing the recipients' distress than support of which they are aware. However, Maisel and Gable (2009) found that even invisible support can be problematic when the provider's intentions behind their supportive gesture did not include being understanding, validating, or caring; thus, invisible support can be ineffective or, worse, harmful, when not delivered skillfully.

interactions were associated with greater benefits and fewer risks than social support interactions in daily life (Gable et al., 2012; Study 2). It is important to note that there are still risks involved in sharing a positive event; the interaction partner could respond in an unsupportive manner or not respond at all, which would diminish perceptions of available support. However, the risks are reduced compared to when a negative event is shared because the event is good and does not carry all the additional potential costs associated with sharing a negative event.

To describe how capitalization responses may efficiently and directly contribute to perceptions of the quality of one's social support network, Gable et al. (2012) used the analogy of the test button on a smoke detector. You do not want to set your house on fire in order to determine if the smoke detector is working properly. However, you can push the red test button on a regular day when there is no fire danger and this will enhance your confidence that the smoke detector will work properly in a real emergency. Taking the analogy one step farther, if there is an actual fire and the smoke detector does work properly, getting to safety, putting out the fire, and dealing with the aftermath of the emergency become your primary concerns; appropriate appreciation for the working smoke detector will likely fall by the wayside.

Similarly, sharing positive events with someone is a relatively safe way to assess his ability to be responsive to the self. If the response does not convey understanding, validation, and caring this signals that the person may not be responsive if a negative event does occur and one is in need of help dealing with the problem (i.e., a real fire that needs putting out). On the other hand, capitalization responses that are supportive may signal that the other person has one's best interests in mind and is likely to be responsive in the context of a stressor. An initial empirical test of these ideas offered tentative support. Active-constructive (and not passive or destructive) responses to capitalization attempts during a daily diary study were associated with greater perceptions of the availability of social support for stressors 2 months later, controlling for initial perceptions of support availability (Gable et al., 2012; Study 3). Actual social support receipt for stressors during the diary study did not predict perceptions of support availability at a later time. More research is needed to replicate this initial finding and understand its implications for the broader social support findings.

The second, but to date not empirically explored, reason to suspect that capitalization processes influence stress buffering processes is that capitalization responses carry information about the value, importance, and relevance of the positive event. An active-constructive response conveys that the event is important and the discloser did something right, which should influence feelings of control and self-efficacy. These resources in turn should also be effective at both buffering against stress and attaining personal goals. This prediction is based on a long history of emphasizing the social aspects the self.

For example, Cooley (1902) and Mead (1934) proposed that evaluations of the self are based on the imagined evaluations of others, especially significant others (see also Higgins' Self-Discrepancy Theory, 1989; and sociometer theory, Leary, 2005; Leary & Baumeister, 2000). Capitalization attempts have the potential to influence both chronic and situational perceived control and self-efficacy. Thus, in a very concrete way, interactions with close others become part of the self-concept. Although direct research on these ideas is needed, the proposed links between capitalization responses from close other and evaluations of the self are consistent with work by Rusbult and her colleagues on *The Michelangelo Phenomenon* (see Rusbult, Finkel, & Kumashiro, 2010, for review). The Michelangelo Phenomenon describes how a close other can promote (or inhibit) one's striving toward the ideal self by perceiving that one is already at the ideal and behaving toward one as if that ideal self already exists. In this way positive interactions can shape the self. Again, we see this as a next important area of research on capitalization.

LIMITING CONDITIONS AND MODERATORS OF CAPITALIZATION

Although the links between capitalization responses and personal and interpersonal outcomes are reliable, people vary in the process. In particular, one might want to know if capitalization is only an important process for happy people and relatively satisfied relationship partners. That is, perhaps capitalization is only beneficial for those who are already pretty well off. There is good evidence, however, that the opposite may, in fact, be true. For example, research suggests that making the most out of positive events is actually most beneficial for those who have the fewest positive experiences. In a longitudinal study, Hurley and Kwon (2013) found that those who had few positive events and uplifts had levels of well-being similar to those who had greater frequencies of positive events, but only when they were also high on savoring (the capacity to attend to and enhance positive experiences). Thus, savoring and making the most out of positive events buffered people from the negative impact of having few positive events, relative to those who were low on savoring.

Even more compelling, Hershenberg, Davila, and Leong (2014) found that women with higher depressive symptoms reported similar levels of positive changes in affect after sharing a positive event and receiving a supportive response. That is, even though when given the choice to share a positive event or negative event, women with more depressive symptoms preferred to share a negative event, when they did share a positive event they received just as much benefit as those with fewer depressive symptoms. Finally, in a recent study, Otto, Laurenceau, Siegel, and Belcher (2015) examined capitalization process in couples in which one member was experiencing a serious health challenge. Specifically, they examined the sharing negative and positive events in couples in which the woman was coping with early stage breast cancer. Their results showed that capitalization attempts were positively associated with intimacy for both members of the couples. In addition, perceived partner responsiveness to capitalization attempts was associated with increases in intimacy and decreases in negative affect. Most impressive, the capitalization effect remained significant even when controlling for the sharing of negative events. This study highlights that even under highly stressful circumstances, such as facing a health crisis, capitalization still matters.

Although these studies suggest that capitalization processes are similar across different levels of well-being, and in some cases may actually be more beneficial for those at higher risk, research has also demonstrated that there are important individual differences that moderate capitalization processes. Given the impact that capitalization responses have on the self, it should not be surprising that self-esteem is one such moderator. Smith and Reis (2012), in both a daily experience study and laboratory study, found that those with low self-esteem perceived less supportive capitalization responses from their partners. However, importantly, the differences between high and low self-esteem individuals' partner perceptions were only seen when participants' relationships were threatened (either experimentally through priming or on days following a conflict with the partner). When not under relationship threat, high and low self-esteem individuals perceived similar responsiveness from their partners following capitalization attempts. Self-esteem, or more accurately perceptions of another person's self-esteem, may also have an impact on the likelihood of sharing positive events in the first place. MacGregor and Holmes (2011) found that when people believed that a potential target for capitalization attempts had low self-esteem they were reluctant to share positive events with those people. Their data suggest that this reluctance to capitalize with low self-esteem individuals seems to stem from the expectation that the interaction would not be beneficial for the would-be discloser because a supportive response was not likely. Although not yet tested empirically, potential capitalizers may also refrain from sharing with those who they believe to have low self-esteem because they want to spare them from unfavorable social comparisons or even to avoid appearing lacking in empathy themselves.

There is also evidence that attachment orientations moderate capitalization processes. In an observational study, dating couples shared positive events and their discussions were videotaped (Shallcross, Howland, Bernis, Simpson, & Frazier, 2011). Results showed that insecurely attached participants perceived less responsiveness from their partners than warranted by outside raters. In addition, insecurely attached participants also reported they were less responsive to their partners when they disclosed positive events, a perception that was echoed by the observer ratings. These patterns were especially noted in avoidantly attached participants and anxiously attached participants with avoidant partners. Similarly, in a diary study of romantic couples we (Gosnell & Gable, 2013) examined how attachment security moderated perceptions of capitalization support. The results showed that high avoidance was associated with lower perceptions of partner responsiveness in daily life. In addition, we examined whether attachment security moderated the links between capitalization support and daily emotions, relationship satisfaction, and life satisfaction. The results showed that anxiety predicted the strength of the association between daily relationship and life satisfaction and partners' capitalization responses. Specifically, those high on anxious attachment reported more well-being and satisfaction when partners were responsive than those lower on anxiety; conversely highly anxious people reported bigger decreases in these outcomes when partners were less responsive, compared to securely attached participants. Overall, the evidence suggests that attachment insecurity moderates responses to capitalization attempts, perceptions of partners' capitalization responses, and the impact that those responses have on personal and relationship outcomes.

CONCLUDING COMMENTS

Earlier in this chapter, we noted two ubiquitous proverbs regarding the different benefits of sharing negative and positive events with others. A good deal of research has shown that sharing negative events with others can reduce the impact of those events; however less research has been devoted to understanding the role that others play in helping us make the most of positive events. The work on capitalization shows that it is highly valuable to have responsive partners to turn to when things go right. It is valuable not only for the individual but also for building and maintaining close relationships among the responders and disclosers. More broadly speaking, the work on capitalization processes in close relationships suggests that relationship science needs to pay attention to how relationship processes unfold outside of the contexts of stress, threat, and conflict.

REFERENCES

Altermatt, E. R. (2011). Capitalizing on academic success: Students' interactions with friends as predictors of school adjustment. *The Journal of Early Adolescence*, 31(1), 174–203. doi:10.1177/0272431610379414

Altermatt, E. R., & Ivers, I. E. (2011). Friends' responses to children's disclosure of an achievement-related success: An observational study. *Merrill-Palmer Quarterly: Journal of Developmental Psychology*, 57(4), 26.

Barbee, A. P., Derlega, V. J., Sherburne, S. P., & Grimshaw, A. (1998). Helpful and unhelpful forms of social support for HIV-positive individuals. *HIV and social interaction* (pp. 83–105) Thousand Oaks, CA: Sage Publications, Inc.

Bolger, N., & Eckenrode, J. (1991). Social relationships, personality, and anxiety during a major stressful event. *Journal of Personality and Social Psychology*, 61, 440–449.

Bolger, N., Zuckerman, A., & Kessler, R. C. (2000). Invisible support and adjustment to stress. *Journal of Personality and Social Psychology*, 79(6), 953–961.

Bryant, F. B. (1989). A four-factor model of perceived control: Avoiding, coping, obtaining, and savoring. *Journal of Personality*, 57, 773–797.

Bryant, F. B. (2003). Savoring beliefs inventory (SBI): A scale for measuring beliefs about savouring. *Journal of Mental Health*, 12(2), 175–196.

Bryant, F. B., Smart, C. M., & King, S. P. (2005). Using the past to enhance the present: Boosting happiness through positive reminiscence. *Journal of Happiness Studies*, 6, 227–260.

Burns, A. B., Brown, J. S., Sachs-Ericsson, N., Plant, E. A., Curtis, J. T., Fredrickson, B. L., & Joiner, T. E. (2008). Upward spirals of positive emotion and coping: Replication, extension, and initial exploration of neurochemical substrates. *Personality and Individual Differences*, 44(2), 360–370.

Cheung, E. O., Gardner, W. L., & Anderson, J. F. (2015). Emotionships: Examining people's emotion-regulation relationships and their consequences for well-being. *Social Psychological and Personality Science*, 6(4), 407–414. doi:10.1177/1948550614564223

Cohen, S., Doyle, W. J., Skoner, D. P., Rabin, B. S., & Gwaltney, J. M., Jr. (1997). Social ties and susceptibility to the common cold. *Journal of the American Medical Association*, 277, 1940–1944.

Collins, N., & Feeney, B. (2000). A safe haven: An attachment theory perspective on support seeking and caregiving in intimate relationships. *Journal of Personality and Social Psychology*, 78, 1053–1073.

Cooley, C. H. (1902). *Human nature and the social order*. New York: Scribner.

Coyne, J. C., Wortman, C. B., & Lehman, D. R. (1988). *The other side of support: Emotional over involvement and miscarried helping.*

Cunningham, M. R., & Barbee, A. P. (2000). Social support. In C. Hendrick & S. S. Hendrick (Eds.), *Close relationships: A sourcebook* (pp. 273–285). Thousand Oaks, CA: Sage.

Demir, M., & Davidson, I. (2013). Toward a better understanding of the relationship between friendship and happiness: Perceived responses to capitalization attempts, feelings of mattering, and satisfaction of basic psychological needs in same-sex best friendships as predictors of happiness. *Journal of Happiness Studies*, 14(2), 525–550.

Diener, E., Suh, E. M., Lucas, R. E., & Smith, H. L. (1999). Subjective well-being: Three decades of progress. *Psychological Bulletin*, 125(2), 276–302.

Dunkel-Schetter, C., & Bennett, T. L. (1990). Differentiating the cognitive and behavioral aspects of social support. In B. R. Sarason, I. G. Sarason, & G. R. Pierce (Eds.), *Social support: An interactional view* (pp. 267–296). New York: John Wiley & Sons, Inc.

Emmons, R. A., & McCullough, M. E. (2003). Counting blessings versus burdens: An experimental investigation of gratitude and subjective well-being in daily life. *Journal of Personality and Social Psychology*, 84, 377–389.

English, T., & John, O. P. (2013). Understanding the social effects of emotion regulation: The mediating role of authenticity for individual differences in suppression. *Emotion*, 13, 314–329.

Feeney, B. C. (2004). A secure base: Responsive support of goal strivings and exploration in adult intimate relationships. *Journal of Personality and Social Psychology*, 87, 631–648.

Feeney, B. C., & Collins, N. L. (2014). A new look at social support: A theoretical perspective on thriving through relationships. *Personality and Social Psychology Review*, 19(2), 1–35.

Finch, J. F., Okun, M. A., Pool, G. J., & Ruehlman, L. S. (1999). A comparison of the influence of conflictual and supportive social interactions on psychological distress. *Journal of Personality*, 67, 581–621. doi:10.1111/1467–6494.00066

Fisher, J. D., Nadler, A., & Whitcher-Alagna, S. (1982). Recipient reactions to aid. *Psychological Bulletin*, 91(1), 27.

Fredrickson, B. L. (1998). What good are positive emotions? *Review of General Psychology*, 2, 300–319.

Fredrickson, B. L., & Joiner, T. (2002). Positive emotions trigger upward spirals toward emotional well-being. *Psychological Science*, 13, 172–175.

Gable, S., Gonzaga, G., & Strachman, A. (2006). Will you be there for me when things go right? supportive responses to positive event disclosures. *Journal of Personality and Social Psychology*, 91, 904–917.

Gable, S. L., Gosnell, C. G., Maisel, N., & Strachman, A. N. (2012). Safely testing the alarm: Responses to personal events. *Journal of Personality and Social Psychology*, 103 (6), 949–962.

Gable, S. L., Reis, H. T., & Elliot, A. (2000). Behavioral activation and inhibition in everyday life. *Journal of Personality and Social Psychology*, 63, 221–233.

Gable, S. L., Reis, H. T., Impett, E., & Asher, E. R. (2004). What do you do when things go right? The intrapersonal and interpersonal benefits of sharing positive events. *Journal of Personality and Social Psychology*, 87, 228–245.

Gleason, M. E., Iida, M., Bolger, N., & Shrout, P. E. (2003). Daily supportive equity in close relationships. *Personality and Social Psychology Bulletin*, 29(8), 1036–1045.

Gosnell, C. L. (2014). The ego-depleting nature of social support provision. *Unpublished doctoral dissertation*. University of California, Santa Barbara.

Gosnell, C.G., & Gable, S. L. (2013). Attachment and capitalizing on positive events. *Attachment and Human Development*, 15(3), 281–302.

Gross, J. J. (2013). Emotion regulation. Taking stock and moving forward. Emotion, 13, 359–365. doi:10.1037/a0032135

Harlow, R. E., & Cantor, N. (1995). To whom do people turn when things go poorly? Task orientation and functional social contacts. *Journal of Personality and Social Psychology*, 69, 329–340.

Hershenberg, R., Davila, J., & Leong, S. H. (2014). Depressive symptoms in women and the preference and emotional benefits of discussing positive life events.. *Journal of Social and Clinical Psychology*, 33(9), 767–788.

Hobfoll, S. E. (2001). The influence of culture, community, and the nested-self in the stress process: Advancing conservation of resources theory. *Applied Psychology*, 50(3), 337–421.

Holt-Lunstad, J., & Uchino, B. N. (2015). Social support and health. *Health behavior: Theory, research, and practice (5th ed.)*. (pp. 183–204) Jossey-Bass, San Francisco, CA.

Hurley, D. B., & Kwon, P. (2013). Savoring helps most when you have little: Interaction between savoring the moment and uplifts on positive affect and satisfaction with life. *Journal of Happiness Studies*, 14(4), 1261–1271. doi:10.1007/s10902-012-9377-8

Hurst, C. (2010). *Tell them something good: The well-being and behavioral outcomes of disclosing positive news to coworkers.* Unpublished doctoral dissertation. University of Florida.

Jose, P. E., Lim, B. T., & Bryant, F. B. (2012). Does savoring increase happiness? A daily diary study. *The Journal of Positive Psychology,* 7(3), 176–187. doi:10.1080/17439760.2012.671345

Kane, H. S., McCall, C., Collins, N. L., & Blascovich, J. (2012). Mere presence is not enough: Responsive support in a virtual world. *Journal of Experimental Social Psychology,* 48(1), 37–44.

Kaul, M., & Lakey, B. (2003). Where is the support in perceived support? The role of generic relationship satisfaction and enacted support in perceived support's relation to low distress. *Journal of Social and Clinical Psychology,* 22(1), 59–78.

Lakey, B., Adams, K., Neely, L., Rhodes, G., Lutz, C. J., & Sielky, K. (2002). Perceived support and low emotional distress: The role of enacted support, dyad similarity, and provider personality. *Personality and Social Psychology Bulletin,* 28(11), 1546–1555.

Lakey, B., & Cassady, P. B. (1990). Cognitive processes in perceived social support. *Journal of Personality and Social Psychology,* 59, 337–343.

Lambert, N. M., Gwinn, A. M., Baumeister, R. F., Strachman, A., Washburn, I. J., Gable, S. L., & Fincham, F. D. (2013). A boost of positive affect: The perks of sharing positive experiences. *Journal of Social and Personal Relationships,* 30(1), 24–43. doi:10.1177/0265407512449400

Langston, C. A. (1994). Capitalizing on and coping with daily-life events: Expressive responses to positive events. *Journal of Personality and Social Psychology,* 67, 1112–1125.

Leary, M. R. (2005). Sociometer theory and the pursuit of relational value: Getting to the root of self-esteem. *European Review of Social Psychology,* 16(1), 75–111.

Leary, M. R., & Baumeister, R. F. (2000). The nature and function of self-esteem: Sociometer theory. In M. P. Zanna (Ed.), *Advances in experimental social psychology* (Vol. 32, pp. 1–62). San Diego, CA: Academic Press.

Lemay, E. P., Jr., Clark, M. S., & Feeney, B. C. (2007). Projection of responsiveness to needs and the construction of satisfying communal relationships. *Journal of Personality and Social Psychology,* 92(5), 834–853.

Logan, J. M., & Cobb, R. J. (2013). Trajectories of relationship satisfaction: Independent contributions of capitalization and support perceptions. *Personal Relationships,* 20(2), 277–293. doi:10.1111/j.1475-6811.2012.01408.x

MacGregor, J. C. D., & Holmes, J. G. (2011). Rain on my parade: Perceiving low self-esteem in close others hinders positive self-disclosure. *Social Psychological and Personality Science,* 2(5), 523–530. doi:10.1177/1948550611400098

Maisel, N. C., & Gable, S. L. (2009). The paradox of received social support. *Psychological Science,* 20(8), 928–932.

Maisel, N. C., Gable, S. L., & Strachman, A. (2008). Responsive behaviors in good times and in bad. *Personal Relationships,* 15, 317–338.

Mead G. H. (1934). *Mind, self, and society.* Chicago: University of Chicago Press.

Murray, S. L., Holmes, J. G., & Collins, N. L. (2006). Optimizing assurance: The risk regulation system in relationships. *Psychological Bulletin,* 132(5), 641–666.

Murray, S. L., Holmes, J. G., & Griffin, D. W. (2000). Self-esteem and the quest for felt security: how perceived regard regulates attachment processes. *Journal of Personality and Social Psychology,* 78(3), 478.

Nezlek, J. B., & Gable, S. L. (2001). Depression as a moderator of relationships between positive daily events and day-to-day psychological adjustment. *Personality and Social Psychology Bulletin*, 27, 1692–1704.

Otto, A. K., Laurenceau, J. P., Siegel, S. D., & Belcher, A. J. (2015). Capitalizing on everyday positive events uniquely predicts daily intimacy and well-being in couples coping with breast cancer. *Journal of Family Psychology*, 29(1), 69–79.

Pagani, A. F., Donato, S., & Iafrate, R. (2013). Actively dealing with good fortune? confirmatory factor analysis and gender invariance of the perceived responses to capitalization attempts (PRCA) scale. *TPM-Testing, Psychometrics, Methodology in Applied Psychology*, 20(2), 101–116.

Pasch, L. A., & Bradbury, T. N. (1998). Social support, conflict, and the development of marital dysfunction. *Journal of Consulting and Clinical Psychology*, 66(2), 219.

Quoidbach, J., Berry, E. V., Hansenne, M., & Mikolajczak, M. (2010). Positive emotion regulation and well-being: Comparing the impact of eight savoring and dampening strategies. *Personality and Individual Differences*, 49(5), 368–373. doi:10.1016/j.paid.2010.03.048

Reis, H. T., Clark, M. S., & Holmes, J. G. (2004). Perceived partner responsiveness as an organizing construct in the study of intimacy and closeness. In D. J. Mashek & A. Aron (Eds.), *Handbook of closeness and intimacy* (pp. 201–225). Mahwah, NJ: Lawrence.

Reis, H. T., Smith, S. M., Carmichael, C. L., Caprariello, P. A., Tsai, F., Rodrigues, A., & Maniaci, M. R. (2010). Are you happy for me? How sharing positive events with others provides personal and interpersonal benefits. *Journal of Personality and Social Psychology*, 99(2), 311–329. doi:10.1037/a0018344

Rimé, B. (2009). Emotion elicits social sharing of emotion: Theory and empirical review. *Emotion Review*, 1, 60–85.

Rini, C., Schetter, C. D., Hobel, C. J., Glynn, L. M., & Sandman, C. A. (2006). Effective social support: Antecedents and consequences of partner support during pregnancy. *Personal Relationships*, 13(2), 207–229.

Rusbult, C. E., Finkel, E. J., & Kumashiro, M. (2009). The Michelangelo Phenomenon. *Current Directions in Psychological Science*, 18(6), 305–309.

Shallcross, S. L., Howland, M., Bemis, J., Simpson, J. A., & Frazier, P. (2011). Not "capitalizing" on social capitalization interactions: The role of attachment insecurity. *Journal of Family Psychology*, 25(1), 77–85. doi:10.1037/a0021876

Shorey, R. C., & Lakey, B. (2011). Perceived and capitalization support are substantially similar: Implications for social support theory. *Personality & Social Psychology Bulletin*, 37(8), 1068–1079. doi:10.1177/0146167211406507

Shrout, P. E., Herman, C. M., & Bolger, N. (2006). The costs and benefits of practical and emotional support on adjustment: A daily diary study of couples experiencing acute stress. *Personal Relationships*, 13(1), 115.

Smith, S. M., & Reis, H. T. (2012). Perceived responses to capitalization attempts are influenced by self-esteem and relationship threat. *Personal Relationships*, 19(2), 367–385. doi:10.1111/j.1475-6811.2011.01367.x

Tugade, M. M., & Fredrickson, B. L. (2004). Resilient individuals use positive emotions to bounce back from negative emotional experiences. *Journal of Personality and Social Psychology*, 86, 320–333.

Uchino, B. N., Cacioppo, J. T., & Kiecolt-Glaser, J. K. (1996). The relationship between social support and physiological processes: A review with emphasis on underlying mechanisms and implications for health. *Psychological Bulletin*, 119, 488–531.

Zaki, J., & Williams, W. C. (2013). Interpersonal emotion regulation. *Emotion*, 13, 803–810. doi:10.1037/a0033839

Zautra, A. J., Schultz, A. S., & Reich, J. W. (2000). The role of everyday events in depressive symptoms for older adults. In G. M. Williamson & D. R. Shaffer (Eds.), *Physical illness and depression in older adults: A handbook of theory, research, and practice* (pp. 65–91). New York: Kluwer Academic/Plenum.

6

The positive implications of sex for relationships

AMY MUISE, JAMES J. KIM, JAMES K. MCNULTY,
AND EMILY A. IMPETT

Romantic relationships are vital to our physical health and psychological well-being (e.g., Diener & Seligman, 2002; House, Landis, & Umberson, 1988), and sexuality is a key factor that shapes the quality of romantic relationships. In fact, people who are the most satisfied with their sex lives are also the most satisfied with their relationships, and this is true for both dating and married couples (Brezsnyak & Whisman, 2004; Sprecher, 2002). Despite the importance of sex for relationships, couples face numerous challenges to having and maintaining a satisfying sexual relationship. Empirical research reveals that sexual desire tends to peak in the beginning stages of romantic relationships as intimacy is rapidly developing (Baumeister & Bratlavsky, 1999), and then often declines over time as partners become more secure and comfortable in the relationship (see review by Impett, Muise, & Peragine, 2014). As a result, romantic partners will inevitably encounter times in which their sexual interests differ (Impett & Peplau, 2003), and couples may disagree about when and how frequently to engage in sex or the specific activities in which they wish to engage (Blumstein & Schwartz, 1983; O'Sullivan & Byers, 1996). In a national study of couples married fewer than 5 years, disagreements about sexual frequency were one of the top three most cited arguments between partners (Risch, Riley, & Lawler, 2003), and many long-term couples find themselves in situations in which they have divergent sexual interests (Davies, Katz, & Jackson, 1999; Mark, 2012; Mark & Murray, 2012). Further, conflicts of interest about sex are one of the most common reasons why couples seek marital therapy (Rosen, 2000), and can be one of the most difficult types of conflict to successfully resolve (Sanford, 2003). Given the importance of sex for romantic relationships, these sexual difficulties are likely to threaten couples' global evaluations of the relationship. In fact, normative declines in sexual satisfaction may partially explain normative declines in marital satisfaction commonly observed in longitudinal research on marriage (e.g., Meltzer, McNulty, Jackson, & Karney, 2014).

But the positive side of this connection between sexual and relationship quality is that good sex is one powerful mechanism for enhancing relationships. When couples can successfully navigate sexual issues, feelings of closeness and intimacy in the relationship can be strengthened (Dawson, Fallis, & Rehman, 2010; Rehman et al., 2011). In this chapter, we will describe evidence demonstrating the importance of sexuality in relationships, and we will review research that sheds light on how couples can maintain sexual desire and satisfaction as they face declines or changes in desire over time as well as differences in their sexual interests. In the first section of the chapter, we describe the ways in which sex can benefit relationships, focusing on the roles of both sexual frequency and sexual satisfaction in shaping high-quality relationships. In the second section, we focus our attention on understanding how couples can stave off declines in sexual desire and satisfaction, with a focus on the individual differences and relationship factors that contribute to the maintenance of desire and sexual satisfaction over time. We then conclude the chapter by highlighting what we see as promising directions for future research on sex and relationships.

We want to acknowledge a few important caveats at the outset of the chapter. Although sexual aspects such as attraction, frequency, and communication have implications for the quality of casual relationships and new dating relationships (Fletcher, Kerr, Li, & Valentine, 2014; Lehmiller, VanderDrift, & Kelly, 2014), the current chapter is focused primarily on sexuality in the context of *established* romantic relationships. In addition, we acknowledge that sexuality in the context of romantic relationships also has a dark side. For example, many couples face specific sexual dysfunctions, such as erectile dysfunction and vaginismus (i.e., pain during sex) (e.g., Ferenidou et al., 2008), and sexual coercion is a stark reality, even in the context of established relationships (Brousseau, Bergeron, Hébert, & McDuff, 2011; O'Leary & Williams, 2006). These negative aspects of sexuality can be challenging – even devastating – for many people and couples, and are clearly in need of research attention. In line with the focus of this volume, however, our primary aim in this chapter is to highlight the positive side of sexuality in relationships – that is, to focus on the ways in which sex can lift people up and contribute to happy, flourishing relationships that last.

GOOD SEX IS GOOD FOR RELATIONSHIPS

Love is an ice cream sundae, with all the marvelous coverings.
Sex is the cherry on top.

– Jimmy Dean

Sexuality is a key factor that shapes the quality of romantic relationships. As noted earlier, research has consistently demonstrated that people who are the most satisfied with their sex lives are also the most satisfied with their romantic relationships (Brezsnyak & Whisman, 2004; Byers, 2005; McNulty, Wenner, & Fisher, 2015; Sprecher, 2002; Yeh, Lorenz, Wickrama, Conger, & Elder, 2006). In one of the strongest demonstrations of the association between a healthy sexual relationship and relationship satisfaction and vice versa, McNulty et al. (2015) used two eight-wave longitudinal studies of marriage to demonstrate that sexual satisfaction at one wave of measurement positively predicted changes in marital satisfaction from that wave to the next and that marital satisfaction at one wave positively predicted changes in sexual satisfaction from that wave to the next.

Sex and affection frequency in romantic relationships

Given the importance of sexual satisfaction to relationships, it is crucial to understand what makes for a satisfying sexual relationship. Does the frequency with which couples engage in sex or other affectionate activities lead to higher levels of sexual satisfaction? The answer appears to be "yes." Both men and women report feeling more satisfied with their sex lives when their frequency of engaging in sex is high (e.g., Cheung et al., 2008; Laumann, Gagnon, Michael, & Michaels, 1994; McNulty et al., 2015; Rahmani, Khoei, & Gholi, 2009). Interestingly, the multi-wave, longitudinal research described earlier indicates this association is bidirectional, such that sexually satisfied couples pursue sex more frequently, and frequent sex leads to increases in sexual satisfaction (McNulty et al., 2015). Further, the association between sexual frequency and sexual satisfaction is consistent for both men and women, and this has also been documented in individuals living in non-Western countries such as China (Cheung et al., 2008) and Iran (Rahmani et al., 2009). Finally, the association does not appear to be unique to heterosexual couples; it has also emerged in samples of same-sex couples (Blair & Pukall, 2014; Blumstein & Schwartz, 1983).

Do the implications of sexual frequency extend beyond sexual satisfaction? The answer to this question also appears to be "yes." Call and colleagues (1995) reported that (low) sexual frequency was the second strongest correlate of marital dissatisfaction, ranking only behind age and controlling for other important predictors of sexual frequency, such as relationship duration and whether or not couples had children living in the home. Further, in a study using data from the National Survey of Families and Households, Yabiku and Gager (2009) found that lower sexual frequency was associated with higher rates of relationship dissolution, particularly for cohabiting (compared to married) couples. Further, other work suggests that factors that affect relationship satisfaction may do so through their implications for the sexual relationship (Fisher &

McNulty, 2008; Meltzer & McNulty, 2010). For example, Meltzer and McNulty (2010) found that positive body image was positively associated with marital satisfaction for both partners, and these associations were fully mediated by sexual frequency and sexual satisfaction. In other words, women who evaluated their bodies more positively were happier in their marriages because they had more frequent, satisfying sex. Finally, other research indicates that established couples who report more frequent sex also report greater satisfaction with their lives overall (Muise, Schimmack, & Impett, 2015). In fact, the difference in well-being between having sex once a week compared to less than once a month is greater than the difference in well-being between making $75,000 a year compared to $25,000 (Muise et al., 2015). Of course, engaging in other affectionate and intimate behaviors also promotes sexual and relationship satisfaction (Heiman et al., 2011; Muise, Giang, & Impett, 2014), an issue we address in more detail later in this chapter. In fact, some research suggests the association between affectionate behaviors, such as kissing and cuddling, and relationship quality is as strong or stronger than the association between sexual frequency and relationship quality (Heiman et al., 2011).

Engaging in more frequent sex can also buffer romantic couples against other negative relationship outcomes. Both attachment insecurity (for review, see Cassidy & Shaver, 1999) and neuroticism (e.g., Karney & Bradbury, 1997) have been consistently associated with relationship dissatisfaction. However, research has shown that the negative effects of both factors are attenuated for people who engage in more frequent sex. Russell and McNulty (2011) demonstrated that neuroticism was unassociated with marital satisfaction among spouses who engaged in relatively frequent sex. Given that sexual activity enhances positive affect, this effect may have emerged because such positive affect offsets the implications of negative affect so frequently experienced by people high in neuroticism. Likewise, Little, McNulty, and Russell (2010) demonstrated that attachment avoidance was not associated with marital satisfaction among spouses who engaged in more frequent sex. This effect was mediated by expectancies for partner availability, suggesting that more frequent sex assuaged such partners' automatic concerns of abandonment.

There are some theoretical reasons to expect sex differences in the implications of sexual frequency. From an evolutionary perspective, men desire more frequent sex than women due to differences in parental investment (Trivers, 1972), whereby the reproductive costs of engaging in frequent sexual activity tend to be lower for men than for women (e.g., Buss & Schmitt, 1993). Some evidence supports this perspective by showing that men and women report different levels of desired sexual frequency (Baumeister, Cantonese, & Vohs, 2001). Interestingly, however, recent research indicates that the association between sexual frequency and sexual satisfaction is no stronger among married men than it is among married women (McNulty et al., 2015). In two longitudinal studies of marriage, increased sexual frequency was as strongly predictive of positive changes in sexual satisfaction among women as it was among men.

One reason for the equally strong association between sexual frequency and satisfaction among men and women in established relationships, despite their different sexual appetites, may be that the actual levels of sex that occur in relationships reflect a compromise in the desires of the male and female partner. Indeed, in same-sex relationships, where decisions about sexual frequency are made by partners of the same gender, female same-sex couples report having sex less frequently than male same-sex couples or mixed-sex couples (Blumstein & Schwartz, 1983), although in other research female same-sex couples reported a significantly longer *duration* of sexual activity than men and women in mixed-sex relationships or men in same-sex relationships (Blair & Pukall, 2014). In fact, duration of sex in that study was associated with self-reported sexual and relationship satisfaction, suggesting that researchers should consider other aspects of couples' sex lives beyond frequency, such as duration, when looking at correlates of sexual and relationship quality.

Given that sexual frequency is important for relationship quality, the fact that sexual frequency tends to decline with age (Waite et al., 2009) could pose a problem for the maintenance of relationship satisfaction over time. Nevertheless, non-penetrative sex, such as kissing, cuddling and caressing, does not seem to decline (Waite et al., 2009), which suggests one way some spouses may stay happy despite declines in sexual frequency. Indeed, there is evidence that non-penetrative sex is important to satisfaction as well. In a recent study of mixed-sex couples in midlife and older adulthood conducted in five countries, affectionate behaviors such as kissing, cuddling and caressing were associated with increased sexual satisfaction for both men and women (Heiman et al., 2010). Interestingly, despite women's tendency to focus more on relational aspects of sexuality relative to men (see review by Diamond, 2004), these associations were strongest for men and significant predictors of men's (but not women's) general relationship satisfaction. Of course, these findings need to be considered in light of the fact that age-related declines in sexual desire may stem in part from hormonal changes (DeLamater & Sill, 2005), which may lessen the importance of penetrative sex. Nevertheless, another set of studies of younger couples also highlights the importance of affection to sexual and relationship satisfaction (Muise, Giang, & Impett, 2014). In particular, couples who spent a longer duration engaging in post sex affection (i.e., kissing, cuddling, caressing) felt more satisfied with the sexual experience and with their relationship as a whole. In fact, the duration of after sex affection was a stronger predictor of sexual and relationship satisfaction than the amount of time spent engaging in foreplay or sex itself, and this was true for both men and women.

Engaging in affectionate behaviors may help couples maintain satisfaction during times when sexual frequency in their relationship is low. Couples who are able to move beyond the notion that penetrative sex is the primary or only mode of sexual expression and incorporate a broader repertoire of sexual and affectionate behaviors seem better able to maintain or experience heightened sexual satisfaction in older adulthood (Hinchliff & Gott, 2008; Potts, Grace, Vares, & Gavey, 2006). In addition, Ahlborg et al. (2005) found that during pregnancy and the post-partum period when sexual frequency was lower than pre-pregnancy levels, couples remained affectionate, with the majority of parents reporting daily kisses and caresses. Of course, the cross-sectional nature of these studies makes it impossible to draw causal conclusions. Future longitudinal research may benefit from examining whether affectionate behaviors can compensate for the temporarily lower levels of sexual satisfaction that couples experience during times in a relationship when the frequency of penetrative sex may be low, such as during times of stress and change.

Sexual satisfaction and relationship quality

Although the frequency with which couples engage in sex as well as other affectionate activities shape relationship quality, it is likely that how people *feel* about their sex lives may be a better predictor of how they feel about their relationships than the frequency with which they engage in sex or the duration of sex. Indeed, McNulty et al. (2015) demonstrated that the effects of sexual frequency on relationship satisfaction were indirect, such that they emerged through sexual satisfaction. In other words, having a satisfying sexual relationship appears to be most important to relationship quality, regardless of how one gets there.

A recent thematic analysis of responses to the question "How would you define sexual satisfaction?" revealed two main themes (Pascoal, Narciso, & Pereira, 2014). The first theme focuses on the positive aspects of an individual's sexual experience, such as pleasure, positive feelings, arousal, sexual openness, and orgasm. The second theme emphasizes relational aspects, such as mutuality of pleasure, romance, expression of feelings, creativity, acting out desires, and frequency of sexual activity. These two themes are further supported by a quantitative study designed to create and validate a new scale for measuring sexual satisfaction (Stulhofer, Busko, & Brouillard, 2010). Again, the research suggested sexual satisfaction has two main dimensions, one that is self or ego focused and reflects satisfaction with personal sensations and experiences, and one that is partner or relationship focused and reflects satisfaction with a partner's sexual engagement. Taken together, these qualitative and quantitative studies highlight that in addition to the obvious role of personal sexual pleasure in promoting sexual satisfaction, relational aspects such as partner engagement are vital to people's experience of sexual satisfaction.

As noted earlier, in both dating and married couples, and across the lifespan, people's satisfaction with their sex lives is closely linked with their feelings of satisfaction with their relationship as a whole (Brezsnyak & Whisman, 2004; Byers, 2005; Davies et al., 1999; Laumann et al., 2006; McNulty et al., 2015; Sprecher, 2002; Yeh et al., 2006). In fact, in a multi-national study of individuals from 29 countries, Laumann et al. (2006) demonstrated that individuals who were the most sexually satisfied were also the happiest with their romantic relationships and with their lives in general. Extensive research has also shown that couples who enjoy positive, satisfying sexual relationships have more stable relationships than couples who are less sexually satisfied or who report experiencing sexual problems (e.g., Edwards & Booth, 1994; Sprecher, 2002). In fact, as noted earlier, sexual dissatisfaction or incompatibility is a key reason why couples ultimately break up and dissolve their relationships (Kurdek, 1991; Sprecher, 1994). Importantly, this association appears to be synchronous as opposed to directional. As noted earlier, in two eight-wave, longitudinal studies of marriage, McNulty et al. (2015) demonstrated that sexual satisfaction at one wave positively predicted changes in marital satisfaction from that wave to the next and that marital satisfaction at one wave positively predicted changes in sexual satisfaction from that wave to the next. Interestingly, once the bidirectional association between sexual and relationship satisfaction was controlled, frequency of sex had no direct effects on changes in relationship satisfaction, supporting the idea that sexual interactions primarily have benefits to the extent that they are satisfying.

The importance of sexual satisfaction is also highlighted by research demonstrating that, like sexual frequency, sexual satisfaction explains and attenuates the effects of critical individual difference factors on relationship quality. For example, Fisher and McNulty (2008) demonstrated that sexual satisfaction mediated the effects of neuroticism on marital satisfaction – that is, the low marital satisfaction of people high in neuroticism was accounted for by their low sexual satisfaction. Likewise, Little et al. (2010) demonstrated that sexual satisfaction moderated the effects of attachment anxiety on global relationship satisfaction, such that anxiety was unrelated to marital satisfaction among intimates who were satisfied with their sexual relationships. This finding is important because it demonstrates that even those who are high in attachment anxiety – who tend to report lower relationship quality – can benefit from engaging in satisfying sex with a close partner.

STAVING OFF DECLINES IN SEXUAL INTIMACY OVER TIME

I wonder if it's possible to have a love affair that lasts forever.
– Andy Warhol

The importance of sex for the quality of relationships described in the previous section highlights the need to understand how some couples are able to either stave off such declines or remain satisfied despite them. Indeed, although sexual desire tends to decline or waver over the course of a relationship on average (Call et al., 1995; Simms & Meana, 2010), romantic love, which is characterized by high sexual interest, engagement, and intensity, does not decline for everyone (Acevedo & Aron, 2009) and not everyone experiences accompanying declines in relationship satisfaction (Lavner & Bradbury, 2010; Simms & Meana, 2010). From their review of the literature, Acevedo and Aron (2009) concluded that although the obsessive element of passionate love (i.e., the "honeymoon" phase) decreases over time, the romantic elements – including strong sexual desire – can be maintained in long-term relationships. In fact, many couples in long-term marriages report that sexual activity remains an important component of their relationship, albeit not as prominent or experienced as intensely as during the earlier stages of the relationship (Hinchliff & Gott, 2004). Even for the many romantic partners who experience discrepancies in sexual desire or have divergent sexual interests, some are able to navigate these differences with greater success and maintain satisfaction even in the face of sexual disagreements. In this section, we focus on how couples can maintain sexual desire and satisfaction over the course of a long-term relationship. We review research on who and under what circumstances people are able to stave off declines in sexual desire and satisfaction, including work on sexual motives, sexual communal motivation, cognition, and sexual communication. We also discuss non-traditional approaches to understanding "great sex" and the maintenance of relationships over time.

Sexual motives

Although research suggests that, in general, engaging in more frequent sex with a romantic partner is associated with greater sexual and relationship satisfaction, research on sexual motivation suggests that not all sexual experiences are similarly satisfying. For example, research guided by self-determination theory (e.g., Deci & Ryan, 2000) has found that people experience greater psychological well-being and relationship quality when they engage in sex for motives that are more self-determined in nature such as "because I enjoy being sexual" and "for the pleasure of sharing a special and intimate experience," compared to when they engage in sex for motives that are more controlling in nature such as "because I would feel bad to withhold from my partner" and "because I feel pressured by my partner to have sex" (Brunell & Webster, 2013). Similarly, research indicates that sexual interactions characterized by higher levels of autonomy, competence, and relatedness are also associated with more positive sexual experiences (Smith, 2007). Furthermore, research guided by approach-avoidance motivational theory (for a review, see Gable & Impett, 2012) has shown that when people reported engaging in sex to pursue positive outcomes in their relationship, such as to enhance intimacy or express love for their partner (i.e., approach goals), they felt more positive emotions and both partners reported higher sexual and relationship satisfaction (Impett, Peplau, & Gable, 2005; Muise, Impett, & Desmarais, 2013). In contrast, when people engaged in sex to avoid negative outcomes in their relationship, such as to avoid conflict or a partner's disappointment (i.e., avoidance goals), they experienced more negative emotions and relationship conflict and both partners reported lower sexual and relationship satisfaction. In one longitudinal study of long-term married and cohabiting couples, people who had sex more frequently for avoidance goals over the course of a 3-week daily experience study reported lower sexual satisfaction at a 4-month follow-up and had partners who felt less sexually satisfied and committed to maintaining their relationship 4 months later (Muise et al., 2013). As such, research on sexual motivation suggests that some sexual experiences contribute more strongly to relationship quality and well-being than others.

Research guided by approach-avoidance motivational theory has also shown that individuals who are motivated by approach goals such as to deepen their relationship with their partner or promote growth and development in their relationship are more likely to sustain high levels of sexual desire for their partner over time (Impett et al., 2008). Two daily experience studies of dating, cohabiting, and married couples revealed that on days when people engaged in sex with their partner for approach goals, both partners reported higher sexual desire and in turn, felt more satisfied with the sexual experience and the relationship. In contrast, on days when people engaged in sex for avoidance goals such as to avoid disappointing their partner, not only did they feel lower desire and satisfaction, but their partners reported lower desire and satisfaction as well (Muise et al., 2013). This research has also shown that people who pursue sex for approach goals are able to maintain high levels of sexual desire even on days that would ordinarily be the most threatening to couples, such as when they have disagreements with their partner. In a 14-day daily experience study of college students in dating relationships, sexual desire was generally higher on days when people reported experiencing more frequent positive events and was lower on days with more frequent negative events, but people who were more approach-motivated were even able to maintain high desire in the face of more negative relationship events

(Impett et al., 2008). Therefore, engaging in sex to pursue positive outcomes for the partner or relationship, such as enhancing closeness, is one way that couples can maintain satisfying sexual relationships over time.

Sexual communal motivation

Another way people in romantic relationships may also differ in their sexual motivations is in the extent to which they are communally motivated to meet their partner's sexual needs. *Communal strength* is defined as the motivation to give to a partner to enhance that partner's well-being without the expectation of direct reciprocation, as opposed to giving *quid pro quo* where a favor is contingent upon receiving something in return (Mills, Clark, Ford, & Johnson, 2004). As such, communally motivated people are more willing to sacrifice their own self-interests for the sake of their partner or their relationship (Mills et al., 2004). Recently, theories of communal motivation have been applied to the sexual domain of relationships. *Sexual communal strength* is the extent to which people are motivated to be non-contingently responsive to their partner's sexual needs (Muise, Impett, Kogan, & Desmarais, 2013). People high in sexual communal strength report being more likely to have sex with their partner when they are not entirely in the mood, being open-minded about their partner's preferences, communicating with their partner about their sexual likes and dislikes (both learning about their partner's preferences and sharing their own), and ensuring that the sexual relationship is mutually satisfying (Muise & Impett, 2012).

Interestingly, people who are communally motivated to meet their partner's sexual needs compared to those who are less communal reap important benefits for both the *self* and their *partner*. In a sample of long-term couples who had been together for an average of 11 years, people who were higher in sexual communal strength felt more sexual desire for their partner and had more enjoyable sexual experiences (Muise et al., 2013). More intuitively, the partners of people high in sexual communal strength also reaped important benefits. People with communally motivated partners reported that their partners were, in fact, highly responsive to their needs during sex and in turn, they felt more satisfied with and committed to their relationships (Muise & Impett, 2015). Related research suggests that, at times, changing sexual habits (or making *sexual transformations*) for a partner can benefit the relationship (Burke & Young, 2012). In one study, romantic couples reported how frequently they made sexual changes for their partners (e.g., had sex more frequently than personally desired or engaged in activities that were not their preference), and how they felt about making these sexual changes. People who made more (compared to less) frequent sexual changes for their partners had partners who reported being more satisfied in their relationship. In addition, people who felt more positive about changing their sexual habits for a partner felt more satisfied with their relationships and had partners who reported feeling more satisfied as well.

Being communally motivated to meet a partner's sexual needs also helps couples maintain sexual desire over time. In one study, in comparison to people lower in sexual communal strength, people who were highly motivated to meet their partner's sexual needs in a relationship engaged in sex more for approach goals, such as to enhance intimacy with their partner, over the course of a 3-week diary study and reported higher levels of daily sexual desire as a result (Muise et al., 2013). In addition, whereas people low in sexual communal strength declined in desire over time in their relationship, people high in sexual communal strength began the study with slightly higher desire and were able to maintain sexual desire over a 4-month period of time (Muise et al., 2013). Communally motivated people are even motivated to meet their partner's needs in situations when it is not particularly easy – for example, in situations in which their partner is interested in sex but their own desire for sex is low. In these situations, communally motivated people remain motivated to pursue benefits for their partner, such as making their partner feel loved and desired, instead of focusing on what they personally have to lose from engaging in sex, such as feeling too tired (Day, Muise, Joel, & Impett, 2015). As a result of their increased motivation to pursue benefits for their partner and decreased motivation to avoid costs to themselves, they are more likely to engage in sex in these situations and both partners report greater sexual and relationship satisfaction as a result. Taken together, the research on sexual communal motivation suggests that pursuing benefits for a partner and the relationship is associated with higher sexual desire and can lead to enhanced sexual fulfillment and relationship quality for both partners.

Researchers have also examined how narcissistic tendencies influence sexual satisfaction over time. In many ways, narcissists are the opposite of highly communal people – instead of being focused on meeting their partner's needs, they tend to have low levels of empathy, focus on themselves in their communication, and exploit others for their own gains (Campbell, Foster, & Finkel, 2002). In a longitudinal study, McNulty and Widman (2013) assessed sexual narcissism, which captures four facets of narcissism in the sexual domain, including sexual exploitation, sexual entitlement, low sexual empathy, and sexual skill (Widman & McNulty, 2010). Interestingly, one facet of sexual narcissism – high perceived sexual skill – was associated with *higher* sexual and relationship satisfaction as reported by both members of the couple. However, by and large sexual narcissism was associated with negative sexual and relational outcomes; three of the four facets of sexual narcissism, sexual exploitation, sexual entitlement, and low sexual empathy, predicted declines in sexual and relationship satisfaction for both partners over the first 5 years of marriage. Taken together, the research on sexual communal motivation and narcissism suggests that sexual responsiveness to a partner's needs and engaging in sex to pursue benefits for a partner may help couples to stave off declines in sexual desire and satisfaction over time.

Cognition

Although sex itself is a physical act, sexual satisfaction is an evaluative cognition. Accordingly, it may be difficult to gain the fullest understanding of sexual satisfaction without also understanding its cognitive elements. One of the most basic tenets of social cognition is that people tend to evaluate social objects in a manner that is consistent with their initial expectancies for those objects through processes of perceptual confirmation (Wyer & Srull, 1986). The same may be true for sexual evaluations; what intimates expect from their sexual relationships may shape the way they perceive those relationships. Of course, not all events are subject to the influence of expectations. Very concrete information, such as how frequently a couple has sex, is less open to interpretation and thus less susceptible to the perceptual influences of expectations (Neff & Geers, 2013) (though expectations could still predict people's willingness to engage in sex). As numerous scholars have noted, women's sexual experiences are more influenced by contextual factors such as acculturation, education, and religion (Baumeister, 2000; Peplau, 2003). Therefore, expectations about a sexual relationship may more strongly influence women's sexual satisfaction than they influence men's, whereas men's sexual satisfaction may be more strongly influenced by objective aspects such as frequency.

In one study, both partners reported their sexual satisfaction and sexual frequency as well as completed a 7-day daily experience study about how sexually satisfied they expected to be in their relationship (McNulty & Fisher, 2008). Six months later both partners again reported their sexual satisfaction and sexual frequency. For women, but not men, sexual expectancies (i.e., how satisfied they expected to feel with their sexual relationship with their partner) predicted changes in their sexual satisfaction over this 6-month period of time. More specifically, women who expected to be more satisfied with their sex lives over time were, in fact, more satisfied 6 months later. For men, in contrast, changes in sexual frequency over the 6-month period predicted changes in their sexual satisfaction. Engaging in less frequent sex at the 6-month follow-up compared to the beginning of the study was associated with lower sexual satisfaction for men. In sum, whereas women's expectations for their sexual experiences appear to play a role in shaping their sexual evaluations, men's sexual evaluations may be grounded in more objective aspects of sex, such as frequency.

But expectations are not the only cognition likely to affect sexual satisfaction and the sexual relationship. Recent research also suggests that people's implicit beliefs about how sexual satisfaction is maintained over time in a relationship have implications for their sexual and relationship quality. A robust body of research demonstrates that people's implicit theories regarding whether particular behaviors are innate or take effort to cultivate have important implications for the way people approach and ultimately engage in such behaviors (Dweck, 2008). Following Knee (1998), who applied this distinction to relationships, Maxwell, Muise, MacDonald, Day, Rosen and Impett (invited resubmission) developed a measure of two implicit theories intimates may have regarding sexual relationships: sexual growth beliefs and sexual destiny beliefs. *Sexual growth* believers think that sexual satisfaction is maintained by work and effort, whereas *sexual destiny* believers think that sexual satisfaction results from finding a highly compatible partner, their sexual "soulmate." The results of five studies showed that sexual growth believers were more responsive sexual partners and reported higher sexual and relationship satisfaction as a result. In contrast, sexual destiny believers used their sexual compatibility with their partner as a barometer for relationship quality and as such, were more sensitive to sexual disagreements and experienced lower sexual and relationship satisfaction.

Lastly, people are motivated to view their relationships positively and these cognitive processes help to maintain romantic relationships over time (Murray et al., 2011), at least for those in healthy relationships at the outset (see McNulty, O'Mara, & Karney, 2008; O'Mara, McNulty, & Karney, 2011). Recent research has applied theory about cognitive relationship maintenance mechanisms to the sexual domain (de Jong & Reis, in press). This research has revealed that romantic partners tend to positively construe their sexual relationship such that they view their current partner as their ideal sexual partner and feel optimistic about their future sex lives. People higher in commitment are more likely to positively construe their sexual relationships, which reflects a motivational process serving to bolster people's resolve to persist in their relationships. Assuming such processes are occurring in healthy, well-functioning relationships, they may predict better sexual outcomes over time. Taken together, this research suggests that a person's expectations for their sexual relationship and their beliefs about how sexual satisfaction is maintained over time have implications for how much their sexual desire declines over time, how they react to such declines, and thus the quality and maintenance of their relationships.

Sexual communication

Another factor that influences the association between sexual and relationship satisfaction is sexual communication. Couples who report higher-quality communication about their sex lives also report higher sexual and relationship satisfaction (Byers, 2005). In fact, general self-disclosure as well as disclosure about specific sexual likes and dislikes contributes to romantic partners' feelings of sexual satisfaction (Byers & Demmons, 1999). In one study, researchers found that it is not just communication outside the bedroom that is important, but communicating with a partner *during* sex also has implications for sexual quality. People who communicate, either verbally or nonverbally, with their partner during sex reported higher levels of sexual satisfaction (Babin, 2012). In fact, couples who reported using more sexual terms during sexual interactions with their partner reported higher satisfaction with sexual communication, and also greater overall relational quality and feelings of closeness (Hess & Coffelt, 2012). Using more sexual terms with a partner might indicate that these couples are talking about sex more frequently or have greater comfort with sexual communication and this is accounting for their increased relationship quality.

Sexual self-disclosure may also be one way for couples to maintain sexual desire and satisfaction over the course of long-term relationships (MacNeil & Byers, 2009). As mentioned previously, people who are high in sexual communal strength (i.e., those who are motivated to meet their partner's sexual needs) are more likely to maintain sexual desire over time (Muise et al., 2013) and one way they report meeting their partner's sexual needs is through effective sexual communication. In response to an open-ended question about the strategies they use to meet their partner's needs, communal people indicated that they try to learn about a partner's sexual likes and dislikes and incorporate what they learn into their sexual activities (Muise & Impett, 2012). Individual differences in romantic attachment also influence comfort with sexual communication as well as sexual and relationship satisfaction. Securely attached individuals (i.e., those who are comfortable with intimacy and closeness) generally have committed, stable, and satisfying romantic relationships and enjoy sex in the context of relationships (Birnbaum et al., 2006).

One key reason why secure people have satisfying sex lives and relationships seems to be that they are better able to communicate their sexual needs and understand the needs of their partner. In general, more open and effective sexual communication is associated with greater sexual and relationship satisfaction (e.g., Byers & Demmons, 1999; Sprecher, 2006), and secure individuals tend to be better able to communicate their sexual needs compared to insecure individuals (i.e., those high in attachment anxiety or attachment avoidance) (Shaver & Mikulincer, 2005). In one study, secure individuals reported less inhibited sexual communication compared to anxious and avoidant individuals, and this was found to mediate the relationship between attachment and levels of sexual satisfaction (Davis et al., 2006). Similarly, in a more recent study of partnered gay men, securely attached individuals reported the highest levels of sexual communication and experienced greater relationship quality, and men with securely attached partners were the most likely to report having sex with their partners at least once per week (Starks & Parsons, 2014). Of course, given recent research suggesting that people tend to overestimate how accurate they are in their knowledge of their partner's sexual preferences and the extent to which their sexual preferences are similar and compatible with their romantic partner (de Jong & Reis, 2014), couples may need to strike a balance between disclosure and leaving some preferences and desires for the imagination. Future research may benefit by investigating this issue.

Non-traditional approaches to maintaining sexual intimacy

Traditionally, sex and relationship therapists have focused on minimizing sexual dysfunctions and problems in relationships. However, in recent years, sex therapists and researchers have embraced the idea that sexual fulfillment in relationships does not simply mean the absence of sexual problems and have shifted their focus from treating sexual dysfunction to helping couples achieve sexual fulfillment. In some ways, this new focus mirrors the advantages of approach (versus avoidance) motivations described in the earlier section. Indeed, in her research on optimal sexuality, Peggy Kleinplatz explores what her participants endorse as "great sex" (Kleinplatz & Menard, 2007; Kleinplatz et al., 2009). Kleinplatz and her colleagues conducted qualitative interviews with couples who reported having "great sex" and extracted the common themes that emerged during these interviews. She argues that the picture of great sex that emerges from her research looks radically different than that prescribed by conventional sex therapy or the mainstream media. Eight components of great sex were identified from her interviews: being present, connection, deep sexual and erotic intimacy, extraordinary communication, interpersonal risk-taking and exploration, authenticity, vulnerability, and transcendence (Kleinplatz et al. 2009). Interestingly, orgasm, which is typically viewed as a standard indicator of sexual function, did not emerge as a key component of or even necessary to experience great sex. In fact, in these narratives, great sex had little to do with physical function and was instead more grounded in a deep connection between partners. The fact that these participants were specifically recruited because they reported having very satisfying sex may mean these findings are unique to such couples, as compared to couples who are satisfied by more frequent sex (e.g., Call et al., 1995; McNulty et al, 2015), but it also suggests focusing less on the physical, objective aspects of sex may lead couples to experience enhanced satisfaction.

Researchers have also suggested some non-normative sexual behaviors that have the potential to strengthen relationships. Based on the idea that some people may hold their relationships to standards that those relationships are unable to meet (Finkel et al., 2014), Conley and Moors (2014) suggest that some couples may benefit from employing the tenets of consensually non-monogamous (CNM) or polyamorous relationships. These ideas involve multiple aspects such as: removing the expectations that one person (i.e., a romantic partner) will meet *all* of one's needs; anticipating that sexual desire and attraction for one's partner will waver at times over the course of a long-term relationship; understanding that having multiple loving relationships (whether these are romantic or sexual relationships or not) can be healthy and beneficial; communicating with your partner (or partners) in an open and honest way; and making time to talk about your relationship. It is important to point out that Conley and Moors are not suggesting that everyone should pursue a CNM relationship; instead, they suggest that both researchers and couples may learn strategies from polyamorous relationships that can help to revive romantic partnerships over time. For some couples, this may mean discussing and re-evaluating the terms of their monogamous commitment regularly. For other couples, this may mean accepting attractions to and sexual fantasies about others. For other couples, it may be learning from CNM couples who are likely to have addressed complicated issues in their relationships and studying how CNM couples manage conflict that might present useful strategies for monogamous couples as well. These ideas are ripe for empirical investigation.

CONCLUSIONS AND DIRECTIONS FOR FUTURE RESEARCH

Although in recent years we have gained many important insights about the positive implications of sexuality for relationships, many unanswered questions remain. In this section, we briefly highlight some key directions for future work on the intersection of sexuality and romantic relationships. First, we know that desire discrepancies or conflicts of sexual interest between partners often have negative implications for dating and marital relationships. However, divergent sexual interests are common in long-term relationships and certainly some couples are able to navigate these differences while maintaining high relationship quality. An important avenue for future research is to explore the strategies that couples use to manage sexual disagreements more successfully. Dyadic research that involves interviewing desire-discrepant couples who are both struggling and thriving and observing interactions between partners are promising directions for this line of inquiry. With respect to the latter, recent research on non-sexual problem-solving communication indicates that direct communication can be more effective than more indirect forms (McNulty & Russell, 2010; Overall, Fletcher, Simpson, & Sibley, 2009). Further research may benefit from examining whether the same is true for resolving disagreements about sex. We also know that a combination of compromise and acceptance can help distressed couples improve their relationship satisfaction (Jacobson,

Christensen, Prince, Cordova, & Eldridge, 2000). Applied to the sexual domain of relationships, romantic couples may aim to make changes to their sex life based on each other's sexual preferences or desired sexual frequency when reasonable, in order to reach a compromise. This may include engaging in sexual activities that one partner enjoys, but are not the other partner's preferred activity, or compromising on how frequently the couples engages in sex by pursuing sex at a frequency that is somewhere in between partners' desired frequency. At the same time, however, partners may also aim to accept the things that the other person is not willing to change. For example, if one partner is interested in a specific sexual activity, but their partner is not comfortable doing this, they may have to accept that this activity will not be part of their sex life with this partner. Future research may benefit from addressing these possibilities as well.

Second, a growing body of research suggests that a person's reasons or goals for engaging in sex are crucial for predicting when sex is most enjoyable and when it might detract from relationship satisfaction. But in many situations, relationship partners will choose *not* to engage in sex and decide, instead, to pursue their own personal interests. There is currently no research investigating how and why people decline their partner's sexual advances, as well as whether some ways of delivering sexual rejection are better able to preserve closeness in romantic relationships. On the flip slide, we know virtually nothing about how people can remain satisfied despite receiving sexual rejection from their romantic partner. In short, almost all of the existing work on sex and relationships has focused on what happens when people *do* have sex, and almost none of it has looked at what happens when people *don't* have sex – and if there are particular ways of rejecting a partner and receiving a rejection that can best preserve intimacy in couples.

Third, although there are biological differences, such as sex, that influence sexual desire, research has also revealed that there are important individual difference factors – including individual differences in approach goals, communal motivation, and sexual expectations – that can powerfully shape desire and satisfaction in romantic relationships. Although some of the variance in these and other individual differences may be due to biological individual differences, they may be partially malleable. Nevertheless, we know very little about how they can be modified. The lack of research on this topic likely reflects the challenges in conducting experimental work in the area of sexuality. However, learning whether it is possible to enhance people's approach sexual goals or communal motivation has important implications for improving couples' sexual relationships. In previous research on social goals, Strachman and Gable (2006) manipulated approach and avoidance social goals and found that being primed with approach goals leads to more positive social interactions. It is possible that providing couples with information about the benefits of certain approaches to sexuality in their relationship could have positive effects, and this would be a worthwhile avenue for future research.

Finally, romantic relationships change over time and following important relationship transitions, such as the transition to parenthood, but few studies have followed couples over long periods of time and during these transitional periods to learn about the factors that help couples maintain desire and better navigate sexual changes and differences in a relationship. We believe that longitudinal studies of romantic couples may hold the greatest potential for answering questions about why some relationships thrive over time and others fail. Many couples strive to maintain desire and satisfaction over time, and researchers have much to contribute and much left to learn about the positive implications of sex for relationships.

In today's world, some people expect more from their romantic relationships than ever before (Finkel et al., 2014), including sexual fulfillment. Although we know that high expectations can benefit sexual relationships (McNulty & Fisher, 2008) and relationships more broadly (McNulty & Karney, 2002), we also know that expectations that are difficult or impossible to meet can be a liability (Finkel et al., 2014, McNulty & Karney, 2004). Successfully navigating these challenges and maintaining sexual fulfillment over time has great potential to enhance the quality of a couple's relationship and some of the lines of research described throughout this chapter have begun to shed light on how couples may do this. We hope that our review of the growing literature on positive perspectives of sexuality in relationships highlights how much we have learned and sparks increased interest in a topic that we think is integral to strengthening the quality and longevity of romantic bonds.

REFERENCES

Acevedo, B. P., & Aron, A. (2009). Does a long-term relationship kill romantic love? *Review of General Psychology*, 13, 59–65.

Ahlborg, T., Dahlöf, L. G., & Hallberg, L. R. M. (2005). Quality of the intimate and sexual relationship in first-time parents six months after delivery. *Journal of Sex Research*, 42, 167–174.

Babin, E. (2012). An examination of predictors of nonverbal and verbal communication of pleasure during sex and sexual satisfaction. *Journal of Social and Personal Relationships*, 30, 270–292.

Baumeister, R. F. (2000). Gender differences in erotic plasticity: The female sex drive as socially flexible and responsive. *Psychological Bulletin*, 126, 347–374.

Baumeister, R. F., & Bratslavsky, E. (1999). Passion, intimacy, and time: Passionate love as a function of change in intimacy. *Personality and Social Psychology Review*, 3, 49–67.

Birnbaum, G. E., Reis, H. T., Mikulincer, M., Gillath, O., & Orpaz, A. (2006). When sex is more than just sex: Attachment orientations, sexual experience, and relationship quality. *Journal of Personality and Social Psychology*, 91, 929.

Blair, K. L., & Pukall, C. F. (2014). Can less be more? Comparing duration vs. frequency of sexual encounters in same-sex and mixed-sex relationships. *The Canadian Journal of Human Sexuality*, 23, 123–136.

Blumstein, P., & Schwartz, P. (1983). *American couples: Money, work, sex*. New York: Morrow.

Brezsnyak, M., & Whisman, M. A. (2004). Sexual desire and relationship functioning: The effects of marital satisfaction and power. *Journal of Sex & Marital Therapy*, 30, 199–217.

Brousseau, M. M., Bergeron, S., Hébert, M., & McDuff, P. (2011). Sexual coercion victimization and perpetration in heterosexual couples: A dyadic investigation. *Archives of Sexual Behavior*, 40, 363–372.

Brunell, A. B., & Webster, G. D. (2013). Self-determination and sexual experience in dating relationships. *Personality and Social Psychology Bulletin*, 39, 970–987.

Burke, T. J., & Young, V. J. (2012). Sexual transformations and intimate behaviors in romantic relationships, *Journal of Sex Research*, 49, 454–463.

Buss, D. M., & Schmitt, D. P. (1993). Sexual strategies theory: An evolutionary perspective on human mating. *Psychological Review*, 100, 204–232.

Byers, E. S. (2005). Relationship satisfaction and sexual satisfaction: A longitudinal study of individuals in long-term relationships. *Journal of Sex Research*, 42, 113–118.

Byers, E. S., & Demmons, S. (1999). Sexual satisfaction and sexual self-disclosure within dating relationships. *Journal of Sex Research*, 36, 180–189.

Call, V., Sprecher, S., & Schwartz, P. (1995). The incidence and frequency of marital sex in a national sample. *Journal of Marriage and Family*, 57, 639–652.

Campbell, W. K., Foster, C. A., & Finkel, E. J. (2002). Does self-love lead to love for others?: A story of narcissistic game playing. *Journal of Personality and Social Psychology*, 83, 340–354.

Cassidy, J., & Shaver, P. R. (Eds.). (1999). *Handbook of attachment: Theory, research, and clinical applications*. New York: Guilford Press.

Cheung, M. W. L., Wong, P. W. C., Liu, K. Y., Yip, P. S. F., Fan, S. Y., & Lam, T. (2008). A study of sexual satisfaction and frequency among Hong Kong Chinese couples. *Journal of Sex Research*, 45, 129–139.

Conley, T. D., & Moors, A. C. (2014). More oxygen please!: How polyamorous relationship strategies might oxygenate marriage. *Psychological Inquiry*, 25, 56–63.

Davies, S., Katz, J., & Jackson, J. L. (1999). Sexual desire discrepancies: Effects on sexual and relationship satisfaction in heterosexual dating couples. *Archives of Sexual Behavior*, 28, 553–567.

Davis, D., Shaver, P. R., Widaman, K. F., Vernon, M. L., Follette, W. C., & Beitz, K. (2006). "I can't get no satisfaction": Insecure attachment, inhibited sexual communication, and sexual dissatisfaction. *Personal Relationships*, 13(4), 465–483.

Dawson, J., Fallis, E., & Rehman, U. S. (2010). *Why is this so difficult? Challenges of discussing sexual issues in committed relationships*. Presented at the Canadian Sex Research Forum, Toronto, ON.

Day, L., Muise, A., Joel, S., & Impett, E. A. (2015). To do it or not to do it? How communally motivated people navigate sexual interdependence dilemmas. *Personality and Social Psychology Bulletin*.

Deci, E. L., & Ryan, R. M. (2000). The "what" and "why" of goal pursuits: Human needs and the self-determination of behavior. *Psychological Inquiry*, 11, 227–268.

de Jong, D. C., & Reis, H. T. (2015). We do it best: Commitment and positive construals of sex. *Journal of Social and Clinical Psychology*, 34, 181–202.

de Jong, D. C., & Reis, H. T. (2014). Sexual kindred spirits: Actual and overperceived similarity, complementarity, and partner accuracy in heterosexual couples. *Personality and Social Psychology Bulletin*, 40, 1316–1329.

DeLamater, J. D., & Sill, M. (2005). Sexual desire in later life. *The Journal of Sex Research*, 42, 138–149.

Diamond, L. (2004). Emerging perspectives on distinctions between romantic love and sexual desire. *Current Directions in Psychological Science*, 13, 116–119.

Diener, E., & Seligman, M. E. P. (2002). Very happy people. *Psychological Science*, 13, 81–84.

Dweck, C. S. (2008). Can personality be changed? The role of beliefs in personality and change. *Current Directions in Psychological Science*, 17, 391–394.

Edwards, J. N., & Booth, A. (1994). Sexuality, marriage, and well-being: The middle years. In A. S. Rossi (Ed.), *Sexuality across the life course* (pp. 233–259). Chicago, IL: University of Chicago Press.

Ferenidou, F., Kapoteli, V., Moisidis, K., Koutsogiannis, I., Giakoumelos, A., & Hatzichristou, D. (2008). Presence of a sexual problem may not affect women's satisfaction from their sexual function. *The Journal of Sexual Medicine*, 5, 631–639.

Finkel, E. J., Hui, C. M., Carswell, K. L., & Larson, G. M. (2014). The suffocation of marriage: Climbing Mount Maslow without enough oxygen. *Psychological Inquiry*, 25, 1–41.

Fisher, T. D., & McNulty, J. K. (2008). Neuroticism and marital satisfaction: The mediating role played by the sexual relationship. *Journal of Family Psychology*, 22, 112–122.

Fletcher, G. J., Kerr, P. S., Li, N. P., & Valentine, K. A. (2014). Predicting romantic interest and decisions in the very early stages of mate selection standards, accuracy, and sex differences. *Personality and Social Psychology Bulletin*, 40, 540–550.

Gable, S. L., & Impett, E. A. (2012). Approach and avoidance motives and close relationships. *Social & Personality Psychology Compass*, 6, 95–108. doi:10.1111/j.1751-9004.2011.00405.x.

Heiman, J. R., Long, S. J., Smith, S. N., Fisher, W. A., & Sand, M. S. (2010). Sexual satisfaction and relationship happiness in midlife and older couples in five countries. *Archives of Sexual Behavior*, 40, 741–753.

Hess, J. A., & Coffelt, T. A. (2012). Verbal communication about sex in marriage. *Journal of Sex Research*, 49, 603–612

Hinchliff, S., & Gott, M. (2004). Intimacy, commitment and adaptation: Sexual relationships within long-term marriages. *Journal of Social & Personal Relationships*, 21(5), 595–609.

Hinchliff, S., & Gott, M. (2008). Challenging social myths and stereotypes of women and aging: Heterosexual women talk about sex. *Journal of Women and Aging*, 20, 65–81.

House, J. S., Landis, K. R., & Umberson, D. (1988). Social relationships and health. *Science*, 241, 540.

Impett, E. A., Muise, A., & Peragine, D. (2014). Sexuality in the context of relationships. In D. L. Tolman, L. M. Diamond, J. A. Bauermeister, W. H. George, J. G. Pfaus, & L. M. Ward (Eds.), *APA handbook of sexuality and psychology*, (Vol. 1) (pp. 269–315). Washington, DC: American Psychological Association.

Impett, E. A., Peplau, L. A., & Gable, S. L. (2005). Approach and avoidance sexual motives: Implications for personal and interpersonal well-being. *Personal Relationships*, 12, 465–482.

Impett, E., A., Strachman, A., Finkel, E. J., & Gable, S. L. (2008). Maintaining sexual desire in intimate relationships: The importance of approach goals. *Journal of Personality and Social Psychology*, 94, 808–823.

Impett, E. A., & Peplau, L. A. (2003). Sexual compliance: Gender, motivational, and relationship perspectives. *Journal of Sex Research*, 40, 87–100.

Jacobson, N. S., Christensen, A., Prince, S. E., Cordova, J., & Eldridge, K. (2000). Integrative behavioral couple therapy: An acceptance-based, promising new treatment for couple discord. *Journal of Consulting and Clinical Psychology*, 68, 351–355.

Karney, B. R., & Bradbury, T. N. (1997). Neuroticism, marital interaction, and the trajectory of marital satisfaction. *Journal of Personality and Social Psychology*, 72, 1075–1092.

Kleinplatz, P. J., & Ménard, A. D. (2007). Building blocks toward optimal sexuality: Constructing a conceptual model. *Family Journal: Counseling and Therapy for Couples and Families*, 15, 72–78.

Kleinplatz, P. J., Menard, A. D., Paquet, M-P., Paradis, N., Campbell, M., Zuccarino, D., & Mehak, L. (2009). The components of optimal sexuality: A portrait of "great sex." *Canadian Journal of Human Sexuality*, 18, 1–13.

Knee, C. R. (1998). Implicit theories of relationships: Assessment and prediction of romantic relationship initiation, coping, and longevity. *Journal of Personality and Social Psychology*, 74, 360–370.

Kurdek, L. A. (1991). Sexuality in homosexual and heterosexual couples. In K. McKinney & S. Sprecher (Eds.), *Sexuality in Close Relationships* (pp. 177–191). Hillsdale, NJ: Lawrence Erlbaum Associates.

Laumann, E. O., Gagnon, J. H., Michael, R. T., & Michaels, S. (1994). *The social organization of sexuality: Sexual practices in the United States*. Chicago, IL: University of Chicago Press.

Laumann, E. O., Paik, A., Glasser, D. B., Kang, J. H., Wang, T., Levinson, B., Moreira, E. D., Nicolosi, M., & Gingell, C. (2006). A cross-national study of subjective sexual well-being among older women and men: Findings from the Global Study of Sexual Attitudes and Behaviors. *Archives of Sexual Behavior*, 35, 143–159.

Lavner, J. A., & Bradbury, T. N. (2010). Patterns of change in marital satisfaction over the newlywed years. *Journal of Marriage and Family*, 72(5), 1171–1187.

Lehmiller, J. J., VanderDrift, L. E., & Kelly, J. R. (2014). Sexual communication, satisfaction, and condom use behavior in friends with benefits and romantic partners. *Journal of Sex Research*, 51, 74–85.

Little, K. C., McNulty, J. K., & Russell, V. M. (2010). Sex buffers intimates against the negative implications of attachment insecurity. *Personality and Social Psychology Bulletin*, 36, 484–498.

MacNeil, S., & Byers, E. S. (2009). Role of sexual self-disclosure in the sexual satisfaction of long-term heterosexual couples. *Journal of Sex Research*, 46, 3–14.

Mark, K. P. (2012). The relative impact of individual sexual desire and couple desire discrepancy on satisfaction in heterosexual couples. *Sexual and Relationship Therapy*, 27, 133–146.

Mark, K. P., & Murray, S. H. (2012). Gender differences in desire discrepancy as a predictor of sexual and relationship satisfaction in a college sample of heterosexual romantic relationships. *Journal of Sex and Marital Therapy*, 38, 198–215.

Maxwell, J., Muise, A., MacDonald, G., Day, L. C., Rosen, N. O., Impett, E. A., & (invited resubmission). Sexpectations: The influence of implicit beliefs about sexual relationships on sexual satisfaction.

McNulty, J. K., & Fisher, T. D. (2008). Gender differences in response to sexual expectancies and changes in sexual frequency: A short-term longitudinal study of sexual satisfaction in newly married couples. *Archives of Sexual Behavior, 37*, 229–240.

McNulty, J. K., & Karney, B. R. (2002). Expectancy confirmation in appraisals of marital interactions. *Personality and Social Psychology Bulletin, 28*, 764–775.

McNulty, J. K., & Karney, B. R. (2004). Positive expectations in the early years of marriage: Should couples expect the best or brace for the worst? *Journal of Personality and Social Psychology, 86*, 729–743.

McNulty, J. K., O'Mara, E. M., & Karney B. R. (2008). Benevolent cognitions as a strategy of relationship maintenance: "Don't sweat the small stuff" . . . but it is not all small stuff. *Journal of Personality and Social Psychology, 94*, 631–646.

McNulty, J. K., & Russell, V. M. (2010). When "negative" behaviors are positive: A contextual analysis of the long-term effects of problem-solving behaviors on changes in relationship satisfaction. *Journal of Personality and Social Psychology, 98*, 587–604.

McNulty, J. K., Wenner, C. A., & Fisher, T. D. (2015). Longitudinal associations among marital satisfaction, sexual satisfaction, and frequency of sex in early marriage. *Archives of Sexual Behavior*, Advanced online publication.

McNulty, J. K., & Widman, L. (2013). The implications of sexual narcissism for sexual and marital satisfaction. *Archives of Sexual Behavior, 42*, 1021–1032.

Meltzer, A. L., & McNulty, J. K. (2010). Body image and marital satisfaction: Evidence for the mediating role of sexual frequency and sexual satisfaction. *Journal of Family Psychology, 24*, 156–164.

Meltzer, A. L., McNulty, J. K., Jackson, G. L., & Karney, B. R. (2014). Sex differences in the implications of partner physical attractiveness for the trajectory of marital satisfaction. *Journal of Personality and Social Psychology, 106*, 418–428.

Mills, J., Clark, M. S., Ford, T. E., & Johnson, M. (2004). Measurement of communal strength. *Personal Relationships, 11*, 213–230.

Muise, A., Giang, E., & Impett, E. A. (2014). Post sex affectionate exchanges promote sexual and relationship satisfaction. *Archives of Sexual Behavior, 43*, 1391–1402.

Muise, A., & Impett, E. A. (2012, September). Are you game? The benefits of sexual communal strength. Paper presented at the 38th Annual Meeting of the Canadian Sex Research Forum, Ottawa, ON, Canada.

Muise, A., & Impett, E. A. (2015). Good, giving and game: The relationship benefits of communal sexual responsiveness. *Social Psychological and Personality Science, 6*, 164–172. doi:10.1177/1948550614553641

Muise, A., Impett, E. A., & Desmarais, S. (2013). Getting it on versus getting it over with sexual motivation, desire, and satisfaction in intimate bonds. *Personality and Social Psychology Bulletin, 39*, 1320–1332.

Muise, A., Impett, E. A., Kogan, A., & Desmarais, S. (2013). Keeping the spark alive: Being motivated to meet a partner's sexual needs sustains sexual desire in long-term romantic relationships. *Social Psychological and Personality Science, 4*, 267–273.

Muise, A., Schimmack, U., & Impett, E. A. (2015). Sex and well-being: Does having more frequent sex actually make you happier? Advanced online publication.

Murray, S. L., Griffin, D. W., Derrick, J. L., Harris, B., Aloni, M., & Leder, S. (2011). Tempting fate or inviting happiness? Unrealistic idealization prevents the decline of marital satisfaction. *Psychological Science, 22*(5), 619–626.

Neff, L. A., & Geers, A. L. (2013). Optimistic expectations in early marriage: A resource or vulnerability for adaptive relationship functioning? *Journal of Personality and Social Psychology*, 105, 38–60.

O'Leary, K. D., & Williams, M. C. (2006). Agreement about acts of aggression in marriage. *Journal of Family Psychology*, 20, 656–662.

O'Mara, E. M., McNulty, J. K., & Karney B. R. (2011). Positively biased appraisals in everyday life: When do they benefit mental health and when do they harm it? *Journal of Personality and Social Psychology*, 101, 415–432.

O'Sullivan, L. F., & Byers, E. S. (1996). Gender differences in responses to discrepancies in desired level of sexual intimacy. *Journal of Psychology and Human Sexuality*, 8, 49–67.

Overall, N. C., Fletcher, G. J. O., Simpson, J. A., & Sibley, C. G. (2009). Regulating partners in intimate relationships: The costs and benefits of different communication strategies. *Journal of Personality and Social Psychology*, 96, 620–639.

Pascoal, P. M., Narciso, I. D. S. B., & Pereira, N. M. (2014). What is sexual satisfaction? Thematic analysis of lay people's definitions. *Journal of Sex Research*, 51, 22–30.

Peplau, L. A. (2003). Human Sexuality: How Do Men and Women Differ? *Current Directions in Psychological Science*, 12, 37–40.

Potts, A., Grace, V. M., Vares, T., & Gavey, N. (2006). "Sex for life"? Men's counter-stories on "erectile dysfunction", male sexuality and ageing. *Sociology of Health and Illness*, 28, 306–329.

Rahmani, A., Khoei, E. M., & Gholi, L. A. (2009). Sexual satisfaction and its relation to marital happiness in Iranians. *Iranian Journal of Public Health*, 38, 77–82.

Rehman, U. S., Janssen, E., Newhouse, S., Heiman, J., Holtzworth-Munroe, A., Fallis, E., & Rafaeli, E. (2011). Marital satisfaction and communication behaviors during sexual and nonsexual conflict discussions in newlywed couples: A pilot study. *Journal of Sex & Marital Therapy*, 37, 94–103.

Risch, G. S., Riley, L. A., & Lawler, M. G. (2003). Problematic issues in the early years of marriage: Content for premarital education. *Journal of Psychology and Theology*, 31, 253–269.

Rosen, R. (2000). Prevalence and risk factors of sexual dysfunction in men and women. *Current Psychiatry Reports*, 2, 189–195.

Russell, V. M., & McNulty, J. K. (2011). Frequent sex protects intimates from the negative implications of their neuroticism. *Social Psychological and Personality Science*, 2, 220–227.

Sanford, K. (2003). Problem-solving conversations in marriage: Does it matter what topics couples discuss. *Personal Relationships*, 10, 97–112.

Shaver, P. R., & Mikulincer, M. (2005). Attachment theory and research: Resurrection of the psychodynamic approach to personality. *Journal of Research in Personality*, 39, 22–45.

Simms, K. E., & Meana, M. (2010). Why did passion wane? A qualitative study of married women's attributes for declines in desire. *Journal of Sex and Marital Therapy*, 36, 360–380.

Smith, C. V. (2007). In pursuit of "good" sex: Self-determination and the sexual experience. *Journal of Social and Personal Relationships*, 24, 69–85.

Sprecher, S. (1994). Two sides to the breakup of dating relationships. *Personal Relationships*, 1, 199–222.

Sprecher, S. (2002). Sexual satisfaction in premarital relationships: Associations with satisfaction, love, commitment, and stability. *Journal of Sex Research*, 39, 190–196.

Sprecher, S. (2006). Sexuality. In P. Noller & J. Feeney (Eds.), *Close relationships* (pp. 267–286). Thousand Oaks, CA: Sage Publications, Inc.

Starks, T.J., & Parsons, J.T. (2014). Adult attachment among partnered gay men: Patterns and associations with sexual relationship quality. *Archives of Sexual Behavior*, 43, 107–117.

Strachman, A., & Gable, S. L. (2006). What you want (and don't want) affects what you see (and don't see): Avoidance social goals and social events. *Personality and Social Psychology Bulletin*, 32, 1446–1458.

Štulhofer, A., Buško, V., & Brouillard, P. (2010). Development and bicultural validation of the New Sexual Satisfaction Scale. *Journal of Sex Research*, 47, 257–268.

Trivers, R. (1972). Parental investment and sexual selection. In B. Campbell (Ed.), *Sexual selection and the descent of man* (pp. 136–179). New York: Aldine de Gruyter.

Waite, L. J., Laumann, E. O., Das, A., & Schumm, L. P. (2009). Sexuality: Measures of partnerships, practices, attitudes, and problems in the National Social Life, Health, and Aging Study. *The Journals of Gerontology Series B: Psychological Sciences and Social Sciences*, 64B (Suppl 1), i56–i66.

Widman, L., & McNulty, J. K. (2010). Sexual narcissism and the perpetration of sexual aggression. *Archives of Sexual Behavior*, 39, 926–939.

Wyer, R. S., & Srull, T. K. (1986). Human cognition in its social context. *Psychological Review*, 93, 322–359.

Yabiku, S. T., & Gager, C. T. (2009). Sexual frequency and the stability of marital and cohabiting unions. *Journal of Marriage and Family*, 71, 983–1000.

Yeh, H. C., Lorenz, F. O., Wickrama, K. A. S., Conger, R. D., & Elder G. H., Jr. (2006). Relationships among sexual satisfaction, marital quality, and marital instability at midlife. *Journal of Family Psychology*, 20, 339.

7

The power of diagnostic situations: how support and conflict can foster growth and security

NICKOLA C. OVERALL, YUTHIKA U. GIRME,
AND JEFFRY A. SIMPSON

Intimate relationships are a central ingredient of health and well-being. Close relationships help people live longer, healthier, and more meaningful lives, in part because support from intimate partners helps individuals traverse the challenges of life (Uchino, Cacioppo, & Kiecolt-Glaser, 1996). But well-intended support can also backfire and undermine coping and reduce relationship satisfaction (e.g., Bolger, Zuckerman, & Kessler, 2000; Brock & Lawrence, 2009). Moreover, just as they generate love and happiness, intimate partners can also cause pain and heartache. Relationship conflict is common, and it often leads to depression and poorer health outcomes (Beach, Fincham, & Katz, 1998; Kiecolt-Glaser & Newton, 2001). Unresponsive or neglectful caregiving can also cultivate attachment insecurity – relatively enduring orientations that undermine people's ability to be happy in relationships (Bowlby, 1969, 1973, 1980).

Developing satisfying and long-lasting relationships is a tough job considering that both positive elements of relationships, such as support, and negative features of relationships, such as conflict and rejection, can undermine well-being. However, instead of being impediments to optimal relationship development, such difficulties can actually be opportunities for growth, even for insecure individuals who typically respond in destructive ways during support and conflict interactions. These situations offer the potential for growth because partners' support and conflict behavior provides "diagnostic" information regarding the partners' underlying motives, regard, and dependability (Kelley et al., 2003; Rusbult & Van Lange, 2003). For example, when a partner gives the specific kind of support that a recipient needs, this reveals that he or she is a reliable and sensitive caregiver (Reis, Clark, & Holmes, 2004). Similarly, when a partner puts his or her personal dissatisfactions aside to solve relationship problems and be caring during relationship conflicts, the partner is demonstrating that he or she is committed, invested, and trustworthy (Rusbult & Van Lange, 2003).

In the current chapter, we discuss the power of these diagnostic situations to foster growth and security in intimate relationships. We first consider when and how support enacted by intimate partners can be costly and beneficial to support recipients and then illustrate how the right kind of support that matches recipients' needs can promote resilience and growth, especially for those who need it most. We then consider how conflict can improve relationships, not merely by resolving relationship problems, but also by providing an opportunity for partners to establish or reconfirm that they are invested and committed. By identifying the types of partner support and conflict behaviors that "work" for different types of people, we provide insights into how to facilitate relationship happiness and stability, particularly among individuals who typically experience difficulties sustaining happy relationships.

PROVIDING THE RIGHT KIND OF SUPPORT FOSTERS RESILIENCE, GROWTH, AND SECURITY

Support from close others can have sweeping benefits, including reducing distress, bolstering self-esteem, and protecting psychological and physical health when individuals are confronted with major life challenges (Cacioppo & Kiecolt-Glaser, 1996; Collins & Feeney, 2000; Conger, Rueter, & Elder, 1999; Feeney, 2004; Uchino, Wethington, & Kessler, 1986). Partner support also helps individuals thrive by aiding the pursuit and achievement of personal goals (Feeney, 2004; Feeney & Collins, 2014; Overall, Fletcher, & Simpson, 2010). Moreover, by providing reassurance and conveying positive regard, support from intimate partners can generate feelings of being loved and supported, which in turn fosters greater closeness and satisfaction (Cutrona & Suhr, 1992; Feeney & Collins, 2003; Gleason, Iida, Shrout, & Bolger, 2008; Pasch, Bradbury, & Sullivan, 1997; Sullivan, Pasch, Johnson, & Bradbury, 2010; Verhofstadt, Buysse, Ickes, Davis, & Devoldre, 2008).

Unfortunately, even though perceiving support can be tremendously beneficial, the actual provision of support by intimate partners can have surprising costs. Support behaviors that are direct, overt, and visible to support recipients – dubbed *visible* support – can heighten recipients' anxiety and depressed mood (Bolger & Amarel, 2007; Bolger et al., 2000), reduce feelings of self-efficacy (Howland & Simpson, 2010), and undermine recipients' confidence about achieving their goals (Girme, Overall, & Simpson, 2013). In addition, the overprovision of support (i.e., getting more support than is desired) forecasts lower relationship satisfaction (Brock & Lawrence, 2009; Cutrona, 1996). All of these costs of support are believed to occur because overt support increases the salience of stressors, signals that recipients may be unable to cope on their own, and creates feelings of indebtedness to partners (Bolger et al., 2000). Thus, even when visible support helps people feel more cared for and connected, its provision can impinge on people's need for autonomy (self-direction) and competence (ability to achieve), thereby hindering recipients' well-being and goal achievement (Ryan & Deci, 2000, 2002).

These costs of visible support have led Bolger and his colleagues to conclude that partner support should be most effective when it is *invisible* (i.e., when it goes unnoticed by recipients) and avoids undermining recipients' sense of autonomy and competence (Bolger & Amarel, 2007; Bolger et al., 2000; Shrout, Herman, & Bolger, 2006). Invisible support is indexed by a mismatch between the reports of support providers and support recipients, where partners report providing support, but recipients fail to perceive it (e.g., Bolger et al., 2000; Gleason et al., 2008; Maisel & Gable, 2009; Shrout et al., 2006). Specific types of invisible support behaviors have also been identified during couples' discussions, including subtle and indirect behaviors that de-emphasize who is the support provider and who is the support recipient and shift the focus of the problem away from the support recipient onto others who have experienced similar issues (Girme et al., 2013; Howland & Simpson, 2010). This body of research has shown that the enactment of invisible support is associated with reductions in depressed mood and anxiety (Bolger et al., 2000; Shrout et al., 2006), increased self-efficacy (Howland & Simpson, 2010), more positive perceptions that others perceive the self as capable (Bolger & Amarel, 2007), and greater goal achievement over time (Girme et al., 2013).

However, knowing that partners *are* supportive, available, and responsive is also critical to feeling secure and happy in relationships (Reis et al., 2004). Compared to visible support, invisible support may do little to fulfill recipients' needs for connection or relatedness. For example, when support is clearly perceived and visibly provided during support exchanges, it produces greater relationship closeness and quality (e.g., Feeney & Collins, 2003; Overall et al., 2010; Pasch et al., 1997; Sullivan et al., 2010). Indeed, perceiving the partner as being responsive and supportive may be paramount in many support interactions, trumping autonomy and competence needs and overriding potential hits to personal coping or self-efficacy. For example, Maisel and Gable (2009) found that invisible support resulted in greater sadness and reduced feeling of closeness in recipients when partners were perceived as being less understanding and less responsive. When accompanied by positive perceptions of the partner's understanding and validation, visible support did *not* generate more negative moods in recipients and, instead, generated greater relationship closeness (also see Gleason et al., 2008).

Viewed as a whole, the existing literature indicates that different types of support are likely to meet different types of needs in support recipients. The key to effective support, therefore, should be proper *matching* of the type of support to the primary needs of the recipient in the particular context in which a support transaction is occurring (Cutrona, 1990). For example, when recipients desire emotional reassurance, but their partner provides practical guidance, recipients perceive their partner as less sensitive and evaluate the support more negatively (Cutrona, Shaffer, Wesner, & Gardner, 2007). The same is true with regard to visible versus invisible support. Although early work demonstrated that visible forms of emotional support undermined coping (e.g., Bolger et al., 2000), recent research has shown that when individuals are distressed when discussing their goals with their partners, receiving visible emotional support is associated with recipients feeling more supported and more confident about achieving their personal goals (Girme et al., 2013). In contrast, when discussing goal strivings with partners is not distressing, receiving more visible emotional support reduces recipients' goal-related confidence and feelings of efficacy (Girme et al., 2013). A similar pattern might arise with practical support. For example, recipients may be more appreciative of visible practical support if they really lack the resources to accomplish their goals (Cutrona, 1990).

In sum, the enactment of support by intimate partners can both facilitate and hinder recipients' needs for relatedness, competence, and autonomy. The benefits of support should be maximized (and its potential costs minimized) when enacted support meets the contextual needs of recipients. Invisible support should be most effective in contexts in which visible support impinges on people's sense of competence and autonomy needs (e.g., Bolger & Amarel, 2007; Bolger et al., 2000) or recipients cannot bolster their sense of competence by reciprocating support they have received (e.g., Gleason et al., 2008). In contrast, visible support will be most beneficial when recipients are experiencing emotional distress and need their partner's care and comfort (e.g., Girme et al., 2013) or want evidence of their partner's understanding and responsiveness (e.g., Maisel & Gable, 2009). In addition, the provision of emotional support (e.g., listening, offering comfort, soothing) versus practical support (e.g., giving advice, guidance, and/or tangible aid) addresses very different needs, so each type of support should be most effective when it matches the current desires, needs, and demands of support recipients (Cutrona et al., 2007).

Needless to say, providing the right kind of support is not easy. However, partners who are able to responsively tailor their support provision to recipients' needs may not only help recipients navigate stressful challenges and achieve their personal goals; they may also demonstrate to recipients that they (partners) can be counted on to be a "safe haven" in times of need and a "secure base" from which to embark on life's endeavors (see Feeney & Collins, 2014; Reis et al., 2004). Indeed, as we discuss next (and summarize in Table 7.1), support interactions can offer an *opportunity* for partners to show insecure individuals that they (partners) are sensitive and reliable caregivers, which in turn may enhance trust in relationships.

Meeting the needs of avoidantly attached support recipients

One important individual difference that shapes how people respond to partner support is attachment avoidance. According to Bowlby (1969, 1973, 1980), people who become highly avoidant have been rejected by their prior caregivers, especially during times of need. As a result, highly avoidant individuals believe they cannot trust and depend on close others and, therefore, eschew closeness and intimacy and become rigidly self-reliant (Mikulincer & Shaver, 2003). Highly avoidant individuals' deep distrust of others, and their strong motivation to avoid depending on their partners, produces a unique style of regulating distress – suppressing their attachment needs and defensively withdrawing from their attachment figures, especially when they are upset (Simpson & Rholes, 2012). Accordingly, when highly avoidant individuals are stressed and could benefit from support, they distance themselves from their partners rather than seek support (Collins & Feeney, 2000; Simpson, Rholes, & Nelligan, 1992). Highly avoidant support recipients also exaggerate their partners' lack of responsiveness, perceiving them as less supportive and caring than they really are (Collins & Feeney, 2004; Rholes et al., 2011). And, because they do not believe they can rely on their partners, avoidant individuals often respond to partners' support attempts with hostility and withdrawal to prevent becoming vulnerable to hurt by their partners (Rholes, Simpson, Campbell, & Grich, 2001; Rholes, Simpson, & Oriña, 1999; Simpson et al., 1992).

The striving for independence associated with attachment avoidance might suggest that more subtle, invisible forms of support that do not threaten individuals' sense of autonomy and competence could be one effective way to support highly avoidant people without triggering the distancing strategies they display when feeling dependent on their partners. However, maintaining independence from partners is a defensive priority arising from deep-seated beliefs that partners cannot be relied on to be good, available, and responsive caregivers (Bowlby, 1973). Thus, it is not that avoidant individuals do not want love and support or do not have strong relatedness needs; they do (Mikulincer, Birnbaum, Woddis, & Nachmias, 2000; Mikulincer, Gillath, & Shaver, 2002). Rather, avoidant individuals deny these needs in order to protect themselves from the neglect and hurt they believe will happen if they expect love and support from their partners. Paradoxically, despite their defensive focus on sustaining independence, we think it is these foundational beliefs that account for why prior research has shown that avoidant individuals are more reactive to their partner's enacted support, including both responding negatively when their partner fails to provide support (e.g., Rholes et al., 1999) and responding more positively when their partner provides the clear, direct support they need to believe their partner is actually "there" for them (e.g., Simpson et al., 1992).

This point becomes clear when considering the specific conditions in which highly avoidant support recipients react negatively in support contexts – when their partners confirm avoidant individuals' negative expectations by providing low levels of support. Rholes et al. (1999), for example, found that highly distressed avoidant women were angrier when their partners offered them lower levels of support, but not when their partner's support was higher. Collins and Feeney (2004) also found that highly avoidant individuals appraised low (but not high) amounts of support more negatively, and they performed more poorly during a speech task when their partners provided low (but not high) support. Thus, rather than being happy relying on their own abilities and resources, highly avoidant individuals show poorer coping in the *absence* of support.

The underlying fear of dependence and expectations of neglect, which lie at the core of avoidance, also mean that partner support must be especially clear and salient to benefit avoidant support recipients. Indeed, high levels of support may break through avoidant defenses by sharply contradicting the negative expectations of avoidant people and providing them with undeniable evidence of their partner's availability. For example, although Simpson and his colleagues (1992) found that highly avoidant recipients sought less support from their partners when they were more distressed, avoidant recipients were the *most calmed* by very high levels of partner support. Studying the transition to parenthood, Rholes and his colleagues (2011) found that lower levels of perceived cooperative care from partners predicted increases in depressive symptoms across time in avoidant individuals, but higher levels of cooperative care forecasted reductions in depressive symptoms (also see Girme, Overall, Simpson, & Fletcher, 2015).

Thus, when low levels of support convey that partners are unreliable, unavailable, or neglectful, highly avoidant support recipients fare more poorly. However, when very high levels of support provide irrefutable evidence of the partner's availability, this allows highly avoidant individuals to safely experience their partner's care and support, ensuring that their defensive self-reliance and distancing do not hamper the support provision process. Partner support, however, still needs to remain sensitive to the discomfort that avoidant individuals tend to experience during intimate, emotionally imbued interactions. This explains why highly avoidant support recipients are more calmed when their partners offer specific advice or concrete solutions to problems (practical support) rather than encouraging intimacy or disclosure of emotions (emotional support; Simpson, Winterheld, Rholes, & Oriña, 2007; also see Mikulincer & Florian, 1997). Thus, higher levels of practical support that focus on offering helpful advice may provide the evidence that most avoidant support recipients need to believe their partners are really there for them, without the intimacy and vulnerability that often comes with receiving emotional caregiving. Confirming this notion, Girme, et al. (2015) recently demonstrated that the defensive responses highly avoidant recipients demonstrate at low levels of support are overturned when partners provide very high levels of practical support.

The complex emotional and behavioral reactions of highly avoidant support recipients highlight two important points. Delivering the right kind of support (1) provides diagnostic information regarding the degree to which partners are sensitive and reliable caregivers, and (2) is contingent on meeting the specific needs of particular support recipients. Thus, the right kind of support for avoidant recipients involves a higher level of practical support that: (1) provides irrefutable evidence of the partner's availability and thus contradicts expectations that partners will be neglectful or rejecting, but also (2) does not pull for too much emotional disclosure and intimacy, which may require too much vulnerability to lower avoidant defenses effectively (see Table 7.1). The more couples encounter support contexts, the more partners who provide this type of support can demonstrate they are reliable and can be trusted, which in turn should improve relationship outcomes and may even build greater attachment security across time. Supporting this latter proposition, greater trust that the partner is available and dependable predicts decreases in attachment avoidance across time (Arriaga, Kumashiro, Finkel, VanderDrift, & Luchies, 2014). Importantly, trust should be built up by partners who consistently provide evidence that they can be counted on to support highly avoidant recipients both when they need it and how they need it.

Meeting the needs of anxiously attached support recipients

According to Bowlby (1969, 1973, 1980), attachment anxiety arises when attachment figures have sometimes responded to bids for support with love and care, but at other times responded with anger or rejection. These experiences create a profound hunger for emotional closeness and intimacy, coupled with intense fears of rejection and abandonment. Unlike highly avoidant people, who cope with their negative expectations by downplaying relatedness needs and by striving to prevent dependence, highly anxious individuals manage their fears by continually seeking reassurance and constantly trying to obtain their partner's care, positive regard, and support (Mikulincer & Shaver, 2003). Unfortunately, their hyperactivated relatedness needs mean that anxious individuals exhibit intense, ruminative reactions to distressing situations (Shaver & Mikulincer, 2007) and engage in clingy, emotionally manipulative strategies to seek support (Collins & Feeney, 2000). Unfortunately, the more recipients engage in this type of support seeking, the less partners tend to respond with positive support behaviors (Barbee &

TABLE 7.1. *Examples of partner behavior in diagnostic contexts that foster growth and security*

		Facilitating resilience, growth, and security in insecurely attached individuals		
Diagnostic context	Partners' behavior	Demonstrates	Meeting the needs of highly avoidant individuals	Meeting the needs of highly anxious individuals
Support	Partner support that is responsive to the contextual needs of recipients *Example: visible forms of care and reassurance to recipients who are upset/distressed; invisible forms of support to recipients who need to feel efficacious and competent to deal with impending stressors*	Partner is reliable and dependable	High levels of practical support that provide irrefutable evidence that the partner is a safe haven	Global perceptions of the partner's support and availability that provide reassurance the partner is a secure base
Conflict	Conflict behavior that is responsive to the contextual needs of recipients *Example: minimizing anger and engaging in accommodation for minor problems; engaging in conflict and expressing negative affect for major problems*	Partner is invested and committed	Softening communications and conflict recovery behaviors that demonstrate the partner has good intentions	Accommodation behaviors and emotional expressions (e.g., guilt) that illustrate the partner is committed to and values the relationship

Cunningham, 1995; Don, Mickleson, & Barbee, 2013). Moreover, because highly anxious individuals are sensitive to signs that their partners are not giving them what they crave, they tend to experience more negative emotions when their partners fail to provide sufficient support (Rholes et al., 1999).

Their persistent and intense need for closeness and support suggests that invisible forms of support should not be effective – and might even be detrimental – for anxious support recipients. Instead, highly anxious recipients might be most receptive to and soothed by high levels of clear, direct, and visible support. However, partner support is often relatively ineffective at soothing highly anxious support recipients (e.g., Collins & Feeney, 2000; Moreira et al., 2003; Simpson et al., 1992), and highly anxious recipients evaluate the partner support they do receive more negatively (e.g., Collins & Feeney, 2004; Gallo & Smith, 2001; Priel & Shamai, 1995; Simpson, Rholes, Campbell, & Wilson, 2003). We think this is because highly anxious individuals have an insatiable desire for closeness and reassurance that is difficult for partners to fulfill, particularly in interactions that create expectations that the partner should provide care and support, such as when anxious individuals are in the role of the support recipient. Thus, in stressful support-based exchanges, even high levels of partner support may not gratify highly anxious individuals' craving for love and support.

Can anxious individuals ever reap the benefits of caring and supportive partners? Thus far, we have discussed the consequences of specific types of support enacted by partners in support-relevant contexts. Although the actual receipt of support provided by partners is not uniformly beneficial to recipients, more general perceptions that partners are supportive and caring have consistently positive effects on personal and relationship well-being (e.g., Kaul & Lakey, 2003; Lakey, 2013; Uchino & Garvey, 1997; Wethington & Kessler, 1986). These broader, more stable perceptions may typically arise from couples' everyday exchanges that indicate the partner is a constant source of positivity and regard (Lakey, 2013). In addition, although the support delivered during support exchanges may not immediately soothe recipients, seeing the partner attempting to provide support during these events may accumulate across time to generate more general and positive perceptions of partner support. Thus, although their overwhelming distress and insatiable appetite for support may make highly anxious recipients difficult to console during support interactions, more global perceptions that their partner is caring, available, and supportive is likely to have very positive effects on highly anxious individuals.

Research outside the context of acute and potentially distressing support exchanges does indicate that perceptions of support may have benefits for highly anxious individuals. For example, although they do not experience day-to-day supportive events more positively than other people, highly anxious individuals believe such events are more likely to have positive consequences for the survival of their relationships (Campbell, Simpson, Boldry, & Kashy, 2005). Exaggerated daily expressions of affection by partners also help anxious individuals feel more loved and regarded (Lemay & Dudley, 2011). During the transition to parenthood, highly anxious parents also experience more stable relationship satisfaction, fewer depressive symptoms, and reductions in attachment anxiety when they possess more positive perceptions of spousal support – that is, perceiving that their partner is dependable and provides a sense of emotional security (Rholes et al., 2001; Rholes et al., 2011; Simpson et al., 2003). Moreover, highly anxious individuals report reductions in attachment anxiety across time when they perceive that their partners are validating and supporting their personal goals, thereby providing a secure base for them to thrive more independently (Arriaga et al., 2014).

In sum, the specific constellation of needs associated with avoidance and anxiety highlight that different support processes foster resilience, growth, and security in highly avoidant and highly anxious individuals (Overall & Simpson, 2015). Their deep-seated fear of dependence and resulting defensive focus on independence means that highly avoidant support recipients need undisputed evidence that their partner is a safe haven, which may build trust and reduce avoidance across time. In contrast, their overdependence and vigilant focus on relatedness limits the degree to which partners can console highly anxious individuals in the midst of stressful interactions. However, global perceptions that the partner is supportive and caring may serve as a secure base that promotes strength and happiness in highly anxious individuals. These unique dynamics once again highlight that when support matches the specific needs of support recipients, it can create the conditions for optimal personal and relationship development (see Table 7.1).

RELATIONSHIP CONFLICTS AS OPPORTUNITIES FOR REPAIR AND GROWTH

It seems rather obvious that support tends to be good for relationships and the people in them, but perhaps more surprising is the fact that support can also be bad. It is also obvious that conflict can be damaging to both partners and relationships, but it may come as a bit more surprising that conflict can actually be *good* for relationships. Conflict can definitely take a toll on partners and relationships. For example, couples that have more frequent conflict are more likely to report declines in satisfaction and their relationship is more likely to dissolve (e.g., Kluwer & Johnson, 2007; Le, Dove, Agnew, Korn, & Mutso, 2010; Orbuch, Veroff, Hassan, & Horrocks, 2002). On the other hand, avoiding conflict and loyally maintaining positivity in the face of persistent relationship problems also leads to declining relationship satisfaction, particularly if relationship problems remain unresolved (e.g., Cohan & Bradbury, 1997; Drigotas, Whitney, & Rusbult, 1995; Gottman & Krokoff, 1989; McNulty, 2010; Overall, Fletcher, Simpson, & Sibley, 2009; Overall, Sibley, & Travaglia, 2010). Indeed, there is now a solid body of research showing that solving relationship problems often requires directly engaging in conflict, even when that involves high levels of anger and hostility (e.g., Cohan & Bradbury, 1997; Gottman & Krokoff, 1989; Heavey, Layne, & Christensen, 1993; Karney & Bradbury, 1997; McNulty & Russell, 2010; Overall et al., 2009).

Maximizing a relationship's potential can occur only if the source of major relationship conflicts are addressed and improved (Overall & Simpson, 2013). Beyond this, however, conflict can also be an opportunity for relationship repair and growth because, if conflicts are managed well, they can provide valuable, diagnostic information about the partner, which in turn can improve relationships. In particular, partners' conflict-related behaviors and emotions reveal the degree to which partners are truly committed and can be trusted to put aside their own desires for the good of the relationship (Rusbult & Van Lange, 2003). During conflict, when hurt and anger often run high, the typical "gut response" is to protect the self by derogating, blaming, or attacking the partner and/or by withdrawing altogether. When partners are able to transform this initial impulse into a more controlled effort to resolve the problem by voicing concerns in a calm, forgiving, and constructive manner – called *accommodation* – this helps to build and maintain closeness and satisfaction (e.g., Rusbult, Bissonnette, Arriaga, & Cox, 1998; Rusbult, Verette, Whitney, Slovik, & Lipkus, 1991). These benefits occur because accommodation requires high levels of self-control and commitment (Finkel & Campbell, 2001; Rusbult, Arriaga, & Agnew, 2001), which signal the partner's dedication and pro-relationship motives. Thus, when people see their partners accommodating during heated conflicts, they may experience greater trust and commitment over time (Wieselquist, Rusbult, Foster, & Agnew, 1999).

Sometimes even negative emotional and behavioral responses by the partner can be signs that the partner is invested and committed to the relationship (Baker, McNulty, & Overall, 2014). For example, people who are more dependent and strongly committed to their relationship tend to experience greater hurt feelings when they encounter conflict. More intense hurt feelings, in turn, motivate stronger efforts to restore closeness and repair the relationship bond, which has important interpersonal benefits (Lemay, Overall, & Clark, 2013). As with accommodation behavior, because hurt feelings arise when people care about and are committed to their relationship, individuals respond more positively to partners who express or are perceived to be experiencing hurt feelings (Lemay et al., 2013), which can lead people to feel more secure and satisfied in their relationship (Overall, Girme, Lemay, & Hammond, 2014).

In contrast to hurt feelings, the expression of anger often elicits and intensifies hostility during most conflict interactions (Lemay et al., 2012; Overall et al., 2009). However, anger also instigates attempts to address the root cause of conflicts and produce desired changes (Canary, Spitzberg, & Semic, 1998; Lemay et al., 2012). Moreover, although expressions of anger and hostile attempts to change a problem typically exacerbate negativity in the short-term, these behaviors can be effective at improving relationship problems across time, which in turn produces higher levels of relationship satisfaction (Cohan & Bradbury, 1997; McNulty & Russell, 2010; Overall et al., 2009). Two underlying mechanisms may explain these long-term benefits. First, expressions of anger and hostility clearly convey the seriousness of the problem and thus can motivate important changes in one or both partners (Overall et al., 2009; Overall & Simpson, 2013). Second, once initial self-protective resistance dissipates, people may often understand that their partners' anger and hostile problem engagement is a sign that they want change because they are truly invested in and care about the relationship (e.g., Gottman, 1998; Heavey et al., 1993).

How can inhibiting negativity via accommodation and expressing hurt, anger, and hostility both promote relationship improvement and growth? Similar to support contexts, whether accommodation or expressing negative affect maintains satisfaction, improves relationships, and conveys commitment depends on contextual factors. McNulty and Russell (2010), for instance, found that blaming and demanding conflict behaviors led to more satisfying and stable relationships for couples that were facing serious problems, but resulted in increased problems and dissatisfaction when problems were relatively minor. This pattern most likely arises because when problems are very serious, partners' anger and hostile behaviors are more likely to reflect and be perceived as strident attempts to maintain and improve the relationship (McNulty & Russell, 2010; Overall et al., 2009). In contrast, when problems are minor, disproportionate anger and hostility probably produces feelings of unfair derogation and rejection, thereby eliciting reciprocal negativity and undermining conflict resolution. Indeed, during routine conflicts, maintaining positivity and demonstrating that irritations and personal preferences are not worth endangering the relationship (by accommodating) should foster greater affection, trust, and stability (McNulty, 2010).

Just as problem severity shapes the importance and underlying meaning of accommodation versus hostility, so should the orientations and dispositions of people who are on the receiving end of these behaviors. For example, people who believe that facing conflict can cultivate relationship growth may be more likely to respond positively to their partners' hostile attempts to improve relationship-relevant problems (Knee, Patrick, & Lonsbary, 2003). More securely attached people, who have learned they can rely on others' love and acceptance during hard times (Bowlby, 1969), also approach conflict situations with greater confidence and more optimistic attributions (Collins, 1996; Collins et al., 2006), are less likely to feel the sting of negativity from their partners (Campbell et al., 2005; Simpson et al., 1996), and may be more likely to view negative emotions and behaviors as signs that their partner is trying to improve the relationship. In contrast, the threat inherent in conflict situations should trigger the concerns and defensive strategies of highly anxious and avoidant individuals, particularly when the partner displays intense emotions (Simpson & Rholes, 1994, 2012). To successfully traverse relationship conflicts, therefore, partners may need to accommodate the particular needs of anxious and avoidant individuals. And, as when providing the right kind of support, partners who are responsive to the specific concerns of insecure individuals should not only prevent insecurities from impeding problem resolution, but also facilitate greater stability and security by demonstrating they are committed and truly willing to put the needs of the relationship above their own desires and goals (see Table 7.1; also see Overall & Simpson, 2015).

Meeting the needs of avoidantly attached individuals

Highly avoidant individuals deal with their deep distrust of others by keeping a safe emotional distance from their partners, which provides them a sense of independence and personal control. During conflict, however, avoidant individuals must contend in some way with the needs and dissatisfaction of their partners while also being the target of their partner's influence attempts. Not surprisingly, these elements of conflict can impinge on the independence that avoidant individuals strive to retain, activating their defenses. Avoidant individuals tend to exhibit greater anger and withdrawal both during conflict discussions and when their partners try to influence them (e.g., Overall & Sibley, 2009; Simpson et al., 1996). These reactions encourage emotional distance and minimize the influence of partners by forcing them to back off, to cease seeking change, or to accept less intimacy, thereby helping avoidant individuals feel more in control and safe from the threat of dependence (Overall & Lemay, 2015).

Expressions of negative emotions, hostile demands, or direct influence attempts by partners should exacerbate these distancing strategies and confirm the negative expectations of avoidant people – that partners are intentionally malicious and uncaring. To bypass avoidant defenses and facilitate some kind of resolution, partners need to adopt a softer approach that accommodates the core defenses and needs of highly avoidant individuals. To test this possibility, Overall, Simpson and Struthers (2013) examined the emotional and behavioral responses of both partners as couples engaged in conflict discussions in which partners asked highly avoidant individuals to change their thoughts or behaviors in some important way. As predicted, avoidant individuals responded with greater anger, disengagement, and withdrawal, which resulted in poorer conflict resolution. However, partners were able to down-regulate these defensive reactions when they "softened" their communication through (1) reducing direct influence attempts that challenged avoidant targets' independence (e.g., by downplaying the severity of the problem, acknowledging progress made, validating the targets' point of view), and (2) offering clear evidence that avoidant targets were valued (e.g., by reducing friction, inhibiting negativity, expressing positive regard). These softening behaviors are sensitive to the fragility underlying highly avoidant individuals' need to sustain independence, and they contradict the hostile intentions that avoidant individuals often anticipate from their partners.

By being responsive to the specific concerns and needs associated with avoidance, partners can enhance their relationships by resolving conflicts and improving major relationship problems. Partners' responsiveness might also help avoidant people develop more secure beliefs and expectations by clearly demonstrating they (partners) *can* be trusted, and they are not the cold, selfish partners that avoidant individuals fear (Overall & Simpson, 2015; Simpson & Overall, 2014). Salvatore, Kuo, Steele, Simpson, and Collins (2011) have provided some evidence for these positive, long-term effects by examining the degree to which partners recovered from conflict during a "cool-down" task that immediately followed couples' discussions of a major relationship problem. Attachment insecurity (primarily avoidance), which had been assessed 20 years earlier in infancy, predicted poorer conflict recovery, and insecure individuals whose partners could not "move beyond the conflict" were less likely to be together 2 years later. However, when insecure individuals were involved with partners who displayed greater positivity and repair attempts during conflict recovery, their relationships were more likely to remain intact. Partners' better conflict recovery should signal that they (partners) can let go of negativity and blame, which may have helped these couples maintain their relationships over time (also see Arriaga et al., 2014). Similar behaviors that are careful to not highlight the dangers of dependence and also strongly contradict the negative expectations associated with avoidance also bolster avoidant individuals' trust and commitment (see Farrell, Simpson, Overall, & Shallcross, in press).

Meeting the needs of anxiously attached individuals

The craving for closeness and fear of abandonment, which lies at the core of attachment anxiety, also makes conflict challenging for highly anxious individuals (Simpson & Rholes, 2012). Conflict inevitably carries the possibility of rejection, threatens the relationship bond, and can undermine feelings of love and acceptance. Moreover, highly anxious individuals maximize the negative implications of conflict by perceiving it, and their partner's negative behaviors, as an indication that the relationship is in jeopardy (Collins, 1996; Collins et al., 2006). Accordingly, highly anxious individuals experience more pronounced distress during relationship conflicts (Campbell et al., 2005; Simpson et al., 1996; Tran & Simpson, 2009) and they find it difficult to "move past" their hurt feelings to handle conflict in constructive ways (Simpson et al., 1996; Tran & Simpson, 2009). Instead, anxious individuals tend to "protest" the loss of the relationship bond with exaggerated emotional displays and try to control and cling to their partners to re-establish proximity and closeness (Shaver & Mikulincer, 2007; Overall et al., 2014).

Demonstrating that conflict can provide an opportunity to appreciate the partner's care and regard, recent research has shown that anxious individuals' responses to conflict do elicit evidence of their partner's commitment, which they so desperately crave. Overall et al. (2014) examined the emotional reactions and proximity-maintaining strategies exhibited by highly anxious individuals when faced with daily conflict and during couples' discussions of serious relationship conflicts. Highly anxious individuals experienced more pronounced hurt feelings when they dealt with conflict, which triggered guilt-inducing attempts to regain their partner's care and reassurance involving exaggerated emotional expressions of hurt and appeals to their partner's love, concern, or relationship obligations. These tactics are commonly used in close relationships to induce guilt, which typically motivates partners to apologize, provide reassurance, and make amends. Because guilt-induction tactics work to the extent that a partner cares about and is invested in the relationship, guilt provides strong evidence of the partner's commitment (Baumeister, Stillwell, & Heatherton, 1994), which is exactly what anxious individuals want. Accordingly, Overall et al. (2014) found that when highly anxious individuals successfully induced guilt in their partners, they reported more positive evaluations of their partner's commitment and relationship satisfaction across time.

These results suggest that anxious individuals may use conflict situations to test (or diagnose) their partner's level of commitment. The resulting negative emotions induced in partners generate the reassurance that highly anxious individuals desire, which in turn bolsters their feelings of relationship security and satisfaction. Partners should also be able to produce the same benefits (and bypass some of the costs associated with guilt induction) if they enter conflicts with direct expressions of care and regard for their partners (see Lemay & Dudley, 2011; Simpson & Overall, 2014). As described earlier, accommodation during conflict directly communicates love, commitment, and trustworthiness, thereby soothing anxious individuals. To test this proposition, Tran and Simpson (2009) assessed feelings of acceptance and accommodation behavior during couples' conflict discussions. Highly anxious individuals felt less accepted and exhibited less accommodation, as did their partners. However, highly committed partners were able to prevent the reactivity of their highly anxious mates from infecting their own responses by displaying greater accommodation. Moreover, when partners were highly committed, and thus displayed greater accommodation, highly anxious individuals felt greater acceptance and behaved more positively (also see Tran & Simpson, 2011). Similar to the long-term benefits of guilt, by demonstrating strong commitment, these more positive dynamics during conflict interactions should help anxious individuals feel more secure and satisfied over time.

In sum, although relationship conflicts are often unpleasant, the way in which partners manage conflict can improve relationship problems and provide diagnostic evidence of the partner's genuine commitment and true relationship intentions. Moreover, because conflicts are attachment-relevant situations that activate the concerns and destructive reactions of insecure people, they also provide opportunities for partners to soothe the concerns of avoidant and anxious individuals, elicit more constructive reactions from them, and eventually build more secure and satisfying relationships. As with support contexts, the types of partner behaviors that facilitate relationship improvement and help insecure individuals depend on contextual needs (see Table 7.1). When serious problems need to be addressed, and attachment security removes the potential damage that can be caused by harsh problem-solving behaviors, even partner anger and hostility – if expressed appropriately – can facilitate problem resolution, demonstrate investment, and enhance relationship maintenance. Partner behavior needs to take a different, more measured tone with people who are avoidant in order to prevent and down-regulate their defensive strategies, which serve to maintain independence. However, by conveying that partners have benevolent, loving intentions, softer repair efforts focused on moving the relationship forward can facilitate greater commitment in avoidant individuals and enhance relationship maintenance. Anxious individuals also feel happier and more secure when their partners' emotional and behavioral responses during conflict provide clear evidence they (partners) are committed and value the relationship. These examples illustrate once more that precarious situations can be important opportunities for relationship and personal growth.

CONCLUSIONS

Relationships come with major risks. Relying on intimate partners for support makes individuals vulnerable to pain if partners are not adequately responsive. Relationship conflicts inevitably occur, which carry the risk of rejection and exploitation, especially when partners are not sufficiently invested in the relationship. However, these dilemmas also provide opportunities for relationship and personal growth. Partners who are responsive to the specific needs of support recipients can help them weather challenges and demonstrate that they (partners) are reliable and sensitive caregivers. Partners who are upset by relationship conflict and strive to solve problems can reveal just how much they truly care about the relationship. And when partners regulate their own dissatisfaction in ways that are sensitive to the needs of insecure individuals, they demonstrate their high levels of investment and commitment. Thus, by exposing the partner's dependability, commitment, and trustworthiness, these diagnostic contexts have the power to solidify and enhance relationships.

It is in some ways ironic that the power of diagnostic contexts that foster growth may be strongest for those who find these situations most difficult, but it is the possible risks and vulnerabilities of *needing support* and *confronting conflict* that make these contexts so influential (Overall & Simpson, 2015). It is within these specific situations that a partner's behavior can convincingly counteract the negative beliefs and expectations of highly avoidant and anxious people. As the research reviewed in this chapter demonstrates, partners' responsive support and sensitive conflict behavior can temper the concerns and damaging responses of insecurely attached people, create more constructive interactions, and build greater commitment, trust, satisfaction, and security in them.

We focused on support and conflict situations because support is a key component of all attachment-based relationships, conflict can be a significant source of distress in almost all relationships, and both situations can damage relationships if they are not managed well. Many other dyadic contexts might also be used to gauge a partner's level of love, commitment, and/or trustworthiness, offering even more opportunities to facilitate growth and security. For example, more satisfying and frequent sexual activity generates expectations that partners are available, which helps maintain relationship satisfaction in insecure individuals (see Little, McNulty, & Russell, 2010; Muise, Kim, McNulty, & Impett, Chapter 6, this volume). Sharing and capitalizing on positive events is also an important contributor to maintaining quality relationships (see Gable & Anderson, Chapter 5, this volume), but can be difficult to negotiate with insecure individuals because anxious people disclose in demanding ways and avoidant people shy away from emotional intimacy (see Shallcross, Howland, Bemis, Simpson, & Frazier, 2011). And enacting or asking for sacrifices to sustain relationships can have both positive and negative effects, depending on each partner's goals and motives (Day & Impett, Chapter 10, this volume; Farrell et al., in press). As with the situations discussed in this chapter, partner responses that promote optimal relationship development and enhance security critically depend on *matching* the specific needs of people within those interactions. Future research that investigates the different ways in which partners meet this challenge are likely to extend our understanding of how couples can leverage the power of diagnostic situations to sustain and strengthen their intimate relationships.

REFERENCES

Arriaga, X. B., Kumashiro, M., Finkel, E. J., VanderDrift, L. E., & Luchies, L. B. (2014). Filling the void: Bolstering attachment security in committed relationships. *Social Psychological and Personality Science*, 5, 398–406.

Baker, L. T., McNulty, J., & Overall, N. C. (2014). When negative emotions benefit relationships. In W. G. Parrott (Ed.), *The positive side of negative emotions* (pp. 101–125). New York: Guilford.

Barbee, A. P., & Cunningham, M. R. (1995). An experimental approach to social support communications: Interactive coping in close relationships. *Communication Yearbook*, 18, 381–413.

Baumeister, R. F., Stillwell, A. M., & Heatherton, T. F. (1994). Guilt: An interpersonal approach. *Psychological Bulletin*, 115, 243–267.

Beach, S. R. H., Fincham, F. D., & Katz, J. (1998). Marital therapy in the treatment of depression: Toward a third generation of therapy and research. *Clinical Psychology Review*, 18, 635–661.

Bolger, N., & Amarel, D. (2007). Effects of social support visibility on adjustment to stress: Experimental evidence. *Journal of Personality and Social Psychology*, 92(3), 458–475.

Bolger, N., Zuckerman, A., & Kessler, R. C. (2000). Invisible support and adjustment to stress. *Journal of Personality and Social Psychology*, 79, 953–961.

Bowlby, J. (1969). *Attachment and loss*, Vol. 1: *Attachment*. New York: Basic Books.

Bowlby, J. (1973). *Attachment and loss*, Vol. 2: *Separation*. New York: Basic Books.

Bowlby, J. (1980). *Attachment and loss*, Vol. 3. *Loss*. New York: Basic Books.

Brock, R., & Lawrence, E. (2009). Too much of a good thing: Underprovision versus overprovision of partner support. *Journal of Family Psychology*, 23, 181–192.

Campbell, L., Simpson, J. A., Boldry, J., & Kashy, D. A. (2005). Perceptions of conflict and support in romantic relationships: The role of attachment anxiety. *Journal of Personality and Social Psychology*, 88, 510–531.

Canary, D. J., Spitzberg, B. H., & Semic, B. A. (1998). The experience and expression of anger in interpersonal settings. In P. A. Andersen & L. K. Guerrero (Eds.), *Handbook of communication and emotion: Research, theory, applications, and contexts* (pp. 189–213). San Diego, CA: Academic Press.

Cohan, C. L., & Bradbury, T. N. (1997). Negative life events, marital interaction, and the longitudinal course of newlywed marriage. *Journal of Personality and Social Psychology*, 73, 114–128.

Collins, N. L. (1996). Working models of attachment: Implications for explanation, emotion, and behavior. *Journal of Personality and Social Psychology*, 71, 810–832.

Collins, N. L., & Feeney, B. C. (2000). A safe haven: An attachment theory perspective on support seeking and caregiving in intimate relationships. *Journal of Personality and Social Psychology*, 78, 1053–1073.

Collins, N. L., & Feeney, B. C. (2004). Working models of attachment shape perceptions of social support: Evidence from experimental and observational studies. *Journal of Personality and Social Psychology*, 87, 363–383.

Collins, N. L., Ford, M. B., Guichard, A. C., & Allard, L. M. (2006). Working models of attachment and attribution processes in intimate relationships. *Personality and Social Psychology Bulletin, 32*, 201–219.

Conger, R. D., Rueter, M. A., & Elder, G. H. (1999). Couple resilience to economic pressure. *Journal of Personality and Social Psychology, 76*(1), 54–71.

Cutrona, C. E. (1990). Stress and social support – in search of optimal matching. *Journal of Social and Clinical Psychology, 9*, 3–14.

Cutrona, C. E. (1996). Social support as a determinant of marital quality. In G. R. Pierce, B. R. Sarason, and I. G. Sarason (Eds.), *Handbook of social support and the family*, pp. 173–194. New York: Plenum Press.

Cutrona, C. E., Shaffer, P. A., Wesner, K. A., & Gardner, K. A. (2007). Optimally matching support and perceived spousal sensitivity. *Journal of Family Psychology, 21*, 754–758.

Cutrona, C. E., & Suhr, J. A. (1992). Controllability of stressful events and satisfaction with spouse support behaviors. *Communication Research, 19*, 154–174.

Don, B. P., Mickelson, K. D., & Barbee, A. P. (2013). Indirect support seeking and perceptions of spousal support: An examination of a reciprocal relationship. *Personal Relationships, 20*, 655–668.

Drigotas, S. M., Whitney, G. A., & Rusbult, C. E. (1995). On the peculiarities of loyalty: A diary study of responses to dissatisfaction in everyday life. *Personality and Social Psychology Bulletin, 21*, 596–609.

Farrell, A. K., Simpson, J. A., Overall, N. C., & Shallcross, S. L. (in press). Buffering avoidantly attached romantic partners in strain test situations. *Journal of Family Psychology*.

Feeney, B. C., (2004). A secure base: Responsive support of goal strivings and explorations in adult intimate relationships. *Journal of Personality and Social Psychology, 87*(5), 631–648.

Feeney, B. C., & Collins, N. L. (2003). Motivations for caregiving in adult intimate relationships: Influences on caregiving behavior and relationship functioning. *Personality and Social Psychology Bulletin, 29*(8), 950–968.

Feeney, B. C., & Collins, N. C. (2014). A new look at social support: A theoretical perspective on thriving through relationships. *Personality and Social Psychology Review*, Published online before print August, 14, 2014, doi:10.1177/1088868314544222

Finkel, E. J., & Campbell, W. K. (2001). Self-control and accommodation in close relationships: An interdependence analysis. *Journal of Personality and Social Psychology, 81*, 263–277.

Gallo, L. C., & Smith, T. W. (2001). Attachment style in marriage: Adjustment and responses to interaction. *Journal of Social and Personal Relationships, 18*, 263–289.

Girme, Y. U., Overall, N. C., & Simpson, J. A. (2013). When visibility matters: Short-term versus long-term costs and benefits of visible and invisible support. *Personality and Social Psychology Bulletin, 39*, 1441–1454.

Girme, Y. U., Overall, N. C., Simpson, J. A., & Fletcher, G. J. O. (2015). "All or Nothing": Attachment avoidance and the curvilinear effects of partner support. *Journal of Personality and Social Psychology, 108*, 450–475.

Gleason, M. E. J., Iida, M., Shrout, P. E., Bolger, N. (2008). Receiving support as a mixed blessing: Evidence for dual effects of support on psychological outcomes. *Journal of Personality and Social Psychology, 94*(5), 824–838.

Gottman, J. M. (1998). Psychology and the study of marital processes. *Annual Review of Psychology, 49*, 169–197.

Gottman, J. M., & Krokoff, L. J. (1989). Marital interaction and satisfaction: A longitudinal view. *Journal of Consulting and Clinical Psychology*, 57, 47–52.

Heavey, C. L., Layne, C., & Christensen, A. (1993). Gender and conflict structure in marital interaction: A replication and extension. *Journal of Consulting and Clinical Psychology*, 61, 16–27.

Howland, M., & Simpson, J. A. (2010). Getting in under the radar: A dyadic view of invisible support. *Psychological Science*, 21, 1878–1885.

Karney, B. R., & Bradbury, T. N. (1997). Neuroticism, marital interaction, and the trajectory of marital satisfaction. *Journal of Personality and Social Psychology*, 72, 1075–1092.

Kaul, M., & Lakey, B. (2003). Where is the support in perceived support? The role of generic relationship satisfaction and enacted support in perceived support's relation to low distress. *Journal of Social and Clinical Psychology*, 22(1), 59–78.

Kelley, H. H., Holmes, J. G., Kerr, N. L., Reis, H. T., Rusbult, C. E., & Van Lange, P. A. M. (2003). *An atlas of interpersonal situations*. New York: Cambridge University Press.

Kiecolt-Glaser, J. K., & Newton, T. L. (2001). Marriage and health: His and hers. *Psychological Bulletin*, 127, 427–503.

Kluwer, E. S., & Johnson, M. D. (2007). Conflict frequency and relationship quality across the transition to parenthood. *Journal of Marriage and the Family*, 69, 1089–1106.

Knee, C. R., Patrick, H., & Lonsbary, C. (2003). Implicit theories of relationships: Orientation toward evaluation and cultivation. *Personality and Social Psychology Review*, 7, 41–55.

Lakey, B. (2013). Social support process in relationships. In J. A. Simpson & L. Campbell (Eds.), *Oxford handbook of close relationships* (pp. 711–729). New York: Oxford University Press.

Le, B., Dove, N. L., Agnew, C. R., Korn, M. S., & Mutso, A. A. (2010). Predicting nonmarital romantic relationship dissolution: A meta-analytic synthesis. *Personal Relationships*, 17, 377–390.

Lemay, E. P., Jr., & Dudley, K. L. (2011). Caution: Fragile! Regulating the interpersonal security of chronically insecure partners. *Journal of Personality and Social Psychology*, 100, 681–702.

Lemay, E. P., Jr., Overall, N. C., & Clark, M. S. (2012). Experiences and interpersonal consequences of hurt feelings and anger. *Journal of Personality and Social Psychology*, 103, 982–1006.

Little, K. C., McNulty, J. K., & Russell, M. (2010). Sex buffers intimates against the negative implications of attachment insecurity. *Personality and Social Psychology Bulletin*, 36, 484–498.

Maisel, N. C., & Gable, S. L. (2009). The paradox of received social support: The importance of responsiveness. *Psychological Science*, 20(8), 928–932.

McNulty, J. K., & Russell, V. M. (2010). When "negative" behaviors are positive: A contextual analysis of the long-term effects of interpersonal communication. *Journal of Personality and Social Psychology*, 98, 587–604.

Mikulincer, M., Birnbaum, G., Woddis, D., & Nachmias, O. (2000). Stress and accessibility of proximity-related thoughts: Exploring the normative and intraindividual components of attachment theory. *Journal of Personality and Social Psychology*, 78, 509–523.

Mikulincer, M., & Florian, V. (1997). Are emotional and instrumental supportive interactions beneficial in times of stress? The impact of attachment style. *Anxiety, Stress & Coping*, 10, 109–127.

Mikulincer, M., Gillath, O., & Shaver, P. R. (2002). Activation of the attachment system in adulthood: Threat-related primes increase the accessibility of mental representations of attachment figures. *Journal of Personality and Social Psychology*, 83, 881–895.

Mikulincer, M., & Shaver, P. R. (2003). The attachment behavioral system in adulthood: Activation, psychodynamics, and interpersonal processes. In M. P. Zanna (Ed.), *Advances in experimental social psychology* (Vol. 35). San Diego, CA: Academic Press.

Moreira, J. M., Silva, M. F., Moleiro, C., Aguiar, P., Andrez, M., Bernardes, S., & Afonso, H. (2003). Perceived social support as an offshoot of attachment style. *Personality and Individual Differences*, 34, 485–501.

Orbuch, T. L., Veroff, J., Hassan, H., & Horrocks, J. (2002). Who will divorce: A 14-year longitudinal study of black couples and white couples. *Journal of Social and Personal Relationships*, 19, 179–202.

Overall, N. C., Fletcher, G. J. O., & Simpson, J. A. (2010). Helping each other grow: Romantic partner support, self-improvement and relationship quality. *Personality and Social Psychology Bulletin*, 36, 1496–1513.

Overall, N. C., Fletcher, G. J. O., Simpson, J. A., & Sibley, C. G. (2009). Regulating partners in intimate relationships: The costs and benefits of different communication strategies. *Journal of Personality and Social Psychology*, 96, 620–639.

Overall, N. C., Girme, Y. U., Lemay, E. P., Jr., & Hammond, M. T. (2014). Attachment anxiety and reactions to relationship threat: The benefits and costs of inducing guilt in romantic partners. *Journal of Personality and Social Psychology*, 106, 235–256.

Overall, N. C., & Lemay, E. P., Jr. (2015). Attachment and dyadic regulation processes. In J. A. Simpson & W. S. Rholes (Eds.), *Attachment theory and research: New directions and emerging themes*. New York: Guilford.

Overall, N. C., & Sibley, C. G. (2009). Attachment and dependence regulation within daily interactions with romantic partners. *Personal Relationships*, 16, 239–261.

Overall, N. C., Sibley, C. G., & Travaglia, L. K. (2010). Loyal but ignored: The benefits and costs of constructive communication behavior. *Personal Relationships*, 17, 127–148.

Overall, N. C., & Simpson, J. A. (2015). Attachment and dyadic regulation processes. *Current Opinion in Psychology*, 1, 61–66.

Overall, N. C., & Simpson, J. A. (2013). Regulation processes in close relationships. In J. A. Simpson & L. Campbell (Eds.), *The Oxford handbook of close relationships* (pp. 427–451). New York: Oxford University Press.

Overall, N. C., Simpson, J. A., & Struthers, H. (2013). Buffering attachment avoidance: Softening emotional and behavioral defenses during conflict discussions. *Journal of Personality and Social Psychology*, 104, 854–871.

Pasch, L., Bradbury, T. N., & Sullivan, K. T. (1997). Social support in marriage: An analysis of intraindividual and interpersonal components. In G. R. Pierce, B. Lakey & I. G. Sarason (Eds.), *Sourcebook of social support and personality* (pp. 229–256). New York: Plenum Press.

Priel, B., & Shamai, D. (1995). Attachment style and perceived social support: Effects on affect regulation. *Personality and Individual Differences*, 19(2), 235–241.

Reis, H. T., Clark, M. S., & Holmes, J. (2004). Perceived partner responsiveness as an organizing construct in the study of intimacy and closeness. In D. J. Mashek and A. Aron (Eds.), *Handbook of closeness and intimacy* (pp. 201–225). Mahwah, NJ: Laurence Erlbaum.

Rholes, W. S., Simpson, J. A., Campbell, L., & Grich, J. (2001). Adult attachment and the transition to parenthood. *Journal of Personality and Social Psychology*, 81, 421–435.

Rholes, S. W., Simpson, J. A., Kohn, J. L., Wilson, C. L., Martin III, A. M., Tran, S., & Kashy, D. A. (2011). Attachment orientations and depression: A longitudinal study of new parents. *Journal of Personality and Social Psychology*, 100(4), 567–586.

Rholes, W. S., Simpson, J. A., & Oriña, M. M. (1999). Attachment and anger in an anxiety-provoking situation. *Journal of Personality and Social Psychology*, 76, 940–957.

Rusbult, C. E., Arriaga, X. B., & Agnew, C. R. (2001). Interdependence in close relationships. In G. J. O. Fletcher & M. S. Clark (Eds.), *Blackwell handbook of social psychology: Interpersonal processes* (pp. 359–387). Malden, MA: Blackwell.

Rusbult, C. E., Bissonnette, V. L., Arriaga, X. B., & Cox, C. L. (1998). Accommodation processes during the early years of marriage. In T. N. Bradbury (Ed.), *The developmental course of marital dysfunction* (pp. 74–113). New York: Cambridge University Press.

Rusbult, C. E., & Van Lange, P. A. M. (2003). Interdependence, interaction, and relationships. *Annual Review of Psychology*, 54, 351–375.

Rusbult, C. E., Verette, J., Whitney, G. A., Slovik, L. F., & Lipkus, I. (1991). Accommodation processes in close relationships: Theory and preliminary empirical evidence. *Journal of Personality and Social Psychology*, 60, 53–78.

Ryan, R. M., & Deci, E. L. (2000). Self-determination theory and the facilitation of intrinsic motivation, social development, and well-being. *American Psychologist*, 55, 68–78.

Ryan, R. M., & Deci, E. L. (2002). Overview of self-determination theory: An organismic dialectical perspective. In R. M. Ryan & E. L. Deci (Eds.), *Handbook of self-determination research*. Rochester, NY: The University of Rochester Press.

Salvatore, J. E., Kuo, S. I., Steele, R. D., Simpson, J. A., & Collins, W. A. (2011). Recovering from conflict in romantic relationships: A developmental perspective. *Psychological Science*, 22.

Shallcross, S. L., Howland, M., Bemis, J., Simpson, J. A., & Frazier, P. (2011). Not "capitalizing" on social capitalization interactions: The role of attachment insecurity. *Journal of Family Psychology*, 25, 77–85.

Shaver, P. R., & Mikulincer, M. (2007). Adult attachment strategies and the regulation of emotion. In J. J. Gross (Ed.), *Handbook of emotion regulation* (pp. 446–465). New York: Guilford Press.

Shrout, P. E., Herman, C. M., & Bolger, N. (2006). The costs and benefits of practical and emotional support on adjustment: A daily diary study of couples experiencing acute stress. *Personal Relationships*, 13, 115–134.

Simpson, J. A., & Overall, N. C. (2014). Partner buffering of attachment insecurity. *Current Directions in Psychological Science*, 23, 54–59.

Simpson, J. A., & Rholes, W. S. (1994). Stress and secure base relationships in adulthood. In K. Bartholomew & D. Perlman (Eds.), *Advances in personal relationships (Vol. 5): Attachment processes in adulthood* (pp. 181–204). London: Kingsley.

Simpson, J. A., & Rholes, W. S. (2012). Adult attachment orientations, stress, and romantic relationships. In T. Devine & A. Plante (Eds.), *Advances in Experimental Social Psychology* (Vol. 45, pp. 279–328). New York: Elsevier.

Simpson, J. A., Rholes, W. S., Campbell, L., & Wilson, C. L. (2003). Changes in attachment orientations across the transition to parenthood. *Journal of Experimental Social Psychology*, 39, 317–331.

Simpson, J. A., Rholes, W. S., & Nelligan, J. S. (1992). Support-seeking and support-giving within couples in an anxiety-provoking situation: The role of attachment styles. *Journal of Personality and Social Psychology*, 62, 434–446.

Simpson, J. A., Rholes, W. S., & Phillips, D. (1996). Conflict in close relationships: An attachment perspective. *Journal of Personality and Social Psychology*, 71, 899–914.

Simpson, J. A., Winterheld, H. A., Rholes, S., & Oriña, M. (2007). Working models of attachment and reactions to different forms of caregiving from romantic partners. *Journal of Personality and Social Psychology*, 93, 466–477.

Sullivan, K. T., Pasch, L. A., Johnson, M. D., & Bradbury, T. N. (2010). Social support, problem solving, and the longitudinal course of newlywed marriage. *Journal of Personality and Social Psychology*, 98, 631–644.

Tran, S., & Simpson, J. A. (2009). Prorelationship maintenance behavior: The joint roles of attachment and commitment. *Journal of Personality and Social Psychology*, 97, 685–698.

Tran, S., & Simpson, J. A. (2011). Attachment, commitment and relationship maintenance: When partners really matter. In L. Campbell, J. La Guardia, J. Olson, & M. Zanna (Eds.), *The Ontario Symposium: Vol. 10. The science of the couple* (pp.95–117). New York: Psychology Press.

Uchino, B. N., Cacioppo, J. T., & Kiecolt-Glaser, J. K. (1996). The relationship between social support and physiological processes: A review with emphasis on underlying mechanisms and implications for health. *Psychological Bulletin*, 119, 448–531.

Uchino, B. N., & Garvey, T. S. (1997). The availability of social support reduces cardiovascular reactivity to acute psychological stress. *Journal of Behavioral Medicine*, 20, 15–27.

Verhofstadt, L. L., Buysse, A., Ickes, W., Davis, M., Devoldre, I. (2008). Support provision in marriage: The role of emotional similarity and empathic accuracy. *Emotion*, 8(6), 792–802.

Wethington, E., & Kessler, R. C. (1986). Perceived support, received support, and adjustment to stressful life events. *Journal of Health and Social Behavior*, 27(1), 78–89.

Wieselquist, J., Rusbult, C. E., Foster, C. A., & Agnew, C. R. (1999). Commitment, prorelationship behavior, and trust in close relationships. *Journal of Personality and Social Psychology*, 77, 942–966.

8

The role of passion in optimal relationships

ROBERT J. VALLERAND AND NOÉMIE CARBONNEAU

Our relationships represent one of the most important facets of our existence. Hundreds of studies underscore the fact that we have an innate need to belong (Baumeister & Leary, 1995) or to relate to others (Deci & Ryan, 2000). Such a need directs us to interact with other people on an ongoing basis in a number of relationships involving parents, sibling, friends, workmates, and romantic partners. In this chapter, we suggest that the construct of passion can open up a window on our relationships and shed some light on the processes that affect the relationships in our lives. Furthermore, the quality of the passion that we have for the important activities in our lives has the potential to affect our relationships for better or for worse. This should not surprise us as passionate activities are central in people's lives (Vallerand, 2010; Vallerand et al., 2003, Study 1) and as such these activities should be centrally related to a sizeable portion of our relationships and help determine if our relationships will develop in an optimal fashion or not.

We would like to submit that there are at least two ways through which one can develop optimal relationships. One is by experiencing positive activity experiences and the second by avoiding negative experiences. To make a financial comparison, there are at least two ways to maximize the amount of money in one's bank account: to make frequent and substantial deposits and to make relatively few withdrawals. Similarly, making sure that your passion leads to positive outcomes (deposits) and not to negative outcomes (withdrawals) are two ways to experience happiness. As we will see in this chapter, one type of passion (harmonious passion) provides both types of contribution and should lead to the most optimal relationships. As we shall see, the situation is different and not as positive with a second type of passion (obsessive passion).

In this chapter, we focus on three ways in which passion matters for interpersonal relationships. We first posit that one's passion for a given activity can affect our relationships with the people with whom we interact within the purview of the passionate activity. For example, passion for playing basketball may influence the quality of friendships that one will develop and maintain with his or her basketball teammates and the opponents as well. Second, passion for a given activity may also influence the quality of relationships that one has with people in other spheres of life. Thus, having an obsessive passion for research may lead one to neglect his or her family life. Finally, one can have a passion for a romantic relationship. In this case, the passion is for a relationship with the romantic partner. For instance, having a harmonious passion for the loved one should allow the person to fully engage in the relationship while experiencing positive outcomes both within and outside the relationship. In all three cases, the outcomes induced by passion can be profound and important. These issues will be addressed, in turn. However, first, we present the Dualistic Model of Passion (Vallerand, 2010, 2015; Vallerand et al., 2003) that serves as the underlying conceptualization of this research.

THE DUALISTIC MODEL OF PASSION

In line with Self-Determination Theory (Deci & Ryan, 2000), we posit that individuals are motivated to explore their environment in order to grow as individuals. In so doing, they engage in a variety of activities. Of these, only a few will be perceived as particularly enjoyable and important and to have some resonance with how we see ourselves. In fact, these activities come to be so self-defining that they represent central features of one's identity. For instance, those who have a passion for playing basketball, playing the guitar, or doing research do not merely engage in these activities, they *see themselves* as "basketball players," "guitar players," and "scientists." The Dualistic Model of Passion (DMP) defines passion as a strong inclination toward a specific object, activity, concept, or person (e.g., a romantic partner) that one loves (or at least strongly likes) and highly values, that is part of one's identity, and in which we invest time and energy on a regular basis. Furthermore, it is proposed that there are two types of passion, obsessive and harmonious, that can be distinguished in terms of how the passionate activity has been internalized into one's identity. Past research has shown that values and regulations concerning non-interesting activities can be internalized in either a controlled or an autonomous fashion (Deci et al., 1994; Sheldon, 2002; Vallerand, Fortier, & Guay, 1997). Similarly, it is posited that activities that people love or strongly like will also be internalized in the person's identity to the extent that these are highly valued and meaningful for the person.

Obsessive passion results from a controlled internalization of the activity into one's identity and self. A controlled internalization originates from intra and/or interpersonal pressure typically because certain contingencies are attached to the activity such as feelings of social acceptance or self-esteem, or because the sense of excitement derived from activity engagement is uncontrollable. In other words, with such internalization people engage in the activity for much more than the activity itself as they seek additional benefits they may derive from engagement such as a boost in self-esteem (Mageau, Carpentier, & Vallerand, 2011). People with an obsessive passion can thus find themselves in the position of experiencing an uncontrollable urge to partake in the activity they view as important and enjoyable, especially if the beloved activity represents the only source of self-esteem. They then feel that they cannot help but to engage in the passionate activity as ego-invested, rather than integrative self-processes (Hodgins & Knee, 2002), are at play and come to control the person. Consequently, they risk experiencing conflicts and other negative affective, cognitive, and behavioral consequences during and after activity engagement.

Conversely, harmonious passion results from an autonomous internalization of the activity into the person's identity. An autonomous internalization occurs when individuals have freely accepted the activity as important for them without any contingencies attached to it. This type of internalization emanates from the intrinsic and integrative tendencies of the self (Deci & Ryan, 2000; Ryan & Deci, 2003) where activity engagement is in line with personal values. It produces a motivational force to engage in the activity willingly and engenders a sense of volition and personal endorsement about pursuing the activity. When harmonious passion is at play, individuals do not experience an uncontrollable urge to engage in the passionate activity, but rather freely choose to do so. With this type of passion, the activity occupies a significant but not overpowering space in the person's identity and is in harmony with other aspects of the person's life. In other words, with harmonious passion the authentic integrating self (Deci & Ryan, 2000) is at play allowing the person to fully partake in the passionate activity with an openness that is conducive to positive experiences (Hodgins & Knee, 2002). Consequently, people with a harmonious passion have access to optimal self-processes and should experience a number of positive outcomes both during (e.g., positive affect, concentration) and after task engagement (e.g., satisfaction, general positive affect).

Research provides strong support for the DMP. Thus, much support exists for the existence of the two types of passion as defined by the DMP in a number of activities and field settings (see Vallerand, 2010, 2015 for reviews). Furthermore, the Passion Scale has been validated and has demonstrated high levels of predictive, discriminant, construct, and external validity, as well as good internal consistency in a number of activities (e.g., Castelda, Mattson, Mackillop, Anderson, & Donovick, 2007; MacKillop, Anderson, Castelda, Mattson, & Donovick, 2006; Stenseng, 2008; Vallerand et al., 2003, Study 1; Vallerand, Rousseau, Grouzet, Dumais, & Grenier, 2006, Study 1). In addition, research has also shown that the scale displays invariance as a function of gender, language, and types of activities (Marsh et al., 2013).

The differential effects of the harmonious and obsessive passions have been supported in over a hundred studies and with respect to a variety of outcomes. Thus, obsessive passion has been found to positively predict negative emotions, rumination, anxiety, and depression, and to be either negatively related or unrelated to indices of well-being such as vitality and meaning in life (e.g., Mageau et al., 2005; Philippe et al., 2009, Study 1; Philippe, Vallerand, Adrianarisoa, & Brunel, 2009, Study 1; Ratelle, Vallerand, Mageau, Rousseau, & Provencher, 2004; Rousseau & Vallerand, 2003; Vallerand et al., 2003, Study 1; Vallerand et al., 2006, Studies 2 and 3; Vallerand et al., 2007, Studies 1 and 2; see Vallerand, 2008, 2010, 2015, for reviews). On the other hand, harmonious passion has been found to positively predict indices of positive emotions, flow (i.e., feeling immersed in the activity; Csikszentmihalyi, 1975), and life satisfaction and vitality (e.g., Carpentier, Mageau, & Vallerand, 2012; Lafrenière, Vallerand, Donahue, & Lavigne, 2009; Mageau, Vallerand, Rousseau, Ratelle, & Provencher, 2005; Philippe, Vallerand, & Lavigne, 2009, Study 1; Rousseau & Vallerand, 2003; Vallerand et al., 2003, Study 1; Vallerand et al., 2006, Studies 2 and 3; Vallerand et al., 2007, Studies 1 and 2; see Vallerand, 2008, 2010, 2015 for reviews). Of additional importance, experimental research has shown that the two types of passion can be experimentally induced and lead to the same effects as those obtained in correlational studies using the Passion Scale (e.g., Bélanger et al., 2013b; Lafrenière, Vallerand, & Sedikides, 2013, Study 2).

PASSION AFFECTS RELATIONSHIPS WITH OTHERS ENGAGED IN THE PASSIONATE ACTIVITY

Passion and optimal vs. less than optimal relationships

While engaging in their passionate activity, people are likely to meet and interact with a variety of people. In fact, it appears that roughly 80 percent of people engage in their passionate activity with at least one other person (Lecoq & Rimé, 2009, Study 2).Chances are, then, that one's passion for a given activity will affect the behavior displayed with these other persons with whom we engage in this activity and, consequently, the quality of our relationships with others. People driven by passion are often described as "magnetic" because they are full of zest and energy. Thus, passion may attract others. But does this attraction translate into friendships? And if so, does the quality of these relationships vary as a function of the type of passion? In a study of massively multiplayer online role-playing games such as *World of Warcraft*, Utz, Jonas, and Tonkens (2012) asked a large number of gamers to complete the Passion Scale and scales assessing the number of friends online that they have. Controlling for the number of weekly hours played, results from regression analyses revealed that both the harmonious and obsessive passions positively predicted the number of friends online. These findings thus suggest that the higher one's passion for the activity, the more friendships in the gaming activity. Thus, passion seems to matter.

Although important, the above study by Utz et al. did not follow participants from "Time 0," that is, from the first time people met. Thus, we don't know if people were friends before they started playing role-playing games. So, the question remains: Do people *develop* better-quality friendships as a function of passion and does the type of passion come into play in the new relationships that they develop? Research conducted in a variety of settings, including work, sports, and study groups, has addressed these issues. For instance, in one study, Philippe, Vallerand, Houlfort, Lavigne, and Donahue, (2010, Study 3) followed basketball players during a 1-week basketball camp to ascertain the quality of new relationships they would develop. Athletes completed the Passion Scale early in the camp and subsequently, toward the end of camp, they were asked to assess the quality of the *new* relationships that they developed during camp using the Quality of Interpersonal Relationship Scale (QIRS; Senécal, Vallerand, & Vallières, 1992). The QIRS assesses the extent to which relationships one has with other people (in this case, other basketball players at camp) are enriching, satisfying, and so on. Results from correlational analyses revealed that the more athletes had a harmonious passion for basketball, the more they developed *new* friendships of high quality during the basketball camp. Obsessive passion was not found to affect the quality of these relationships. Thus, harmonious, but not obsessive, passion seems to positively affect the development of new relationships of high quality. These findings were replicated in another study with students who did not know each other initially and who interacted in study groups over a whole semester (Philippe, Vallerand, Houlfort et al., 2010, Study 4).

What the above findings suggest is that passion matters with respect to developing new relationships. But what about existing relationships? Are these relationships affected in the same way by our passion as the new relationships that we develop? Does the quality of such relationships vary over time or does it remain stable as a function of passion? In their study on massively multiplayer online role-playing games such as *World of Warcraft*, Utz et al. (2012) found that controlling for the number of weekly hours played, only harmonious passion positively predicted the *quality* of existing friendships. These findings were also obtained by Philippe, Vallerand, and Houlfort et al. (2010) in a number of settings, including work and leisure. In addition, Paradis, Martin, and Carron (2012) also found that harmonious passion predicted higher levels of cohesion than obsessive passion in both recreational and competitive teams of different sports. Finally, Stenseng, Forest, and

Curran (2015) showed that harmonious (but not obsessive) passion predicted belongingness with recreational athletes.

Passion, emotions, and relationships

It would appear from the above that harmonious passion facilitates both the development and the maintenance of high-quality relationships. The next issue, then, is to determine the nature of the mediating processes involved in these effects. In particular, why does harmonious passion foster positive relationships? One likely candidate is emotion. One major emotion theory, the Broaden-and-Build theory (Fredrickson, 2001), posits that positive emotions allow people to open up to themselves (having full access to the self) but also to their surroundings and to others (Fredrickson, 2001; Waugh & Fredrickson, 2006). Thus, when in such a positive state, people smile, touch, laugh, and engage in a positive sharing of the activity while remaining attuned to others with an openness that is conducive to positive relationships (Waugh & Fredrickson, 2006). This is in line with the writings by emotion theorists (e.g., Frijda & Mesquita, 1994) that emotions serve some social functions. Indeed, much research reveals that emotions serve to communicate with others. For instance, emotional behavior displayed at sporting events such as smiling, slapping hands (giving "high fives"), and talking loudly to others convey that one is experiencing positive emotions such as happiness and is willing to share one's joy with others. Such emotions are likely to lead to more positive interactions with others both at the dyadic (Waugh & Fredrickson, 2006) and the group level (Haidt, 2003). In contrast, blushing is a manifestation of being shy and may be provoked by the acknowledgement of the superiority of another person (Frijda & Mesquita, 1994). Shyness may also lead others to feel uncomfortable especially in cultures in which social status differences are undesirable. From a self-related perspective, guilt may lead one to engage in reparatory behavior while anger may lead one to restore justice sometimes through aggressive acts.

It should be noted that if positive emotions send a positive signal to others and open us up in a way so as to connect fully and positively with others, then negative emotions send the opposite message. Most negative emotions send the signal to the person experiencing the emotions that there is something wrong and that they should take time to correct the situation (Mandler, 1975). In doing so, negative emotions constrict the self instead of opening it up. Thus, instead of connecting with others, the person is then likely to shy away from others. And if we look unhappy, we may keep others at bay, as people typically do not want to interact with unhappy people (Fowler & Christakis, 2008).

In light of the above, experiencing positive emotions while engaging in an activity with other people may bring us closer to these other people. Much research reveals that when harmonious passion is at play, people experience positive affective states. It then follows that harmonious passion should therefore facilitate the development and maintenance of high-quality relationships through its effects on positive affect. Conversely, because negative emotions turn other people off and the fact that obsessive passion facilitates the experience of negative affect (see Vallerand, 2010, 2015), then, this type of passion should undermine the development and maintenance of high-quality relationships within the purview of the passionate activity.

These different hypotheses on the nature of the mediating processes were tested by Philippe, Vallerand, Houlfort, et al. (2010) in their studies on passion and relationships discussed previously. In a study on study groups (Philippe, Vallerand, Houlfort, et al., 2010, Study 4), students who met for the first time at the beginning of the term completed the Passion Scale toward their studies in management. Then, at the end of the term, 15 weeks later, they indicated the positive and negative emotions experienced within their study groups over the semester and reported on the positive (connectedness) and negative (seclusion) interpersonal aspects that they had experienced during the term. Furthermore, participants were asked to rate their perceptions of each of their teammates' quality of interpersonal relationships developed with the other people in the study group over the semester on the positive and negative interpersonal dimensions. Results from the structural equation modeling analyses appear in Figure 8.1. As can be seen, harmonious passion positively predicted positive affect, but negatively predicted negative affect, experienced over the semester. Conversely, obsessive passion was unrelated to positive affect and positively predicted negative affect. In turn, positive and negative affect experienced in the study group over the semester respectively predicted the positive and negative relationship assessments performed by *both* the participants and their fellow students. These basic findings were also obtained in 3 other studies, including one with middle-age workers (Philippe et al., 2010, Study 1) and one short-term longitudinal study that took place with teenagers who had never met each other before in a basketball camp over a full week and that included both athletes and coaches' report of the quality of athletes' new relationships developed during camp (Philippe et al., 2010, Study 3).

Research reviewed above involved the quality of relationships with teammates and workmates. What characterizes such relationships is that people are at the same level with no one having a higher status than the other. Other research conducted with relationships of different status revealed that passion also matters. For example, in studies dealing with the coach–athlete relationship, it was found that athletes' harmonious passion toward their sport was positively related to relationship satisfaction with their coach, whereas obsessive passion was negatively related to some and unrelated to the other indices (Lafrenière, Jowett, Vallerand,

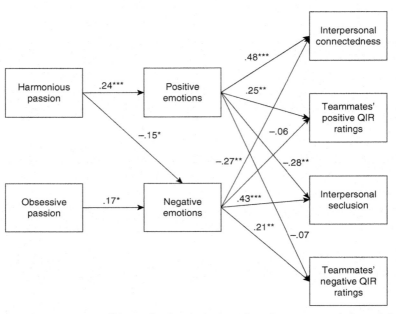

FIGURE 8.1   Passion, affect, and relationships within the activities (adapted from Philippe et al., 2010, Study 4).
*For sake of clarity, covariances are not presented. Note: QIR: Quality of interpersonal relationships.

Donahue, & Lorimer, 2008, Study 1). Furthermore, in a second study, involving coaches, Lafrenière and colleagues (2008, Study 2) showed that positive emotions mediated the impact of harmonious passion on the quality of the coach–athlete relationships. Thus, the same basic findings obtained by Philippe, Vallerand, Houlfort, et al. (2010) were replicated with positive emotions serving as mediators of the harmonious passion quality of the relationships that coaches have with their athletes. Obsessive passion did not contribute to quality of the relationship.

In sum, these findings reveal that passion for an activity contributes to making *new* friends as well as preserving such friendships once developed. Further, the type of passion matters as the positive effects come from harmonious and not obsessive passion. In fact, obsessive passion may even detract from making new friends. In addition, in line with the suggestion of emotion theorists (e.g., Fredrickson, 2001), positive and negative affect mediated the effects of harmonious and obsessive passion, respectively. Finally, the same processes seem at play whether relationships involve people of the same or different status (e.g., a supervisor or a coach). As posited by emotion theorists (Frijda, 2007), emotions do serve some important social functions, including that of helping us connect with others.

PASSION FOR AN ACTIVITY AFFECTS RELATIONSHIPS IN OTHER AREAS OF ONE'S LIFE

The DMP posits that there is a second relevant context where passion for an activity may affect our relationships. This other situation takes place when one's passion for a given activity influences our relationships in another life domain. For instance, does my involvement in basketball help or detract from my family life? Here again, the DMP posits that it depends on the type of passion at play. Specifically, having an obsessive passion toward an activity can lead to negative effects on relationships in other life contexts. This is because with obsessive passion, one cannot let go of the passionate activity and conflict between the passionate activity and relationships outside of it arises. At some point, such conflict takes its toll and negative effects on such relationships take place. Such should not be the case for harmonious passion as more than one goal or activity can peacefully coexist without the person experiencing any conflict among them (see Bélanger et al., 2013a).

Initial research by Utz et al. (2012) on passion for gaming has provided preliminary support for the above hypothesis as it was found that obsessive passion for gaming *negatively* predicts both the number of *offline* friends (or friends outside the online gaming activity) that they have as well as the quality of such friendships. No relationships were found with harmonious passion. Although the research of Utz and colleagues supports the role of passion in relationships outside the passionate activity, it did not look at the role of conflict in such a relationship. Much research has shown that obsessive passion for a given activity leads one to experience conflict between the passionate activity and other aspects of the person's life (e.g., Caudroit, Boiché, Stephan, Le Scanff, & Trouilloud, 2011; Stenseng, 2008; Vallerand et al., 2003, Study 1; Vallerand, Paquet, Philippe, & Charest, 2010; Young, De Jong, & Medic, 2014) and that it is not the case with harmonious passion. It can thus be suggested that the negative effects of obsessive passion on relationships outside of the passionate activity are mediated by the conflict that arises between the activity one is passionate about and relationships outside the activity. Some support for this hypothesis was obtained in a study by Séguin-Lévesque and colleagues (2003). These authors looked at the role of passion for the Internet in romantic conflict. Their results showed that controlling for the number of hours that people engaged in the Internet, obsessive passion for the Internet predicted conflict with one's spouse, whereas harmonious passion was unrelated to it. Thus, it is not necessarily the number of hours devoted to the passionate activity that is the major problem (although it can be!), but rather the type of passion at play and to what extent such passionate engagement conflicts with one's love life.

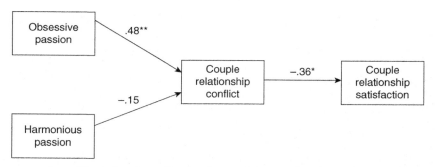

FIGURE 8.2   The role of conflict in the passion–couple relationship satisfaction (adapted from Vallerand, Ntoumanis, et al., 2008, Study 3).
*For sake of clarity, covariances are not presented.

Vallerand, Ntoumanis, et al. (2008, Study 3) subsequently tested more directly the mediating role of subjective conflict between passion for soccer and the quality of one's romantic relationship. English soccer fans were asked to complete a questionnaire that contained the Passion Scale toward soccer, a scale assessing perceptions of subjective conflict between soccer and the loved one (adapted from Séguin et al., 2003), and the Perceived Relationship Quality Components Inventory (Fletcher et al., 2000). Structural equation modeling analyses were conducted. The results appear in Figure 8.2. As can be seen, the results revealed that obsessive passion for one's soccer team predicted conflict between soccer and the loved one. Conflict, in turn, negatively predicted satisfaction with the relationship. Harmonious passion was unrelated to these variables. In other words, conflict does mediate the role of obsessive passion in the quality of one's romantic relationship but harmonious passion is not involved in such effects.

In sum, findings from the above studies in this second research area reveal that having an obsessive passion for a given activity undermines the number (Utz et al., 2012) as well as the quality of friendships (Utz et al., 2012) outside the realm of the passionate activity. In addition, obsessive passion for activities such as the Internet and being a soccer fan can also undermine the quality of one's romantic relationship (Séguin-Lévesque et al., 2003; Vallerand et al., 2008, Study 3). Furthermore, conflict mediates this relationship (Vallerand et al., 2008, Study 3). Harmonious passion toward a given activity is unrelated to conflict and decreases in relationship satisfaction. Future research using a longitudinal design is necessary in order to rule out the alternative hypothesis that it is a negative relationship with one's spouse that triggers conflict with other life activities and leads to obsessive passion for such activities. Further, additional research is needed in order to determine whether and how harmonious passion can increase the quality of one's relationship in other life spheres. One possibility may be positive experiences in the passionate activity. For instance, Carpentier et al. (2012) found that harmonious passion for one's favorite activity leads to the experience of flow in a second activity (i.e., one's studies) that, in turn, leads to psychological well-being. It is possible that flow experiences also facilitate high-quality relationships, although this effect remains to be empirically substantiated. In any event, it appears that passion for an activity can have important implications for the quality of our relationships outside the realm of the passionate activity. Future research is needed to explore whether obsessive passion for an activity can also affect other types of relationships (e.g., parents, siblings) outside the passionate activity as well as determine whether harmonious passion may positively contribute to these relationships and identify the nature of the processes through which such effects may take place.

PASSION IN ROMANTIC RELATIONSHIPS

The final area where passion affects relationships pertains to the impact that one's passion for the loved one can have on the quality of the romantic relationship. Thus, here the passion is for another person within the romantic relationship. In this section, we first briefly present the implications of the DMP for a romantic relationship and compare it to two other models that deal with romantic passion. We then review research on passion and conflict in romantic relationships from the perspective of the DMP.

The dualistic model of passion as applied to romantic involvement

The DMP posits that passion can be experienced not only toward an activity and object but toward a person as well. Thus, based on the DMP, romantic passion is defined as *a strong inclination toward a romantic partner that one loves and who becomes part of our identity, in a relationship that is deemed important and into which significant time and energy is invested.* Thus, in line with this definition, being "romantically involved" means much more than loving the person. It also means investing time and energy in the relationship and to highly valuing this relationship. In addition, in line with the DMP, it also means internalizing the loved one in our identity. Thus, in line with Self-Expansion Theory (Aron, Aron, & Smollan, 1992), the loved one becomes part of our identity. However, contrary to Self-Expansion Theory, we posit that such internalization is not unidimensional but rather can take one of two forms, thereby leading to the two types of passion. In line with Self-Determination Theory (Deci & Ryan, 2000), if the loved one is internalized through the autonomous internalization process (e.g., you love your partner and he or she is important to you purely for whom he or she is), a harmonious passion will develop. Conversely, if the internalization is controlled in nature (e.g., you love him or her and he or she is important to you because of the prestige you derive from your relationship with him or her), an obsessive passion will develop toward the loved one.

The present perspective on romantic passion can be compared to two important theoretical perspectives in which passion for romantic relationships plays a role, namely Hatfield and colleagues' conceptualization of passionate love (e.g., Hatfield & Rapson, 1990, 1993; Hatfield & Walster, 1978) and Sternberg's Triangular Theory of Love (e.g., Sternberg 1986, 1988). First, some similarities exist among the three models. For instance, all models agree on the importance of considering passion in romantic relationships as it represents a major experience of such relationships. Second, all three models also agree that passion can lead to important outcomes. However, the three models disagree on at least two counts. First, there is some disagreement on the nature of passion. While Hatfield and her colleagues consider passion to be an emotion (i.e., passionate love) and Sternberg sees it as mostly sexual in nature, the DMP focuses on the motivational dimension of romantic involvement. Furthermore, while the other models consider passion as unidimensional in nature, the DMP posits the existence of two different types of romantic passion (namely harmonious and obsessive passions) that represent two different ways of engaging in the relationship. Thus, the DMP posits that passion can differ both in terms of quantity (high or low passion, as do the other passion models) and quality, with harmonious passion representing a higher quality of engagement in the relationship than obsessive passion.

A second area of disagreement between the present perspective and the other models pertains to outcomes. Hatfield and colleagues posit that a contingency exists between outcome valence (positive or negative) and reciprocity of love. Specifically, these authors assume that reciprocated love is associated with fulfillment and ecstasy in the passionate lover, whereas unrequited love leads to emptiness, anxiety, or despair (Hatfield & Sprecher, 2010; Hatfield & Walster, 1978). On the other hand, Sternberg's model does not clearly specify how (sexual) passion leads to outcomes without being integrated with the other two dimensions (i.e., commitment and intimacy) of his triangular model of love. Although it agrees that the partner's behavior can affect outcomes derived from one's relationship, the DMP also posits that one's own passion for the loved one can, in and of itself, lead to outcomes over the beyond the effects of the romantic partner. This is because the quality of one's engagement in the relationship varies as a function of the type of passion (harmonious vs. obsessive passion) for the loved one. Harmonious passion leads to more positive outcome than obsessive passion. Thus, in addition to making important distinctions with respect to the nature of romantic passion, the DMP offers novel predictions as pertains to the processes through which personal and relational outcomes come about as a function of passion type. In sum, the DMP differs significantly from other passion models.

In line with the above, one of the major contributions of the DMP is that it is hypothesized that the two types of passion have different types of impact on both personal and relational outcomes when in a relationship. The quality of such outcomes will differ largely because of the way that one's passion will lead us to act toward our romantic partner while engaged in the romantic relationship. In line with research with other passionate activities, it is proposed that romantic involvement is experienced more positively when fueled by harmonious passion relative to obsessive passion. This is because of the adaptive nature of harmonious passion and the non-defensive and open form of involvement it promotes in the relationship. The person is not in the relationship to compete and to "win" or be better than the loved one but to share and cooperate with him or her. Conversely, with obsessive passion a more defensive position is taken where one is oriented toward personal benefits in a dyadic context thereby influencing behavior in the relationship in a way that paradoxically minimizes the experience of positive outcomes and even facilitates that of negative outcomes. Thus, just like in friendships, one's passion should have a lot to say in the outcomes we derive from our romantic relationship.

Romantic passion and relational outcomes

In line with the above, the DMP posits that because people are passionate for their romantic relationship, they will be active and will self-initiate behaviors and strategies that will influence relationship outcomes. Thus, although certain situations may be out of your control (e.g., if your partner is cheating on you, chances are that you will feel rather bad and may even be depressed), in general, we have some control over most situations. Thus, what the DMP posits is that we are not strictly pawns to the behavior of our partner. Indeed, how we choose to interact with our partner also affects the quality of the relationship for better or for worse. In other terms, the quality of our romantic relationship involvement as influenced by our romantic passion determines in large part the quality of relationship outcomes that my partner and I will derive from the relationship. In line with the DMP, harmonious passion should typically lead to more positive outcomes than obsessive passion.

A series of three studies conducted by Ratelle et al. (2013) tested the relative role of harmonious and obsessive passions in relational outcomes. Fletcher et al. (2000) have suggested that perceived relationship quality is a multidimensional construct comprised of six distinct dimensions, namely satisfaction, commitment, trust, sexual passion, intimacy, and love. In a series of three studies, Ratelle et al. (2013) investigated how the two types of romantic passion were related to each of these components of relationship quality. In the first study, male and female university students completed the

Relationship Passion Scale as well as Fletcher's Perceived Relationship Quality Components Inventory (PQRCI). This latter scale assesses the six components of relationship quality presented above. The Romantic Passion Scale assesses the two types of romantic passion. For instance, a harmonious passion item was "[m]y relationship with my partner is in harmony with my other life domains," whereas an obsessive passion item was "I have almost obsessive feelings for my partner." Results of a series of statistical analyses supported the psychometric properties of the Romantic Passion Scale. Regression analyses were performed for all dimensions of relationship quality with harmonious and obsessive passions as predictors and while controlling for gender. Results showed that harmonious passion was a strong positive predictor of all evaluative components whereas obsessive passion predicted decreasing levels of trust and increasing levels of commitment and love. Furthermore, the authors found the contribution of harmonious passion to all components of relationship quality to be statistically higher than that of obsessive passion.

Results of this study show a clear pattern of results for harmonious passion, but the picture is not as clear for obsessive passion. Obsessive passion was characterized by two components of optimal relationships, namely love and commitment, which is not surprising given that central features of romantic passion include love of the romantic partner and time and energy investment in the relationship. Meanwhile, obsessive passion was not associated with the benefits of experiencing intimacy and satisfaction in the relationship, and was even associated with distrust for the partner. This paradoxical finding reflects the fact that individuals experiencing obsessive passion appear to be trapped in a rigid persistence pattern whereby they stay in the relationship despite the absence of positive experiences and the occurrence of some negative ones. This state of affairs may result from the fact that with obsessive passion self-esteem is contingent on the romantic relationship one is passionate about (Mageau et al., 2011; see also Knee, Canevello, Bush, & Cook, 2008).

The results of Study 1 showed that the harmonious and obsessive passions were differently associated with indices of relationship quality. However, these results were obtained considering only one partner of the couple. In Study 2, Ratelle and colleagues (2013) studied both partners of couples in order to examine the relative contribution of the participant's own harmonious and obsessive passion and that of the partner's in predicting relationship quality. Such a comparison allowed the authors to test more directly the relative role of the person's passion and that of his or her partner in predicting relationship outcomes. This point is important as it deals directly with the assumption of the DMP that we are not simply pawns merely reacting to our partner's type of involvement. Rather we also contribute to the relational outcomes that we experience through the type of passion we bring to the relationship. Participants of Study 2 were both partners of heterosexual couples who completed the Romantic Passion Scale, as well as the PRQCI (Fletcher et al., 2000).

Results yielded four findings of interest. First, the effects of one's own passion obtained in Study 1 were replicated: harmonious passion led to more positive effects on the various dimensions of relationship quality than obsessive passion. Second, the passion of the partner made a significant contribution to relationship satisfaction over and beyond the passion of the participant him or herself. For instance, controlling for women's own harmonious and obsessive passion, men's harmonious passion positively predicted women's general satisfaction with the relationship. In fact, in this case men's harmonious passion proved to be a better positive predictor of women's satisfaction with their sex life than women's own harmonious passion! Men's obsessive passion for the loved one was a significant negative predictor of women's satisfaction with their sex life. Women's passion also influenced outcomes for men although such effects were not as strong as those of men's passion. Third, in line with the DMP, one's own passion had much more important effects on relational outcomes than partner's passion, again reinforcing the view that the quality of our own involvement in the relationship carries a lot of weight in terms of what we derive from the relationship. Thus, through one's own passion for the partner, outcomes are in large part self-engendered. Fourth and final, it should be noted that the results of Study 2 revealed that there was *no* support for the matching of passion types among partners of a given couple (i.e., there was no matching for passion types in couples). However, it was found that for those limited couples who were matched on passion type, there were some effects but only for men. For instance, when both partners were predominantly obsessively passionate, men reported being least satisfied and least in love. Future research is needed to identify the determinants of passion matching as it may yield insights into the phenomenon of "collective passion" (e.g., Drnovsek, Cardon, & Murnieks, 2009).

In the last study of the Ratelle et al. (2013, Study 3) paper, the authors assessed the predictive role of passion as pertains to relationship continuity over time. Because of its positive relation to indices of adaptive couple functioning, harmonious passion was expected to promote a lasting relationship. Conversely, because of its associated negative features, and especially the distrust of one's partner, obsessive passion was expected to facilitate relationship dissolution. Study 3 aimed at testing these predictions, using a 3-month prospective design. Participants had been in a romantic relationship for close to 5 years. At Time 1, they completed an online questionnaire that contained the Romantic Passion Scale and the PRQCI. The questionnaire at Time 2 contained questions about whether the participants were still involved in the same romantic relationship or not. Results from a multiple regression analysis revealed that harmonious passion predicted remaining in the relationship, while obsessive passion predicted being out of the relationship, even after controlling for gender and quality of the relationship at Time 1. In other words, having a harmonious romantic passion for a relationship with our partner positively contributes to the relationship being experienced as positive and, further, predicts if both partners will remain in the relationship. Future research is needed to identify the nature of the personal and interpersonal factors that mediate such effects.

On the role of romantic passion in conflicted situations

The Ratelle et al. (2013) research looked at romantic passion and its relationships to romantic satisfaction in general. However, passion should also affect how partners behave in specific situations. One such situation deals with conflict. How romantic partners behave when conflict arises is a central aspect of romantic relationships (e.g., Fincham, Stanley, & Beach, 2007; Gottman, 2011; Gottman & Notarius, 2000). Contrary to what some people believe, the issue is not whether conflict takes place or not but rather what one does when it arises. Research by Gottman (1994, 1998) has convincingly shown that how partners handle conflict is a strong indicator of the partners' feelings of satisfaction for their marriage as well as the length of that marriage. As Gottman and colleagues (e.g., Gottman, Driver, & Tabares, 2002; Gottman & Ryan, 2005) argue, the clues to a couple's future breakup or longevity lie in the way they argue.

Some specific conflict behaviors appear to be especially corrosive to relationship happiness. Gottman (1998, 2011) has identified four of them that he labels the "four horsemen of the apocalypse": criticism, contempt, defensiveness, and stonewalling. Criticism refers to using blame to attack the personality or character rather than the behavior of one's partner. Contempt is defined as attacking the partner's sense of self with the intention to insult him/her and includes mockery, name-calling, and hostile humor. Contempt conveys disgust with the partner and, according to Gottman and Silver (1999, p. 29), it is "the worst of the four horsemen." Defensiveness refers to any form of self-defense that includes denying responsibility for a problem, excuse making, cross-complaining (i.e., meeting the partner's complaint immediately with another complaint), and whining. Finally, stonewalling is a conversational behavior used in an attempt to isolate oneself from the interaction and includes ceasing to respond, keeping an icy distance, changing the subject, and leaving the room. The four horsemen of the apocalypse have been shown to predict deterioration of marital satisfaction and to be strong predictors of early divorcing (Gottman, 1994, 2011; Gottman & Notarius, 2000).

Research conducted by Gottman and colleagues reveals that what happens *during* a conflict matters greatly for the relationship and those involved in it. However, recently, Salvatore, Kuo, Steele, Simpson, and Collins (2011) have argued that what happens *following* a conflict is also of great importance. For example, post-conflict behaviors seeking to repair the damage done and reconnecting with the partner, such as apologies and affiliative physical contact, have positive effects such as facilitating the restoration of relationship commitment and closeness (Tsang, McCullough, & Fincham, 2006), enhancing both relationship satisfaction and stability (e.g., McCullough et al., 1998), and maintaining perceptions of partner care and intimacy (Alvaro, 2001).

Romantic passion (either harmonious or obsessive) is marked by great emotional involvement and intense focus and preoccupation with one's object of love. Such intense involvement in the relationship would appear to set the stage for high levels of emotional reactivity when couple conflict occurs. However, the type of behavior that will be emitted during the conflict should be determined, in part, by the type of passion that the person holds. With harmonious passion, the integrated self (Deci & Ryan, 2000) is at play, allowing the person to invest in the relationship in a mindful (Brown & Ryan, 2003), non-defensive (Hodgins & Knee, 2002) manner and with a secure sense of self. Harmonious passion should therefore prevent engaging in the "four horsemen" and promote engagement in reparative behaviors following conflicts. Conversely, because obsessive passion is entrenched primarily in an ego-invested sense of self (Deci & Ryan, 2000; Hodgins & Knee, 2002; see also Knee et al., 2013) and is associated with a fragile and contingent self-esteem, this type of passion should lead one to protect the self and therefore to engage in less than optimal relational behaviors, including "the four horsemen of the apocalypse" and to refrain oneself from engaging in reparative behaviors following conflicts.

These hypotheses have recently been tested in two studies by Carbonneau and Vallerand (2013). In this research, we scrutinized the role of both forms of romantic passion in conflict and reparative behaviors. In Study 1, young adults who had been engaged in a romantic relationship for over 4 years completed the Romantic Passion Scale as well as two scales assessing behavior generally displayed toward the partner during conflict. The first scale assessed destructive behavior and was based on the four horsemen of the apocalypse (e.g., Gottman, 1994, 2011; Gottman & Silver, 1999). A sample item is the following: "During conflicts … I tell myself that my partner can be so stupid sometimes." The second scale assessed reparative behaviors following conflict (e.g., "After a conflict, I hug my partner"). Results from multiple regression analyses revealed that harmonious passion negatively predicted engaging in damaging behaviors while it positively predicted the use of reparative behaviors following conflict. Conversely, obsessive passion positively predicted engaging in damaging behavior and did not significantly predict the use of reparative behaviors following conflicts. Of importance, these findings held even when we statistically controlled for relationship length.

Although the above findings from Study 1 provided support for hypotheses derived from the DMP as to the differential role of both types of romantic passion in conflict situations, there were some methodological limitations. Specifically, the severity of conflict that participants referred to when completing the two behavior scales was not controlled for. It is plausible that people with a harmonious passion for the relationship remembered mild conflicts whereas those with an obsessive passion remembered more severe ones. If such a situation took place, this would explain why obsessive passion would engender a less positive behavioral pattern than harmonious passion. Another important limitation deals with the recall methodology. In this study, participants were asked to report their behavior in general based on their recollections of past events. However, research reveals that it is preferable to collect people's responses as soon as possible following an event to prevent memory from coming into play.

In a second study, we (Carbonneau & Vallerand, 2013, Study 2) conducted a diary study that addressed these limitations. In this study, participants were followed over a 10-day period in order to assess the role of romantic passion in damaging and reparative behavior each time that a conflict occurred during the 10-day period. The results fully replicated those of Study 1. Furthermore, these results were obtained even after controlling for conflict severity and relationship length. These results underscore the fact that the findings of Study 1 were not due simply to recall or conflict severity biases. Passion does seem to matter as pertains to adaptive (or maladaptive) behavior during and after conflict.

On taking part in passionate activities with the romantic partner

Many studies have shown associations between time romantic partners spend together and the quality of their relationship (e.g., Kilbourne et al., 1990; Kingston & Nock, 1987). Spending time together in joint activities would appear to be relationship enhancing as such activities encourage interdependence, which is conducive to greater closeness and commitment between the partners (Canary et al., 1993; Flanagan et al., 2002). But taking part in joint activities with one's partner may not be beneficial for the couple if the partners find themselves constantly arguing or if one or both partners become overly competitive (Segrin & Flora, 2005). Whether taking part in a joint activity with one's partner is relationship enhancing or not may well depend on the type of passion one has for the activity . . . and for one's partner. We recently conducted a study aimed at examining this question (Carbonneau, Rochette, & Vallerand, 2014; Rochette, Carbonneau, & Vallerand, 2015). A total of 214 young adults currently involved in a romantic relationship were recruited for this study. They were asked to identify an activity that they love, find important, and regularly engage in together with their partner. They then completed the Passion Scale with regards to this specific activity, and also completed the Romantic Passion Scale. We also assessed the emotions that participants typically experience when they take part in their passionate activity with their partner and whether they thought that taking part in the activity with their partner has strengthened their romantic relationship. Results of structural equation modeling analyses revealed that participants' harmonious passion for their partner and for the activity both positively contributed to the prediction of the positive emotions experienced during activity engagement. In turn, the more positive emotions participants experienced, the more they reported that engaging in the passionate activity had contributed to the strengthening of their relationship with their partner. The reverse was found with obsessive passion. Specifically, obsessive passion for the romantic partner and for the passionate activity both predicted negative emotions experienced during activity engagement, which was negatively associated with perceiving the joint activity as relationship-enhancing. It has to be noted that these results were found while controlling for the level of excitement of the activity. This is important as sharing stimulating (vs. less intense) activities is associated more strongly with relationship quality (Reissman, Aron, & Bergen, 1993). Overall, these results suggest that taking part in a shared activity with the loved one does not ensure positive outcomes; the type of passion one has toward the activity and toward the partner matter greatly as they differently predict affective and relational outcomes.

Overall, the findings in this section on romantic passion are clear: romantic passion does matter in love relationships. Future research will be needed to pursue these initial efforts. Observational studies as well as diary and longitudinal studies assessing people's passion and outcomes are needed in order to determine how the two types of passion and outcomes influence themselves over time in leading to optimal relational and personal outcomes.

CONCLUSION

Research reviewed in this chapter reveals that passion matters as pertains to optimal friendships and romantic relationships. A number of conclusions can be made with respect to friendships. First, passion for a given activity determines the number and quality of friendships that one develops and maintains within the sphere of this activity: The more harmonious the passion, the more positive the relationships. Obsessive passion is either unrelated or negatively related to the quality of one's friendships. Second, research reveals that emotions mediate these relationships. Specifically, positive emotions mediate the positive effects of harmonious passion on relationships, while negative emotions mediate the effects of obsessive passion on relationships. There is a bonus effect. Through its negative relationship with negative emotions, harmonious passion also protects one against the negative effects of negative emotions on relationships. Thus, harmonious passion would appear to yield the complete package as pertains to relationships: promoting the positive and protecting against the negative. Third, the same processes seem at play in both the development of new high-quality relationships and the maintenance of such relationships. Fourth, the same findings are observed whether relationships involve people of the same or different status (e.g., a supervisor or a coach). However, it should be underscored that in their study, Lafrenière et al. (2008) did not assess negative emotions and thus could not test the path from obsessive passion to negative emotions to relationship quality. Future research is needed to test this path and to replicate the overall findings with a variety of one-up relationships in areas such as work and school. Finally, fifth, these affective mediating processes are not only experienced by the passionate performers, but are also being picked up by the people with whom they engage in the activity as was found in the Philippe et al. research. In other terms, the impact of passion on relationship quality does not simply take place in the heads of passionate individuals but rather fully extends to other people with whom they engage in the passionate activity. As posited by emotion theorists (Frijda, 2007), emotions do serve some important social functions, including that of helping us connect with others.

A second conclusion of importance deals with the impact that one's passion for a given activity (e.g., work) can have on relationships in another life domain (family life). The more obsessive the passion, the more negative the effects. Conflict between the passionate activity and the other life domain mediates the effects of obsessive passion on other life outcomes. Harmonious passion is unrelated to conflict and its negative effects on relational outcomes in other life spheres. These findings extend in the interpersonal sphere the findings that showed that passion for a given activity can affect intrapersonal outcomes in another sphere of functioning (e.g., Vallerand et al., 2010). Thus, through its impact in life conflict of different types, obsessive passion can negatively affect both intrapersonal and interpersonal outcomes. Future research is needed in order to extend these findings with other types of interpersonal outcomes such as friendships and relationships with siblings and parents and relatives.

Finally, one can also have a passion for the loved one and such romantic passion can have important effects on both personal and relational outcomes experienced within the romantic realm. The more harmonious the romantic passion, the more positive the personal and relational outcomes that one will experience. Obsessive passion can lead to some negative outcomes such as personal suffering, lower levels of relational satisfaction, and relationship breakups. These differential outcomes may result from different conflict and repair behaviors triggered by one's obsessive passion. Whereas obsessive passion leads to high levels of conflict and low quality of repair behavior toward the loved one, harmonious passion leads to the opposite, more adaptive, pattern. It is thus hardly surprising that harmonious passion leads to more positive romantic outcomes, including the longevity of the relationship. Finally, taking part in a shared activity even if highly exciting with the loved one does not ensure positive outcomes. The type of passion one has toward the activity and toward the partner both matter greatly as they differently predict affective and relational outcomes.

Overall, then, the development and maintenance of optimal relationships are affected in a variety of ways through our passion for activities and for our romantic relationships. Clearly, the passion we have for these activities greatly influences how we engage in these activities that, in turn, influence the quality of our relationship with others. To the extent that we are harmoniously passionate toward such activities, including the romantic relationship, we are likely to develop and maintain positive relationships.

REFERENCES

Alvaro, J.A. (2001). An interpersonal forgiveness and reconciliation intervention: The effect on marital intimacy. *Dissertation Abstracts International: Section B. The Science and Engineering*, 62(3B), pp. 1608.

Aron, A., Aron E.N., & Smollan, D. (1992). Inclusion of other in the self scale and the structure of interpersonal closeness. *Journal of Personality and Social Psychology*, 63, 596–612.

Bélanger, J.J., Lafrenière, M.-A.K., Vallerand, R.J., & Kruglanski, A.W. (2013a). Driven by fear: The effect of success and failure information on passionate individuals' performance. *Journal of Personality and Social Psychology*, 104(1), 180–195.

Bélanger, J.J., Lafrenière, M.-A.K., Vallerand, R.J., & Kruglanski, A.W. (2013b). When passion makes the heart grow colder: The role of passion in alternative goal suppression. *Journal of Personality and Social Psychology*, 104(1), 126–147.

Brown, K.W., & Ryan, R.M. (2003). The benefits of being present: Mindfulness and its role in psychological well-being. *Journal of Personality and Social Psychology*, 84, 822–848.

Canary, D.J., Stafford, L., Hause, K.S., & Wallace, L.A. (1993). An inductive analysis of relational maintenance strategies: Comparisons among lovers, relatives, friends and others. *Communication Research Reports*, 10, 5–14.

Carbonneau, N., Rochette, S., & Vallerand, R.J. (2014). *The unique contribution of passion for one's partner and passion for an activity that is shared with the partner in the prediction of affective and relational outcomes.* Paper in preparation.

Carbonneau, N., & Vallerand, R.J. (2013). On the role of harmonious and obsessive romantic passion in conflict behavior. *Motivation and Emotion, 37*, 743–757.

Carpentier, J., Mageau, G.A., & Vallerand, R.J. (2012). Ruminations and flow: Why do people with a more harmonious passion experience higher well-being? *Journal of Happiness Studies*, 13(3), 501–518. doi:10.1007/s10902-011-9276-4

Castelda, B.A., Mattson, R.E., MacKillop, J., Anderson, E.J., & Donovick, P.J. (2007). Psychometric validation of the Gambling Passion Scale (GPS) in an English-speaking university sample. *International Gambling Studies*, 7, 173–182.

Caudroit, J., Boiché, J., Stephan, Y., Le Scanff, C., & Trouilloud, D. (2011). Predictors of work/family interference and leisure-time physical activity among teachers: The role of passion towards work. *European Journal of Work and Organizational Psychology*, 20(3), 326–344.

Csikszentmihalyi, M. (1975). *Beyond boredom and anxiety*. San Francisco, CA: Jossey Bass.

Deci, E.L., Eghrari, H., Patrick, B.C., & Leone, D.R. (1994). Facilitating internalization: The self-determination perspective. *Journal of Personality*, 62, 119–142.

Deci, E.L., & Ryan, R.M. (2000). The "what" and "why" of goal pursuits: Human needs and the self-determination of behavior. *Psychological Inquiry*, 11, 227–268.

Fincham, F.D., Stanley, S.M., & Beach, S. (2007). Transformative processes in marriage: An analysis of emerging trends. *Journal of Marriage and Family*, 69, 275–292. doi:10.1111/j.1741-3737.2007.00362.x

Flanagan, K.M., Clements, M.L., Whitton, S.W., Portney, M.J., Randall, D.W., & Markman, H.J. (2002). Retrospect and prospect in the psychological study of marital and couple relationships. Dans J.P. McHale & W.S. Grolnick (Eds), *Retrospect and prospect in the psychological study of families* (pp. 99–125). Mahwah, NJ: Lawrence Erlbaum Associates Publishers.

Fletcher, G.J., Simpson, J.A., & Thomas, G. (2000). The measurement of perceived relationship quality components: A confirmatory factor analytic approach. *Personality and Social Psychology Bulletin*, 26, 340–354.

Fowler, J.H., & Christakis, N.A. (2008). Dynamic spread of happiness in a large social network: longitudinal analysis over 20 years in the Framingham Heart Study. *BMJ: British Medical Journal*, 337.

Fredrickson, B.L. (2001). The role of positive emotions in positive psychology: The Broaden-and Build Theory of positive emotions. *American Psychologist*, 56, 218–226.

Frijda, N.H. (2007). *The laws of emotion*. Mahwah, NJ: Lawrence Erlbaum Associates.

Frijda, N.H., & Mesquita, B. (1994). The social roles and functions of emotions. Dans S. Kitayama & H.R. Markus (Eds), *Emotion and culture: Empirical studies of mutual influence* (pp. 51–87). Washington, DC: American Psychological Association.

Gottman, J.M. (1994). *What predicts divorce? The relationship between marital processes and marital outcomes*. Hillsdale, NJ: Erlbaum.

Gottman, J.M. (1998). Psychology and the study of marital processes. *Annual Review of Psychology*, 49, 169–197.

Gottman, J.M. (2011). *The science of trust: Emotional attunement for couples*. New York, NY: W. W. Norton.

Gottman, J.M., Driver, J., & Tabares, A. (2002). Building the sound marital house: An empirically-derived couple therapy. In A.S. Gurman and N.S. Jacobson (Eds.), *Clinical handbook of couple therapy* (3rd ed., pp. 373–399). New York, NY: Guilford Press.

Gottman, J.M., & Notarius, C.I. (2000). Decade review: Observing marital interaction. *Journal of Marriage and the Family*, 62, 927–947.

Gottman, J.M., & Ryan, K. (2005). The mismeasure of therapy: Treatment outcomes in marital therapy research. In W.M. Pinsof & J.L. Lebow (Eds.), *Family psychology: The art of the science* (pp. 65–89). New York, NY: Oxford University Press.

Gottman, J.M., & Silver, N. (1999). *The seven principles for making marriage work.* New York: Three Rivers Press.

Haidt, J. (2003). The moral emotions. In R.J. Davidson, K.R. Scherer, & H.H. Goldsmith (Eds.), *Handbook of affective sciences* (pp. 852–870). New York: Oxford University Press.

Hatfield, E., & Rapson, R.L. (1990). Passionate love in intimate relationships. In B.S. Moore & A.M. Isen (Eds.), *Studies in emotion and social interaction. Affect and social behavior* (pp. 126–151). New York: Cambridge University Press.

Hatfield, E., & Rapson, R. (1993). Love and attachment processes. In M. Lewis & J.M. Haviland (Eds.), *Handbook of emotions* (pp. 595–604). New York: Guilford Press.

Hatfield, E., & Sprecher, S. (1986). Measuring passionate love in intimate relationships. *Journal of Adolescence*, 9, 383–410.

Hatfield, E., & Walster, G.W. (1978). *A new look at love.* Reading, MA: Addison-Wesley.

Hodgins, H.S., & Knee, C.R. (2002). The integrating self and conscious experience. In E.L. Deci & R.M. Ryan (Éds.), *Handbook of self-determination research* (pp. 87–100). Rochester, NY: University of Rochester Press.

Kilbourne, B.S., Howell, F., & England, P. (1990). A measurement model for subjective marital solidarity: Invariance across time, gender, and life cycle stage. *Social Science Research*, 19, 62–81.

Kingston, P.W., & Nock, S.L. (1987). Time together among dual-earner couples. *American Sociological Review*, 52, 391–400.

Knee, C.R., Canevello, A., Bush, A.L., & Cook, A. (2008). Relationship-contingent self-esteem and the ups and downs of romantic relationships. *Journal of Personality and Social Psychology*, 95, 608–627.

Knee, C.R., Hadden, B.W., Porter, B., & Rodriguez, L.M. (2013). Self-determination theory and romantic relationship processes. *Personality and Social Psychology Review*, 17, 307–324.

Lafrenière, M-A.K., Jowett, S., Vallerand, R.J., Donahue, E.G., & Lorimer, R. (2008). Passion in sport: On the quality of the coach-player relationship. *Journal of Sport and Exercise Psychology*, 30, 541–560.

Lafrenière, M-A.K., Vallerand, R.J., Donahue, E.G., & Lavigne, G.L. (2009). On the costs and benefits of gaming: The role of passion. *CyberPsychology & Behavior*, 12.

Lafrenière, M.-A.K., Vallerand, R.J., & Sedikides, C. (2013). On the relation between self-enhancement and life satisfaction: The moderating role of passion. *Self and Identity*, 12, 516–530.

Lecoq, J., & Rimé, B. (2009). Les passions: aspects émotionnels et sociaux. *Revue Européenne de Psychologie Appliquée/European Review of Applied Psychology*, 59, 197–209.

MacKillop, J., Anderson, E.J., Castelda, B.A., Mattson, R.E., & Donovick, P.J. (2006). Divergent validity of measures of cognitive distortions, impulsivity, and time perspective in pathological gambling. *Journal of Gambling Studies*, 22, 339–354.

Mageau, G., Carpentier, J., & Vallerand, R.J. (2011). The role of self-esteem contingencies in the distinction between obsessive and harmonious passion. *European Journal of Social Psychology*, 6, 720–729.

Mageau, G.A., Vallerand, R.J., Rousseau, F.L, Ratelle, C.F., & Provencher, P.J. (2005). Passion and gambling: Investigating the divergent affective and cognitive consequences of gambling. *Journal of Applied Social Psychology*, 35, 100–118.

Mandler, G. (1975). *Mind and Emotion*. New York, NY: John Wiley & Sons Inc.

Marsh, H.W., Vallerand, R.J., Lafreniere, M.A.K., Parker, P., Morin, A.J.S., Carbonneau, N., . . . Paquet, Y. (2013). Passion: Does one scale fit all? Construct validity of two-factor passion scale and psychometric invariance over different activities and languages. *Psychological Assessment*, 25, 796–809.

McCullough, M.E., Rachal, K.C., Sandage, S.J., Worthington, E.L. Jr., Brown, S.W., & Hight, T.L. (1998). Interpersonal forgiving in close relationships: II. Theoretical elaboration and measurement. *Journal of Personality and Social Psychology*, 75, 1586–1603.

Paradis, K., Martin, L., & Carron, A.V. (2012). Examining the relationship between passion and perceptions of cohesion in athletes. *Sport & Exercise Psychology Review*, 8, 22–31.

Philippe, F.L., Vallerand, R.J., Andrianarisoa, J., & Brunel, P. (2009). Passion in referees: Examining their affective and cognitive experiences in sport situations. *Journal of Sport and Exercise Psychology*, 31, 1–21.

Philippe, F., Vallerand, R.J., Houlfort, N., Lavigne, G.L., & Donahue, E.G. (2010). Passion for an activity and quality of interpersonal relationships: The mediating role of emotions. *Journal of Personality and Social Psychology*, 98, 917–932.

Ratelle, C.F., Carbonneau, N., Vallerand, R.J., & Mageau, G.A. (2013). Passion in the romantic sphere: A look at relational outcomes. *Motivation and Emotion*, 37, 106–120.

Ratelle, C.F., Vallerand, R.J., Mageau, G.A., Rousseau, F.L., & Provencher, P. (2004). When passion leads to problematic outcomes: A look at gambling. *Journal of Gambling Studies*, 20, 105–119.

Reissman, C., Aron, A., & Bergen, M.R. (1993). Shared activities and marital satisfaction: Causal direction and self-expansion versus boredom. *Journal of Social and Personal Relationships*, 10, 243–254.

Rochette, S., Carbonneau, N., & Vallerand, R.J. (2015). *The unique contribution of passion for one's partner and passion for an activity that is shared with the partner in the prediction of affective and relational outcomes*. Poster presented at the 16th annual conference of the Society for Personality and Social Psychology (SPSP), Long Beach, California.

Rousseau, F.L., & Vallerand, R.J. (2003). Le rôle de la passion dans le bien-être subjectif des aînés [The role of passion in the subjective well-being of elderly individuals]. *Revue Québécoise de Psychologie*, 24, 197–211.

Salvatore, J., Kuo, S.I., Steele, R.D., Simpson, J.A., & Collins, W.A. (2011). Recovering from conflict in romantic relationships: A developmental perspective. *Psychological Science*, 22, 376–383.

Segrin, C., & Flora, J. (2005). *Family communication*. Mahwah, NJ: Lawrence Erlbaum Associates Publishers.

Séguin-Lévesque, C., Laliberté, M.-L., Pelletier, L.G., Blanchard, C., & Vallerand, R.J. (2003). Harmonious and obsessive passion for the Internet: Their associations with the couple's relationships. *Journal of Applied Social Psychology*, 33, 197–221.

Senécal, C.B., Vallerand, R.J., & Vallières, E.F. (1992). Construction et validation de l'échelle de la Qualité des Relations Interpersonnelles (EQRI) [Construction and validation on the Quality of Interpersonal Relationships Scale (QIRS)]. *European Review of Applied Psychology*, 42, 315–322.

Sheldon, K.M. (2002). The Self-Concordance Model of healthy goal-striving: When personal goals correctly represent the person. In E.L. Deci & R.M. Ryan (Eds.), *Handbook of self-determination research* (pp. 65–86). Rochester, NY: The University of Rochester Press.

Stenseng, F. (2008). The two faces of leisure activity engagement: Harmonious and obsessive passion in relation to intrapersonal conflict and life domain outcomes. *Leisure Sciences*, 30, 465–481.

Stenseng, F., Forest, J., & Curran, T. (2015). Positive emotions in recreational sport activities: The role of passion and belongingness. *Journal of Happiness Studies*, 16, 1117–1129.

Sternberg, R.J. (1986). A triangular theory of love. *Psychological Review*, 93, 119–153.

Sternberg, R.J. (1988). Triangulating love. In R.J. Sternberg & M.L. Barnes (Eds.), *The psychology of love* (pp. 1119–138). New Haven, CT: Yale University Press.

Tsang, J.A., McCullough, M.E., & Fincham, F.D. (2006). The longitudinal association between forgiveness and relationship closeness and commitment. *Journal of Social and Clinical Psychology*, 25, 448–472.

Tucker, P., & Aron, A. (1993). Passionate love and marital satisfaction at key transition points in the family life cycle, *Journal of Social and Clinical Psychology*, 12, 135–147.

Utz, S., Jonas, K.J., & Tonkens, E. (2012). Effects of passion for massively multiplayer online role-playing games on interpersonal relationships. *Journal of Media Psychology: Theories, Methods, and Applications*, 24, 77–86.

Vallerand, R.J. (2008). On the psychology of passion: In search of what makes people's lives most worth living. *Canadian Psychology*, 49, 1–13. (invited paper, CPA Presidential Address).

Vallerand, R.J. (2010). On passion for life activities: The dualistic model of passion. In M.P. Zanna (Ed.), *Advances in experimental social psychology* (Vol. 42, pp. 97–193). New York: Academic Press.

Vallerand, R.J. (2015). *The psychology of passion*. New York: Oxford University Press.

Vallerand, R.J., Blanchard, C.M., Mageau, G.A., Koestner, R., Ratelle, C.F., Léonard, M., ... Marsolais, J. (2003). Les passions de l'âme: On obsessive and harmonious passion. *Journal of Personality and Social Psychology*, 85, 756–767.

Vallerand, R.J., Fortier, M.S., & Guay, F. (1997). Self-determination and persistence in a real-life setting: Toward a motivational model of high school dropout. *Journal of Personality and Social Psychology*, 72, 1161–1176.

Vallerand, R.J., Ntoumanis, N., Philippe, F., Lavigne, G.L., Carbonneau, N., Bonneville, A., Lagacé-Labonté, C., & Maliha, G. (2008). On passion and sports fans: A look at football. *Journal of Sport Sciences*, 26, 1279–1293.

Vallerand, R.J., Paquet, Y., Philippe, F.L., & Charest, J. (2010). On the role of passion in burnout: A process model. *Journal of Personality*, 78, 289–312.

Vallerand, R.J., Rousseau, F.L., Grouzet, F.M.E., Dumais, A., & Grenier, S. (2006). Passion in sport: A look at determinants and affective experiences. *Journal of Sport & Exercise Psychology*, 28, 454–478.

Vallerand, R.J., Salvy, S.J., Mageau, G.A., Elliot, A.J., Denis, P., Grouzet, F.M.E., & Blanchard, C.M. (2007). On the role of passion in performance. *Journal of Personality*, 75, 505–534.

Waugh, C.E., & Fredrickson, B.L. (2006). Nice to know you: Positive emotions, self-other overlap, and complex understanding in the formation of a new relationship. *The Journal of Positive Psychology*, 1, 93–106.

Young, B.W., de Jong, G.C., & Medic, N. (2014). Examining relationships between passion types, conflict, and negative outcomes in masters athletes. *International Journal of Sport and Exercise Psychology*, 13, 132–149

9

The dyadic nature of ideal and partner perceptions in romantic relationships

LORNE CAMPBELL AND SARAH MOROZ

My biggest mistake was lovin' you too much and lettin' you know
'Cause now you've got me where you want me and you're gonna let me go

In these song lyrics, sung originally by Marvin Gaye (Holland, Dozier, & Holland, 1964), it is clear that one partner in the relationship is not as satisfied as the other and intends to end the relationship. It is also clear that the about to be jilted lover is painfully aware of his or her partner's feelings and intentions. These lyrics acknowledge the dyadic nature of relationships: that partner's actions influence each other's outcomes (Kelley et al., 1983). Romantic relationships involve individuals, typically two at one time (Fletcher, Simpson, Campbell, & Overall, 2015), but the relationship cannot be understood by focusing only on the thoughts, feelings, and behavior of individuals in relationships; instead, they need to be understood in terms of the mutual influence that exists between these individuals over time (e.g., Berscheid, 1999; Reis, 2007).

Such a dyadic focus was part of the Ideal Standards Model (ISM; Fletcher, Simpson, Thomas, & Giles, 1999; Simpson, Fletcher, & Campbell, 2001) at its inception, but only recently have the dyadic consequences of the ISM been empirically and systematically tested. The ISM makes unique predictions regarding the evaluation and maintenance of relationships, and the goal of this chapter is to briefly outline the basic tenets of the ISM in order to particularly highlight research investigating the dyadic consequences of the model. We end by making suggestions for future research.

THE IDEAL STANDARDS MODEL

The ISM (Fletcher et al., 1999; Simpson, Fletcher, & Campbell, 2001) proposes that people possess images of their ideal partner, or an abstract concept of the qualities that they would like their potential or current romantic partner to have. Ideals comprise three overlapping components: perceptions of the self, partner, and relationships (Baldwin, 1992). Individual's images of their ideal partners reflect their self-perceptions, the qualities they would like their partner to possess, and the type of relationship that they would like to have. Individuals' ideals are linked to their self-perceptions such that more positive self-evaluations are associated with higher standards, and vice versa (Campbell, Simpson, Kashy, & Fletcher, 2001).

According to the ISM, the ideals that people use as evaluative criteria for their romantic partners should reflect evolutionarily relevant relationship goals. Principles derived from evolutionary theories (see Buss & Schmitt, 1993; Gangestad & Simpson, 2000) suggest that people ought to judge ideal partners on three basic dimensions: (a) their capacity for intimacy and commitment, (b) their attractiveness and general health, and (c) their social status and resources. These three dimensions reflect evolutionary theories of human mating that integrate "good-provider" and "good-genes" perspectives (Gangestad & Simpson, 2000). Each dimension represents a different way of obtaining a mate and promoting one's own reproductive fitness (Buss & Schmitt, 1993). By being attentive to a partner's capacity for intimacy and commitment, individuals should increase their chances of finding a cooperative, committed partner who is likely to be a devoted parent. By focusing on attractiveness and health, individuals are more likely to acquire a mate who is younger, healthier, and perhaps more fertile (especially in the case of men choosing women). And by considering a partner's resources and status, individuals should be more likely to obtain a mate who can ascend social hierarchies and form coalitions with other people who have, or can acquire, valued social status or other resources (especially in the case of women choosing men). Factor analyses of data collected from two independent samples confirmed this tripartite factor structure regarding how individuals evaluate romantic partners (Fletcher et al., 1999).

According to the model, comparisons between these ideal standards and perceptions of the current partner or relationship should serve three basic functions. The magnitude of the discrepancies between ideal standards and perceptions of the current partner-relationship (hereafter referred to as "partner discrepancies") allow individuals to (a) estimate and *evaluate* the quality of their partners and relationships (e.g., to assess the appropriateness of potential of one's current relationship; is this someone I could marry?), (b) *explain* what happens in relationships (e.g., give causal accounts explaining relationship satisfaction, problems, or conflicts; why do my partner and I argue so often?), and (c) *regulate* and make adjustments in relationships (e.g., to predict and possibly control current partners or relationships; how can I make this relationship better?). Large partner discrepancies should indicate to people that they are in an unsatisfactory relationship, which may motivate them to make adjustments in the current relationship (e.g., lower their ideals or enhance their partners) or end the relationship. When people fall short of their partner's ideals, they are in a qualitatively different situation than those who match their partner's ideals. The former may have to engage in different regulatory behaviors to reduce the size of their *partner's* discrepancy. For instance, an individual may have to avoid conflict and showcase his or her best qualities in an effort to more closely meet his or her partner's standards.

A dyadic perspective.

According to the ISM the magnitude of partner discrepancies should not only affect how individuals evaluate their relationships (Fletcher et al., 1999; Campbell et al., 2001), but also affect how the partners of these individuals feel about the relationship (e.g., Sternberg & Barnes, 1985). This is because one of the main functions of ideal standards is to help individuals evaluate the quality of their romantic relationships by accurately identifying areas of strength and weakness in both themselves and their romantic partners (Simpson et al., 2001). We next present empirical evidence supporting this dyadic perspective of the model focusing on three areas of relationship processes: (1) how partners attempt to change each other to regulate their relationships, and the effects of these regulation attempts on the relationship; (2) evaluations of relationship quality associated with comparisons to a partner's ideals, and the accuracy of inferences regarding how closely one matches a partner's ideals; and (3) how individuals may calibrate the accuracy with respect to how closely they match their partner's ideals.

REGULATION PROCESSES IN RELATIONSHIPS

According to the ISM, if a large discrepancy exists between perceptions of one's current and ideal partner, an individual should try to regulate the partner or the relationship to reduce the size of this discrepancy (Fletcher, Simpson, & Thomas, 2000). This can be achieved by attempting to change a partner and/or relationship over time so that the partner more closely matches one's ideals. Alternatively, an individual can decide that the current situation is unsatisfactory and simply terminate the relationship. In contrast, romantic partners may alter their ideals to more closely match their current relationship situation. A study of newly formed dating relationships indeed found that individuals subtly changed their ideals over time to be more consistent with their perceptions of current partners and relationships, but not vice versa (Fletcher et al., 2000). Specifically, individual's perceptions of their partners assessed at the first testing session predicted changes in these individuals' ideals from the first to the second testing session, suggesting they were altering their ideals to be aligned more closely to their partner perceptions.

In the first test of the regulatory functions of ideal standards, as proposed by the ISM, Overall, Fletcher, and Simpson (2006) reported that higher partner discrepancies were associated with greater regulation attempts (i.e., attempts to change the partner to more closely match one's own ideals), and these links operated independently within each of the ISM dimensions (warmth and trustworthiness, attractiveness and vitality, and status and resources). Longitudinal analyses over a six-month period found that higher partner discrepancies predicted increased regulation attempts over time, along with a decline in relationship satisfaction. Reflecting the dyadic nature of these processes, more regulation by partner A, for example in terms of expressing affection, was associated with partner B becoming more aware that they were not living up to partner A's expectations. The target partner also acquired a relatively more negative view of his or her own ability to express affection, apparently motivating this partner to try to become more overtly affectionate over time.

Additional research by Overall, Fletcher, Simpson, and Sibley (2009), conducted in the laboratory setting, focused on situations in which individuals seek to improve their relationships by actively trying to change something they do not like about their partners. These types of conversations are not always pleasant given that asking a partner to change something about himself or herself implies being dissatisfied with the partner, and this has the potential to hurt the feelings of the partner now made aware that he or she falls short of the partner's image of an ideal partner.

Nevertheless, an open discussion of what partners like and do not like about each other can potentially have positive long-term effects. For example, relationship conflict can provide a context where intimates are forced to pay attention to each other's desires and goals, and provide the possibility of working toward a mutually beneficial solution (e.g., Fishtein, Pietromonaco, & Feldman Barrett, 1999). Furthermore, conflict prompts partners to articulate competing interests, understand each other's interests, and negotiate compromises (Fincham, 2003; Fincham & Beach, 1999).

Testing the possible long-term positive effects of regulation attempts for relationships, Overall et al. (2009) had couples discuss aspects of each other that they wanted to see changed while they were being videotaped. The use of exit, voice, loyalty, and neglect behavioral strategies (e.g., Rusbult & Zembrodt, 1983) enacted by each partner was coded by independent raters and relationship perceptions were obtained from each partner at 3-month intervals for 1 year. Consistent with past research (e.g., Overall et al., 2006), the enactment of more active strategies during the discussion (both positive and negative) was viewed by both partners as less successful in promoting the desired change. In the short term, directly communicating to a partner that he or she lacks certain desired qualities was not associated with positive relationship evaluations, even when communicated in a positive nature.

Instead, the use of more positive passive strategies during the discussion (e.g., loyalty, or hoping that something will change without asking for change) was more positively experienced and perceived as more successful at producing change. The results reversed, however, when examining reports obtained over the course of the year. Across time, the use of direct strategies (e.g., voice) produced greater change in the targeted features as reported by both partners. Indirect strategies such as loyalty, in contrast, resulted in absolutely no change over time (see also Overall, Sibley, & Travaglia, 2010). Asking partners to change may create friction or negative feelings between partners in the short term; however, if the problem is eventually worked through, often via additional voice strategies, the couple may end up being better off and more satisfied over time (see also McNulty, 2008, 2010; McNulty & Russell, 2010).

The research on regulation processes in relationships places emphasis on discrepancies that arise when partner A perceives that partner B is falling short of partner A's ideals. The flipside of this discrepancy occurs when partner A does not match up to partner B's ideals. As suggested by Campbell et al. (2001), these two types of discrepancies should be experienced in unique ways by each partner in the relationship. Lackenbauer and Campbell (2012) tested the potentially unique outcomes associated with each type of ideal discrepancy across a series of five studies. They found that participants who perceived their partners as discrepant from the participant's ideal standards experienced more dejection-related emotions (e.g., dissatisfied, upset) and a more promotion-focused regulatory style (i.e., focusing on behaviors to enact in order to achieve a relationship goal), suggesting that such partner discrepancies activate nurturance-related concerns. Consistent with regulatory focus theory (Higgins, 1997), a promotion focus in this instance should generate promotion behaviors intended to reduce the discrepancy in order to achieve the desired relationship outcomes. These findings are also consistent with findings from Overall et al. (2006), who showed that people enact behaviors aimed at regulating or changing their partners to more closely match their own ideal standards in order to achieve relationship-relevant goals.

Perceiving that one is discrepant from one's partner's ideal standards, on the other hand, was associated with agitation-related emotions (e.g., guilt, anxiety) and a prevention focus (i.e., focusing on behaviors to avoid in order to reach a relationship goal). This supports the notion that this form of discrepancy leads to concerns about negative outcomes that could occur and, thus, activates security-related concerns (Lackenbauer & Campbell, 2012). This type of discrepancy and resulting regulatory focus may also lead to behavior aimed at preventing feared negative outcomes. For instance, Campbell et al. (2001) suggested that an individual may have to focus on avoiding conflict and emphasizing his or her best qualities to more closely meet his or her partner's standards. Especially for people involved in generally satisfying and committed relationships, this prevention strategy could reduce the partner discrepancy and maintain relationship satisfaction.

SATISFACTION AND ACCURACY

The hypothesis derived from the ISM that individuals should report higher levels of relationship satisfaction when they perceive their partners to more closely match their ideals has consistently received support (e.g., Campbell et al., 2001; Fletcher et al., 1999; Overall et al., 2006, 2009). The dyadic nature of the results of the research on the regulation in relationships, however, also implies that individuals' relationship satisfaction should be linked with how they are perceived by their partners in addition to how they perceive their partners. For instance, if partner A feels that partner B closely matches their ideals, then partner A should feel satisfied with their relationship. However, partner A's relationship satisfaction should also be affected by how closely they match partner B's ideals. Campbell et al. (2001; study 2) tested this hypothesis by asking both members of a large sample of dating couples to report their ideal standards, and how closely their partners matched their ideals. Smaller partner discrepancies predicted greater relationship quality as reported by both members of the dyad. Individuals whose partners more closely matched their ideals reported greater perceived relationship quality, but reported relationship quality was also uniquely predicted by how closely participants matched their *partner's* ideals (as reported by their partner). This "partner" effect has been replicated many times (e.g., Campbell, Overall, Rubin, & Lackenbauer, 2013; Overall et al., 2006, 2009).

This partner effect also implies that individuals' satisfaction with their relationship may, at least to some degree, be associated with an accurate assessment of how closely they compare to their partner's ideals. Prior research examining people's inference of their partner's assessment of the self has argued, and empirically demonstrated, however, that such inferences are biased by individuals' own self-evaluations (e.g., Murray, Holmes, & Griffin, 2000). Nevertheless, because personal well-being and desired outcomes depend on the actions and continued investment of the partner (Kelley et al., 1983), people should be strongly motivated to make accurate judgments of their partners' evaluations.

In two large dyadic samples, Campbell et al. (2013) tested the degree to which individuals accurately inferred how closely they matched their partner's ideals, and if such accurate inferences accounted for the association between the perceived discrepancies of one partner and the relationship satisfaction of the other partner. In both samples, inferences regarding the degree to which the self matched the partner's ideals were uniquely associated with the partner's actual ideal discrepancies, in addition to individuals' own partner and self-evaluations (the focus of prior research). Overall, individuals are fairly accurate in their assessments of how well they match their partner's ideals. Additionally, across both studies inferences about the partner's discrepancies partially mediated the partner effect (i.e., for the warmth/ trustworthiness and vitality/attractiveness dimensions). Thus, when individuals were more discrepant from their partner's ideals on these dimensions, they experienced lower relationship satisfaction partially because they accurately inferred that they were more discrepant from their partner's ideal. These effects also occurred beyond other projection processes shown by prior research. This research established that relationship partners do accurately infer how closely they match their partner's ideals, inviting the further question of how this accuracy is achieved.

SOURCES OF ACCURACY

There are examples from prior research suggesting that interpersonal behavior clearly contains certain observable cues that allow individuals to make accurate inferences about others, including the thoughts, feelings, and behaviors of romantic partners. For example, many studies have demonstrated that individuals' inferences of partner responsiveness are significantly affected by responsive cues enacted during a discussion with the partner (e.g., Maisel, Gable and Strachman, 2008; for a more complete review of perceived responsiveness, see Reis, Clark, & Holmes, 2004). In relation to ideals, recall that past research has shown that regulation attempts enacted by a relationship partner are related to more negative self-evaluations by the targeted partner, as well as inferences by the targeted partner that they did not live up to their partner's standards (Overall et al., 2006). Similarly, a study by Overall and Fletcher (2010) indicated that the perception of regulation attempts from one's partner is negatively associated with inferences about how closely one matched the partner's ideals. Inferred consistency was, in turn, associated with poorer relationship evaluations and more negative evaluations of the self-attributes targeted by the partner's regulation attempts. Perceived regulation also led directly to more attempts by the individual to change the targeted features – a direct behavioral outcome. Overall and Fletcher noted that although the use of negative regulation strategies produced much the same pattern of results after a 6-month time lag, the use of positive regulation strategies actually led to greater inferred ideal consistency.

Previous research has also shown that interpersonal behavior provides individuals with accurate cues from which inferences can be made even in "zero acquaintance" scenarios (that is, when the perceiver has not previously engaged with the target). For instance, a study by Stillman and Maner (2009) investigated raters' ability to judge women's sociosexuality after watching a video of them completing a task with a male confederate. Their results showed a high correlation between judgments of the women's sociosexuality and the women's self-reported sociosexuality, indicating that the women's behavior was, to some degree, honestly communicating the extent of her sexual (un)restrictedness. Indeed, the researchers identified numerous cues enacted by the women which were used by the raters to infer her socio-sexuality, including eyebrow flashes, glancing at the confederate, and a lack of attention paid to the task (Stillman & Maner, 2009). Previous research in the same area has demonstrated that sociosexuality can be inferred with relative accuracy even when presented with very little information. One study found that perceivers' ratings of male sociosexuality correlated well with self-reported sexuality after perceivers were exposed to a one-minute silent video of the men being interviewed (Gangestad, Simpson, DiGeronimo, & Biek, 1992).

Finally, inferences of personality traits have more generally been linked to behavioral cues as well. As early as the 1930s, researchers were interested in the accuracy with which raters could perceive personality traits based on thin-slice exposure; that is, exposure to audio or video recordings that are so short as to lack meaningful content. For instance, Estes (1938) showed that first-impression judgments provided a more accurate rating of personality traits such as impulsivity, dominance and apathy than could be attributed to chance. More recent research has shown that first-impression ratings after brief exposure to recorded beha-viors can be reliably predictive of such variables as job performance and success, deception, trustworthiness, voting behavior, anxiety, and sexual orientation, among many others (Ambady & Rosenthal, 1992; Ambady, Hallahan, & Conner, 1999).

Consistent with the important role of interpersonal behavior in the development of accurate interpersonal inferences, Campbell et al. (2013; study 2) hypothesized that romantic partners likely convey their evalua-tions of each other via their behavior, with this process being one way that romantic partners develop accurate inferences of how closely they match their partner's ideals. Specifically, they examined the possibility that indi-viduals may display differing patterns of interpersonal behavior based on how closely their partners match their ideals, and that inferences about partner discrepancies may be influenced by these behaviors. This possibi-lity was investigated using a conflict resolution setting, where couples were asked to discuss while being videotaped an issue that had caused friction in their relationship. When individuals reported larger discrepancies between their ideals and partner perceptions, they were observed to behave in a more negative, and less positive, manner toward their partner during the discussion. The partners of individuals engaging in more negative, and less positive, behaviors during the discussion were then more accurate when inferring how closely they matched their partner's ideals. In other words, both positive and negative partner behaviors partly mediated the association between partners' pre-discussion perceived discrepancies and actors' post-discussion inferences, indicating that partners' behaviors during the discussion were providing actors with critical diagnostic information, which was then incorporated into their assessment of the partners' discrepancies.

CONCLUSIONS AND FUTURE DIRECTIONS

... relationship scholars seek laws governing individuals' *interactions* with each other – or the influence each person's behavior exerts on his or her partner's behavior. Thus, the tissue of a relationship, and the object of study, is the oscillating rhythm of influence observed in the interactions of two people.

(Berscheid, 1999, p. 261).

In these two lines, Ellen Berscheid both defined the nature of a close, dyadic relationship and the optimal approach to investigating relationship processes. Relationships exist at the intersection of two individuals, and to assess the laws governing these interactions, relationship scholars need to study how partners influence each other. In this chapter we have focused on theoretical and empirical work emphasizing dyadic influences in relationships from the perspective of the Ideal Standards Model (ISM), work that heeds Berscheid's advice. There are at least three important themes to this body of work that we discuss below.

1. Dyadic consequences of perceived discrepancies

It is important to always keep in mind that in relationships, individuals are not only evaluating their partner, their partner is also evaluating them. Indeed, when an individual communicates a desire for his or her partner to make personal and/or interpersonal changes, it is important to assess the implications of these regulation attempts for (a) both partners, as well as the (b) relationship, particularly (c) over time (Overall et al., 2006, 2009). Asking for change may be hurtful to the relationship in the short-term, but *not* asking for change may be devastating to the relationship in the long-term. If this body of research had not assessed how individuals feel when asked to make changes by their partner, the dyadic nature of motivations for engaging in this pro-relationship behavior would not have been discovered and therefore this behavior would not be adequately understood. Additionally, if this research did not follow the dyadic effects of regulation attempts in relationships over time, advice columnists could not be blamed for suggesting that research supports the notion that asking each other to make changes is *bad* for relationships.

Additionally, whereas individuals are not as satisfied in relationships when they perceive their partner as not closely matching their own image of an ideal partner, there is a robust finding showing that individuals are also uniquely less satisfied in relationships when they fail to match their partner's image of an ideal partner (as rated by their *partner*). Although both the "actor" and "partner" are less satisfied when a discrepancy exists between the actor's ideal standards and partner perceptions, there are unique emotional and motivational outcomes associated with each discrepancy (i.e., these discrepancies had different "negative" consequences). When individuals feel their partner does match their own ideals, they tend to feel more dejection related emotions and adopt a promotion focus mindset. When individuals do not match their partner's ideals, however, they tend to feel more agitation related emotions and adopt a prevention focus mindset. What these differences mean for how intimates go about addressing problems in their relationship is an important next step in this research.

Another future direction for this research is to determine if the dyadic effects discussed above vary across the three ideal standard dimensions in meaningful ways across context and/or time. For example, could there be a different emotional reaction based on which dimension the discrepancy is on in different relationship contexts? For instance, if someone perceived him or herself to not match his or her partner's ideal standards, would it make a difference if that discrepancy was on the attractiveness dimension or the status/resources dimension when at the beginning of the relationship compared to in an established relationship? Also, would regulatory attempts have positive long-term outcomes when enacted in relatively new compared to established relationships, or for personal characteristics that are difficult to change? Also, are optimal relationships those in which partners are in agreement with each other's ideals and perceptions of each other? Research on these questions is needed.

2. Interpersonal accuracy of partner evaluations

According to the ISM, one of the main functions of ideal standards is to help individuals evaluate the health of a romantic relationship by identifying areas of strength and weakness in both a romantic partner and the self (Simpson et al., 2001). The findings of Campbell et al. (2013) provide evidence for this diagnostic function of ideal standards by showing that individuals are accurately picking up on how they are being assessed compared to their partner's ideals.

But why might it be important in relationships to develop this type of interpersonal accuracy in partner evaluations? Judgments are guided by both accuracy goals involving the desire to make a correct conclusion and directional goals involving the desire to reach a particular conclusion (Kunda, 1990). This distinction relates to the differences between epistemic and esteem needs within close relationships (Gagné & Lydon, 2004). Whereas individuals are often motivated to view their relationship in a positive manner (Murray,

1999) and avoid threatening thoughts and feelings (e.g., Simpson, Ickes, & Blackstone, 1995), there are also instances (e.g., deciding whether to escalate commitment to the relationship, making important relationship decisions) where individuals are motivated to gather information in an attempt to better understand their relationship (De La Ronde & Swann, 1998; Swann, De La Ronde, & Hixon, 1994). These processes can operate simultaneously (Lackenbauer, Campbell, Rubin, Fletcher, & Troister, 2010). However, the nature of the content and function of ideal standards may be particularly well suited for gathering information to meet epistemic relationship needs relative to more globally measured constructs. Future research needs to better understand the relationship contexts that shift the focus from more, compared to less, accuracy, as well as from more, or less, positive bias.

3. The calibration of inferred ideal discrepancies

Campbell et al. (2013) were the first to demonstrate that individuals are picking up and using information communicated to them by their partner's behavior during important relationship interactions. This information is used to generate accurate inferences regarding how closely they match their partner's ideal, at least on the warmth/trustworthiness dimension. This calibration of inferred ideal discrepancies from a partner's behavior is consistent with the previously discussed perspective on accuracy motives in relationship. Specifically, situations that are diagnostic for the relationship should activate accuracy motives, and as relationships develop and partners interact across more domains, they are also likely to navigate many relationship diagnostic situations (e.g., Braiker & Kelley, 1979). Over time, therefore, there are many opportunities in relationships to be exposed to information conveying the presence and magnitude of a partner's discrepancies that should result in a greater correspondence between inferred and actual ideal discrepancies between partners. Future research repeatedly measuring couples over time, and across different diagnostic situations, could provide further evidence of how individuals develop more accurate inferences of their partner's regard as couples enter and exit diagnostic situations.

Future research should follow couples over time to get a sense of the trajectory of accuracy in relationships, and how the development of accuracy is associated (or not) with important relationship outcomes. Additionally, following couples over time allows for assessing different contexts that may be particularly relevant to each of the three ideal dimensions at different times. For example, over time an individual's physical appearance can significantly change, becoming more or less fit, strengthening the association between relationship processes and perceived discrepancies on the health/vitality dimension. Additionally, over time individuals may experience significant changes to their career status (e.g., getting a promotion; losing a job) that could make perceived discrepancies on the status/resources dimension particularly relevant. It is possible that current research guided by the ISM has not found consistent effects for the health/vitality or status/resources dimensions because they have not adequately assessed couple's perceptions in these contexts.

CODA

Perhaps the most consistent theme in the study of romantic relationships is the pivotal importance of individuals feeling understood, valued, and supported by their partner (Reis, 2007). This theme mirrors Berscheid's (1999) focus on interactions between partners when studying relationship processes, and is the primary theme of the research, guided by the Ideal Standards Model (ISM), discussed in the chapter. Overall, the degree to which individuals match their partner's ideal standards has very important dyadic and relationship outcomes.

REFERENCES

Ambady, N., Hallahan, M., & Conner, B. (1999). Accuracy of judgments of sexual orientation from thin slices of behavior. *Journal of Personality and Social Psychology*, 77(3), 538–547.

Ambady, N., & Rosenthal, R. (1992). Thin slices of expressive behavior as predictors of interpersonal consequences: A meta-analysis. *Psychological Bulletin*, 111(2), 256–274.

Baldwin, M. W. (1992). Related schemas and the processing of social information. *Psychological Bulletin*, 112, 461–484.

Berscheid, E. (1999). The greening of relationship science. *American Psychologist*, 54(4), 260–266.

Braiker, H. B., & Kelley, H. H. (1979). Conflict in the development of close relationships. In R. L. Burgess & T. L. Huston (Eds.), *Social Exchange in Developing Relationships* (pp 135–168). New York: Academic Press, Inc.

Buss, D. M., & Schmitt, D. P. (1993). Sexual strategies theory: An evolutionary perspective on human mating. *Psychological Review*, 100, 204–232.

Campbell, L., Overall, N. C., Rubin, H., & Lackenbauer, S. D. (2013). Inferring a partner's ideal discrepancies: Accuracy, projection, and the communicative role of interpersonal behaviour. *Journal of Personality and Social Psychology*, 105, 217–233.

Campbell, L., Simpson, J. A., Kashy, D. A., & Fletcher, G. J. (2001). Ideal standards, the self, and flexibility of ideals in close relationships. *Personality and Social Psychology Bulletin*, 27(4), 447–462.

De La Ronde, C., & Swann, Jr, W. B. (1998). Partner verification: Restoring shattered images of our intimates. *Journal of Personality and Social Psychology*, 75(2), 374–382.

Estes, S. G. (1938). Judging personality from expressive behavior. *The Journal of Abnormal and Social Psychology*, 33(2), 217–236.

Fincham, F. D. (2003). Marital conflict correlates, structure, and context. *Current Directions in Psychological Science*, 12(1), 23–27.

Fincham, F. D., & Beach, S. R. (1999). Conflict in marriage: Implications for working with couples. *Annual Review of Psychology*, 50(1), 47–77.

Fishtein, J., Pietromonaco, P. R., & Barrett, L. F. (1999). The contribution of attachment style and relationship conflict to the complexity of relationship knowledge. *Social Cognition*, 17(2), 228–244.

Fletcher, G. J. O., Simpson, J. A., Campbell, L., & Overall, N. C. (2015). Pair-bonding, romantic love, and evolution: The curious case of Homo sapiens. *Perspectives on Psychological Science*, 10(1), 20–36.

Fletcher, G. J. O., Simpson, J. A., & Thomas, G. (2000). Ideals, perceptions, and evaluations in early relationship development. *Journal of Personality and Social Psychology*, 79, 933–940.

Fletcher, G. J. O., Simpson, J. A., Thomas, G., & Giles, L. (1999). Ideals in intimate relationships. *Journal of Personality and Social Psychology*, 76(1), 72–89.

Gagné, F. M., & Lydon, J. E. (2004). Bias and accuracy in close relationships: An integrative review. *Personality and Social Psychology Review*, 8(4), 322–338.

Gangestad, S. W., & Simpson, J. A. (2000). The evolution of human mating: Trade-offs and strategic pluralism. *Behavioral and Brain Sciences*, 23(4), 573–587.

Gangestad, S. W., Simpson, J. A., DiGeronimo, K., & Biek, M. (1992). Differential accuracy in person perception across traits: Examination of a functional hypothesis. *Journal of Personality and Social Psychology*, 62(4), 688–698.

Higgins, E. T. (1997). Beyond pleasure and pain. *American Psychologist*, 52(12), 1280–1300.

Holland, B., Dozier, L., & Holland, E. (1964). Baby Don't Do It [recorded by Marvin Gaye]. On How Sweet It Is to Be Loved by You [Record]. Detroit, Michigan: Tamla Records.

Kelley, H. H., Berscheid, E., Christensen, A., Harvey, J. H., Huston, T. L., Levinger, G., McClintock, E., Peplau, L. A., & Peterson, D. (1983). *Close relationships*. New York: Freeman.

Kunda, Z. (1990). The case for motivated reasoning. *Psychological Bulletin*, 108(3), 480–498.

Lackenbauer, S. D., & Campbell, L. (2012). Measuring up: The unique emotional and regulatory outcomes of different perceived partner-ideal discrepancies in romantic relationships. *Journal of Personality and Social Psychology*, 103(3), 472–488.

Lackenbauer, S. D., Campbell, L., Rubin, H., Fletcher, G. J., & Troister, T. (2010). The unique and combined benefits of accuracy and positive bias in relationships. *Personal Relationships*, 17(3), 475–493.

Maisel, N.C., Gable, S. L., & Strachman, A. M. Y. (2008). Responsive behaviors in good times and in bad. *Personal Relationships*, 15, 317–338.

McNulty, J. K. (2008). Forgiveness in marriage: Putting the benefits into context. *Journal of Family Psychology*, 22, 171–175.

McNulty, J. K. (2010). Forgiveness increases the likelihood of subsequent partner transgressions in marriage. *Journal of Family Psychology*, 24, 787–790.

McNulty, J. K., & Russell, V. M. (2010). When "negative" behaviours are positive: A contextual analysis of the long-term effects of problem-solving behaviors on changes in relationship satisfaction. *Journal of Personality and Social Psychology*, 98, 587–604.

Murray, S. L. (1999). The quest for conviction: Motivated cognition in romantic relationships. *Psychological Inquiry*, 10(1), 23–34.

Murray, S. L., Holmes, J. G., & Griffin, D. W. (2000). Self-esteem and the quest for felt security: How perceived regard regulates attachment processes. *Journal of Personality and Social Psychology*, 78(3), 478–498.

Overall, N. C., Fletcher, G. J. O., & Simpson, J. A. (2006). Regulation processes in intimate relationships: The role of ideal standards. *Journal of Personality and Social Psychology*, 91, 662–685.

Overall, N. C., Fletcher, G. J. O., Simpson, J. A., & Sibley, C. G. (2009). Regulating partners in intimate relationships: The costs and benefits of different communication strategies. *Journal of Personality and Social Psychology*, 96, 620–639.

Overall, N. C., Sibley, C. G., & Travaglia, L. K. (2010). Loyal but ignored: The benefits and costs of constructive communication behavior. *Personal Relationships*, 17(1), 127–148.

Reis, H. T. (2007). Steps toward the ripening of relationship science. *Personal Relationships*, 14, 1–23.

Reis, H. T., Clark, M. S., & Holmes, J. G. (2004). Perceived partner responsiveness as an organizing construct in the study of intimacy and closeness. In D. J. Mashek & A. Aron (Eds.), *Handbook of Closeness and Intimacy* (pp. 201–225). Mahwah, NJ: Lawrence Erlbaum Associates, Inc.

Rusbult, C. E., & Zembrodt, I. M. (1983). Responses to dissatisfaction in romantic involvements: A multidimensional scaling analysis. *Journal of Experimental Social Psychology*, 19(3), 274–293.

Simpson, J. A., Fletcher, G. J. O., & Campbell, L. (2001). The structure and function of ideals standards in close relationships. In G. J. O. Fletcher & M. Clark (Eds.), *Blackwell handbook of social psychology: Interpersonal processes* (pp. 86–106). Oxford, England: Blackwell.

Simpson, J. A., Ickes, W., & Blackstone, T. (1995). When the head protects the heart: Empathic accuracy in dating relationships. *Journal of Personality and Social Psychology*, 69(4), 629–641.

Stillman, T. F., & Maner, J. K. (2009). A sharp eye for her SOI: Perception and misperception of female sociosexuality at zero acquaintance. *Evolution and Human Behavior*, 30, 124–130.

Swann Jr, W. B., De La Ronde, C., & Hixon, J. G. (1994). Authenticity and positivity strivings in marriage and courtship. *Journal of Personality and Social Psychology*, 66(5), 857–869.

10

For it is in giving that we receive: the benefits of sacrifice in relationships

LISA C. DAY AND EMILY A. IMPETT

In "The Gift of the Magi," O. Henry tells the story of a young married couple, Jim and Della, who are too poor to buy each other presents for their first Christmas together. In acts of great sacrifice and love, they each secretly decide to sell their most prized possessions to buy one another gifts. Jim sells his pocket watch to buy Della a comb for her beautiful long hair, and Della sells her hair to buy Jim a chain for his watch. Ironically then, when they each receive their gifts, Jim no longer has the watch for which Della has bought him a chain, and Della no longer has the hair for which Jim has bought her a comb. At first glance, Jim and Della's decisions to give up the possessions they value the most might seem foolish; in the end, their gifts to each other have no use. But, the author is quick to explain that Jim and Della's decisions to sacrifice for each other are in fact very wise decisions, as expressing that we care about the people we love is a greater gift than any material possession.

In this tragic yet beautiful story, O. Henry makes a very insightful observation about the importance of being willing to give up or *sacrifice* things that we strongly desire in order to please our relationship partners. In fact, a growing literature on close relationships supports the moral of the "Gift of the Magi" story – that sacrifices made with the best interests of the partner in mind have the potential to benefit the giver, the recipient, and the relationship (see review by Impett & Gordon, 2008). This work highlights that in interdependent relationships in which partners' interests and outcomes are intertwined, sacrifice is both inevitable and necessary. Not all sacrifices are as major or quite as touching as the ones that Jim and Della made for each other. Instead, most sacrifices tend to be relatively mundane, such as going to your partner's favorite restaurant instead of your own, taking out the trash on your day off, or picking up your child from daycare when it's

This work has been supported by a Social Science and Humanities Research Council (SSHRC) predoctoral fellowship awarded to Lisa C. Day, and a SSHRC Insight Grant and Insight Development Grant awarded to Emily A. Impett.

your partner's turn. But, when taken together, even these small, daily sacrifices can have a significant impact on overall relationship functioning (Impett, Gable, & Peplau, 2005).

In this chapter, we review this growing literature on sacrifice, emphasizing the crucial role that sacrifice plays in optimal relationship development and maintenance. We should note at the outset that we have focused our discussion on sacrifices made in the context of adult romantic relationships because the majority of research on sacrifice has focused on romantic bonds. However, people give to and receive sacrifices from a variety of relationship partners, and developing an understanding of sacrifice within the context of other relationships such as friendship and parent–child relationships is an important endeavor, one that we return to at the end of this chapter. Our chapter is organized into five major sections. In the first section, we define sacrifice and review the ways in which sacrifice has been measured in psychological research. In the second section, we discuss the benefits that a willingness to sacrifice can bring to relationships. In the third section, we present a motivational account of sacrifice and review research showing that people's goals for sacrifice can powerfully impact their own well-being, as well as the quality and success of their relationships. In the fourth section, we review research showing that the way that people regulate the emotions that arise when making a sacrifice – in particular, the extent to which people express or suppress the emotions that they genuinely feel – is a critical element in satisfying relationships. In the fifth section, we conclude by discussing what we see as interesting but currently unanswered questions as well as promising directions for future research on sacrifice.

DEFINING TERMS: WHAT IS SACRIFICE?

Sacrifice has been defined as foregoing immediate self-interest in order to promote the well-being of a partner or a relationship (Impett & Gordon, 2008; Van Lange, Rusbult, Drigotas, Arriaga, Witcher & Cox, 1997). Sacrifices are most frequently discussed in the context of situations in which two people have personal interests that directly conflict with each other. As romantic relationships develop and partners' lives become more intertwined, situations of conflicting interests are inevitable. Romantic partners depend on each other to meet their needs in many domains, including finances, parenting responsibilities, emotional support, and sex (Rusbult & Van Lange, 2003). Over time, and across all of these domains, it is unrealistic to assume that partners' desires or goals will always be perfectly aligned (Gere, Schimmack, Pinkus, & Lockwood, 2011). In some situations of conflicting interests, one partner's interests are directly at odds with the other's, making it difficult or impossible for both partners to get what they want. When these dilemmas arise in relationships, one or both partners will be required to make a sacrifice.

For example, in a situation in which one partner would like to go out dancing on a Friday evening, while the other partner wants to stay home and relax, their interests are directly at odds. If the couple still wants to spend time together, and in the absence of some sort of compromise or choosing to engage in another activity altogether, one partner will get his or her way, while the other partner will not: either the couple will stay at home and relax or go out for a night on the town.

The types of sacrifice that people can make for a romantic partner range in size from small, seemingly mundane sacrifices such as going to a party when you are not in the mood, to larger, more life-altering sacrifices such as learning a new language or choosing to move to a new city or country so that your partner can pursue his or her dream career (Impett & Gordon, 2008). Clearly, couples have more frequent opportunities to make small sacrifices on a day-to-day basis than they do to make large sacrifices that change their lives. Another important distinction is whether sacrifices are *active* or *passive* in nature (Van Lange, Rusbult et al., 1997). When people make an active sacrifice, they do something that they do not particularly want to do either for or with their partner, such as cleaning the house or driving several hours with their partner in the car to run some errands. Passive sacrifices, on the other hand, involve forsaking a desirable activity, such as giving up an afternoon with friends to spend time with your partner's family (Van Lange, Rusbult et al., 1997). In many cases, sacrifices contain both active and passive elements. That is, oftentimes, when people do something that they do not particularly want to do for their partner's sake, they are also giving up things they would like to do in the process.

The situations in which partners' interests conflict can take place in any domain in which partners depend on each other. Research has found that people report making sacrifices in a variety of domains. In terms of smaller, frequent sacrifices, the most commonly reported domains of sacrifice include sacrifices that have to do with friends and family (e.g., spending time with a partner's family or spending less time with one's own family), as well as those that have to do with recreational activities and social obligations (e.g., going to parties or events that one does not want to attend) (Impett et al., 2005). Other common domains of sacrifice include running errands for a partner, making sacrifices in the domains of school and work, making changes to one's health and lifestyle, and changing communication patterns in relationships. In addition to small, daily sacrifices, partners are also sometimes called upon to make more major, life-altering sacrifices. In a study of dating couples who were asked to discuss the most important or meaningful sacrifice that they had made for their partner over the course of their relationship (Impett et al., 2012), common sacrifices involved spending time alone or giving up a sense of personal freedom, sacrificing other interpersonal relationships, providing financial support to one's partner, relocating to a new city or state, turning down potentially lucrative job offers in other geographical regions, limiting college choices to remain in the same area as their partner, and attempting to change personality traits (e.g., neuroticism, jealousy) to please one's partner.

BENEFITS: IS SACRIFICE GOOD FOR RELATIONSHIPS?

Sacrifice is not only necessary in long-term relationships, but it also has the potential to benefit and strengthen relationships. Willingness to engage in sacrifice has unique benefits for the recipient of the sacrifice, the giver of the sacrifice, and the relationship as a whole. The first and most obvious benefit of sacrifice is that – assuming that the recipient wants what the giver provides – the recipient will have his or her immediate needs met. To recall our earlier example of a couple in which the wife wants to go out dancing on Friday night while the husband wants to stay home and relax, if the wife agrees to make a sacrifice and stay in and relax instead of going out, the husband will have his immediate needs for sleep and relaxation met. In addition to receiving the tangible things that they want, recipients of sacrifice also receive less tangible, but arguably more important benefits. When people perceive that their partner is willing to give up their own self-interest to meet their needs, they know that their partner is invested in and cares about the relationship (Joel, Gordon, Impett, & Keltner, 2013; Wieselquist et al., 1999). Thus recipients of sacrifice receive two types of benefits. First, they receive tangible benefits from having their immediate needs met. Second, attribution theory suggests that recipients are also likely to infer that the sacrifice means that their partner is committed, invested, and concerned about their well-being (Kelley, 1973). As such, recipients of sacrifice may derive an added sense of security that comes from knowing that their partner cares about them and is responsive and willing to meet their needs.

Less obvious are the ways in which givers themselves benefit from sacrificing their interests for the good of their partner. Although people incur tangible costs when sacrificing to meet their partner's needs, such as giving up an afternoon with friends in order to run errands with their partner, they also benefit personally by being able to maintain views of themselves as good, responsive relationship partners (Holmes & Murray, 1996). In fact, on days when people report making small sacrifices, they report increased satisfaction with their relationship (Ruppel & Curran, 2012). Further, Reis, Maniaci, and Rogge (2014) found that on days when individuals reported more acts of compassionate love – acts during which one is concerned for a partner's well-being and responsive to his or her needs – their spouses reported higher marital quality.

In fact, sacrifice has been found to uniquely benefit romantic relationships in ways that other costly activities such as daily hassles with a partner do not. In one study, Clark and Grote (1998) found that people who reported engaging in more communal behaviors – such as sacrifice – for their romantic partners and friends experienced enhanced quality of relationships. In this same study, however, when people reported that they had incurred other personal costs that were not meant to benefit a partner, such as experiencing daily hassles, the quality of their friendships and romantic relationships actually declined. This work suggests that small, frequent sacrifices may be the most beneficial to romantic relationships, as they come at a relatively low cost, but also communicate caring concern for one's partner. People who have a strong communal motivation to meet their partners' needs and do so without expectation for reciprocation – that is, those who are high in communal strength (Mills, Clark, Ford, & Johnson, 2004; see also review by Clark & Mills, 2012) – are especially likely to benefit from sacrifice. Research has shown that people who are high in communal strength tend to feel more positive emotions when making sacrifices for their romantic partner, as well as feel more appreciated by their partner and experience increased relationship satisfaction on days when they sacrifice for their partner, as compared to those lower in communal strength (Kogan et al., 2010). Research has also shown that an important reason why highly communal people experience sacrifice as highly rewarding is because they feel more authentic or "true" to themselves when they sacrifice to please their partner, as compared to those who are less communal (Kogan et al., 2010).

Relatedly, communal orientation – the motivation to meet other people's needs in general – has also been found to have benefits in terms of giving to others. For individuals who are high in communal orientation, giving to other people is a part of the self, and integral to one's self-concept. Research on communal orientation suggests that when communally oriented people give to close others, the personal benefits that they receive are largely unintentional. That is, while their primary motivation is to care for others, they often experience unanticipated rewards such as boosts in positive emotions from giving to others (Le, Impett, Kogan, Webster, & Cheng, 2013). Taken together, research on communal strength and communal orientation indicates that highly communal people experience these rewards of sacrifice and giving to others, not because they are motivated to receive them, but because giving up their own self-interest allows them to verify or authenticate an important part of who they are as giving people.

Greater willingness to sacrifice can also be beneficial for romantic relationships as a whole, as reported by both partners in the relationship. Several studies have found that people who are more willing to sacrifice for their romantic partner also report greater relationship satisfaction and stability (Van Lange, Agnew, Harnick, & Steemers, 1997; Van Lange, Rusbult, et al.,

1997). For example, in one study of married couples, people who reported a greater willingness to sacrifice important personal interests for the sake of their romantic partner at the beginning of the study were more satisfied and less likely to have broken up with their partner 1 ½ years later (Van Lange, Rusbult, et al., 1997). Further, when people make costly daily sacrifices for their romantic partner, they tend to perceive their partner as more valuable on subsequent days in order to justify their greater investment in the relationship (Murray et al. 2009). These sacrifices, in turn, impact how the partner on the receiving end feels about the relationship as well. When people perceive that their partner is willing to sacrifice their own interests for the sake of the relationship, they feel a sense of trust that their partner will be responsive to their needs and feel more committed to the relationship as a result (Joel et al., 2013; Wieselquist et al., 1999).

It is important to note that while research has generally shown that people who are more willing to sacrifice have higher relationship satisfaction than those who are less willing, not everyone benefits from an increased willingness to sacrifice. In particular, research has shown that people who are high in attachment anxiety – that is, people who tend to be preoccupied with concerns about being abandoned by their partner and have high needs for reassurance from their partner – do not tend to benefit from sacrifice as much as those who are relatively more securely attached (for a review of attachment research, see Simpson & Rholes, 2012). Research by Ruppel and Curran (2012) has shown that for individuals low in attachment anxiety (those who are relatively more securely attached), the more frequently they make small, daily sacrifices for a romantic partner, the more satisfied they feel with their relationship. However, for people who are relatively more anxiously attached, frequency of daily sacrifice was not associated with relationship satisfaction. The authors suggest that this might be because anxiously attached individuals are so preoccupied with their value to their partner that they might not be able to enjoy the benefits of sacrifice such as the positive feelings associated with meeting a partner's needs and the anticipation of reciprocity.

Sacrifice is often beneficial; however, this is not always the case – in fact sacrifice can even be quite costly – when taken to an extreme. The term unmitigated communion refers to the motivation to meet another person's needs to the exclusion of one's own needs (Helgeson & Fritz, 1998). People who are high in unmitigated communion are excessively concerned with meeting the needs of their romantic partner, so much so that they actually ignore their own needs in an attempt to meet the needs of their partner (Fritz & Helgeson, 1998). Research has shown that unmitigated communion is associated with higher levels of depression and lower levels of subjective well-being (Aube, 2008). Thus, it seems likely that the willingness to sacrifice can be beneficial for romantic relationships as long as partners do not completely lose sight of their own needs and desires. Although no research to date has specifically investigated the role of unmitigated communion in shaping people's willingness to sacrifice or their satisfaction with sacrifice, research stemming from interdependence theory suggests that relationships are the most successful when partners feel that their levels of commitment to the relationship are mutual. For example, in samples of both dating and married couples, Drigotas, Rusbult, and Verette (1999) found that people who perceived their levels of commitment and their partner's levels of commitment to be relatively more equal or mutual experienced enhanced relationship relative to those who perceived a greater discrepancy in commitment between the two partners. Further, recent research has shown that while people who are high in sexual communal strength – those who are highly motivated to meet their partner's sexual needs – are able to maintain sexual desire over time (Muise, Impett, Kogan, & Desmarais, 2013) and have romantic partners who are more satisfied and committed to the relationship (Muise & Impett, 2015), people high in unmitigated communion specific to the domain of sexuality do not reap these same rewards (Muise & Impett, 2014). Fortunately, research suggests that one-sided giving is more the exception than the rule in romantic relationships. In fact, in most romantic relationships, partners display mutual styles of giving – where they take both their own and their partner's needs into account when making decisions – although mutual sacrifice is less common in relationships where there is a power discrepancy between partners (Neff & Harter, 2002a). More research is needed to investigate the conditions under which the willingness to sacrifice can be taken too far, as well as the role of mutuality specifically in the domain of sacrifice in ongoing romantic relationships, a point to which we return at the end of the chapter.

MOTIVATION: WHY DO PEOPLE SACRIFICE?

Given that sacrifice is inherently costly, *why* do romantic partners choose to make sacrifices for one another? A growing body of work suggests that people sacrifice for a variety of reasons and that people's *motivations* for giving up their own self-interest shape the outcomes of sacrifice – and are sometimes more important than the simple act of sacrifice itself. Based on approach-avoidance motivational theory (see reviews by Carver, Sutton, & Scheier, 2000; Elliot & Covington, 2001), people's motivations for sacrifice can be classified into two broad types of goals (see review by Impett & Gordon, 2008). When people sacrifice for approach goals, they focus on trying to bring about positive outcomes in their relationships, such as making their partner happy or increasing intimacy in their relationship. In contrast, when people sacrifice for avoidance goals, they focus on averting negative outcomes, such as feeling guilty, disappointing their partner, or causing conflict in their relationship. For example, consider a man who decides to surprise his wife on their wedding anniversary by cooking her a romantic dinner after the couple has put their kids to bed. Perhaps he went out of his way because he is excited about their anniversary and wants to show his wife how much he loves and appreciates her. Alternatively, he could have forgotten their anniversary last year and wanted to prevent his wife from feeling hurt or let down again. In both of these examples, the man is engaging in the same behaviors (i.e., surprising his wife, preparing a nice dinner), yet he is motivated by two different sorts of goals – goals which research has shown have important implications for the happiness and success of relationships (see review by Gable & Impett, 2012).

In an experience sampling study of individuals in dating relationships who provided reports of daily sacrifices each day for 14 consecutive days, on days when people sacrificed for approach goals such as to make their partner happy or to increase intimacy in the relationship, they experienced boosts in positive emotions and increases in relationship quality (Impett et al., 2005). In contrast, on days when they sacrificed to avoid negative outcomes such as disappointing their partner, feeling guilty, or causing tension in the relationship, they experienced increased negative emotions and relationship conflict. More strikingly, the extent to which people sacrificed for approach versus avoidance goals predicted the success and happiness of relationships over time. Specifically, the more that people sacrificed for approach goals over the course of the 2-week diary study, the more satisfied they were and the more likely they were to still be together with their romantic partner 1 month later. In contrast, the more people sacrificed for avoidance goals, the less satisfied they felt and the more likely they were to have broken up with their partner 1 month later. Thus, the sacrifices that partners made had different consequences depending on whether they were made for approach goals, such as wanting to communicate caring concern for the partner, or for avoidance goals, such as wanting to prevent an argument.

People's goals for sacrifice not only shape their own experiences, but also shape the recipients' experiences as well. In another daily experience study of both members of romantic couples, sacrifice goals predicted increased positive emotions and relationship quality for the recipient of sacrifice, whereas avoidance goals predicted increased negative emotions (Impett, Gere, Kogan, Gordon, & Keltner, 2013). Again in this study, sacrifice goals were associated with the long-term success of relationships, as those who made more approach-motivated sacrifices during the course of the diary study reported greater satisfaction, as did their romantic partners, at a 3-month follow-up, whereas those who made more avoidance-motivated sacrifices and their partners reported less relationship satisfaction and closeness, and had more thoughts about breaking up with their partner 3 months later. Therefore, it is not simply whether or not people sacrifice or the overall frequency of sacrifice that is important for maintaining relationship quality; people's reasons for sacrifice matter as well.

There are important individual differences that shape people's goals for making a sacrifice for their romantic partner. Whereas individuals who are more anxiously attached – those who are fearful of losing their romantic partner – tend to be more willing to sacrifice both for approach and for avoidance goals, people who are more avoidantly attached – those who are more fearful of becoming dependent on their romantic partner – tend to make fewer approach-and more avoidance-motivated sacrifices (Impett & Gordon, 2010). Given that avoidance-motivated sacrifices tend not to provide the same benefits as those made for approach goals, this research suggests that people who are either anxiously or avoidantly attached are less likely than those who are more relatively more securely attached to reap all the potential rewards of sacrificing for a romantic partner.

Why does sacrificing to please one's partner or create intimacy in relationships benefit relationships while sacrificing to avoid conflict seems to ironically backfire? Recent research has begun to shed light on some of the reasons why people's motivations for sacrifice matter. Thus far, research suggests the importance of two mechanisms: the emotions that people feel when they sacrifice in pursuit of different goals and people's self-reported feelings of authenticity. First, regarding the role of emotions, research has shown that the emotions that people experience are a critical reason why approach sacrifice is so beneficial and why avoidance sacrifice can be so costly. The more frequently people sacrifice for approach goals such as to make their partner happy, the greater positive emotions, such as excitement and joy, they tend to experience, and in turn, both partners report feeling more satisfied with their relationship (Impett et al., 2005; Impett et al., 2013). In contrast, the more frequently people sacrifice for avoidance goals such as to avoid conflict or a partner's disappointment, the greater negative emotions, such as frustration and resentment, they tend to experience, and these negative emotions in turn have been shown to diminish both partners' satisfaction and ironically lead to even more conflict in the relationship (Impett et al., 2013). The mediating role of emotions has been demonstrated when partners make sacrifices for each other in the course of daily life and in the laboratory when partners discuss major sacrifices that they have made for each other, demonstrating that emotional experience plays an important role in both smaller, daily sacrifices as well as in more consequential sacrifices. No research to date has looked at the possible moderating role of successfully versus unsuccessfully meeting the goals that people strive to pursue when they make a sacrifice for a partner on the emotions felt during a sacrifice. For example, if a woman sacrifices to avoid conflict with her boyfriend and successfully prevents conflict from ensuing, she might feel frustrated while making the sacrifice, but may experience a sense of relief from successfully meeting her goal.

In addition to emotional experience, the extent to which people feel that they have been genuine or authentic when making a sacrifice for their partner is another important mechanism of the link between sacrifice goals and personal and interpersonal outcomes. Sometimes people feel authentic or "true" to themselves when they sacrifice their self-interest for a romantic partner (Impett et al., 2012; Kogan et al., 2010). Other times, however, people feel as though they are putting on a "false face" or acting disingenuously when they sacrifice or give up their own interests (Neff & Harter, 2002b). Several studies combining experimental, cross sectional, and daily experience methods have shown that when people sacrifice for approach goals, they experience greater feelings of authenticity, and in turn, they experience greater personal well-being and higher quality relationships (Impett, Javam, Le, Asyabi-Eshghi, & Kogan, 2013). In contrast, when people sacrifice to avoid negative outcomes, they often feel that they have been less authentic, and these decreased feelings of genuineness seem to detract from their well-being and the quality of their relationships.

While sacrificing to pursue positive outcomes tends to feel more authentic than doing so to avoid negative outcomes, avoidance-motivated sacrifice does not *always* feel inauthentic. Recent research has shown there are particular people who feel that they are being relatively genuine when they sacrifice for avoidance goals. In particular, people who construe the self as highly interconnected with close others – those with an interdependent self-construal (Markus & Kitayama, 1991) – do not experience declines in authenticity when they sacrifice to pursue avoidance goals such as preventing their partner's disappointment or warding off conflict in their relationship (Impett, Le, Asyabi-Eshghi, Day, & Kogan, 2013). People with an interdependent self-construal are also buffered against drops in emotional well-being and relationship quality when they sacrifice for avoidance goals. Thus, it seems likely that sacrificing for avoidance goals is not costly for highly interdependent people since doing so allows them to maintain the harmony in social interactions that they so highly value (Elliot, Chirkov, Kim, & Sheldon, 2001). Future research is needed to identify other important boundary conditions of the effects of approach and avoidance sacrifice goals on personal and interpersonal outcomes.

EMOTIONAL SUPPRESSION: HOW DO WE DEAL WITH OUR EMOTIONS WHEN WE SACRIFICE?

Despite the fact that many people who sacrifice for their romantic partners reap unintended rewards, they also incur some costs by choosing to give up their own self-interest. As such, not all sacrifices are experienced as inherently joyful. In some cases, people experience negative emotions such as feelings of irritation, resentment, or anger when they sacrifice for their partner. For example, consider a young couple furnishing their first home together. One partner might be particularly excited about shopping for all of the necessities for their new home, while the other might be less than enthused. If the less enthusiastic partner agrees to shop all weekend for furniture, it is possible that he or she will experience negative emotions, such as frustration or boredom at some point from engaging in an undesired activity for an extended period of time. What should people do with the negative emotions that might arise when they do something they are not particularly excited about? Should they express their emotions openly and honestly to their partner or keep them to themselves? Similarly, should people fake or feign interest in something that their partner wants to do if they are not really "feeling it"?

To date, research has focused primarily on one emotion regulation strategy: emotional suppression, defined as attempting to inhibit or conceal the emotions that people experience (Gross, 1998; Gross & John, 2003). In some ways, suppressing one's emotions could be seen as an intuitive way to manage situations of conflicting interests in relationships. The partner who is reluctant to spend the weekend shopping for furniture might try to conceal their disinterest or irritation in an attempt to avoid hurting their partner's feelings. However, a growing body of work on emotion regulation has shown that the suppression of emotions is typically quite costly for both partners in relationships (see review by English, John, & Gross, 2013). For example, people who report that they habitually suppress their emotions tend to experience less positive and more negative emotions in general (Gross & John, 2003), feel less authentic, and show poorer social functioning (John & Gross, 2004; Srivastava, Tamir, McGonigal, John, & Gross, 2009) than those who are less inclined to suppress their emotions.

Similar costs to suppression have been documented in the context of sacrifice. For example, in a study in which couples discussed major sacrifices that they had made for each other over the course of their relationship, increased suppression was associated with decreased authenticity, and in turn with more negative emotions and less positive emotions (Impett et al., 2012). In a related line of work, researchers have shown that people who consistently self-conceal – or hide personal information from their romantic partner – tend to have lower relationship satisfaction and commitment as a result of diminished feelings of autonomy in their relationships. Further, on days when people self-conceal more in their romantic relationships, they feel that their needs for autonomy, relatedness, and competence are met to a lesser degree than on days with less self-concealment, and in turn they tend to feel lower relationship satisfaction and commitment (Uysal, Lin, Knee, & Bush, 2012). Similarly, Impett et al. (2012) also found that suppressing emotions when making daily sacrifices for a romantic partner is costly for both partners in the relationship. In a daily experience study, on days when people suppressed their emotions when sacrificing their self-interest for their romantic partner, both partners reported decreased emotional well-being and relationship quality. The effects of suppression on both partners' outcomes were mediated by authenticity, suggesting that when people suppress their emotions when making a sacrifice for the good of the relationship, they feel less authentic, and these decreased feelings of genuineness or authenticity dampen both partners' well-being and feelings about the relationship. In this study, increased suppression during daily sacrifice was also associated with more frequent thoughts about ending the relationship 3 months later, suggesting that suppression is also related to relationship instability (Impett et al., 2012). Taken together, the results of these studies on suppression and self-concealment suggest that when people are actively trying to conceal their feelings from their partner, they feel that they are not being authentic, or true to themselves, which in turn detracts from both partners' emotional experiences and feelings about the relationship.

Additional research suggests that when one partner suppresses their emotions, to a certain extent, their romantic partner can detect that they are not being genuine and, as a result, they experience decreases in emotional well-being and relationship quality. In one study, the more people reported suppressing their emotions – both when discussing an important sacrifice that they had made for their partner in the lab and when making sacrifices in daily life – the more their romantic partner indicated that they were indeed suppressing their emotions (Impett, Le, Kogan, Oveis, & Keltner, 2014). In other words, suppression was to a certain extent detectable, perhaps due to the fact that there are some nonverbal indicators of suppression identified in previous research such as compromised responsiveness and appearing more withdrawn and hostile (Butler et al., 2003; Butler, Lee, & Gross, 2007) that make suppression detectable. Further, the more people thought their partner suppressed their emotions, the less authentic they perceived them to be, and in turn, perceived partner inauthenticity during sacrifice was associated with poorer personal well-being and relationship quality (Impett, Le et al., 2014).

Suppression is not always costly, however. Recent research has shown that people with an interdependent self-construal actually experience benefits when suppressing negative emotions when sacrificing their self-interest for a romantic partner. In a daily experience study of individuals in dating relationships, on days when interdependent people suppressed negative emotions when making a sacrifice for their romantic partner, they actually felt *more* authentic, and experienced increased emotional well-being and higher quality relationships as a result (Le & Impett, 2013). In contrast, those who had a less interdependent sense of self experienced the typical negative consequences of suppression, including decreased authenticity, poorer emotional well-being, and lower quality relationships. This study suggests that suppression during sacrifice is not always negative, and in fact for some people, it may have positive consequences, likely because suppressing negative emotions helps highly interdependent people maintain the harmony in their close relationships that they so highly value. Future research is needed to replicate these findings and investigate the effects of suppressing emotions during sacrifice on the romantic partners of people who are highly interdependent. It is possible that the partners of highly interdependent people might experience benefits comparable to the benefits experienced by the partner who suppresses his or her emotions. Alternatively, it is possible that being in a relationship with a partner who suppresses his or her emotions when sacrificing for the good of the relationship is almost always costly, regardless of how the giver construes themselves in social interactions with others. Research is needed to test these two possibilities.

It is important to note that emotional suppression is only one of many emotion regulation strategies that partners may use when they experience unpleasant emotions when making a sacrifice. Another strategy that we think has the potential to help people deal with negative emotions in a healthier way than suppression is cognitive reappraisal, defined as attempts to reconstrue an emotionally arousing situation in a non-emotional way (Gross, 2002). For example, if one partner is experiencing boredom or frustration while furniture shopping, he or she could reconstrue the situation as a chance to spend time with their partner, or an opportunity to make their partner feel loved, rather than a waste of their time. Future research should investigate different emotion regulation strategies in addition to suppression to determine how partners can best manage the negative emotions that may arise during sacrifice.

TAKING STOCK: WHERE HAVE WE BEEN AND WHERE ARE WE HEADED?

Given that research on sacrifice has grown tremendously in recent years, the time is ripe to take stock of important questions that have yet to be answered and to look toward the future of research on sacrifice. In the last section of our chapter, we highlight five key areas that we see as places of growth in research on sacrifice including: research on the decision making processes that people engage in when deciding whether or not to sacrifice for a romantic partner; research on the importance of mutuality of sacrifice between partners; research that sheds light on the question regarding whether the decision to sacrifice represents an automatic impulse or more controlled decision; research on how people's feelings about sacrifice might shift over the time from before they make decisions until after the consequences of those decisions have played out; and research on sacrifice in other types of relationships besides romantic relationships such as the relationship between parents and their children.

First, sacrifices sometimes involve quite complex decision making processes that we as relationship scientists know surprisingly little about (see review by Joel, MacDonald, & Plaks, 2013). What kinds of individual and relational factors do people take into account when they make decisions about whether they will pursue their self-interests versus sacrifice for the good of their relationship? We would argue that when people are faced with decisions about whether or not to sacrifice, they are likely to weigh the relevant costs and benefits – both to themselves and to their romantic partner – when making these important decisions. But *what are* the particular costs and benefits that people weigh when they make decisions that hold great importance and perhaps even symbolic value in their relationship? How does the decision making process impact the quality of people's relationships? Preliminary research suggests that people who are high in communal strength make decisions in giving, prosocial ways that ultimately benefit both partners in the relationship, as compared to those who are less communal. For example, several studies from our lab (Day & Impett, 2015) suggest that when people contemplate making sacrifices for their romantic partner, those who are more communally motivated tend to perceive engaging in sacrifice as less costly to the self and more beneficial to their partner. In turn, this decreased focus on the self and increased focus on the partner leads people to be more willing to sacrifice as well as to feel more satisfied with their relationships. In another set of studies in our lab in the domain of sexuality (Day, Muise, Joel, & Impett, 2015), we have found that when people experience situations in which their partner has a high desire for sex but they are less than enthused, highly communally oriented people react to these desire-discrepant situations in ways that enrich rather than detract from the quality of their relationship. In particular, they report that they are less likely than people who are low in communal motivation to be deterred by the costs of sex (e.g., losing time spent sleeping, relaxing, or doing other things). Instead, they are even more motivated by the ways that they can benefit their partner (e.g., making their partner feel desired and valued, creating intimacy in the relationship). Although these findings await replication, they suggest that there are important individual differences that shape how people make decisions about sacrifice – both in general and in the domain of sexuality – and that the ways in which people consider the costs and benefits of sacrifice shape people's emotional experiences and the quality of their romantic relationships.

A second key direction for future work concerns identifying the circumstances under which decisions to sacrifice are automatic versus controlled in nature. Interdependence theorists assert that when partners find themselves in situations of conflicting interests, one or both partners will undergo a *transformation of* their initial self-interested motives into more prosocial motives to benefit their partner (Van Lange, Rusbult et al., 1997). In addition, interdependence theorists have long suggested that the transformation process can happen quite quickly and automatically (Kelley & Thibaut, 1978; Rusbult & Van Lange, 2003). For example, one set of studies has shown that people who are low in trait self-control show a greater willingness to sacrifice (Righetti, Finkenauer, & Finkel, 2013), especially if they are highly communal. This work suggests that some people have a gut instinct to act prosocially, but then later, self-control sets in and allows people to override their automatic inclination to give to others to focus more on what may be best for themselves. This set of studies is also consistent with more recent work on prosocial emotions (Keltner, Kogan, Piff, & Saturn, 2014; Rand, Greene, & Nowak, 2012), which suggests that humans might be inherently motivated to be kind, to act prosocially, and to care for others (Keltner, 2009). On the other hand, though, two additional sets of studies out of independent labs have shown that people who have higher trait self-control are more willing to make sacrifices in romantic relationships than those with lower self-control, suggesting that gut-level impulses to act based on self-interest might need to be overridden in a controlled and effortful manner in order for people to sacrifice (Findley, Carvallo & Bartak, 2014; Pronk & Karremans, 2014).

How can we make sense of these conflicting findings in this literature on self-control and sacrifice? Interestingly, whereas the studies conducted by Righetti et al. (2013) focused on people's willingness to make quite small, oftentimes seemingly mundane sacrifices, the studies conducted by Findley et al. (2014) and one of the studies by Pronk and Karremans (2014) focused on more major sacrifices such as moving across the country away from one's own friends and family. It is possible that when people are called upon to sacrifice something relatively minor for a close, romantic partner, their first instinct might be to act prosocially, as these kinds of sacrifices happen quite frequently and partners might not need to think much about whether they will make a low-cost sacrifice in order to benefit their partner. However, during the less frequent but likely more emotionally charged times when people are called upon to make large, even life-altering sacrifices, their gut instinct might be to act based on their own self-interest, but then with time and cognitive effort, they might be able to override these self-oriented motivations and take broader relationship factors into consideration. It will be important for future research to unpack these conflicting findings, as well as situate them in the broader literature on altruism and helping.

A third key area that is ripe for future research has to do with how people's feelings about sacrifice might change over the course of time. Most of the existing research on sacrifice has examined how people feel about sacrifices *after* they have been made. Much less research has investigated how people feel about sacrifices *before* they are made, or looked at potential changes in people's feelings about sacrifices over time. An important feature of large, costly sacrifices is that they typically involve people having a great deal of lead time in which to make decisions about whether or not to sacrifice. Hence, for costly behaviors, such as moving to a new city so that one's partner can take a better job, people are challenged to make decisions in the distant future based on thoughts and feelings which may change significantly as the event approaches. Work in our lab suggests that as the time for making a major sacrifice for one's partner draws near, people view sacrifices as more costly to the self than when they originally made the decision to sacrifice (Day, Asyabi-Eshghi & Impett, 2015). These findings fit with existing literature on temporal construal theory showing that temporal proximity heightens people's sensitivity to potential obstacles and the possibility of negative outcomes (Liberman & Trope, 1998). To the extent that people's romantic partners are able to pick up on these changing feelings, they may view these "changes of heart" as a potential breach of their partner's earlier agreements or promises. Consistent with this possibility, research has shown that people oftentimes fail to keep promises that they have made to their romantic partner because they promise too ambitiously and do not think about the concrete consequences and costs of what these promises entail when they first make them (Peetz & Kammrath, 2011). In turn, this research shows that people report being less satisfied with their relationships when their partners break the promises that they have made too ambitiously in the past. Based on this work, in future research, it will be important to examine how both the giver and the recipient's feelings about sacrifice and their relationship potentially change over the course of time.

A fourth interesting direction that researchers could take is bettering our understanding of the importance of mutuality of sacrifice in romantic relationships. To date, much of the research on sacrifice has been conducted from the perspective of one romantic partner, typically the person who sacrifices as opposed to the recipient (see Impett, Gere, Kogan, Gordon, & Keltner, 2014 for an exception). Interdependence theory predicts that couples will reap the most benefits when both romantic partners are willing to sacrifice for each other; however, when one partner defects and there is not a mutual give-and-take in relationships, it is possible that both partners will experience fewer benefits (Kelly & Thibaut, 1978). Indeed, research on commitment has shown that when feelings of commitment are not mutual in relationships, partners experience poorer dyadic adjustment (Drigotas et al., 1999). Research that includes data from both members of romantic dyads is needed to determine if there are optimal levels of willingness to sacrifice across partners.

Finally, future research on sacrifice should move beyond what has been an almost exclusive focus on romantic relationships. As we mentioned at the outset of the chapter, the overwhelming majority of research on sacrifice has focused on romantic relationships including dating relationships and marriage. Given that romantic relationships are arguably one of our strongest and most important communal bonds (Clark & Mills, 2012), it is not surprising that research has focused on understanding sacrifice in this context. However, sacrifice is common in other types of relationships, such as among family members and close friends. Perhaps no other relationship involves greater sacrifice than the relationship between parents and their children. In parent-child relationships, sacrifice is essential, and unlike in most adult close relationships, is imbalanced in nature, with care being given completely unilaterally from parent to child, at least in the early parenting years. In some new research on parenting in our lab, we have found that parents who are communally motivated to meet their child's needs experience caring for their children – even when it comes at some cost to the self – as highly rewarding (Le & Impett, 2015). This work also shows that one important reason why communal parents reap benefits is because they feel more authentic when responsively meeting their child's needs. In short, giving to their children is inherently rewarding for communally motivated parents. It will be particularly interesting for future work to examine the sacrifices that adult children make for their parents as they enter older adulthood and require more assistance and care. This new work on parenting highlights the importance of examining the role of sacrifice in other types of relationships beyond romantic relationships.

CONCLUDING COMMENTS

Although making sacrifices for a romantic partner is inherently costly to the self, as we hope to have shown in this chapter, the benefits of sacrificing for a romantic partner frequently outweigh the costs of doing so. Nearly two decades of research on sacrifice corroborate the moral of the "Gift of the Magi" story and show that the willingness to sacrifice for a romantic partner, particularly when those sacrifices are motivated by a desire to make one's partner happy, is beneficial for both partners in the relationship. This research suggests that a critical way to promote optimally functioning and flourishing romantic relationships is for people to focus on what they can give to their partner, rather than what they can receive or get in return. In this chapter, we hope to have shown that, in the context of ongoing close relationships, it is in giving that we truly receive.

REFERENCES

Butler, E. A., Egloff, B., Wilhelm, F. H., Smith, N. C., Erickson, E. A., & Gross, J. J. (2003). The social consequences of expressive suppression. *Emotion*, 3, 48–67. doi:10.1037/1528–3542.3.1.48

Butler, E. A., Lee, T. L., & Gross, J. J. (2007). Emotion regulation and culture: Are the social consequences of emotion suppression culture-specific? *Emotion*, 7, 30–48. doi:10.1037/1528-3542.7.1.30

Carver, C. S., Sutton, S. K., & Scheier, M. F. (2000). Action, emotion, and personality: Emerging conceptual integration. *Personality and Social Psychology Bulletin*, 26, 741–751. doi:10.1177/0146167200268008

Clark, M. S., & Grote, N. K. (1998) Why aren't indices of relationship costs always negatively related to indices of relationship quality? *Personality and Social Psychology Review*, 2, 2–17. doi:10.1207/s15327957pspr0201_1

Clark, M. S., & Mills, J. (2012). Communal (and exchange) relationships. In P. A. M. Van Lange, A. W. Kruglanski, & E. T. Higgins (Eds.), *Handbook of theories of social psychology* (pp. 232–250). Thousand Oaks, CA: Sage Publications.

Day, L. C., Asyabi-Eshghi, B., & Impett, E. A. (2015). I'd move mountains for you: How the passage of time influences people's feelings about making costly sacrifices for a romantic partner. Unpublished manuscript.

Day, L. C., & Impett, E. A. (2015). Communal motivation and decisions about sacrifice in romantic relationships. Unpublished manuscript.

Day, L. C., Muise, A. Joel, S., & Impett, E. A. (2015). To do it or not to do it? How communally motivated people navigate sexual interdependence dilemmas. *Personality and Social Psychology Bulletin*, 41, 791–804.

Drigotas, S. M., Rusbult, C. E., & Verette, J. (1999). Level of commitment, mutuality of commitment, and couple well-being. *Personal Relationships*, 6, 389–409. doi:10.1111/j.1475-6811.1999.tb00199.x

Elliot, A. J., & Covington, M. V. (2001). Approach and avoidance motivation. *Educational Psychology Review*, 13, 73–92. doi:10.1023/A:1009009018235

Elliot, A. J., Chirkov, V. I., Kim, Y., & Sheldom, K. M. (2001). A cross-cultural analysis of avoidance (relative to approach) personal goals. *Psychological Science*, 12, 505–510. doi:10.1111/1467-9280.00393

English, T., John, O. P., & Gross, J. J. (2013). Emotion regulation in close relationships. In J. A. Simpson & L. Campbell (Eds.), *The Oxford handbook of close relationships* (pp. 500–513). New York, NY: Oxford University Press.

Findley, M. B., Carvallo, M., & Bartak, C. P. (2014). The effect of self-control on willingness to sacrifice in close relationships, *Self and Identity*, 13, 334–344. doi:10.1080/15298868.2013.826595

Fritz, H. L., & Helgeson, V. S. (1998). Distinctions of unmitigated communion from communion: Self-neglect and over involvement with others. *Journal of Personality and Social Psychology*, 75, 121–140. doi:10.1037/0022-3514.75.1.121

Gable, S. L., & Impett, E. A. (2012). Approach and avoidance motives and close relationships. *Social and Personality Psychology Compass*, 6, 95–108. doi:10.1111/j.1751-9004.2011.00405.x

Gere, J., Schimmack, U., Pinkus, R. T., & Lockwood, P. (2011). The effects of romantic partners' goal congruence on affective well-being. *Journal of Research on Personality*, 45, 549–559. doi:10.1016/j.jrp.2011.06.010

Gross, J. J. (1998). Antecedent- and response-focused emotion regulation: Divergent consequences for experience, expression, and physiology. *Journal of Personality and Social Psychology*, 74, 224–237. doi:10.1037/0022-3514.74.1.224

Gross, J. J., & John, O. P. (2003). Individual differences in two emotion regulation processes: Implications for affect, relationships, and well-being. *Journal of Personality and Social Psychology*, 85, 348–362. doi:10.1037/0022-3514.85.2.348

Helgeson, V. S., & Fritz, H. L. (1998). A theory of unmitigated communion. *Personality and Social Psychology Review*, 2, 173–183. doi:10.1207/s15327957pspr0203_2

Holmes, J. G., & Murray, S. L. (1996). Conflict in close relationships. In E. T. Higgins, A. W. Kruglanski (Eds.), *Social psychology: Handbook of basic principles* (pp. 622–654). New York, NY: Guilford Press.

Impett, E. A., Gable, S. L., & Peplau, L. A. (2005). Giving up and giving in: The costs and benefits of daily sacrifice in intimate relationships. *Journal of Personality and Social Psychology*, 89, 327–344. doi:10.1037/0022-3514.89.3.327

Impett, E. A., Gere, J., Kogan, A., Gordon, A. M., & Keltner, D. (2014). How sacrifice impacts the giver and the recipient: Insights from approach-avoidance motivational theory. *Journal of Personality*, 82, 390–401. doi:10.1111/jopy.12070

Impett, E. A., & Gordon, A. M. (2008). For the good of others: Toward a positive psychology of sacrifice. In S. J. Lopez (Ed.), *Positive psychology: Exploring the best in people volume 2*, (pp. 79–100). Westport, CT: Praeger Publishers.

Impett, E. A., Javam, L., Le, B. M., Asyabi-Eshghi, B., & Kogan, A. (2013). The joys of genuine giving: Approach and avoidance sacrifice motivation and authenticity. *Personal Relationships*, 20, 740–754. doi:10.1111/pere.12012

Impett, E. A., Kogan, A., English, T., John, O., Oveis, C., Gordon, A. M., & Keltner, D. (2012). Suppression sours sacrifice: Emotional and relational costs of suppressing emotions in romantic relationships. *Personality and Social Psychology Bulletin*, 38, 707–720. doi:10.1177/0146167212437249

Impett, E. A., Le, B. M., Asyabi-Eshghi, B., Day, L. C., & Kogan, A. (2013). To give or not to give? Sacrificing for avoidance goals is not costly for the highly interdependent. *Social Psychological and Personality Science*, 4, 649–657. doi:10.1177/1948550612474673

Impett, E. A., Le, B. M., Kogan, A., Oveis, C., & Keltner, D. (2014). When you think your partner is holding back: The costs of perceived partner suppression during relationship sacrifice. *Social Psychological and Personality Science*, 5, 542–549. doi:10.1177/1948550613514455

Joel, S., Gordon, A., Impett, E. A., MacDonald, G., & Keltner, D. (2013). The things you do for me: Perceptions of a romantic partner's investments promote gratitude and commitment. *Personality and Social Psychology Bulletin*, 39, 1333–1345. doi:10.1177/0146167213497801

Joel, S., MacDonald, G., & Plaks, J. E. (2013). Romantic relationships conceptualized as a judgement and decision making domain. *Current Directions in Psychological Science*. doi:10.1177/0963721413498892

John, O. P., & Gross, J. J. (2004). Healthy and unhealthy emotion regulation: Personality processes, individual differences, and life span development. *Journal of Personality*, 72, 1301–1333. doi:10.1111/j.1467-6494.2004.00298.x

Kelley, H. H. (1973). The processes of causal attribution. *American Psychology*, 28, 107–128.

Kelley, H. H., & Thibaut, J. W. (1978). *Interpersonal relations: A theory of interdependence*. New York, NY: Wiley.

Keltner, D. (2009). *Born to be good: The science of a meaningful life*. New York: W. W. Norton.

Keltner, D., Kogan, A., Piff, P. K., & Saturn, S. R. (2014). The sociocultural appraisals, values, and emotions (SAVE) framework of prosociality: Core processes from gene to meme. *Annual Review of Psychology*, 65, 425–460. doi:10.1146/annurev-psych-010213-115054

Kogan, A., Impett, E. A., Oveis, C., Hui, B., Gordon, A. M., & Keltner, D. (2010) When giving feels good: The intrinsic benefits of sacrifice in romantic relationships for the communally motivated. *Psychological Science, 21,* 1918–1924. doi:10.1177/09567610388815

Le, B. M., & Impett, E. A. (2013). When holding back helps: Suppressing negative emotions during sacrifice feels authentic and is beneficial for highly interdependent people. *Psychological Science, 24,* 1809–1815. doi:10.1177/0956797613475365

Le, B. M., & Impett, E. A. (2015). The rewards of caregiving for communally motivated parents. *Social Psychological and Personality Science, 6,* 758-765.

Le, B. M., Impett, E. A., Kogan, A., Webster, G. D., & Cheng, C. (2013). The personal and interpersonal rewards of communal orientation. *Journal of Social and Personal Relationships, 30,* 695–712. doi:10.1177/0265407512466227

Liberman, N., & Trope, Y. (1998). The role of feasibility and desirability considerations in near and distant future decisions: A test of temporal construal theory. *Journal of Personality and Social Psychology, 75,* 5–18. doi:10.1037/0022-3514.75.1.5

Markus, H. R., & Kitayama, S. (1991). Culture and the self: Implications for cognition, emotion, and motivation. *Psychological Review, 98,* 224–253. doi:10.1037/0033-295X.98.2.224

Mills, J., Clark, M. S., Ford, T. E., & Johnson, M. (2004). Measurement of communal strength. *Personal Relationships, 11,* 213–230. doi:10.1111/j.1475-6811.2004.00079.x

Muise, A., & Impett, E. A. (2015). Good, giving and game: The relationship benefits of communal sexual responsiveness. *Social Psychological and Personality Science, 6,* 164–172. doi:10.1177/1948550614553641

Muise, A., & Impett, E. A. (2014, July). Is it good to be giving in the bedroom? The costs and benefits of communal motivation in the sexual domain. In E. A. Impett (Chair), *What givers receive in communal relationships. Paper presented at the International Association for Relationships Research Conference,* Melbourne, Australia.

Muise, A., Impett, E. A., Kogan, A., & Desmarais, S. (2013). Keeping the spark alive: Being motivated to meet a partner's sexual needs sustains sexual desire in long-term romantic relationships. *Social Psychological and Personality Science, 4,* 267–273. doi:10.1177/1948550612457185

Murray, S. L., Holmes, J. G., Aloni, M., Pinkus, R. T., Derrick, J. L., & Leder, S. (2009). Commitment insurance: Compensating for the autonomy costs of interdependence in close relationships. *Journal of Personality and Social Psychology, 97,* 256–278. doi:10.1037/a0014562

Neff, K., & Harter, S. (2002a). The role of power and authenticity in relationship styles emphasizing autonomy, connectedness or mutuality among adult couples. *Journal of Social and Personal Relationships, 19,* 835–857. doi:10.1177/0265407502196006

Neff, K., & Harter, S. (2002b). The authenticity of conflict resolutions among adult coupes: Does women's other-oriented behavior reflect their true selves? *Sex Roles, 47,* 403–417. doi:10.1023/A:1021692109040

Peetz, J., & Kammrath, L. (2011). Only because I love you: Why people make and why they break promises in romantic relationships. *Journal of Personality and Social Psychology, 100,* 887–904. doi:10.1037/a0021857

Pronk, T. M., & Karremans, J. C. (2014). Does executive control relate to sacrificial behaviour during conflicts of interests? *Personal Relationships, 21,* 168–175. doi:10.1111/pere.12024

Rand, D. G., Greene, J. D., & Nowak, M. A. (2012). Spontaneous giving and calculated greed. *Nature, 489,* 427–430. doi:10.1038/nature11467

Reis, H., Maniaci, M., & Rogge, R. (2014). The expression of compassionate love in everyday compassionate acts. *Journal of Social and Personal Relationships*, 31, 651–676. doi:10.1177/0265407513507214

Righetti, F., Finkenauer, C., & Finkel, E. J. (2013). Low self-control promotes the willingness to sacrifice in close relationships. *Psychological Science*, 24, 1533–1540. doi:10.1177/0956797613475457

Ruppel, E. K., & Curran, M. A. (2012). Relational sacrifices in romantic relationships Satisfaction and the moderating role of attachment. *Journal of Social and Personal Relationships*, 29, 508–529. doi:10.1177/0265407511431190

Rusbult, C. E., & Van Lange, P. A. (2003). Interdependence, interaction, and relationships. *Annual Review of Psychology*, 54, 351–375. doi:1146/annurev. psych.54.101601.145059

Srivastava, S., Tamir, M., McGonigal, K. M., John, O. P., & Gross, J. J. (2009). The social costs of emotional suppression: A prospective study of the transition to college. *Journal of Personality and Social Psychology*, 96, 883–897. doi:10.1037/a0014755

Uysal, A., Lin, H. L., Knee, C. R., & Bush, A. L. (2012). Personality and Social Psychology. *Personality and Social Psychology Bulletin*, 38, 39–51. doi:10.1177/0146167211429331

Van Lange, P. A. M., Agnew, C. R., Harinck, R., Steemers, G. E. (1997). From game theory to real life: How social value orientation affects willingness to sacrifice in ongoing close relationships. *Journal of Personality and Social Psychology*, 73, 1330–1344. doi:10.1037/0022-3514.73.6.1330

Van Lange, P. A., Rusbult, C. E., Drigotas, S. M., Arriaga, X. B., Witcher, B. S., & Cox, C. L. (1997). Willingness to sacrifice in close relationships. *Journal of Personality and Social Psychology*, 72, 1373–1395. doi:10.1037/0022-3514.72.6.1373

Wieselquist, J., Rusbult, C. E., Foster, C. A., & Agnew, C. R. (1999). Commitment, pro-relationship behavior, and trust in close relationships. *Journal of Personality and Social Psychology*, 77, 942–966. doi:10.1037/0022-3514.77.5.942

11

For better or worse: compassionate goals create good relationships in good times and bad

JENNIFER CROCKER AND AMY CANEVELLO

People in good relationships are healthier and happier than people in poor-quality relationships, or people who lack relationships altogether (e.g., Baumeister & Leary, 1995; Uchino, 2004). But how can people create the kinds of relationships that are good for their health and well-being? Creating and maintaining high-quality relationships can be challenging; people must confront the risk of rejection and fears that they will be exploited or that the relationship partner won't be there when needed. Close relationships inevitably involve occasional divergence of interests, relationship issues, temptations, and conflicts. If not handled constructively, conflicts can undermine relationship quality, leading to dissolution of relationships, resulting in feelings of loss, failure, or rejection.

Relationship scientists have identified types of people who tend to have better or worse relationships, as well as relationship processes that characterize better and worse relationships. For example, people with low self-esteem, insecure attachment styles, or high rejection sensitivity tend to have unhappier relationships than people with high self-esteem, secure attachment styles, or low rejection sensitivity (e.g., Downey & Feldman, 1996; Mikulincer & Shaver, 2003; Murray, Holmes, & Griffin, 2000). And relationships characterized by mutual support, responsiveness, and trust fare better than relationships lacking these processes (Reis, Clark, & Holmes, 2004; Rempel, Holmes, & Zanna, 1985). Yet, in our view, these findings by themselves do not indicate how to create the good relationships people want. How can people change their level of self-esteem, sensitivity to rejection, or insecure attachment to relationship partners? Furthermore, most people realize that they *should* be supportive, responsive to their relationship partners' needs, and communicate constructively, yet they sometimes find it difficult to do these things.

In this chapter, we describe a program of research suggesting that intentions toward relationship partners – specifically, *compassionate goals* to be constructive and supportive – are a key to creating good relationships. When people strive to be supportive and constructive toward their relationship partners, they tend to become more supportive and responsive over time. Their relationship partners notice and respond in kind, becoming more supportive and responsive themselves. Over time, the mutual support and responsiveness that these intentions foster improve the quality of relationships for both people. Thus, intentions to be supportive and constructive can be the starting point of creating good relationships. Furthermore, the positive dynamics that characterize these relationships can result in increased self-esteem, greater feelings of security in the relationship, and less concern about rejection.

Our research suggests that by carefully setting their intentions toward relationship partners, people can create the good relationships they want. Furthermore, goals to be constructive and supportive foster good relationships regardless of one's level of self-esteem, attachment insecurity, or sensitivity to rejection. They do so for a variety of relationship types, from relationships between previously unacquainted college roommates, to romantic couples, and they do so in good times and in bad times, when issues and conflicts arise. Thus, this approach is quite practical; it provides a framework that people can use to create good relationships.

EGOSYSTEM AND ECOSYSTEM: MOTIVATIONAL ORIENTATIONS IN RELATIONSHIPS

Our research on compassionate goals and their consequences for relationships began with the idea that all human relationships are shaped by two fundamentally important motivational systems, which we call the egosystem and the ecosystem.

Egosystem motivational orientation

Most animals, including humans, are motivated by self-preservation (Henry & Wang, 1998). The egosystem reflects this motivation in interpersonal relationships. In the egosystem, people prioritize their own needs and desires over those of others (Crocker & Canevello, 2015; Hadden, Øverup, & Knee, 2014). When people are driven by egosystem motivation, they "manage" others using strategies such as ingratiation, manipulation, or intimidation (Crocker & Canevello, 2015). They have *self-image goals*; they try to display their desirable qualities and conceal their undesirable qualities to get what they want from others (Crocker & Canevello, 2008).

In the egosystem, people aren't always selfish; they may sacrifice or give to their relationship partners to be seen as helpful or indispensable, or to obtain something in return (Crocker & Canevello, 2012). Apparent selflessness can be motivated by self-image goals to demonstrate one's generosity to others, earn respect or admiration, or make others feel indebted (Cialdini, Brown, Lewis, Luce, & Neuberg, 1997). For example, people high in unmitigated communion seem to prioritize others' needs over their own, to the point of self-sacrifice (Fritz & Helgeson, 1998; Helgeson, 1994). However, people high in unmitigated communion attempt to establish interpersonal control by being intrusive, overly nurturant and overly protective; they try to establish or strengthen relationships by making others need them (Helgeson & Fritz, 2000). People high in unmitigated communion prioritize others' needs over their own needs for selfish reasons, such as earning others' love and admiration (Helgeson & Fritz, 1998).

Ecosystem motivational orientation

All mammals, including humans, have another motivational system that fosters caring about and caring for others (Henry & Wang, 1998). Without the motivation to care for others, mammals' offspring would not survive. The ecosystem reflects this motivation in interpersonal relationships. When people are driven by ecosystem motivation, they care about the well-being of others and try to be supportive and constructive and not harm others (Crocker & Canevello, 2015). They have compassionate goals to be constructive and supportive and not harm others.

In the ecosystem people do not necessarily sacrifice themselves for others, nor are they always selflessly giving to others at the expense of their own needs and well-being. Self-sacrifice is unsustainable, because it harms the self. In the ecosystem people tend to give to others in ways that are good for others *and* the self (Crocker & Canevello, 2012).

Do compassionate goals reflect only ecosystem motivation, or do they also reflect egosystem motivation? Several findings from our research on ecosystem motivation in college students suggest that compassionate goals reflect a distinct motivational orientation consistent with ecosystem motivation (Crocker & Canevello, 2008). When people have compassionate goals, they report that their most important goals make them feel, clear, peaceful, and loving. At those times, they believe that it is important that people take care of each other. They feel closer to others and less lonely. They tend to view interpersonal relationships in nonzero-sum terms, believing that it is possible to find win-win solutions to problems that are good for both people in a relationship. These qualities characterize people who tend to be chronically high in compassionate goals, and they fluctuate along with compassionate goals within people over time (Crocker & Canevello, 2008, 2012). Thus, compassionate goals reflect a state in which people feel connected to and care about others, and view their relationships differently.

Traits or states?

Are egosystem and ecosystem motivation psychological states, or fixed personality traits? In other words, are some people motivated by the egosystem, whereas others are motivated by the ecosystem, or is everyone motivated by each system at different times? If egosystem and ecosystem motivations are relatively fixed traits, then people might want to seek out ecosystem-motivated relationship partners, and avoid egosystem-motivated relationship partners (or vice versa). On the other hand, if they fluctuate, then people might want to understand factors that prompt them or their relationship partners to be more or less driven by the egosystem and ecosystem.

Our research suggests that egosystem and ecosystem motivation are both traits and states. These motivations vary between people (consistent with personality traits) and also vary within people over time (consistent with psychological states) in studies that repeatedly assess people's compassionate and self-image goals toward relationship partners (see Crocker & Canevello, 2012, for a discussion). In one study, approximately 40 percent of the variability in the goals occurred between people, consistent with personality traits. The remaining 60 percent of the variance occurred within people consistent with psychological states. These within-person fluctuations were not simply random, they related systematically to things that were going on in people's emotional lives and in their relationships. These findings suggest that people can shift from egosystem to ecosystem and vice versa, and that we may be able to identify the situational, personal, and relationship factors that prompt these shifts.

COMPASSIONATE GOALS AND OTHER PROSOCIAL ORIENTATIONS

How are compassionate goals related to other prosocial orientations? Researchers have developed several measures of tendencies to engage in prosocial behaviors derived from differing theoretical perspectives and programs of research. However, the similarities and differences among these measures have rarely been systematically examined, and to our knowledge no research has examined whether compassionate goals are a distinct aspect of prosocial orientations, or simply a new name for existing measures and constructs.

In three studies (Canevello & Crocker, in preparation), we examined associations among eight measures of prosocial orientations: empathic concern for others in distress (Davis, 1983), compassionate love for strangers (Sprecher & Fehr, 2005), endorsement of communal norms that people should respond to each others' needs (Clark, Ouellette, Powell, & Milberg, 1987), communion (i.e., interpersonal warmth and kindness; Bakan, 1966;

Spence, Helmreich, & Holahan, 1979), and unmitigated communion (i.e., the tendency to sacrifice one's own needs for the sake of others; Fritz & Helgeson, 1998). The measures were moderately to strongly correlated, but not so strongly correlated to suggest that they were redundant or interchangeable. Furthermore, compassionate goals explained unique variance in outcomes related to relationship functioning and psychological well-being, indicating that our measure of compassionate goals assesses an aspect of prosocial orientations not captured by existing measures and constructs. Factor analyses on the individual items in all of these measures showed that the compassionate goals items loaded on a separate factor, and no items from other measures loaded with the compassionate goals items, supporting the conclusion that compassionate goals add something new to measures of prosocial orientations.

Conceptually, intentions to be supportive and constructive are distinct from empathic concern (an emotional response to others' distress), communion (describing oneself as kind and warm), communal orientation (endorsement of a norm that people *should* respond to others' needs), unmitigated communion (feeling that one *must* help, even at the expense of the self), and compassionate love for strangers (a mix of empathic concern, altruism, and intentions to help directed toward strangers, often distant strangers). Although these other constructs may sometimes involve intentions to be constructive and supportive because people genuinely care about the well-being of others, they may also involve emotional responses without intentions (as when people feel concern for strangers in faraway places), or helping motivated by norms or obligation, rather than caring.

Overall, these findings suggest that although several measures of prosocial orientations bear a family resemblance, they are not identical twins. Compassionate goals, in particular, capture unique aspects of prosocial orientations – intentions to be constructive and supportive – and explain variance in outcomes that is not captured by other measures.

DEVELOPING GOOD RELATIONSHIPS

College roommate relationships are sometimes wonderful, blossoming into life-long friendships, and sometimes terrible, deteriorating into conflict or complete disengagement. When college students are randomly matched with roommates they didn't know prior to college, they also provide a natural laboratory for studying how people create good (or bad) relationships. In three longitudinal studies of first-year college students, including two studies of previously unacquainted roommate pairs, we have examined how compassionate goals shape relationship processes and outcomes over time (e.g., Canevello & Crocker, 2010; Crocker & Canevello, 2008).

Support. Good relationships between fully functioning adults are *mutually supportive*; both people in the relationship give and receive support. In a longitudinal study of students over the first semester of college, we found that those who were chronically high in compassionate goals toward their friends (i.e., those who tended, over time, to want and try to be supportive and constructive and not harmful in their friendships) increased in the amount of support they perceived was available to them over the first semester of college (Crocker & Canevello, 2008, Study 1). However, this increase in perceived available support was experienced only by students who were high in compassionate goals *and* low in self-image goals. When students had high self-image goals, reflecting an egosystem motivational perspective, it didn't matter how much they had compassionate goals; their perceived available social support did not increase over time.

In a second study (Crocker & Canevello, 2008, Study 2) we explored this finding in more depth. We recruited first-semester roommate pairs who were unacquainted prior to college, and asked each member of the pair to report on how much support they gave to their roommate, and how much support they received from their roommate at the start of the study and at the conclusion 3 weeks later. We found once again that students who were chronically high in compassionate goals increased in the support they said they gave to their roommates over the 3 weeks. Their roommates concurred with these reports, but only when the support provider was low in self-image goals. When support providers had high self-image goals and high compassionate goals, providers' compassionate goals were unrelated to increases in the support their roommates reported receiving.

Furthermore, recipients tended to reciprocate the support they received; when they received increased support, they gave increased support back to the provider. Thus, students with high compassionate goals and low self-image goals created mutually supportive relationships over time.

Responsiveness. Responsive people are understanding, validating, and caring (Gable & Reis, 2006). They are warm, sensitive to their partners' feelings, and want to make their partners feel comfortable, valued, listened to, and understood. In good relationships, people are responsive and perceive their relationship partners as responsive. Reis and his colleagues have suggested that perceived partner responsiveness is key to creating intimacy and closeness in relationships (Reis et al., 2004). Of course, almost everyone wants their relationship partners to be understanding, validating, and caring. The challenge is how to increase the responsiveness of relationship partners.

We proposed that when people have compassionate goals, they not only perceive their relationship partners as more responsive, they actually create more responsive partners. Two longitudinal studies of first-year college roommates support this idea (Canevello & Crocker, 2010). In one study, both members of roommate pairs completed measures of compassionate goals and their own responsiveness and their perceptions of their roommate's responsiveness at the start of the semester, once a week for 10 weeks, and at the end of the semester (Canevello & Crocker, 2010, Study 1). Students who had higher compassionate goals over the 10 weeks of the study became more responsive to their roommates over the semester, which in turn predicted increases in how responsive they perceived their roommates were to them. Thus, people with compassionate goals come to perceive their roommates as more responsive over time. Furthermore, their roommates noticed that they were more responsive, and became more responsive as well. Thus, one roommate's compassionate goals predicted increases in mutual responsiveness in the relationship over time. When people have compassionate goals, they create mutually responsive relationships (Wieselquist, Rusbult, Foster, & Agnew, 1999).

In a second study, we examined the implications of these processes for relationship quality – a composite of closeness, satisfaction, and commitment (Canevello & Crocker, 2010, Study 2). In this study, both members of roommate pairs completed measures of compassionate goals, their responsiveness, and their roommate's responsiveness, as well as reporting on their relationship quality each day for 21 days. On days students' compassionate goals were higher than usual (i.e., higher than their own average level of compassionate goals), they were more responsive to their roommates, they perceived their roommates as more responsive to them, and their feelings of closeness, satisfaction, and commitment were higher. Furthermore, their roommates noticed the increased responsiveness, and roommates' relationship quality improved as well. Analyses of change from day to day and from the beginning to the end of the study showed that compassionate goals predict increased responsiveness, increased perceptions of partners' responsiveness, and increased relationship quality over time.

These findings suggest that people can create mutually responsive and therefore better-quality relationships when they have compassionate goals toward their relationship partners.

Trust. In addition to mutual support and responsiveness, trust is another key to good relationships. Trust allows people to take the sort of risks that build close relationships, such as disclosing personal vulnerabilities and weaknesses, and caring about another despite the possibility that one will be hurt (Murray, Holmes, & Collins, 2006; Rempel et al., 1985). According to Rempel and colleagues, "Trust is certainly one of the most desired qualities in any close relationship" (Rempel et al., 1985, p. 95).

Trust typically develops in relationships over time (Rempel et al., 1985). Initially, people base trust on relationship partners' trustworthy behaviors. Later, as the relationship evolves, people draw inferences about the intentions of their relationship partners to decide if their partners are trustworthy. But these processes mean that, particularly at the initial stages of relationships, trust depends on relationship partners acting in a trustworthy manner. People are willing to trust others only when others prove that they are trustworthy.

This approach is problematic, because the default stance of "trust only after others prove themselves trustworthy" can impede the development of closeness (e.g., Murray et al., 2006). When people hold back from taking risks in a relationship, such as refraining from disclosing personal information, relationship partners may likewise decide not to take risks, and refrain from disclosing information.

How can people be the starting point of creating trust in relationships, rather than waiting for others to demonstrate their trustworthiness? We proposed that when people have compassionate goals, they become more trusting in their relationships. In our first study of college students (Crocker & Canevello, 2008, Study 1) we included measures of trust at the beginning and end of the study. Students chronically high in compassionate goals developed greater interpersonal trust over the first semester of college, although, as in the findings on support, we observed this effect only among students who also were low in self-image goals.

Our next studies examined how compassionate goals create trust. We hypothesized that people with compassionate goals disclose personal information to relationship partners regardless of their initial level of trust, because they want to be constructive and supportive. In our weekly study of first-semester roommate pairs, we included measures of trust and disclosure in each weekly measurement, as well as at the start and end of the study (Jiang, Crocker, Canevello, Lewis, & Black, 2014, Study 1). Compassionate goals one week predicted increased disclosure to roommates the following week, controlling for initial levels of trust. Roommates noticed the increased disclosure, and disclosed more in return. Thus, when participants had compassionate goals, they created increased sharing of personal information by both people in the roommate relationship. Furthermore, this increased disclosure predicted increases in trust in both roommates.

These findings have important implications for creating trust in relationships. First, it is not necessary to wait for others to prove their trustworthiness before taking risks in relationships. Indeed, regardless of their initial level of trust, students with compassionate goals disclose more to their roommates, presumably because they want to be supportive and constructive. Second, when people do disclose personal information, relationship partners tend to reciprocate, creating a relationship context in which people can be more open with each other. Third, this disclosure leads to increased trust in both people. Finally, it is noteworthy that students' own disclosure to their roommates, not their roommate's disclosure to them, predicted students' increased trust. In other words, increases in trust do not depend on whether or not relationship partners reciprocate disclosure.

RIPPLE EFFECTS

Thus far, we have seen that compassionate goals foster positive relationship processes, including mutual support, responsiveness, disclosure, and trust, in relatively new relationships. These positive processes, in turn, predict improved relationship quality over time. The benefits of compassionate goals extend beyond relationship quality, however.

Reduced insecurity. Insecure attachment styles impede the formation of close, mutually supportive relationships in adulthood (see Mikulincer & Shaver, 2003, for a review). People who are highly anxious about whether their relationship partners care for them and will be there when needed tend to drive others away with their excessive demands for reassurance, and people with avoidant attachment styles tend to be excessively independent and feel uncomfortable with closeness.

We hypothesized that positive relationship processes sparked by compassionate goals toward relationship partners lead to decreased insecurity in those relationships. In our two longitudinal studies of college roommates, we tested this hypothesis (Canevello, Granillo, & Crocker, 2013). We included measures of anxiety and avoidance in the roommate relationship at the beginning and end of our 3-week study of roommate pairs, and in each weekly survey in our ten-week study of roommates. Compassionate goals toward college roommates consistently predicted increased relationship security in the roommate relationship (i.e., decreased anxiety and avoidance) across 3 weeks (Study 1), and within weeks, from week to week, and across 3 months (Study 2). These findings suggest that people can become more secure in their relationships over time if they have compassionate goals toward their relationship partners.

Increased need satisfaction. Self-determination theory posits that people thrive when their fundamental psychological needs for autonomy, competence, and relatedness are satisfied (see Deci & Ryan, 2000, for a review; Patrick, Knee, Canevello, & Lonsbary, 2007). We hypothesized that compassionate goals foster satisfaction of these fundamental needs, particularly the need for relatedness.

In our 3-week study of college roommates, we included a measure of need satisfaction (autonomy, competence, and relatedness) at pretest and posttest. As hypothesized, when students chronically had compassionate goals toward their roommates, both their and their roommates' need satisfaction increased from pretest to posttest (Canevello & Crocker, 2011a, Study 2). Surprisingly, compassionate goals predicted not only increased relatedness, but also increased competence and autonomy. When people have compassionate goals, they *want or try* to be supportive and not harm others. Thus, compassionate goals may directly foster feelings of autonomy. And when people have compassionate goals, they may feel more competent because giving support to others increases feelings of competence.

Changing beliefs about relationships. The positive relationship processes that follow when people have compassionate goals lead to more positive experiences in relationships, and therefore could potentially change people's beliefs about how relationships in general work. In our studies of college roommates, we have investigated whether compassionate goals predict belief change in positive directions.

People with growth beliefs about relationships believe that difficulties can lead to growth and strengthening of relationships (Knee, 1998). Growth beliefs predict positive outcomes in relationships, particularly when relationship problems occur (see Knee, Patrick, & Lonsbary, 2003, for a review). In two studies, we found that compassionate goals predict increased growth beliefs about relationships (Canevello & Crocker, 2011a).

People with nonzero-sum beliefs about relationships believe that it is possible to find solutions to problems or difficulties in which both people's needs can be met, and that success for one person need not result in setbacks for others. Compassionate goals predict increased nonzero-sum beliefs about relationships over time (Crocker & Canevello, 2012).

Thus, when people have compassionate goals, they develop more optimistic and helpful beliefs about the nature of relationships in general, which could lead to more constructive approaches when relationship difficulties arise.

Growth goals. People with compassionate goals not only increase in the belief that growth is possible in relationships; they also develop stronger desires for personal growth. We hypothesized that when people have compassionate goals toward relationship partners, they want to grow in ways that will better enable them to be supportive and constructive in their relationships.

In two studies, we found that compassionate goals predict increased growth goals in relationships over time (Mischkowski, Crocker, Niiya, Canevello, & Moeller, 2014). Furthermore, increases in the desire to grow in relationships predicted subsequent increases in the desire to grow in academics. Finally, the increased desire to grow in academics predicted increased academic engagement (Mischkowski et al., 2014, Study 2). Thus, in these studies compassionate goals in roommate relationships not only had ripple effects for relationships; they also had positive ripple effects on students' academics.

Well-being. Because people in good relationships are healthier and happier than people in bad relationships or those who lack relationships altogether, we hypothesized that compassionate goals, and the positive relationship processes that follow from them, might have beneficial effects on psychological well-being.

We first tested whether compassionate goals predict decreased anxiety and symptoms of depression in a longitudinal study of first-semester college students. Students chronically high in compassionate goals showed decreased anxiety and symptoms of depression over the first semester of college (Crocker, Canevello, Breines, & Flynn, 2010, Study 1). We replicated this finding in our weekly study of first-semester college roommates, and showed that this decrease in psychological distress was explained by increases in the social support that students gave to their roommates, but interestingly not by the support they received in return (Crocker et al., 2010, Study 2). Thus, consistent with accumulating research on the benefits of giving for psychological well-being, compassionate goals predict decreased distress through their association with giving support.

In another investigation, we examined whether compassionate goals predict change in self-esteem and regard from others (Canevello & Crocker, 2011b). Consistent with other findings, we found that students with chronically high compassionate goals are more responsive to their roommates, and their increased responsiveness predicts increases in their self-esteem. In this study, we also examined whether one student's compassionate goals predict change in the regard their roommate has for them, and in the roommate's self-esteem. We found that roommates noticed the increased responsiveness of students with compassionate goals, and roommates' esteem for the students increased as a result. Furthermore, because roommates reciprocated the increase in responsiveness, showing more responsiveness back to the students, the roommates' self-esteem also increased.

Finally, we tested whether higher self-esteem predicts increased compassionate goals. Indeed, students with higher self-esteem developed more compassionate goals. Thus, we found evidence for a "virtuous cycle" in which compassionate goals predict increased self-esteem for both students and their roommates, via increased responsiveness, which in turn predicts increased compassionate goals.

Summary. Taken together, these results suggest that compassionate goals instigate a cascade of positive relationship processes, relationship outcomes, and individual outcomes in the context of new relationships. Furthermore, they have beneficial consequences for relationship partners, as well. When people have compassionate goals, they become more supportive, responsive, and trusting, and their relationship partners become more supportive, responsive, and trusting in return. These processes have benefits for the relationship quality of both people. In addition, as a result of these positive relationship processes, people feel more secure in their relationships, feel that their fundamental needs are better satisfied, develop healthier, relationship-promoting beliefs, are more motivated to grow as a person, and their psychological well-being improves. These findings suggest that, as people enter into new relationships, when they have compassionate goals they can create relationships that are good for themselves and good for others.

MAINTAINING ONGOING RELATIONSHIPS

The research we have described to this point suggests that compassionate goals help people get new relationships off to a good start. But once a relationship is well-established, do the goals people have toward their relationship partners matter? There are good reasons to think that goals might matter less in established relationships, because people in ongoing relationships have well-developed habits, patterns of behavior, and beliefs about their relationship, their partner, and themselves that might not change much over time. On the other hand, even in established relationships compassionate goals might predict important relationship dynamics.

We have recently begun to examine the role of compassionate goals in established relationships such as friendships and romantic relationships. Because this line of work is relatively new, we know less about the implications of compassionate goals in these contexts. What we do know, however, suggests that compassionate goals are beneficial even after a relationship is off to a good start.

Compassionate goals and gratitude in friendships

When people express feelings of gratitude, they strengthen relationships with responsive interaction partners (Algoe, 2012). Thus, gratitude maintains and builds ongoing relationships. We hypothesized that when people have compassionate goals, they give to their friends for more friend-centered reasons (e.g., to help the friend and prevent harm), and less self-centered reasons (e.g., to demonstrate their own positive qualities, such as being a good person). Furthermore, we hypothesized that the reasons people have for giving to their friends predict their friends' feelings of gratitude; when people have friend-centered reasons for giving, their friends will feel more gratitude, and when people have self-centered reasons for giving, their friends will feel less gratitude.

In a test of these hypotheses, we recruited nearly 100 same-sex friendship pairs. Each member of the pairs completed measures of compassionate goals, reasons for giving to their friend, and feelings of gratitude (Canevello & Crocker, 2015). Results showed that people with more compassionate goals are more likely to have friend-centered, and less likely to have self-centered, reasons for giving. Friend-centered reasons for giving, but not self-centered reasons, predicted how much gratitude their friends expressed. Thus, compassionate goals can help to bind friends together by shaping the reasons people have for giving, and in turn their friends' feelings of gratitude.

By having compassionate goals, and giving for friend-centered reasons, people can foster gratitude in their friends.

Compassionate goals and romantic relationships

Romantic relationships are another type of ongoing relationship that might be affected by people's compassionate goals. A recent longitudinal study of dating couples suggests that compassionate goals are important in these relationships as well. For example, compassionate goals toward partners strongly predicted relationship quality, and even though the dating couples in our study had very high-quality relationships at the start of the study, compassionate goals predicted increased relationship quality over time. Furthermore, people with compassionate goals feel increasingly close to their partner over time (Haynes, Crocker, Canevello, & Lewis, 2014; see also Hadden, Smith, & Knee, 2014 for similar findings). Preliminary analyses indicate that people with compassionate goals also show increases in love for their partners, caring about their partner, relationship satisfaction, non-zero-sum views of the relationship, and growth goals (unpublished data, 2014). Thus, when people have compassionate goals toward their romantic partner, they continue to create higher-quality, closer relationships with romantic partners.

In sum, although we have only recently begun to investigate the implications of compassionate goals in maintaining and improving ongoing relationships, initial evidence suggests that compassionate goals can strengthen ongoing friendships and romantic relationships.

Getting through the rough patches

Even in the best relationships, disagreements, issues, and conflicts will arise (Rusbult, Johnson, & Morrow, 1986). It is tempting to think that when people have compassionate goals, they encounter fewer personal struggles in their lives and less conflict in their close relationships. Perhaps people with compassionate goals experience fewer conflicts, are oblivious to conflicts that do arise, are conflict avoidant, or refuse to acknowledge troubles in their relationships. Evidence on this point is mixed; people with high levels of compassionate goals do not always have fewer conflicts and difficulties in their relationships than people with low levels of compassionate goals (Canevello & Crocker, 2015; Crocker & Canevello, 2008). However, people with compassionate goals construe and respond to conflicts and difficulties in more positive ways. That is, they view life's hurdles as opportunities for growth, take more constructive approaches to solving relationship problems, create trust by disclosing more during discussions about conflicts, forgive transgressions for relationship-promoting reasons, and adopt more productive strategies for overcoming difficulties. These responses to conflicts and difficulties have positive consequences for the self and others, such as increased relationship satisfaction and more optimism that relationships will last after conflict discussions. Thus, compassionate goals promote positive relationship processes during times of conflict – when people need them most.

GROWTH-SEEKING

People with compassionate goals want to learn and grow in order to overcome problems and setbacks. That is, they seek growth opportunities. As noted previously, people with compassionate goals strive for personal growth in their daily lives (Mischkowski et al., 2014). We hypothesized that this motivation to learn and grow persists when people with compassionate goals face difficult circumstances. In a first test of this hypothesis, we examined the association between compassionate goals and growth-seeking (unpublished data). The growth-seeking scale includes items such as, "When I'm faced with a difficult or stressful life situation, I'm likely to view it as an opportunity to learn and grow" (Dykman, 1998). Compassionate goals correlated positively with growth-seeking. Furthermore, in our weekly study of first-semester college roommates, students with compassionate goals toward their roommates at the beginning of the semester increased in growth-seeking across the semester, suggesting that compassionate goals promote increased growth-seeking over time (unpublished data). When we tested the reverse association – whether growth-seeking at the beginning of the semester led to changes in compassionate goals over the semester – growth-seeking did not predict increased compassionate goals over time. These findings suggest that compassionate goals promote seeking out growth and development in difficult times, but not vice versa. We speculate that wanting to be supportive of others gives people a reason to seek growth rather than stay stuck in the difficulty. Compassionate goals may enable people to transcend the potential ego-threats that difficulties can pose.

APPROACHES TO INTERPERSONAL PROBLEMS AND DIFFICULTIES

In addition to being more growth oriented in the face of difficulty, we hypothesized that people with compassionate goals adopt more constructive approaches to overcoming interpersonal problems and difficulties. Specifically, we hypothesized that when people have compassionate goals they (1) view relationship problems as a mutual concern, assuming that if one person in the relationship has a problem, it's a problem for both people because it affects the partner and relationship; (2) feel a sense of shared responsibility for working through and solving relationship issues; (3) address relationship problems promptly rather than avoid talking about problems or ignore or deny them; (4) try to identify root causes of the problem so that the underlying cause can be addressed; and (5) listen to the other person with the goal of understanding their partners' feelings and perspective, which allows them to identify and clarify misunderstandings between them and their partners. We developed a measure of these constructive approaches to relationship problems and examined the association between compassionate goals and constructive approaches in studies of college roommates and friendship, romantic, and marital dyads (Canevello, Crocker, Lewis, & Hartsell, 2014).

Across five studies, people with compassionate goals reported more constructive approaches to problems. In our ten-week study of college roommates, we found that on weeks students had more compassionate goals than usual, they also had more constructive approaches to interpersonal problems. Furthermore, compassionate goals predicted increased constructive approaches from one week to the next, and from the beginning to the end of the first semester of college. Thus, when people have compassionate goals they not only have constructive approaches to interpersonal problems in the moment; they also become more likely to take constructive approaches in the future.

Compassionate goals and the constructive approaches to interpersonal problems they foster have positive consequences for people and their relationship partners. In our ten-week study of college roommates, students' constructive approaches to interpersonal problems one week related to feeling less upset with their roommates that same week and predicted decreased upset feelings the following week, controlling for compassionate goals. Further, students who became more constructive in their approaches to problems with their roommate across the semester also became less upset with their roommates over that semester, again controlling for compassionate goals.

We examined the consequences of compassionate goals and their resulting constructive approaches to problems more closely in a sample of married couples who discussed a recent relationship problem in our laboratory. People higher in compassionate goals and constructive approaches to the conversation felt that they had better communication during the discussion; this positive communication was corroborated by their partners and predicted less relationship distress and higher relationship quality, feeling that they made more progress during the discussion, and greater willingness to discuss the problem again in the future in both relationship partners.

Thus, when people have compassionate goals, they view problems as mutual concerns that affect the relationship, feel that both partners share responsibility for improving relationships, talk about problems as they occur, listen, clarify misunderstandings, and work to identify root causes of relationship problems. This constructive approach to interpersonal problems predicts less negative feelings toward others over time, and during discussions about relationship problems, having compassionate goals and approaching the discussion in a constructive way has benefits for both people.

CREATING TRUST DURING CONFLICTS

How people deal with relationship issues and conflicts can either build or undermine trust. We hypothesized that when people have compassionate goals toward relationship partners, they will take risks in self-disclosure by discussing their real issues, their feelings, and by providing honest feedback to their partners, because they want to be constructive and supportive. We tested this hypothesis in a study of 110 dating couples (Jiang et al., 2014, Study 2). Couples came to the laboratory, completed a range of measures about their relationship, including measures of compassionate goals, trust, perceived responsiveness of their partners, and how much they disclose in their relationships. They then discussed a conflict or issue in their relationship. Following the discussion, both members of the couple completed several questionnaires about the conflict discussion.

Results showed that participants' compassionate goals prior to the discussion predicted their disclosure during the discussion. This association remained when we controlled for initial levels of disclosure, trust, perceived partner responsiveness, and partners' compassionate goals, suggesting that people with compassionate goals disclose more during conflict discussions regardless of their level of trust or perceived safety during the discussion. Furthermore, the more people disclosed during the conflict discussion, the more they trusted their partners after the discussion. This link between disclosure and trust remained when we statistically controlled for compassionate goals, initial disclosure, trust, perceived responsiveness, and partners' goals, and was not due to how much partners disclose during the discussion; it was participants' own disclosure that predicted their increased trust.

Although this finding might surprise some readers, we think of the conflict discussion as being similar to team-building exercises in which people fall, and are caught by their teammates. Building trust doesn't depend on how many times a team member catches his or her teammates; trust is built by being the one to fall. Likewise, trust is built by taking the risk to disclose. If people only disclose when they know it is safe to do so, their trust is unlikely to increase.

FORGIVENESS

The ability to forgive close relationship partners is a crucial feature of healthy relationships (Fenell, 1993). When partners transgress, forgiveness is key to repairing damage to the relationship. People can forgive their partners for selfish reasons (e.g., because they are financially dependent on their partners) or for relationship-promoting reasons (e.g., because they had worked through the problem together and were better able to understand partners' perspectives). We hypothesized that after experiencing a relationship transgression, people with compassionate goals toward partners evaluate their relationship and their partner more positively, and they feel less hurt and disappointed because they have relationship-promoting reasons for forgiving their partners.

We asked two samples of people in romantic relationships about the last time they felt hurt or wronged by their partners. Across samples, those who had compassionate goals for partners had more relationship-promoting reasons for forgiving them, and these reasons for forgiveness led people to have higher-quality relationship, feel less tension with partners, have greater esteem for partners, feel less hurt by and disappointed in partners, and feel that they had come to terms with the event (Canevello, 2014). Importantly, reasons for forgiveness had these positive consequences, regardless of how much participants forgave their partners. Thus, compassionate goals and reasons for forgiving partners benefit relationships, regardless of how much people forgive partners.

In a third study, we explored whether compassionate goals and relationship-promoting reasons for forgiveness had consequences for relationship partners. The first two studies could not rule out the possibility that when people have compassionate goals, they have positive illusions about their partners, even after partners hurt them. Thus, the benefits of compassionate goals may have been imagined by partners, or they might reflect a defensive response to the threat of a transgression. We reasoned that if the effects of people's compassionate goals were real, their partners would be able to detect their relationship-promoting reasons for forgiveness, which would then have positive consequences for partners. In a third study, 49 romantic couples wrote about a time when their partners had hurt them. We then informed each person of the event that the other had described and asked how they felt after that event. We found that when one person had compassionate goals following a perceived transgression, partners were more likely to perceive them as having relationship-promoting reasons for forgiveness, which in turn led partners to report greater relationship quality, less stress in the relationship, more disclosure, and have more peaceful, clear, and loving affect toward partners.

In sum, compassionate goals create good relationships not only when things are going well, but also during times of conflict and when relationship partners transgress.

WHEN RELATIONSHIPS END

Although some relationships last for a lifetime, many – if not most – relationships at work, with friends, with romantic partners, and even with spouses eventually end. Despite the benefits of compassionate goals for relationships, even people with compassionate goals will sometimes choose to end their relationships. We hypothesize that compassionate goals influence both the reasons people have for ending relationships and their reactions to the ending of a relationship.

Reasons for ending relationships

Because people with compassionate goals care about both their own and others' well-being, we hypothesized that they consider their partners' needs as well as their own when they choose to end relationships (see Crocker & Canevello, 2015 for a discussion). Whereas some relationship theories assume that people break off relationships when they believe their own needs can be better met in another relationship and they don't stand to lose much by breaking off the relationship (Drigotas & Rusbult, 1992; Rusbult, Drigotas, & Verette, 1994), we hypothesize that people with compassionate goals consider their partner's needs as well. They may choose to break up a relationship when they determine that the relationship is bad for their partner as well as for themselves, because both people's needs matter.

In a preliminary test of this idea, we developed a questionnaire assessing reasons for breaking up a relationship (Crocker & Canevello, 2014, Study 1, unpublished data). As predicted, people with compassionate goals were more likely to say that they would take their partner's needs and well-being into account as a reason for breaking off a relationship. For example, they were more likely to agree with items such as "When deciding whether to break up, I consider what is best for both my partner and me" and "If a relationship is good for me but not my partner, then we should consider breaking up." In a subsequent study, we replicated this finding and showed that it was not explained by socially desirable responding (Crocker & Canevello, 2014, Study 2, unpublished data).

Thus, compassionate goals might not predict whether a relationship lasts or breaks up, but they do predict the reasons people give for leaving versus staying, and how compassionate they are toward their partners when breaking off a relationship (Crocker & Canevello, 2015).

Reactions to relationship breakups

People who experience the loss of a relationship can suffer from low self-esteem, symptoms of depression, and other signs of emotional distress

(Slotter, Gardner, & Finkel, 2010). Evidence that compassionate goals predict decreases in symptoms of depression and anxiety and higher self-esteem over time suggests that compassionate goals might predict *decreased* distress over the breakup of a relationship. On the other hand, evidence that compassionate goals predict improvements in relationship quality, including closeness, satisfaction, and commitment, which previous research shows are associated with greater feelings of loss (e.g., Simpson, 1987; Sprecher, Felmlee, Metts, Fehr, & Vanni, 1998), suggests that people with compassionate goals might experience a greater sense of loss following the ending of a relationship. That is, compassionate goals might predict *increased* distress following relationship breakups because compassionate goals foster relationship quality.

We hypothesized that compassionate goals predict increased breakup distress when relationships end – specifically, that part of breakup distress that is unrelated to symptoms of depression or low self-esteem. In four studies, we examined whether compassionate goals toward romantic partners predict more breakup distress (Haynes et al., 2014). Compassionate goals toward an ex-partner predicted feeling more upset about a breakup in a sample of people who had experienced a breakup, and this link held when we controlled for several known predictors of breakup distress, symptoms of depression, and low self-esteem (Haynes et al., 2014, Study 1). Compassionate goals predicted breakup distress through feeling a loss of self when people imagined breaking up with a current romantic partner (Haynes et al., 2014, Studies 2A and 2B). In a longitudinal study of dating couples, we tested a path model and found that compassionate goals predict increased closeness, which in turn predicts feeling loss of self when imagining a breakup, which predicts distress about the breakup.

These findings point to the cost of compassionate goals; because people with compassionate goals draw closer to relationship partners over time, they feel a greater loss of self following the end of a relationship, and therefore are more distressed. However, our findings suggest that compassionate goals predict a less unhealthy form of distress, not associated with low self-esteem or symptoms of depression.

REMAINING QUESTIONS

Overall, our research on compassionate goals suggests that they foster a variety of positive relationship processes, resulting in better-quality relationships for people with compassionate goals and their relationship partners. Furthermore, when people are chronically high in compassionate goals over time, they experience a cascade of benefits, including increased feelings of security in the relationship, increases in helpful beliefs about relationships, increased desire for personal growth, and improved psychological well-being. Thus, our findings suggest that compassionate goals are a useful tool that can help people create good relationships. However, a number of questions remain.

What types of relationships benefit from compassionate goals?

Most of the research we have conducted to date has focused on new relationships, specifically relationships between college roommates who did not know each other prior to college. Are the benefits of compassionate goals limited to new relationships between people who are initially strangers?

Recent studies of friendship dyads, dating couples, and married couples suggest that compassionate goals have benefits for all of these types of relationships. Indeed, where we have tested them, our studies show a remarkable similarity across relationship types. We have not yet explored work relationships, family relationships, mentoring relationships, and so on. We expect that compassionate goals would have similar benefits for all of these types of relationships.

Whose relationships benefit from compassionate goals?

A related question is whether certain types of people benefit more from having compassionate goals than others. In our research, we find that some people tend to be higher in compassionate goals than others. For example, women tend to be higher in compassionate goals than men, on average (Crocker & Canevello, 2008), and people who are high in self-esteem tend to have more compassionate goals than low-self-esteem people.

Yet, when we have searched for types of people who do not benefit or especially benefit from having compassionate goals, we have generally come up empty-handed. The benefits associated with compassionate goals are surprisingly robust. For example, men benefit from compassionate goals as much as women, and low self-esteem people benefit as much as high-self-esteem people. That does not mean that moderator variables that limit who benefits from compassionate goals will not be discovered in future research. To date, however, we have not found any consistent evidence that benefits of compassionate goals accrue only to some personality characteristics or types of people.

The one limitation that has emerged in research concerns other goals that people have. Specifically, some benefits of compassionate goals seem to be limited to people who do not have self-image goals (Crocker & Canevello, 2008).

What about relationship partners' goals?

Do the benefits of compassionate goals depend on whether people's relationship partners also have compassionate goals? Where we have looked at this issue in our research, we have found that the benefits of compassionate goals do not require that both people in a relationship have them. Indeed, our research suggests that compassionate goals are contagious; when one partner is high in compassionate goals, over time the other partner becomes higher in compassionate goals as well (Canevello & Crocker, 2010). Thus, people do not need to wait for their relationship partner to develop compassionate goals to begin experiencing the benefits of having them.

At the same time, people tend to find that their relationships are better if their partner has compassionate goals toward them. Their partners are more supportive and responsive, share more information about their feelings and problems, and approach problems in a more constructive fashion. These behaviors are noticeable and improve relationship quality.

Can people shift their goals?

One of the most important issues still to be resolved is whether people can choose to have compassionate goals. We know that people have more compassionate goals at some times and less at other times. But this does not necessarily mean that people can choose the motivational system that governs their behavior, choosing compassionate goals even when they are dispositionally insecure, situationally threatened, or their relationship partner is motivated by the egosystem.

We suspect that, at least under certain circumstances, people do have a choice about whether they are motivated by the egosystem or the ecosystem and by compassionate goals or self-image goals. Specifically, when people understand the benefits associated with compassionate goals for themselves, people they care about, and their relationships, and have the cognitive resources to think through the consequences of their actions, they can choose to act with the intention to be supportive and constructive.

If compassionate goals are so helpful to relationships, why don't people always have and act on them?

Given benefits of compassionate goals for relationships, it may seem puzzling that people do not have them all of the time. In an intriguing line of research, Gilbert and his colleagues have examined fears that people have related to compassion – both giving it and receiving it (Gilbert, McEwan, Matos, & Rivis, 2011). For example, people express fears of being exploited by others, of vulnerable people being drawn to them and draining their emotional resources, and of encouraging dependence in others. These findings suggest that when people feel that their emotional resources are limited, such as when they feel stressed, anxious, or worthless, they may have less capacity for compassionate goals.

Even when people express compassionate goals, they may not always act on them. Some people might express compassionate goals when they do not actually have them, because they are socially desirable; "nice" people should have compassionate goals. In our studies, controlling for socially desirable responding rarely changes our results, so we do not see this as a major concern. We think it is more likely that some people find it difficult to hold compassionate goals in working memory, particular when they are distracted, stressed, preoccupied by other things, or feeling threatened. Thus, even sincere, well-intended people may forget their intention to be compassionate when the demands of daily life impinge on them.

CONCLUSIONS

Our research suggests that intentions toward relationship partners – specifically, *compassionate goals* to be constructive and supportive – are a key to creating good relationships. By carefully setting their intentions toward relationship partners, people can usually create the good relationships they want. Furthermore, compassionate goals foster good relationships regardless of one's level of self-esteem, attachment insecurity, or sensitivity to rejection. They do so for a variety of relationship types, from relationships between previously unacquainted college roommates to romantic couples, and they do so in good times and in bad times, when issues and conflicts arise. They also lead to more compassion for partners when dissolving relationships. Thus, this approach is quite practical; it provides a framework that people can use to create the kinds of good relationships that contribute to health and well-being.

REFERENCES

Algoe, S. B. (2012). Find, remind, and bind: The functions of gratitude in everyday relationships. *Social and Personality Psychology Compass*, 6, 455–469.

Bakan, D. (1966). *The duality of human existence*. Chicago, IL: Rand McNally.

Baumeister, R. F., & Leary, M. R. (1995). The need to belong: Desire for interpersonal attachments as a fundamental human motivation. *Psychological Bulletin*, 111, 497–529. doi:10.1037/0033-2909.117.3.497

Canevello, A. (2014). *Compassionate goals and reasons for forgiveness*. Manuscript in preparation.

Canevello, A., & Crocker, J. (2010). Creating good relationships: Responsiveness, relationship quality, and interpersonal goals. *Journal of Personality and Social Psychology, 99,* 78–106. doi:10.1037/a0018186

Canevello, A., & Crocker, J. (2011a). Changing relationship growth belief: Intrapersonal and interpersonal consequences of compassionate goals. *Personal Relationships, 18,* 370–391.

Canevello, A., & Crocker, J. (2011b). Interpersonal goals, others' regard for the self, and self-esteem: The paradoxical consequences of self-image and compassionate goals. *European Journal of Social Psychology, 41,* 422–434. doi:10.1002/ejsp.808

Canevello, A., & Crocker, J. (2015). *Measures of prosocial orientations: Family resemblances and unique associations.* Manuscript under review.

Canevello, A., Crocker, J., Lewis, K., & Hartsell, J. (2014). *Compassionate goals, constructive approaches to interpersonal problems, and upset feelings in relationships.* Manuscript in preparation.

Canevello, A., Granillo, M. T., & Crocker, J. (2013). Predicting change in relationship insecurity: The roles of compassionate and self-image goals. *Personal Relationships, 20,* 587–618.

Cialdini, R. B., Brown, S. L., Lewis, B. P., Luce, C., & Neuberg, S. L. (1997). Reinterpreting the empathy-altruism relationship: When one into one equals oneness. *Journal of Personality and Social Psychology, 73,* 481–494.

Clark, M. S., Ouellette, R., Powell, M. C., & Milberg, S. (1987). Recipient's mood, relationship type, and helping. *Journal of Personality and Social Psychology, 53,* 94–103. doi:10.1037/0022-3514.53.1.94

Crocker, J., & Canevello, A. (2008). Creating and undermining social support in communal relationships: The role of compassionate and self-image goals. *Journal of Personality and Social Psychology, 95,* 555–575. doi:10.1037/0022-3514.95.3.555

Crocker, J., & Canevello, A. (2012). Consequences of self-image and compassionate goals. In P. Devine & A. Plant (Eds.), *Advances in experimental social psychology,* Vol 45. (pp. 229–277). San Diego, CA: Academic Press.

Crocker, J., & Canevello, A. (2015). Relationships and the self: Egosystem and ecosystem. In M. Mikulincer, P. R. Shaver, J. A. Simpson, & J. F. Dovidio (Eds.), *APA handbook of personality and social psychology, Volume 3: Interpersonal relations.* (pp. 93–116). Washington, DC: American Psychological Association.

Crocker, J., & Canevello, A. (2014). [Reasons for breaking up a romantic relationship]. Unpublished raw data.

Crocker, J., Canevello, A., Breines, J. G., & Flynn, H. (2010). Interpersonal goals and change in anxiety and dysphoria in first-semester college students. *Journal of Personality and Social Psychology, 98,* 1009–1024. doi:10.1037/a0019400

Davis, M. H. (1983). Measuring individual differences in empathy: Evidence for a multidimensional approach. *Journal of Personality and Social Psychology, 44,* 113–126. doi:10.1037/0022-3514.44.1.113

Deci, E. L., & Ryan, R. M. (2000). The "what" and "why" of goal pursuits: Human needs and the self-determination of behavior. *Psychological Inquiry, 11,* 227–268.

Downey, G., & Feldman, S. I. (1996). Implications of rejection sensitivity for intimate relationships. *Journal of Personality and Social Psychology, 70,* 1327–1343. doi:10.1037/0022-3514.70.6.1327

Drigotas, S. M., & Rusbult, C. E. (1992). Should I stay or should I go? A dependence model of breakups. *Journal of Personality and Social Psychology, 62,* 62–87. doi:10.1037/0022-3514.62.1.62

Dykman, B. M. (1998). Integrating cognitive and motivational factors in depression: Initial tests of a goal orientation approach. *Journal of Personality and Social Psychology*, 74, 139–158.

Fenell, D. L. (1993). Characteristics of long-term first marriages. *Journal of Mental Health Counseling*, 15, 446–460.

Fritz, H. L., & Helgeson, V. S. (1998). Distinctions of unmitigated communion from communion: Self-neglect and overinvolvement with others. *Journal of Personality and Social Psychology*, 75, 121–140.

Gable, S. L., & Reis, H. T. (2006). Intimacy and the self: An iterative model of the self and close relationships. In P. Noller & J. A. Feeney (Eds.), *Close relationships: Functions, forms and processes* (pp. 211–225). Hove, England: Psychology Press/ Taylor & Francis (UK).

Gilbert, P., McEwan, K., Matos, M., & Rivis, A. (2011). Fears of compassion: Development of three self-report measures. *Psychology and Psychotherapy: Theory, Research, and Practice*, 84, 239–255.

Hadden, B. W., Øverup, C. S., & Knee, C. R. (2014). Removing the ego: Need fulfillment, self-image goals, and self-presentation. *Self and Identity*, 13, 274–293.

Hadden, B. W., Smith, C. V., & Knee, C. R. (2014). The way I make you feel: How relatedness and compassionate goals promote partner's relationship satisfaction. *The Journal of Positive Psychology*, 9, 155–162.

Haynes, P. K., Crocker, J., Canevello, A., & Lewis, K. (2014). *Compassionate goals and breakup distress*. Manuscript under review

Helgeson, V. S. (1994). Relation of agency and communion to well-being: Evidence and potential explanations. *Psychological Bulletin*, 116, 412–428.

Helgeson, V. S., & Fritz, H. L. (1998). A theory of unmitigated communion. *Personality and Social Psychology Review*, 2, 173–183. doi:10.1207/s15327957pspr0203_2

Helgeson, V. S., & Fritz, H. L. (2000). The implications of unmitigated agency and unmitigated communion for domains of problem behavior. *Journal of Personality*, 68, 1031–1057.

Henry, J. P., & Wang, S. (1998). Effects of early stress on adult affiliative behavior. *Psychoneuroendocrinology*, 23, 863–875.

Jiang, T., Crocker, J., Canevello, A., Lewis, K., & Black, A. (2014). *Creating trust through self-disclosure: Compassionate goals predict increased trust in oneself and in relationship partners*. Manuscript in preparaton.

Knee, C. R. (1998). Implicit theories of relationships: Assessment and prediction of romantic relationship initiation, coping, and longevity. *Journal of Personality and Social Psychology*, 74, 360–370.

Knee, C. R., Patrick, H., & Lonsbary, C. (2003). Implicit theories of relationships: Orientations toward evaluation and cultivation. *Personality and Social Psychology Review*, 7, 41–55.

Mikulincer, M., & Shaver, P. R. R. (2003). The attachment behavioral system in adulthood: Activation, psychodynamics, and interpersonal processes. In M. P. Zanna (Ed.), *Advances in experimental social psychology* (Vol. 35, pp. 53–152). San Diego, CA: Academic.

Mischkowski, D., Crocker, J., Niiya, Y., Canevello, A., & Moeller, S. J. (2014). *Compassionate goals for relationships predict increased academic growth goals and academic engagement*. Manuscript under review. Columbus, OH: Ohio State University.

Murray, S. L., Holmes, J. G., & Collins, N. L. (2006). Optimizing assurance: The risk regulation system in relationships. *Psychological Bulletin*, 132, 641–666. doi:10.1037/0033–2909.132.5.641

Murray, S. L., Holmes, J. G., & Griffin, D. W. (2000). Self-esteem and the quest for felt security: How perceived regard regulates attachment processes. *Journal of Personality and Social Psychology*, 78, 478–498. doi:10.1037/0022–3514.78.3.478

Patrick, H., Knee, C. R., Canevello, A., & Lonsbary, C. (2007). The role of need fulfillment in relationship functioning and well-being: A self-determination theory perspective. *Journal of Personality and Social Psychology*, 92, 434–457.

Reis, H. T., Clark, M. S., & Holmes, J. G. (2004). Perceived partner responsiveness as an organizing construct in the study of intimacy and closeness. In D. Mashek & A. P. Aron (Eds.), *Handbook of closeness and intimacy* (pp. 201–225). Mahwah, NJ: Erlbaum.

Rempel, J. K., Holmes, J. G., & Zanna, M. P. (1985). Trust in close relationships. *Journal of Personality and Social Psychology*, 49, 95–112.

Rusbult, C. E., Drigotas, S. M., & Verette, J. (1994). The investment model: An interdependence analysis of commitment processes and relationship maintenance phenomena. In D. J. Canary & L. Stafford (Eds.), *Communication and relational maintenance* (pp. 115–139). San Diego, CA: Academic Press.

Rusbult, C. E., Johnson, D. J., & Morrow, G. D. (1986). Determinants and consequences of exit, voice, loyalty, and neglect: Responses to dissatisfaction in adult romantic involvements. *Human Relations*, 39, 45–63. doi:10.1177/001872678603900103

Simpson, J. A. (1987). The dissolution of romantic relationships: Factors involved in relationship stability and emotional distress. *Journal of Personality and Social Psychology*, 53, 683–692.

Slotter, E. B., Gardner, W. L., & Finkel, E. J. (2010). Who am I without you? The influence of romantic breakup on the self-concept. *Personality and Social Psychology Bulletin*, 36, 147–160.

Spence, J. T., Helmreich, R. L., & Holahan, C. K. (1979). Negative and positive components of psychological masculinity and femininity and their relationships to self-reports of neurotic and acting out behaviors. *Journal of Personality and Social Psychology*, 37, 1673–1682. doi:10.1037/0022–3514.37.10.1673

Sprecher, S., & Fehr, B. (2005). Compassionate love for close others and humanity. *Journal of Social and Personal Relationships*, 22, 629–651. doi:10.1177/0265407505056439

Sprecher, S., Felmlee, D., Metts, S., Fehr, B., & Vanni, D. (1998). Factors associated with distress following the breakup of a close relationship. *Journal of Social and Personal Relationships*, 15, 791–809.

Uchino, B. N. (2004). *Social support and physical health: Understanding the health consequences of our relationships*. New Haven, CT: Yale University Press.

Wieselquist, J., Rusbult, C. E., Foster, C. A., & Agnew, C. R. (1999). Commitment, pro-relationship behavior, and trust in close relationships. *Journal of Personality and Social Psychology*, 77, 942–966.

12

Synchrony in positive social relationships

TANYA VACHARKULKSEMSUK

Cooking a meal together with friends; casually practicing tennis with a hitting partner well-matched in skill level; jumping and cheering in unison with others at a little league game – these instances of human behavior are just a few examples of *synchrony*, each characterized by shared and coordinated movements *with other people*. This chapter examines synchrony as a positive, nonverbal phenomenon that is essential to optimal relationship development. Although much past research focuses on localized displays or behaviors, like smiling and laughing, as indicators of a positive relationship, here I review a broader, Gestalt approach to understanding healthy, high-quality social interactions. After all, if most human activity involves coordinating one's actions with those of other people (Reis & Collins, 2004), then widening one's scope to capture whole bodies moving with each other helps gain complementary insight into interpersonal relationships. This chapter starts with an in-depth definition and description of synchrony, followed by a review of findings showing that synchrony and positive relationships are positively associated with one another. Much of the chapter's review focuses on what I call *behavioral synchrony*. It also touches on other forms of synchrony (i.e., emotional, cognitive, and physiological synchrony), culminating in a newly proposed organizing theory: the Superconductor Theory of Relationships. The chapter closes with a discussion of synchrony more generally and its relationship with interpersonal negativity, and poses open questions, inviting fellow scholars to look into this phenomenon that still has much left to be known in the world of relationships.

BEHAVIORAL SYNCHRONY

Behavioral synchrony is the spontaneous emergence of coordinated movements between two or more people. Colloquially, a couple or group moving

The author is grateful for support of this work from the National Science Foundation (NSF SPRF Award #1306225).

in synchrony is described as displaying "togetherness" or "oneness" – they appear "on the same page," or "on the same wavelength." Synchrony exists underneath the chaos of everyday life in many different types, from the explicit, expected kind, like marching band performances and dance competition routines; to the more subtle kind, like a group of runners seemingly gliding as their common pace puts them in-step with one another, or a pair of friends chatting in a rhythmic back-and-forth fashion about their day's events. To an extent, just thinking of synchronous behaviors evokes positive feelings: admiration for a precisely timed execution of an alley-oop pass in basketball, or awe for a spectacular acrobatic routine. The current chapter focuses primarily on behavioral synchrony with a positive undertone. Mobs or protests – more likely characterized by negative moods and aggressive behavior – may also come to mind, which will be discussed later in this chapter.

As defined in research, behavioral synchrony is coordination of movement that occurs between individuals, featuring similarity of (1) *form*, the manner and style of movements, and (2) *time*, the temporal rhythm of movements (Bernieri, Reznick, & Rosenthal, 1988; Bernieri, Davis, Rosenthal, & Knee, 1994; Kimura & Daibo, 2006). More specifically, behavioral synchrony is movement among a dyad or group of people in-phase with one another and/or is matching in frequency (Clayton, Sager, & Will, 2004; Richardson, Garcia, Frank, Gregor, & Marsh, 2012). In-phase movements are organized in either an exactly matched way, like kangaroo legs launching together; or an exactly opposite way, like human legs striding together. So although physical movements originate from individual people (or legs, in the illustrations just provided), it is through interaction and holistic consideration of those movements that behavioral synchrony exists as a higher-level, collective phenomenon (Katz & Kahn, 1966). Some acts of complementarity, wherein one's behavior is governed by the preceding behavior of another person, would also qualify as synchronous (Fiske, 2000; Markey, Funder, & Ozer, 2003). For example, somebody pulling out a chair is complemented by another person seating oneself in it, or the commonly heard call-and-response format at athletic rallies and events. In both instances, the movement or shout of one person is physically unmatched in form from that of their partners, but the coupled timing of the two actions paired together makes it a holistic instance of synchrony.

Behavioral synchrony is similar to the more widely studied phenomenon of human mimicry, which occurs when one person imitates the behavior of another person (Chartrand & Bargh, 1999; Chartrand, Maddux, & Lakin, 2005). Like synchrony, mimicry involves a match in behavioral *form* (e.g., an interviewee crosses his legs after the interviewer does so, a friend scratches her head after seeing her friend do the same). However, mimicry does not always involve equal temporal lags between each imitation sequence nor always recurs continuously over time. Moreover, in terms of measurement, mimicry studies often observe individual-level behavior, considering one person's behavior toward another; synchrony studies, in a subtly different way, examine behavior at the dyadic or group level. For example, examining mimicry in a marching band would focus on just one member (i.e., "Is member X mimicking other members of the group?"), whereas examining synchrony in a marching band would encompass all the members (i.e., "Is the group in synchrony?"). Despite some synonymous features between synchrony and mimicry, I will use "synchrony" throughout this chapter for simplicity, curating research primarily around emergent, spontaneous types of synchrony.[1]

Numerous studies of human interlimb coordination show that humans spontaneously synchronize – or entrain – to one another (e.g., Haken, Kelso, & Bunz, 1985; Kelso, 1984; Kugler & Turvey, 1987; Kelso, DelColle, & Schöner, 1990; Schmidt, Shaw, & Turvey, 1993; Turvey, Rosenblum, Schmidt, & Kugler, 1986). The Kugler and Turvey (1987) wrist-pendulum paradigm is commonly used to demonstrate this phenomenon, which asks participants sitting side-by-side to each swing a pendulum pivoted at the wrist. Even when participants are asked to swing a wrist pendulum at their own preferred speed and not coordinate their pendulum-swinging movements with that of their partner, their movements eventually become entrained, suggesting unintentional coordination (Richardson, Marsh, & Schmidt, 2005). Other studies utilizing a similar paradigm to observe global body movements, such as postural rocking (Richardson, Marsh, Isenhower, Goodman, & Schmidt, 2007) or forearm swinging (Issartel, Marin, & Cadopi, 2007), replicate the results demonstrating that people spontaneously synchronize with others despite instructions not to.

Importantly, there is a very social basis to synchronized movement, as evidenced by a variety of studies, of humans both young and old. First, in a study by Kirschner and Tomasello (2009), preschoolers (ranging in ages 2.5–4.5 years) were directed to drum with one of three things: a speaker box (audio cue only), a drumming machine (audio and visual cues), or an adult with a drum (audio and visual cues from a social other). Across the research sample, children demonstrated enhanced drumming skill and drumming accuracy when they were paired with a drumming adult. This is a remarkable finding, as it suggests that behavioral synchrony is fundamentally social and starts at a young age. Second, in studies of entrainment, humans show difficulty in resisting the movements of social others, compared to non-social others: even for moving-dot displays described to be pre-recorded human movement versus computer-generated movement (Stanley, Gowen, & Miall, 2007), humans demonstrate greater entrainment behavior.

---

[1] There are many studies that experimentally manipulate synchrony, although they are not the primary focus of this chapter's review.

Taken together, this research suggests that synchrony is a very social phenomenon. Such findings perhaps aren't surprising, given that humans are inherently motivated to engage in and establish positive social relationships (e.g., Baumeister & Leary, 1995; Lakin & Chartrand, 2003). People may achieve these social goals by coordinating with others, helping to reinforce existing social bonds and facilitate new social interactions. In contrast, a lack of coordination disrupts and presents challenges. For instance, people with movement disorders (e.g., dyskinesia, Huntington's disease, cerebral palsy) that may interrupt one's flow of movement and ability to kinetically coordinate with other people more often face social exclusion (Williams, 2007).

SYNCHRONY AND POSITIVE RELATIONSHIPS

The idea of synchrony as related to positive relationships is not new. Tickle-Degnen and Rosenthal (1987, 1990) first proposed behavioral coordination as an essential component of interpersonal rapport, alongside two other components of mutual attentiveness and positivity. Bernieri (1988) observed teacher-student dyads in a classroom, finding a strong positive association between movement synchrony and self-reported scores of rapport from each the teacher and student. These findings stand above and beyond rated friendliness of the interactants, thus highlighting a movement-specific effect. LaFrance (1979) found a similar pattern of association between postural coordination and rapport in psychotherapy sessions. The idea of synchrony also has origins in sociology and anthropology, tracing back to sociologist Durkheim (1912), who theorized the emergence of *collective effervescence* – feeling "as one" in large collectives – when one (unknowingly) sheds one's individuality to partake in collective action or rituals (see also, Haidt, 2012). It is not surprising, then, that many religious activities dating centuries back involve rich amounts of music, singing, and dancing – all of which provide a common tempo to which people move together to (Radcliffe-Brown, 1922). Coordination is at the heart of many cultural rituals that have been around and passed on for centuries, speaking again to the draw humans have toward behaviorally connecting with other people.

More recently, a slew of studies further link behavioral synchrony with positive social consequences. Social interactions characterized by more synchronous movements are associated with greater emotional support satisfaction (Hove & Risen, 2009), newborn infants who show behavioral synchrony with their caretakers' speech patterns show more successful language acquisition later in life (Condon & Sander, 1974), and strangers who achieve synchrony during an initial conversation report greater social connection and rapport (Vacharkulksemsuk & Fredrickson, 2012). A recent study in the context of psychotherapy sessions also validates earlier decades' findings. Specifically, using an advanced technological measure of synchrony (i.e., motion energy analysis), results show an association between greater nonverbal synchrony emerging during a session with self-reported quality of the therapeutic relationships and therapy effectiveness (Ramseyer & Tschacher, 2011). Finally, studies that manipulate behavioral synchrony – rather than observe the spontaneous emergence of it – show that synchrony breeds prosocial outcomes, including compassion (Valdesolo & DeSteno, 2011) and cooperation in adults (Wiltermuth & Heath, 2009; Cohen, Mundry, & Kirschner, 2013), and even preschoolers (Kirschner and Tomasello, 2010). Together, all these studies point to a common conclusion: that when nonverbal movement synchrony is present in an interaction, positive socio-relational outcomes result.

Why is behavioral synchrony such a socially binding experience? One route of effectiveness is simply that behavioral synchrony is a case of the old adage "birds of a feather flock together": feelings of liking and trust typically accompany similarity (e.g., Williams & O'Reilly, 1998; Polzer, Milton, & Swann, 2002). Moving similarly with others signals "hey, we are the same." On the other hand, dissimilarity – on a broad social category like race or gender, or even meaningless distinction like that of nominal groups – signal a "me vs. you" mentality (van Knippenberg & Dijksterhuis, 2000; Ito & Urland, 2003; Montepare & Opeyo, 2002). Behavioral synchrony may also be effective via processes of embodiment, the idea that information processing involves one's own motor experience (see Niedenthal, 2007; Havas, Glenberg, Gutowski, Lucarelli, & Davidson, 2010). That is, one's movements are implicated in the affective and psychological experience of the situation. For example, one's bodily expression of joy and anger involve more shoulder, elbow, pelvis, and trunk motions, compared to feelings of sadness (Gross, Crane, & Fredrickson, 2012). The degree to which one's bodily movements are synchronized or not to other people's, then, may be a barometer for feeling cohesion with others (McNeill, 1995). Critically, in many studies linking behavioral synchrony with positive social relationships, results show that behavioral synchrony is a significant factor above and beyond self-reported feelings of positivity, which underscores a movement-specific ingredient important for positive relationships.

OTHER FORMS OF SYNCHRONY

Whereas behavioral displays of movement synchrony are overt and observable, there are other forms of synchrony – either linked to the behavioral displays or independent of them – that also may contribute to one's feeling or judgment of feeling "as one" with social others. In other words, although one's observed movements may be considered the outward display of what's going on psychologically (i.e., a behavioral nonverbal indicator), other synchronous processes that aren't directly observable may be at play as well.

As psychologists have long established, behaviors and movements are intertwined with emotional, cognitive, and physiological processes. I'll forego specific research citations here, instead pointing out the titles of some of social psychology's top journals that feature integrations of human thoughts, feelings, and biology, like *Cognition & Emotion, Biological Psychology*, and *Social Cognition*. Like many other psychological processes studied in the past, it is quite plausible that movement synchrony may combine in some way with the temporal structure of emotions, cognitions, and/or physiology to effectively promote positivity in social relationships.

Individual-level studies of emotion, cognition, and physiology have primarily been in the forefront of psychology research. Standing in the shadows are also several studies that examine emotion, cognition, and physiology at the dyadic or group level, which shed empirical light on other distinct forms of synchrony. So, rather than what happens when one person is feeling emotions, what happens when both people converge on their feelings? Their cognitive states? Similarly, what about their physiological states? I briefly review past research on each of these types of synchrony now, drawing from psychology and related fields, focusing on their implications for social relationships.

Emotional synchrony

When the emotions of multiple people are considered in-time with one another, emotional synchrony may emerge. Emotional synchrony appears across various streams of literatures under many names, including linkage (Levenson & Gottman, 1983), transmission (Larson & Gillman, 1999), convergence (Anderson, Keltner, & John, 2003), co-regulation (Schoebi, 2008; Butler & Randall, 2013), and coupling (Ferrer & Nesselroade, 2003). When similar emotions are shared and co-experienced across multiple individuals during an interaction, positive relational outcomes result. For example, college roommates over the course of a year who achieved greater emotional similarity reported greater relationship closeness and satisfaction (Anderson, et al., 2003). This emotional synchrony (i.e., emotional convergence, specifically) is thought to have promoted coordination between the roommates, more accurate perceptions of one another, and social validation, which in turn promoted increased self-disclosure and satisfying interactions. Over time, the roommates then operated on a foundation of built trust and continuity of the bond. Emotional synchrony also holds implications for workplace interactions. For example, in a study of work teams, groups of team members who had greater similarity in positive emotions with one another exhibited higher levels of cooperation and team satisfaction, and lower levels of conflict, compared to emotionally dissimilar teams (Barsade, Ward, Turner, & Sonnenfeld, 2000).

Perhaps more intriguing are the consequences of emotional synchrony in the infant-caretaker context, since only nonverbal communication is possible. Around 3 months into an infant's life, coordination of nonverbal behaviors associated with emotional expression (e.g., gaze, touch, proximity, position, facial expressions) between the parent and infant begins to emerge. During this time in the infant's life, research observations reveal sequential occurrences of an initiation for social engagement and a response between the infant and caretaker, with these occurrences featuring a rhythmic back-and-forth and consistent time lag between the initiation and response (Tronick, 1989; Feldman, 2003). Emotional synchrony between the parent and infant measured at 3 and 9 months predicts a suite of complex socio-emotional developmental outcomes for the infant: optimal attachment style at year 1, self-regulatory skills at years 2, 4, and 6, theory of mind skills at year 2, and greater IQ measured at years 2 and 4 (Feldman & Greenbaum, 1997; Feldman, 2007). Together, these findings suggest that emotional synchrony – similarity in time and form of many people's emotions – is a key dynamic ingredient underlying the development and maintenance of positive relationships.

Cognitive synchrony

A co-presence of multiple minds sets a stage for cognitive synchrony to arise. Cognitive synchrony is slightly different from similar phenomena that focus on one person adopting the mindset of another, like perspective-taking (Higgins, 1981; Galinsky, Ku, & Wang, 2005) or theory of mind (Premack & Woodruff, 1978). Common grounding is the joint construction of a conceptual pact among conversation partners (Brennan & Clark, 1996), for example, and is known to have socio-relational benefits. When interactants share a context, culture, or are co-present with one another, cognitive synchrony in the form of common grounding is more likely to emerge: they refer to objects, terms, and information that contribute to a conversation marked by smoothness and rhythmic back-and-forth. In establishing common ground, interactants better coordinate and cooperate, which are defining characteristics of moving a conversation forward (Clark & Wilkes-Gibbs, 1986; Clark & Brennan, 1991). Separately located relationships (e.g., geographically distributed work teams; long-distance relationships), on the other hand, experience more difficulty establishing common ground (Schober, 1998; Kraut, Fussell, Brennan, & Siegel, 2002), and in turn face more conflict (Hinds & Mortensen, 2005). Through common grounding, interactants may also then experience *shared reality*, a sense of established correspondence of inner states with another person (Echterhoff, Higgins, & Levine, 2009), which provides social validation and feelings of connectedness. In contrast, as seen in classic conformity studies, when people are excluded from sharing a common understanding of the world, they become uncomfortable, doubtful, and physically unsettled (Asch, 1956).

Physiological synchrony

Although not overtly visible, people in dyads or groups may indeed get "on the same wavelength" physiologically. Physiological synchrony has been studied under many terms, such as linkage (Levenson & Ruef, 1992; Guastello, Pincus, & Gunderson, 2006), covariation (Waters, West, & Mendes, 2014), and coupling (Konvalinka & Roepstorff, 2012). Here, I define it broadly, considering any instance of individuals' physiological patterns occurring in a temporally organized way with one another. Importantly – like the other cases of synchrony we've talked about – the physiological occurrences under consideration involve two or more people, rather than just one individual's physiological profile. Put another way, instances of physiological synchrony belong to the entire interpersonal system and thus cannot be reduced to the experiences of just one individual (Diamond & Aspinwall, 2003; Feldman, 2007; Sbarra & Hazan, 2008).

Early evidence of physiological synchrony appeared in the context of psychotherapy, where DiMascio, Boyd, and Greenblatt (1957) studied patients and therapists' heart rates. The researchers found that during the pairs' initial dozen sessions, heart rates of both the patient and therapist were similar, especially as the level of conversation depth increased. Physiological synchrony has also been observed between romantic partners (Helm, Sbarra, & Ferrer, 2012). In close relationships, physiological synchrony is theorized to be a central pathway toward intrapersonal benefits like emotional and physiological stability for each the relationship partners, as well as relational-level outcomes like greater satisfaction and health (Butler, 2011; Butler & Randall, 2013). Physiological synchrony also emerges in a variety of other interpersonal contexts, including heart rate and respiratory synchronization between mother and fetus (Van Leeuwen et al., 2009), choir singers singing in unison compared to singing different parts of a piece in unison (Müller & Lindenberger, 2011), and participants and observers of collective rituals (e.g., fire-walking ritual; Konvalinka et al., 2011). Similarly, a study of group arm-waving showed that participants' respiratory rhythms synchronized with others in the group when arm movements were also synchronized (Codrons, Bernardi, Vandoni, & Bernardi, 2014). All these studies demonstrate that humans can indeed connect at a non-conscious, autonomic level. What's more, *even in the absence of shared movement*, participants in the Codrons et al. (2014) study synchronized their breathing. That is, in the sheer presence of others – with or without an associated action – participants were prompted to breathe in a synchronized fashion, suggesting that something inherent to group settings sets a stage for physiological synchrony to arise. And to the extent that physiological reactions are intertwined with emotions and cognitive appraisals, such co-presence with others may be a key condition for other forms of synchrony and associated social benefits to emerge.

As these findings suggest, synching up with other people in various ways – behaviorally, emotionally, cognitively, and/or physiologically – has positive relational benefits. Next, I propose a new theory, inspired by a concept in physics that connects all these forms of synchrony to describe a type of interpersonal relationship and relational process. Named the *superconductor theory of relationships*, the theory offers a unifying framework for thinking about the different forms of synchrony just discussed that have in the past been primarily studied separately. The theory adopts a concept from physics to provide a novel way for viewing pairs and groups of people in a holistic manner – as one system – rather than separate human entities to facilitate formation and maintenance of positive social relationships.

THE SUPERCONDUCTOR THEORY OF RELATIONSHIPS

Why the notion of superconductors? In the physical sense, *superconductors* are materials (e.g., tin, aluminum) that, under specific conditions, conduct electricity without the loss of energy. Many common forms of electricity (e.g., that flowing through a light bulb) are the result of millions of electrons moving chaotically, bouncing off one another with no aim or direction, and in fact leading to energy loss (e.g., in the form of heat). When superconductors are set to temperatures close to absolute zero, however, the aimless electrons synch up – they move, glide, and coordinate with one another in the same direction with zero resistance, and thus no energy loss. This is known as *superconductivity*. Figure 12.1a illustrates these concepts. Conceptualizing this idea in a social-psychological sense, we arrive at the idea of *relational superconductors* (i.e., a dyad-/group-level construct) and *relational superconductivity* (i.e., a relational process by which interactants are coordinating under no resistance).

Social electrons

Adapting the idea of superconductors and superconductivity requires that each of the four reviewed forms of synchrony (i.e., behavioral, emotional, cognitive, physiological) are thought of as electrons, or as I'll call them throughout this chapter, *social electrons*. For example, experienced emotions in an individual may be a type of social electron, as would be a cognitive thought or physiological occurrence. The superconductor theory of relationships proposes that during relational superconductivity, these social electrons between interactants sync up and glide in-step with one another. Emotional

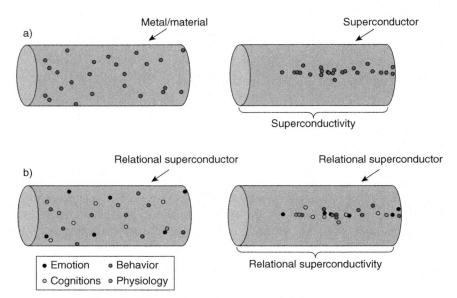

FIGURE 12.1 Simplified illustrations of superconductivity.
(a) Physical superconductivity: The shaded vessel represents a material (e.g., tin, aluminum) and the circles represent electrons (e.g., energy) typically moving with no aim or direction. At temperatures close to absolute zero (shown on right), the aimless electrons in superconductors synchronize – they move, glide, and coordinate with one another in the same direction with zero resistance. This is known as *superconductivity*. (b) Relational superconductivity: The shaded vessel represents a type of dyad or group relationship (e.g., romantic couple, friends, doctor-patient, work colleagues) and the circles represent different types of social electrons (i.e., behavioral, emotional, cognitive, physiological). In cases of *relational superconductivity* (shown on right), the social electrons contained within the relational superconductor synchronize.

convergence across a couple would be a form of relational superconductivity, as would be shared cognitions or physiological linkage described earlier. Indeed, there is the undeniably interrelated nature of each type of social electron; although they are discussed here separately, these various types of social electrons likely combine in an additive or interactive way to characterize relational superconductors and relational superconductivity.

The idea of conceptualizing psychological processes as energy-based is evident in much past work, especially that of emotions. Energy-based metaphors define many psychological constructs, such as affective arousal (Thayer, 1986), emotional energy (Collins, 1993), vitality (Ryan & Frederick, 1997), zest (Miller & Stiver, 1997), and ego-energy (Muraven, Tice, & Baumeister, 1998; Gailliot, et al., 2007). There are also different types of social interactions characterized by varying levels of energy. High-quality connections (Dutton

& Heaphy, 2003) are positive social interactions marked by felt vitality, for example. And in contrast, high-maintenance interactions are those wherein achieving coordination on a joint task consumes more of the interactants' energy than the task actually requires (Finkel, Campbell, Brunell, Dalton, Scarbeck, & Chartrand, 2006). So what's colloquially observed as people "getting" each other or being "on the same page" may actually be a similarity of their observable behavior and underlying affective, cognitive, and/or physiological states – a manifestation of two individuals' social electrons gliding in-step, like coordinated electrons during physical superconductivity. Figure 12.1b illustrates this idea. The superconductor theory of relationships proposes that, like physical superconductors, when the interactants of a relational superconductor are together, they operate without losing energy, and perhaps even give and gain more energy to themselves and others around them. By identifying and studying this unique process of relational super-conductivity, research can help individuals develop positive relationships, and reap the healthy benefits that come from strong social ties.

According to the superconductor theory of relationships proposed here, relational superconductors can be of any human relationship type. Clinical relationships (e.g., doctor-patient, therapist-client) and mentoring relation-ships (e.g., educator-student, mentor-mentee) are specific types of relation-ships that are ripe contexts for studying relational superconductors and the emergence of relational superconductivity. For example, patient-centered aims to more actively involve a patient in medical decision-making compared to traditional care models of an authoritative doctor determining decisions; this care model fosters more effective doctor visits that have been linked with improved patient outcomes, improved doctor-patient communication, and lower health care costs (Epstein, Alper, & Quill, 2004; Epstein & Street, 2007). Similarly, relational mentoring is an interdependent mentor-protégé relation-ship characterized by a focus on growth, learning, and development in one's career world (Ragins & Verbos, 2007). Relational mentoring contrasts tradi-tional models of mentoring that are grounded in principles of exchange, versus communal, relationships. Both patient-centered care and relational mentoring are contexts under which positive psychological capital, such as optimism and resilience, are fostered, as well as meaningfulness and authen-ticity. By investigating these types of relationships under the theoretical lens of relational superconductivity, researchers could simultaneously gain understanding of micro-processes that underlie positive relationships and their context-specific implications.

As mentioned in brief earlier, one way in which synchrony manifests is as complementary behavior, and often seen in hierarchical relationships (Tiedens, Unzueta, & Young, 2007; Tracey, Ryan, & Jaschik-Herman, 2001). Achieving convergence or similarity in emotions, cognitions, behavioral movement, and/or physiology may be especially beneficial in terms of transcending power differences between the interactants, thereby widening the basin for positive outcomes to emerge. Relational superconductivity may be the hallmark process of a doctor and her patient successfully carrying out the principles of patient-centered care, or two people shedding their individual roles and status to operate as "one."

What about other everyday human relationships, like the ones with friends and romantic partners? What can the superconductor theory tell us or do for us in better understanding these everyday relationships? The super-conductor theory of relationships is a new lens for understanding human relationships. By metaphorically considering behavioral, emotional, cogni-tive, and physiological processes as social electrons – and human relationships as a vessel for these social electrons – researchers may develop deeper under-standings of positive relationships. Moreover, the superconductor theory of relationships nudges a scholarly consideration of all psychological processes in tandem with one another, rather than in isolation, to inform relationship science. Relationship science processes, like those detailed in previous chap-ters of this book volume (e.g., *capitalization*, Gable & Anderson; *dyadic regulation*, Overall & Girme; *sacrifice*, Day & Impett), for example, would each be excellent candidates to reconsider using superconductivity as a frame-work. Beyond what's currently known about the specific emotions, cogni-tions, or behaviors underlying each of these processes, the theory offers a novel way of examining processes at a coupled, interdependent level to inform our knowledge about relationships.

What's next?

The superconductor theory of relationships proposed here provides a theoretical framework for setting up future research designed to under-stand synchrony as a positive approach for optimizing relationships. The theory itself – and, in some ways, research on synchrony more broadly – is young. This chapter and theory proposal (intentionally) beg several future research questions: Which types of social electrons are necessary and sufficient for a dyad to achieve relational superconductivity? How might each type of social electron come together to produce relational super-conductivity? Are there additive or interactive effects of different types of social electrons? Does the same profile of "energy" exist for different types of individuals and relationships? Might an alignment of affective electrons be more or less important in romantic relationships versus colleague relationships? Another important issue to address is whether relational superconductivity is a result of automatic or controlled processes. That is, could interaction pairs make a conscious effort to become relational superconductors? Or, is it effective in promoting positive relationships only when it emerges organically and unmanipulated during an interaction? All these questions will be important for advancing the super-conductor theory of relationships, and more broadly, synchrony research. Each is ripe for future relationship science.

A NOTE ON NEGATIVE SYNCHRONY

The chapter has thus far focused on spontaneously emerging synchrony and its benefits for positive relationships. However, it is worth mentioning existing evidence that provides a more balanced approach as research on synchrony in relationships progresses. Alongside examples of positively toned synchrony are examples of negative toned synchrony, such as a charging mob of protestors or soldiers.[2] The "dark side" of synchrony has been studied, with experimental manipulations of movement synchrony significantly pre-dicting participants' greater compliance with instructions to be aggressive, for example (Wiltermuth, 2012). And, cognitive synchrony – in the form of groupthink – is a ripe state for premature consensus in situations of group deliberation or decision-making, particularly among groups that are highly cohesive (Hackman & Morris, 1975; Janis, 1972). Notably, physiological syn-chrony is more likely to arise in situations of negative topics of conversation (Levenson, Carstensen, & Gottman, 1994; Carstensen, Gottman, & Levenson, 1995) and stressful situations (e.g., stressful social evaluation; Waters, et al., 2014). And, there is a significant negative correlation between emergent physiological (Levenson & Gottman, 1983) and hormonal (e.g., cortisol, a measure of stress; Saxbe & Repetti, 2010) synchrony and satisfaction in married couples. The effect is similar in work teams: greater skin conductance synchrony is associated with mutual dislike among member pairs (Kaplan, Burch, & Bloom, 1964), and synchrony of heart rate variation in four-person work teams negatively predicts team members' ratings of team productivity, communication, and ability to work with one another (Henning, Armstead, & Ferris, 2009).

This pattern of results is perhaps not surprising, given that negative emotions have a stronger and clearer physiological profile, compared to positive emotions (Ekman & Friesen, 1978; Levenson, 1992). That is, when traditional measures of physiology (e.g., heart rate, respiration, skin conduc-tance) are examined in contexts of positivity, there is not much variance or evidence of occurrence simply because positive emotions do not register distinctly on such measures. Negative emotions, including fear and anger, arguably evolved to signal threat or danger to oneself, so their connection to humans' physiological states is stronger (Levenson, 1992; Fredrickson, 1998,

---

[2] Although outcomes of mobs, crowds, military marching, and the like are potentially destruc-tive for surrounding onlookers, it is worth noting that the experience for the interactants themselves is reportedly quite pleasant (McNeill, 1996; Ehrenreich, 2009).

2001, 2013). When one's negative affective, cognitive, and/or physiological profile synchronizes with another person's negative profile, then synchrony exacerbates conflict – a couple's social electrons are negatively valenced and fire simultaneously in-step with one another toward destructive outcomes.

During a heated argument or conflict conversation, couples may also appear behaviorally and emotionally synchronized. Often, such interactions are marked by yelling, screaming, defensiveness, criticism, and interactants talking over one another (Gottman, 1998). There is also minimal eye contact, thereby reducing the opportunity for partners to connect and exchange or be receptive of partners' thoughts or feelings (Schrammel, Pannasch, Graupner, Mojzisch, & Velichkovsky, 2009). Rather than being an example of negative synchrony, however, it is perhaps the case that these couples don't even qualify as a relational superconductor. Instead, they are more akin to the idea of *superinsulators*. Remember that, in terms of physics, electrons move together collectively in the same direction, allowing electrical currents to flow with zero resistance or restriction. In the exact opposite way that super-conductors have zero resistance, though, materials called *superinsulators* that – at temperatures close to absolute zero – feature an infinite amount of resistance. Specifically, the electrons within a superinsulator avoid one another, chaotically moving independently of each other with no direction. This means that electrical currents passing through the superinsulator face resistance, and hence energy loss. Superinsulators are mechanistically the exact opposite of superconductors: the former features electrons moving in an independent and disjointed manner from one another, whereas the latter features electrons moving together.

Like physical superinsulators, negative social interactions are character-ized by resistance between the interactants, thus preventing their social electrons from flowing together, and resulting in a loss of energy. Thinking of heated interpersonal arguments in terms of social electrons and resistance has potential implications for advancing solutions and intervention geared for reducing relational conflict. For example, if relational intimacy is a process of mutual and reciprocal responsiveness between relationship partners (Laurenceau, Barrett, & Pietromonaco, 1998; Reis, Clark, & Holmes, 2004), then the lack of coupled social electron flow within that relationship may seriously affect moving the intimacy process forward. Whereas intimacy has a higher likelihood of being generated due to the smooth flow of social electrons in superconductors, intimacy is blocked in superinsulators given that the social electrons fail to interact with one another.

As research on synchrony in relationships progresses, it will be important to integrate what we know about negative relationship processes to ensure a better understanding of synchrony's perils as well. Interestingly, in the physics world, superinsulators and superconductors are currently being considered dualistically to build more efficient systems. In the same way, positive and negative interactions may be considered in tandem to leverage one another toward stronger interpersonal relationships.

CONCLUSION

The goal of this chapter was to illuminate synchrony – behavioral, emotional, cognitive, and physiological – as a positive approach to optimal relationship development. A review of evidence across various research streams of research reveals that synchrony is a unique ingredient underlying positive social relationships. The newly proposed superconductor theory of relationships described in this chapter ties together these various threads, metaphorically capturing a state (i.e., relational superconductivity) that social interactants can achieve. Through relational superconductivity, interactants face minimal energy loss or resistance, in turn experiencing greater relational outcomes.

This work is important for enhancing new and established relationships alike. In moving beyond the individual to consider dyadic and group interactions holistically, we see that synchrony is a subtle, yet powerful platform upon which people create a valuable form of "oneness." So by cultivating moments of synchrony with relationship partners, relationship quality may also increase. Relationship partners may together seek out activities that unlock opportunities for synchrony to arise: trivia night or a book club for couples and groups who would enjoy cognitive synchrony, a fitness activity or local square dance for those who would enjoy physiological and behavioral synchrony, an emotionally-evocative movie or concert for affective synchrony. At face value, these activities are just activities – ways to pass time with another person. Yet they all undeniably tap into synchrony as a process. Alongside the many approaches that currently exist, this dyad-/ group-level phenomenon of synchrony is another one to consider in the repertoire for developing, maintaining, repairing, and optimizing positive social relationships.

REFERENCES

Anderson, C., Keltner, D., & John, O. P. (2003). Emotional convergence between people over time. *Journal of Personality and Social Psychology*, 84, 1054–1068.

Asch, S. E. (1956). Studies of independence and conformity: I. A minority of one against a unanimous majority. *Psychological Monographs: General and Applied*, 70, 1–70.

Barsade, S. G., Ward, A. J., Turner, J. D., & Sonnenfeld, J. A. (2000). To your heart's content: A model of affective diversity in top management teams. *Administrative Science Quarterly*, 45, 802–836.

Baumeister, R., & Leary, M. (1995). The need to belong: Desire for interpersonal attachments as a fundamental human motivation. *Psychological Bulletin*, 117, 497–529.

Bernieri, F. (1988). Coordinated movement and rapport in teacher – student interactions. *Journal of Nonverbal Behavior*, 12, 120–138.

Bernieri, F. J., Davis, J. M., Rosenthal, R., & Knee, C. R. (1994). Interactional synchrony and rapport: Measuring synchrony in displays devoid of sound and facial affect. *Personality and Social Psychology Bulletin*, 20, 303–311.

Bernieri, F. J., Reznick, J. S., & Rosenthal, R. (1988). Synchrony, pseudosynchrony, and dissynchrony: Measuring the entrainment process in mother-infant interactions. *Journal of Personality and Social Psychology*, 54, 243–253.

Brennan, S. E., & Clark, H. H. (1996). Conceptual pacts and lexical choice in conversation. *Journal of Experimental Psychology: Learning, Memory, and Cognition*, 22, 1482–1493.

Butler, E. A. (2011). Temporal interpersonal emotion systems: The "TIES" that form relationships. *Personality and Social Psychology Review*, 15, 367–393.

Butler, E. A., & Randall, A. K. (2013). Emotional coregulation in close relationships. *Emotion Review*, 5, 202–210.

Carstensen, L. L., Gottman, J. M., & Levenson, R. W. (1995). Emotional behavior in long-term marriages. *Psychology and Aging*, 10, 140–149.

Chartrand, T. L., & Bargh, J. A. (1999). The chameleon effect: The perception–behavior link and social interaction. *Journal of Personality and Social Psychology*, 76, 893–910.

Chartrand, T. L., Maddux, W. W., & Lakin, J. L. (2005). Beyond the perception-behavior link: The ubiquitous utility and motivational moderators of nonconscious mimicry. In R. R. Hassin, J. S. Uleman, and J. A. Bargh (Eds.), *The New Unconscious*. New York, NY: Oxford University Press.

Clark, H. H., & Brennan, S. E. (1991). Grounding in communication. *Perspectives on Socially Shared Cognition*, 13, 222–233.

Clark, H. H., & Wilkes-Gibbs, D. (1986). Referring as a collaborative process. *Cognition*, 22, 1–39.

Clayton, M., Sager, R., & Will, U. (2004). In time with the music: The concept of entrainment and its significance for ethnomusicology. *ESEM Counterpoint*, 1, 1–45.

Codrons, E., Bernardi, N. F., Vandoni, M., Bernardi, L. (2014) Spontaneous group synchronization of movements and respiratory rhythms. *PLoS ONE*, 9, e107538. doi:10.1371/journal.pone.0107538

Cohen, E., Mundry, R., & Kirschner, S. (2013). Religion, synchrony, and cooperation. *Religion, Brain & Behavior*, 4, 20–30.

Collins, R. (1993). Emotional energy as the common denominator of rational action. *Rationality & Society*, 5, 203–230.

Condon, W. S., & Sander, L. W. (1974). Neonate movement is synchronized with adult speech: Interactional participation and language acquisition. *Science*, 183, 99–101.

Day, L., & Impett, E. (2015). For it is in giving that we receive: The benefits of sacrifice in relationships. In C. R. Knee and H. T. Reis (Eds.), *Positive Approaches to Optimal Relationship Development*.

Diamond, L. M., & Aspinwall, L. G. (2003). Emotion regulation across the life-span: An integrative perspective emphasizing self-regulation, positive affect, and dyadic processes. *Motivation and Emotion*, 27, 125–156.

DiMascio, A., Boyd, R. W., & Greenblatt, M. (1957). Physiological correlates of tension and antagonism during psychotherapy: A study of "interpersonal physiology." *Psychosomatic Medicine*, 19, 99–104.

Durkheim, E. (1912). *The elementary forms of the religious life* (J.W. Swain, Trans.). New York: Free Press.

Dutton, J. E., & Heaphy, E. D. (2003). The power of high-quality connections. In K. S. Cameron, J. E. Dutton, & R. E. Quinn (Eds.), *Positive organizational scholarship* (pp. 263–278). San Francisco, CA: Berrett-Koehler.

Echterhoff, G., Higgins, E. T., & Levine, J. M. (2009). Shared reality: Experiencing commonality with others' inner states about the world. *Perspectives on Psychological Science*, 4, 496–521.

Ekman, P., & Friesen, W. V. (1978). *Facial action coding system*. Palo Alto, CA: Consulting Psychologists Press.

Epstein, R. M., Alper, B. S., & Quill, T. E. (2004). Communicating evidence for participatory decision making. *Journal of the American Medical Association*, 291, 2359.

Epstein, R. M., & Street, R. L., Jr. (2007) *Patient-centered communication in cancer care: Promoting healing and reducing suffering*. National Cancer Institute, NIH Publ. No. 07–6225. Bethesda, MD. Available at: http://outcomes.cancer.gov/areas/pcc/communication

Feldman, R. (2003). Infant–mother and infant–father synchrony: The coregulation of positive arousal. *Infant Mental Health Journal*, 24, 1–23. doi:10.1002/imhj.10041

Feldman, R. (2007). Parent-infant synchrony: Biological foundations and developmental outcomes. *Current Directions in Psychological Science*, 16, 340–345.

Ferrer, E., & Nesselroade, J. R. (2003). Modeling affective processes in dyadic relations via dynamic factor analysis. *Emotion*, 3, 344–360.

Feldman, R., & Greenbaum, C. W. (1997). Affect regulation and synchrony in mother-infant play as precursors to the development of symbolic competence. *Infant Mental Health Journal*, 18, 4–23. doi:10.1002/(SICI)1097–0355(199721)18:1<4::aid-imhj2>3.0.CO;2-R

Finkel, E. J., Campbell, K. W., Brunell, A. B., Dalton, A. N., Scarbeck, S. J., & Chartrand, T. L. (2006). High-maintenance interaction: Inefficient social coordination impairs self-regulation. *Journal of Personality and Social Psychology*, 91, 456–475.

Fiske, A. P. (2000). Complementarity theory: Why human social capacities evolved to require cultural complements. *Personality and Social Psychology Review*, 4, 76–94.

Fredrickson, B. L. (1998). What good are positive emotions? *Review of General Psychology*, 2, 300–319.

Fredrickson, B. L. (2001). The role of positive emotions in positive psychology: The broaden-and-build theory of positive emotions. *American Psychologist*, 56, 218–226.

Fredrickson, B. L. (2013). Positive emotions broaden and build. In E. Ashby Plant & P.G. Devine (Eds.), *Advances on Experimental Social Psychology*, 47, 1–53. Burlington: Academic Press.

Gable, S. L., & Anderson, J. (2015). Capitalization in close relationships. In C. R. Knee and H. T. Reis (Eds.), *Positive Approaches to Optimal Relationship Development*.

Gailliot, M.T., Baumeister, R. F., DeWall, C. N., Maner, J. K., Plant, E. A., Tice, D. M., … Schmeichel, B. J. (2007). Self-control relies on glucose as a limited energy source: Willpower is more than a metaphor. *Journal of Personality and Social Psychology*, 92, 325–36.

Galinsky, A. D., Ku, G., & Wang, C. S. (2005). Perspective-taking and self-other overlap: Fostering social bonds and facilitating social coordination. *Group Processes & Intergroup Relations*, 8, 109–124.

Gottman, J. M. (1998). Psychology and the study of marital processes. *Annual Review of Psychology*, 49, 169–197.

Gross, M. M., Crane, E. A., & Fredrickson, B. L. (2012). Effort-shape and kinematic assessment of bodily expression of emotion during gait. *Human Movement Science*, 31, 202–221.

Guastello, S. J., Pincus, D., & Gunderson, P. R. (2006). Electrodermal arousal between participants in a conversation: Nonlinear dynamics and linkage effects. *Nonlinear Dynamics, Psychology, and Life Sciences*, 10, 365–399.

Hackman, J. R., & Morris, C. G. (1975). Group tasks, group interaction process, and group performance effectiveness: A review and proposed integration. In L. Berkowitz (Ed.), *Advances in Experimental Social Psychology* (Vol. 16., pp. 1–55). New York, NY: Academic Press.

Haidt, J. (2012). *The righteous mind: Why good people are divided by politics and religion*. New York: Pantheon

Haken, H., Kelso, J. A. S., & Bunz, H. (1985). A theoretical model of phase transitions in humanhand movements. *Biological Cybernetics*, 51, 347–356.

Havas, D. A., Glenberg, A. M., Gutowski, K. A., Lucarelli, M. J., & Davidson, R. J. (2010). Cosmetic use of botulinum toxin-A affects processing of emotional language. *Psychological Science*, 21, 895–900.

Helm, J. L., Sbarra, D., & Ferrer, E. (2012). Assessing cross-partner associations in physiological responses via coupled oscillator models. *Emotion*, 12, 748–762. doi: 10.1037/a0025036

Henning, R. A., Armstead, A. G., & Ferris, J. K. (2009). Social psychophysiological compliance in a four-person research team. *Applied Ergonomics*, 40, 1004–1010.

Higgins, E. T. (1981). Role-taking and social judgment: Alternative developmental perspectives and processes. In J. H. Flavell & L. Ross (Eds.), *Social cognitive development: Frontiers and possible futures* (pp. 119–153). New York: Cambridge University Press.

Hinds, P. J., & Mortensen, M. (2005). Understanding conflict in geographically distributed teams: The moderating effects of shared identity, shared context, and spontaneous communication. *Organization Science*, 16, 290–307.

Hove, M. J., & Risen, J. L. (2009). It's all in the timing: Interpersonal synchrony increases affiliation. *Social Cognition*, 27, 949–960. doi:10.1521/soco.2009.27.6.949

Issartel, J., Marin, L., & Cadopi, M. (2007). Unintended interpersonal co-ordination: "can we march to the beat of our own drum?". *Neuroscience Letters*, 411, 174–179.

Ito, T. A., & Urland, G. R. (2003). Race and gender on the brain: Electrocortical measures of attention to the race and gender of multiply categorizable individuals. *Journal of Personality & Social Psychology*, 85, 616–626.

Janis, I. L. (1972). *Victims of Groupthink: A Psychological Study of Foreign-Policy Decisions and Fiascoes*. Boston, MA: Houghton Mifflin.

Kaplan, H. B., Burch, N. R., & Bloom, S. W. (1964). Physiological covariation and sociometric relationships in small peer groups. In P. H. Leiderman & D. Shapiro (Eds.), *Psychobiological approaches to social behavior* (pp. 92–109). Stanford, CA: Stanford University Press.

Katz, D., & Kahn, R. L. (1966). *The social psychology of organizations*. New York, NY: Wiley.

Kelso, J. A. S. (1984). Phase transitions and critical behavior in human bimanual coordination. *American Journal of Physiology: Regulatory, Integrative, and Comparative*, 246, R1000–R1004.

Kelso, J. A. S., DelColle, J. D., & Schöner, G. (1990). Action-perception as a pattern formation process. In M. Jeannerod (Ed.). *Attention and performance XIII* (Vol. 5, pp. 139–169). Hillsdale, NJ: Erlbaum.

Kimura, M., & Daibo, I. (2006). Interactional synchrony in conversations about emotional episodes: A measurement by "the between-participants pseudosynchrony experimental paradigm." *Journal of Nonverbal Behavior*, 30, 115–126.

Kirschner, S., & Tomasello, M. (2009). Joint drumming: Social context facilitates synchronization in preschool children. *Journal of Experimental Child Psychology*, 102, 299–314.

Kirschner, S., & Tomasello, M. (2010). Joint music making promotes prosocial behavior in 4-year-old children. *Evolution and Human Behavior*, 31, 354–364.

Konvalinka, I., & Roepstorff, A. (2012). The two-brain approach: How can mutually interacting brains teach us something about social interaction? *Frontiers in Human Neuroscience*, 6, 215. doi: 10.3389/fnhum.2012.00215

Konvalinka, I., Xygalatas, D., Bulbulia, J., Schjødt, U., Jegindø, E. M., Wallot, S., & Roepstorff, A. (2011). Synchronized arousal between performers and related spectators in a fire walking ritual. *Proceedings of the National Academy of Sciences*, 108, 8514–8519.

Kraut, R. E., Fussell, S. R., Brennan, S. E., & Siegel, J. (2002). Understanding effects of proximity on collaboration: Implications for technologies to support remote collaborative work. In P. J. Hinds and S. Kiesler (Eds.). *Distributed work* (pp. 137–162). Cambridge, MA: MIT Press.

Kugler, P. N., & Turvey, M. T. (1987). *Information, natural law, and the self-assembly of rhythmic movement*. Hillsdale, NJ: Erlbaum.

LaFrance, M. (1979). Nonverbal synchrony and rapport: Analysis by the cross lag panel technique. *Social Psychology Quarterly*, 42, 66–70.

Lakin, J. L., & Chartrand, T. L. (2003). Using nonconscious behavioral mimicry to create affiliation and rapport. *Psychological Science*, 14, 334–339.

Larson, R. W., & Gillman, S. (1999). Transmission of emotions in the daily interactions of single-mother families. *Journal of Marriage and the Family*, 61, 21–37.

Laurenceau, J. P., Barrett, L. F., & Pietromonaco, P. (1998). Intimacy as an interpersonal process: The importance of self-disclosure, partner disclosure, and perceived partner responsiveness in interpersonal exchanges. *Journal of Personality and Social Psychology*, 74, 1238–1251.

Levenson, R. W. (1992). Autonomic nervous system differences among emotions. *Psychological Science*, 3, 23–27.

Levenson, R. W., Carstensen, L. L., & Gottman, J. M. (1994). The influence of age and gender on affect, physiology, and their interrelations: A study of long-term marriage. *Journal of Personality and Social Psychology*, 67, 56–68.

Levenson, R. W., & Gottman, J. M. (1983). Marital interaction: Physiological linkage and affective exchange. *Journal of Personality and Social Psychology*, 45, 587–597.

Levenson, R. W., & Ruef, A. M. (1992). Empathy: A physiological substrate. *Journal of Personality and Social Psychology*, 63, 234–246.

Markey, P. M., Funder, D. C., Ozer, D. J. (2003). Complementarity of interpersonal behaviors in dyadic interactions. *Personality and Social Psychology Bulletin*, 29, 1082–1090.

McNeill, W. H. (1995). *Keeping together in time: Dance and drill in human history*. Cambridge, MA: Harvard University Press.

Miller, J. B., & Stiver, I. P. (1997). *The healing connection: How women form relationships in therapy and in life*. Boston, MA: Beacon Press.

Montepare, J. M., & Opeyo, A. (2002). The relative salience of physiognomic cues in differentiating faces: A methodological tool. *Journal of Nonverbal Behavior*, 26, 43–59.

Müller, V., & Lindenberger, U. (2011). Cardiac and respiratory patterns synchronize between persons during choir singing. *PLoS ONE*, 6, e24893. doi:10.1371/journal. pone.0024893

Muraven, M., Tice, D. M., & Baumeister, R. F. (1998). Self-control as a limited resource: Regulatory depletion patterns. *Journal of Personality and Social Psychology*, 74, 774–789.

Niedenthal, P. M. (2007). Embodying emotion. *Science*, 316, 1002–1005.

Overall, N. C., & Girme, Y. U. (2015). Dyadic regulation: How intimate partners foster security and growth in close relationships. In C. R. Knee and H. T. Reis (Eds.), *Positive Approaches to Optimal Relationship Development*.

Polzer, J. T., Milton, L. P., & Swann, Jr., W. B. (2002). Capitalizing on diversity: Interpersonal congruence in small work groups. *Administrative Science Quarterly*, 47, 296–324.

Premack, D., & Woodruff, G. (1978). Does the chimpanzee have a theory of mind? *Behavioral and Brain Sciences*, 4, 515–526.

Radcliffe-Brown, A. R. (1922). *The Andaman islanders*. New York: Free Press.

Ragins, B. R., & Verbos, A. K. (2007). Positive relationships in action: Relational mentoring and mentoring schemas in the workplace. In J. E. Dutton & B. R. Ragins (Eds.), *Exploring positive relationships at work: Building a theoretical and research foundation* (pp. 91–116). Mahwah, NJ: Lawrence Erlbaum Associates.

Ramseyer, F., & Tschacher, W. (2011). Nonverbal synchrony in psychotherapy: Coordinated body movement reflects relationship quality and outcome. *Journal of Consulting and Clinical Psychology*, 79, 284–295.

Reis, H. T., Clark, M. S., & Holmes, J. G. (2004). Perceived partner responsiveness as an organizing construct in the study of intimacy and closeness. In D. J. Mashek & A. Aron (Eds.), *Handbook of closeness and intimacy* (pp. 201–225). Mahwah, NJ: Lawrence Erlbaum.

Reis, H. T., & Collins, W. A. (2004). Relationships, human behavior, and psychological science. *Current Directions in Psychological Science*, 13, 233–237.

Richardson, M. J., Garcia, R. L., Frank, T. D., Gregor, M., & Marsh, K. L. (2012). Measuring group synchrony: a cluster-phase method for analyzing multivariate movement time-series. *Frontiers in Physiology*, 3, 1–10.

Richardson, M. J., Marsh, K. L., Isenhower, R. W., Goodman, J. R. L., & Schmidt, R. C. (2007). Rocking together: Dynamics of intentional and unintentional interpersonal coordination. *Human Movement Science*, 26, 867–891.

Richardson, M. J., Marsh, K. L., & Schmidt, R. C. (2005). Effects of visual and verbal interaction on unintentional interpersonal coordination. *Journal of Experimental Psychology: Human Perception and Performance*, 31, 62–79.

Ryan, R. M., & Frederick, C. (1997). On energy, personality, and health: Subjective vitality as a dynamic reflection of well-being. *Journal of Personality*, 65, 529–565.

Saxbe, D., & Repetti, R. L. (2010). For better or worse? Coregulation of couples' cortisol levels and mood states. *Journal of Personality and Social Psychology*, 98, 92–103.

Sbarra, D. A., & Hazan, C. (2008). Co-regulation, dysregulation, self-regulation: An integrative analysis and empirical agenda for understanding adult attachment, separation, loss, and recovery. *Personality and Social Psychology Review*, 12, 141–167.

Schmidt, R. C., Shaw, B. K., & Turvey, M. T. (1993). Coupling dynamics in interlimb coordination. *Journal of Experimental Psychology: Human Perception and Performance*, 19, 397–415.

Schober, M. F. (1998). Different kinds of conversational perspective-taking. In S. R. Fussell & R. J. Kreuz (Eds.), *Social and Cognitive Psychological Approaches to Interpersonal Communication* (pp. 145–174). Mahwah, NJ: Lawrence Erlbaum.

Schoebi, D. (2008). The coregulation of daily affect in marital relationships. *Journal of Family Psychology*, 22, 595–604.

Schrammel, F., Pannasch, S., Graupner, S. T., Mojzisch, A., & Velichkovsky, B. M. (2009). Virtual friend or threat? The effects of facial expression and gaze interaction on psychophysiological responses and emotional experience. *Psychophysiology*, 46, 922–931.

Stanley, J., Gowen, E., & Miall, R. C. (2007). Effects of agency on movement interference during observation of a moving dot stimulus. *Journal of Experimental Psychology: Human Perception and Performance*, 33, 915–926. doi:10.1037/0096–1523.33.4.915

Thayer, R. E. (1986). Activation-deactivation adjective check list: Current overview and structural analysis. *Psychological Reports*, 58, 607–614.

Tickle-Degnen, L., & Rosenthal, R. (1987). Group rapport and nonverbal behavior. In C. Hendrick (Ed.). *Group processes and intergroup relations. Review of personality and social psychology* (Vol. 9, pp. 113–136). Thousand Oaks, CA: Sage Publications.

Tickle-Degnen, L., & Rosenthal, R. (1990). The nature of rapport and its nonverbal correlates. *Psychological Inquiry*, 1, 285–293.

Tiedens, L. Z., Unzueta, M. M. & Young, M. J. (2007). An unconscious desire for hierarchy? The motivated perception of dominance complementary in task partners. *Journal of Personality and Social Psychology*, 93, 402–414.

Tracey, T. J., Ryan, J. M., & Jaschik-Hermann, B. (2001). Complementarity of interpersonal circumplex traits. *Personality and Social Psychology Bulletin*, 27, 786–797.

Tronick, E. Z. (1989). Emotions and emotional communication in infants, *American Psychologist*, 44, 112–119. doi:10.1037/0003-066X.44.2.112

Turvey, M. T., Rosenblum, L. D., Schmidt, R. C., & Kugler, P. N. (1986). Fluctuations and phase symmetry in coordinated rhythmic movement. *Journal of Experimental Psychology: Human Perception and Performance*, 12, 564–583.

Vacharkulksemsuk, T., & Fredrickson, B. L. (2012). Strangers in sync: Achieving embodied rapport through shared movements. *Journal of Experimental Social Psychology*, 48, 399–402. doi:10.1016/j.jesp.2011.07.015

Valdesolo, P., & DeSteno, D. (2011). Synchrony and the social tuning of compassion. *Emotion*, 11, 262–266. doi:10.1037/a0021302

van Knippenberg, A. & Dijksterhuis, A. (2000). Social categorization and stereotyping: A functional approach. *European Review of Social Psychology*, 11, 105–144.

Van Leeuwen, P., Geue, D., Thiel, M., Cysarz, D., Lange, S., Romano, M. C., & Grönemeyer, D. H. (2009). Influence of paced maternal breathing on fetal-maternal heart rate coordination. *Proceedings of the National Academy of Sciences*, 106, 13661–13666.

Waters, S. F., West, T. V., & Mendes, W. B. (2014). Stress contagion: Physiological covariation between mothers and infants. *Psychological Science*, 25, 934–942. doi:10.1177/0956797613518352

Williams, K. D. (2007). Ostracism. *Annual Review of Psychology*, 58, 425–452. doi:10.1146/annurev.psych.58.110405.085641

Williams, K. Y., & O'Reilly, C. A. (1998). Forty years of diversity research: A review. In B. M. Staw & L. L. Cummings (Eds.), *Research in Organizational Behavior* (Vol. 20, pp. 33–140). Greenwich, CT: JAI Press.

Wiltermuth, S. S. (2012). Synchronous activity boosts compliance with requests to aggress. *Journal of Experimental Social Psychology*, 48, 453–456.

Wiltermuth, S. S., & Heath, C. (2009). Synchrony and cooperation. *Psychological Science*, 20, 1–5. doi:10.1111/j.1467-9280.2008.02253.x

PART III

EFFECTIVE INTERVENTIONS

13

Effective interventions for optimal relationships

JUSTIN A. LAVNER AND THOMAS N. BRADBURY

Throughout this volume, multiple lines of evidence highlight the pathways by which different individual characteristics and dyadic processes promote optimal relationship development. Yet we know that the maintenance of these processes also proves elusive for many relationships. Despite newlyweds' initially optimistic beliefs that their relationships will get better over time, relationship satisfaction declines on average during the early years of marriage (Lavner, Karney, & Bradbury, 2013) and the likelihood of divorce is at its peak (Kreider & Ellis, 2011). Scholars have thus worked over the past several decades to devise interventions that will prevent and remediate these adverse outcomes.

What is the best way to intervene to promote optimal relationships? We argue that effective interventions should have one of two aims: helping couples low in distress maintain their satisfaction and avoid deterioration (prevention), and helping couples high in distress regain their satisfaction and improve their relationship (therapeutic intervention). We base this distinction on a growing body of basic research revealing significant variability in couples' marital trajectories, such that some couples begin their marriage highly satisfied and maintain their satisfaction over time whereas others start with low levels of satisfaction that drop precipitously (e.g., Lavner & Bradbury, 2010; Lavner, Bradbury, & Karney, 2012). These basic findings underscore the fact that different couples have different needs from their interventions and necessitate distinguishing "who" interventions are effective for as well as "what" they are effective in doing.

In this chapter, we review the state of the prevention and therapy literatures, providing an overview of the content of the interventions themselves and empirical evidence for their efficacy. We conclude with recommendations for future research to optimize relationship functioning.

PREVENTIVE INTERVENTIONS FOR COUPLES
LOW IN DISTRESS

Given that relationship satisfaction declines on average as relationships progress, a great deal of attention has been devoted to designing interventions that can prevent these declines and help couples maintain their initially high levels of satisfaction. These approaches typically adopt a universal prevention model, in which couples are seen as being more or less equally at risk for adverse outcomes and thus equally needing intervention, which is also similar across couples. The promise of the preventive approach is that it can target couples before they become too entrenched in negative patterns through a program that can fit the needs of many couples. This approach stands in contrast to therapeutic interventions, which are delivered to couples individually on the basis of their clinical distress and individually tailored to their unique needs.

Preventive interventions have taken many forms (see also Rolffs & Rogge, Chapter 15, this volume). Here we focus our review on relationship education, as this is among the most widely used and the most widely studied, as well as a short review of a new class of prevention known as "brief interventions."

Relationship education programs

Relationship education programs are designed to help couples maintain satisfying relationships and prevent distress and dissolution (e.g., Halford, Markman, & Stanley, 2008). These programs are delivered in a group format and typically follow a set curriculum, most commonly focusing on skill-building. For example, in the Prevention and Relationship Enhancement Program (PREP; Markman, Stanley, & Blumberg, 2010), couples are taught communication skills, commitment, friendship, and relationship expectations. The Couple CARE program (Halford, 2011), another widely used relationship education program, emphasizes self-change in areas such as communication, intimacy and caring, managing differences, and sexuality.

A meta-analysis of 86 marriage and relationship education programs showed moderate effects of intervention on relationship quality and communication skills at post-assessment and follow-up, with effect sizes in the .30–.45 range (Hawkins, Blanchard, Baldwin, & Fawcett, 2008). A subsequent meta-analysis of the effects of relationship education on communication skills found that effects were larger and significant for observed communication skills, but not for self-reported communication (Blanchard, Hawkins, Baldwin, & Fawcett, 2009). Despite the promise of these findings, we note that follow-up assessments tended to be brief in duration (3–6 months), with few studies including follow-up of more than 1 year. Accordingly, caution is needed when generalizing the long-term benefits of relationship education.

Indeed, other studies with more extensive follow-up periods cast doubt on the benefits of relationship education. For example, one study of couples receiving PREP showed no difference in their trajectories of communication behavior or eventual dissolution over the first 5 years of marriage (Markman, Rhoades, Stanley, Ragan, & Whitton, 2010). Another recent study of PREP among couples in which at least one partner was in the army found no effect of the intervention on marital quality or marital communication at 2-year follow-up; the intervention group had lower rates of marital dissolution at one site but not at the second site (Stanley et al., 2014). Finally, evidence from a new study of two skills-based interventions (PREP and an acceptance-based model of relationships) showed that couples participating in these interventions had lower dissolution rates at 3-year follow-up compared to couples who had received no treatment, but fared no better than couples who participated in an active control group focused on relationship awareness (described in more detail in the subsequent section; Rogge, Cobb, Lawrence, Johnson, & Bradbury, 2013). Moreover, couples in all three active conditions showed similar changes in relationship quality, and the skills-based interventions produced paradoxical effects in which the respective behavioral targets of the intervention actually showed the worst trajectories over time. These findings dovetail with recent meta-analytic summaries indicating that more rigorous or systematic prevention programs do not produce better effects: institutionalized (i.e., manualized, evaluated) programs did not produce stronger effects than non-institutionalized programs, and programs emphasizing communication skills were no more effective in increasing relationship satisfaction than other types of programs (Hawkins, Stanley, Blanchard, & Albright, 2012). Accordingly, the robustness of the relationship education effects – and skills training in particular – remains in doubt. We now consider evidence for the effectiveness of relationship education in two specific contexts: the transition to parenthood and federal initiatives targeting low-income couples.

Transition to parenthood. Some relationship education programs have been specifically designed around the transition to parenthood, a period when relationship satisfaction commonly declines (see Mitnick, Heyman, & Smith Slep, 2009, for meta-analysis). As with the results from the relationship education literature more generally, results from these studies have been mixed. Results from one study indicated that couples receiving a semi-structured group intervention showed less of a decline in marital satisfaction than control couples, though rates of divorce at the final follow-up 66 months after the birth of the child were similar (Schulz, Cowan, & Cowan, 2006). A different experimental program focused on helping couples become aware of and better manage disagreements before parenthood showed that the positive effects of relationship satisfaction at 3.5-year follow-up were limited to the parents of boys, however, despite more general effects for parental adjustment, co-parenting, and parenting (Feinberg, Jones, Kan, & Goslin, 2010). An initial study of Couple CARE for Parents, an adaption of Couple CARE that combines training in key relationship skills along with infant care information, indicated that women receiving the intervention did not show as much of a decline in relationship satisfaction as women receiving only a maternal parenting education program, but no effects were found for men (Halford, Petch, & Creedy, 2010). Another recent study comparing these interventions showed no main effect on relationship satisfaction, however, though women considered high-risk (e.g., parental divorce, lower education or income, unplanned pregnancy, presence of interpersonal violence) showed less of a decline in relationship satisfaction when receiving the couple-based intervention (Petch, Halford, Creedy, & Gamble, 2012).

Still other evaluations have failed to find any significant effects of relationship education on relationship adjustment during the transition to parenthood. In one, couples participating in a program emphasizing marital virtues did not have significantly higher scores than control group couples on marital virtues, marital quality, marital satisfaction, or the adjustment to parenthood either post-intervention, 3-month post-partum, or 9-month post-partum (Hawkins, Fawcett, Carroll, & Gilliland, 2006). The failure to find significant outcome effects was especially notable given that participants reported being highly satisfied with the program and felt that it was useful in strengthening their marriage. Another study evaluating the efficacy of PREP adapted for Danish couples expecting their first child found similar declines in relationship satisfaction among couples receiving PREP, an information-based control group, and naturally occurring care through 18-month post-partum (Trillingsgaard, Baucom, Heyman, & Elkit, 2012). A meta-analytic review of 21 different interventions targeting the transition to parenthood found small effects for couple communication (d = .28) at the end of intervention, but very limited effects on couple adjustment (d = .09); results from the 11 studies that provided follow-up data (average time of 12 months) were consistent with these patterns (Pinquart & Teubert, 2010). More extensive follow-up data from a study of couples who had received PREP or other forms of premarital education found that receiving premarital education did not change the trajectory of couples' relationship functioning for several years of post-partum (Doss, Rhoades, Stanley, & Markman, 2009b).

Federal initiatives targeting low-income couples. Recent data from two federal initiatives in which relationship education was provided to low-income couples similarly indicate limited effectiveness (for discussion, see M. D. Johnson, 2012, 2013). In one program, Building Strong Families (BSF), voluntary group-based classes on relationship skills education (e.g., communication, conflict management) were provided to unmarried couples who were expecting or just had a baby (Wood, McConnell, Moore, Clarkwest, & Hsueh, 2010). Fifteen months after couples applied for the program, BSF had no effect on couples' relationship stability, the likelihood of marriage, relationship quality, conflict management, fidelity, co-parenting, or father involvement (Wood et al., 2010). There was a pattern of positive results for one of the sites, a pattern of negative results for another site, and no effect on relationship outcomes at the other six sites. Thirty-six months after random assignment, there was a similar pattern of little-to-no effects (Wood, Moore, Clarkwest, & Killewald, 2014). No significant differences were found between treatment and control group couples with regard to their likelihood of being married, marital happiness, conflict management, co-parenting, or family stability.

The second federal program, Supporting Healthy Marriage (SHM), was structured to combine relationship education workshops with supplemental activities and family support services (Hsueh et al., 2012). Whereas BSF consisted primarily of unmarried parents expecting their first child, SHM consisted primarily of married couples (81 percent); the average length of marriage was 6 years. One year after couples had enrolled in the study, there was a general pattern of positive effects: couples receiving the intervention reported significantly higher levels of relationship happiness and higher quality relationship interactions, as well as lower levels of psychological abuse and psychological distress. Men and women also exhibited higher levels of observed positive skills during behavioral interactions. At 30-month follow-up, the intervention group similarly reported higher levels of marital happiness, warmth and support, and positive communication skills, and lower levels of infidelity, psychological abuse, and believing the relationship was in trouble (Lundquist et al., 2014). Treatment effects – though generally positive in nature – were weak, however, with an average effect size of approximately 0.10, falling below standard conventions for an effect to be considered "small" (0.20; Cohen, 1988). Moreover, there were no effects on marital stability, a central target of the program. Taken together, the differences between treatment and control groups may have been statistically different but they were substantively similar.

Summary: Relationship education programs. On the whole, relationship education programs provide some benefit to couples' relationship satisfaction and communication. Nonetheless, these effects are limited in scope and duration, and the program content does not fully meet the needs of diverse, at-risk populations. These results must also be put in the context of program cost: the recent federal initiatives averaged approximately $10,000 per couple (SHM: $9,100; Hsueh et al., 2012; BSF: $11,000; Wood, Moore, Clarkwest, Killewald, & Monahan, 2012), and in general programs are typically given over a series of sessions over several months (Hawkins et al., 2012), thus requiring intensive time and effort. Given the limited benefits of these intensive psychoeducational programs, new efforts are being directed toward developing alternative, brief interventions that require fewer resources and focus more on helping couples use their existing skills. The results from this new class of interventions, though still preliminary in nature, are promising, as described below.

Brief interventions to promote
relationship quality

Like relationship education programs, brief interventions to promote relationship quality target couples low in distress who are not seeking therapy. They are less time intensive and have less of a focus on skill building, however, focusing instead on helping couples be more mindful of their behavioral patterns and harness their existing strengths to keep their relationships healthy.

In one study, couples were randomly assigned to a "Relationship Awareness" condition in which they participated in a one-session intervention designed to increase their awareness of their relationship and the importance of regular relationship maintenance (Rogge et al., 2013). The session focused on helping couples pay more attention to behaviors in their relationship, decide for themselves whether these behaviors were positive or negative, and learn that regular activities such as those captured in films could increase their relationship awareness and maintenance. Couples then watched a film and were led in semi-structured discussions of the themes of the film and how those themes applied to their own relationships. Afterward, couples were provided with a list of 47 popular films and instructed to watch one movie per week for the next month and then discuss the same open-ended questions after each movie. Over a 3-year follow-up, couples who participated in the relationship awareness intervention exhibited declines in hostile conflict (wives only) and stable levels of emotional support compared to no-treatment controls. Especially noteworthy were the significantly lower rates of marital dissolution compared to no-treatment controls (13.3 percent compared to 24.4 percent). As described earlier, these outcomes were similar to the couples randomly assigned to more intensive psychoeducational interventions that explicitly focused on skill-building, suggesting that this type of low-dose, low-cost intervention can prove as beneficial compared to no-treatment controls as existing programs.

The promise of this type of brief intervention is bolstered by findings in which a 21-minute conflict reappraisal writing task promoted relationship quality (Finkel, Slotter, Luchies, Walton, & Gross, 2013). A nonclinical sample of heterosexual married couples (mean duration of marriage = 11 years) was studied for 2 years, with half of the couples randomly assigned to complete the conflict reappraisal task at the end of the first year and two more times at 4-month intervals thereafter (e.g., 16 and 20 months). The control couples received no intervention. The conflict reappraisal task consisted of a seven-minute writing task in which couples were instructed to respond to three prompts regarding a significant disagreement they had experienced with their spouse: (1) how a neutral party might think about the disagreement; (2) what obstacles they encounter when trying to take this neutral third party perspective; and (3) how they might be able to take this perspective in interactions with their partner over the upcoming months. Results indicated that all couples showed significant declines in marital quality over the first year (pre-intervention), but that couples who participated in the intervention were buffered from this decline over the second year (post-intervention), such that their marital quality stabilized during this time. The control couples continued to show significant declines during the second year. Mediational analyses indicated that the intervention served to decrease conflict-related distress, thus promoting marital quality. These findings build on a growing body of work from the social psychology litera-ture highlighting the benefits of brief interventions to promote well-being (e.g., Walton & Cohen, 2011) and dovetail with other findings indicating that self-distancing reduces people's tendency to reason less well about their own problems than they do other people's problems (Grossman & Kross, 2014).

This model of brief intervention is used in the "Marriage Checkup" (Cordova, Warren, & Gee, 2001) as well. Based on motivational interviewing principles (Miller & Rollnick, 1991), this intervention was designed to moti-vate couples to take the steps needed to improve their relationship, either on their own or through couple therapy. It is specifically designed to attract couples with a range of marital functioning, including those who may not typically seek treatment, and intended to be the relationship equivalent of annual physical or dental checkups (Morrill et al., 2011). The program consists of a two-session intervention: a relationship assessment session, which includes standardized measures, an interview, and a problem discussion, along with a tailored individual feedback session (Cordova et al., 2001).

Effectiveness data on the Marriage Checkup highlight its potential benefits. One randomized control trial of 74 couples indicated that couples participating in the Marriage Checkup improved more than a no-treatment control group by post-treatment with regard to their relationship distress, intimacy, acceptance, and motivation to take direct action (Cordova et al., 2005). A recent large-scale randomized trial provides further support for the efficacy of the Marriage Checkup over longer-term follow-up (Cordova et al., 2014). Two hundred and fifteen couples were randomly assigned to treatment (113 couples) or control (102 couples) groups. Treatment couples participated in assessment and feedback visits at the beginning of the study and again 1 year later. All couples completed five assessments during the first year and four additional assessments over the second year. Results indicated small-to-medium effects, such that Marriage Checkup couples were more satisfied and reported significantly more intimacy and acceptance than control couples. Effects were strongest immediately following the Marriage Checkup and then stabilized before diminishing over time, indicating that booster sessions are needed to maintain the benefits of treatment.

Summary: Brief interventions for low distress couples. These findings provide initial evidence to support the efficacy of brief, low-dose interventions as a promising way to help couples maintain their current level of satisfaction. Although the interventions discussed here highlight different areas of relationship maintenance (e.g., relationship awareness, conflict reappraisal, motivating couples to improve on their own), they all aim to capitalize upon couples' existing skills rather than teaching them new skills. This focus on harnessing couples' strengths gives couples greater control over and involvement in maintaining their relationship. This emphasis, along with the low cost and low time investment, makes these programs particularly well-suited for couples low in distress, whose relationships are functioning well and who need only worry about maintaining their already high levels of satisfaction rather than addressing skill deficits in their relationship.

Therapeutic interventions for distressed couples

The research reviewed thus far examines the benefits of interventions designed for low distress couples who want to maintain their satisfaction and/or prevent declines. For couples who are in more serious distress, however, these programs will likely prove insufficient to *improve* the relationship; more intensive treatment is necessary. The clinical need for these types of services is great. Relationship problems are the most frequently cited cause of acute emotional distress in national surveys (Swindle, Heller, Pescosolido, & Kikuzawa, 2000). Approximately 25 percent of intact marriages are considered to be discordant (Beach, Fincham, Amir, & Leonard, 2005; Whisman, Beach, & Snyder, 2008), and 40 percent of first marriages end in divorce, with rates of divorce higher for remarriages (Kreider & Ellis, 2011).

Despite the prevalence of distressed relationships, many couples do not seek therapeutic services. One study found that only 14 percent of couples reported seeking therapy during the first 5 years of marriage (Doss, Rhoades, Stanley, & Markman, 2009a), and other surveys indicate that only 20–35 percent of spouses have ever received counseling (C. A. Johnson et al., 2002; Karney, Garvan, & Thomas, 2003). Strikingly, only 37 percent of participants who had been divorced reported that they received couples therapy prior to the divorce (Johnson et al., 2002), indicating that even couples in severe distress frequently did not access therapy services.

The disconnect between the need for treatment and the actual utilization of couple therapy services is unfortunate given a large body of research supporting the efficacy of couple therapy in the treatment of relationship distress. Below we review two broad classes of couple therapy – behavioral treatments and emotion-focused treatments – that can be used to treat distressed couples. These two treatment types have been the focus of the largest body of scientific study and evidence of their efficacy is now clear (Lebow, Chambers, Christensen, & Johnson, 2012).

Behavioral treatments

Behavioral couple therapy (BCT). Behavioral couple therapy (BCT) has been the most widely studied form of couple therapy and is one of the most widely used: reports from marriage and family therapists indicate that between 30–40 percent identify their primary theoretical orientation as behavioral or cognitive-behavioral (e.g., Beaton, Dienhart, Schmidt, & Turner, 2009). Drawing from behavioral principles, BCT argues that (1) happy marriages can be distinguished from unhappy marriages by the ratio of positives to negatives in the relationship (Stuart, 1969; Jacobson & Margolin, 1979) and (2) couples are distressed because they have not developed or maintained key skills such as providing empathic and supportive communication and problem-solving/decision-making (Weiss, 1980).

BCT takes a skills-oriented, present-focused approach to improving couples' relationships. Based on the theoretical assumptions outlined above, BCT focuses on (1) behavior exchange strategies designed to increase the ratio of positive to negatives in the relationship and (2) communication and problem-solving skills. Behavioral exchange strategies such as "love days" and scheduling positive activities increase couples' positive interactions, and are the initial focus of treatment so that couples experience some positive growth and learn that change is possible (Jacobson & Margolin, 1979). Communication and problem-solving skills training helps couples become more comfortable and adept at sharing their thoughts and feelings and resolving specific challenges in their relationships. Communication training proceeds in a sequential process in which couples receive feedback about their current patterns, learn about more adaptive communication (e.g., listening skills, positive and negative feeling expression), and practice the new communication patterns (Jacobson & Margolin, 1979). Problem-solving training focuses on helping couples define their problems and develop solutions to these problems. Therapists often assign couples homework to practice these discussions at home, and then review these conversations during the following session.

Recent adaptions of BCT have expanded to include a focus on cognitions, driven by the theoretical assumption that a focus on behavior was incomplete without a consideration for partners' interpretations and evaluations of this behavior (D. H. Baucom, Epstein, LaTaillade, & Kirby, 2008; Epstein & Baucom, 2002) and by empirical evidence highlighting the unique role that couples' attributions play in interactional patterns (Bradbury & Fincham, 1992) and in couples' satisfaction and stability (see Bradbury & Fincham, 1990, for review). Interventions in the cognitive domain are thus designed to help couples reassess their cognitions about specific elements of the relationship and the relationship in general so that they view it in a more reasonable and accurate manner.

Empirical support for the effectiveness of BCT has been robust. A meta-analysis and review of different couple therapy models found that BCT was the only model considered "efficacious and specific," the most stringent criteria for empirically supported treatments (Baucom, Shoham, Meuser, Daiutio, & Stickle, 1998). Evidence came from more than two dozen controlled treatment outcome studies, which consistently showed that BCT was more effective than waitlist controls or nonspecific treatments. More recent meta-analyses similarly indicate the effectiveness of BCT compared to no-treatment couples, with an average effect size of 0.59 (Shadish & Baldwin, 2005). The use of communication training/problem solving in particular was shown to lead to larger effects. How clinically representative the samples were (e.g., setting, referrals, therapists) was uncorrelated with effect size, indicating that similar effectiveness is found in tightly controlled laboratory settings and in the community, though more work is needed in this area.

Integrative behavioral couple therapy (IBCT). Integrative Behavioral Couple Therapy (IBCT) grew out of this behavioral tradition. Despite the well-documented efficacy of the behavioral models in producing short-term gains, follow-up results indicated that many of these initial gains could not be maintained over longer periods of time (Snyder, Wills, & Grady-Fletcher, 1991). Moreover, although short-term changes were statistically significant, many couples did not experience clinically significant changes from maritally distressed to satisfied (Jacobson et al., 1984). Accordingly, IBCT built on traditional behavioral approaches to address these limitations and promote more substantial, longstanding changes in couples' functioning.

Perhaps the most notable addition to IBCT is an emphasis on emotional acceptance. This focus comes from the theoretical assumptions that partners often have genuine incompatibilities or irreconcilable differences that are not amenable to change; that the reactions to a behavior may be as problematic as the behavior itself; and that a focus on change can ultimately lead to a resistance to change (Christensen et al., 2004). Emotional acceptance is thus defined as helping partners "convert problems into vehicles for intimacy" and "'let go' of the struggle to change each other" (Jacobson & Christensen, 1998, p. 12–13).

Three primary strategies are used in treatment to facilitate emotional acceptance: empathic joining, unified detachment, and tolerance building (Jacobson & Christensen, 1998). Empathic joining occurs when partners express the vulnerable feelings underlying their reactions, which can often elicit empathy and compassion from the partner and lead to greater closeness. Unified detachment focuses on a more intellectual analysis of the conflict and problematic interaction pattern. Finally, tolerance building strategies are used to help partners let go of the struggle to change their partner and better manage their own reactions. Whereas empathic joining and unified detachment result in deepening intimacy, tolerance interventions result in lessening the intensity and duration of conflict.

IBCT also includes the behavior exchange and communication training interventions found in traditional behavioral couple therapy. Thus, there is still a place for more directive rule-governed change interventions. In general, however, there tends to be more of a focus on contingency-shaped changes in which couples' behaviors are shaped more by their natural consequences (Jacobson & Christensen, 1998).

A small pilot study of 21 couples in which couples were randomly assigned to either TBCT or IBCT showed that IBCT was indeed distinct from TBCT, that therapists were able to implement acceptance-based interventions in IBCT, and that post-treatment results were similar to those in TBCT (Jacobson, Christensen, Prince, Cordova, & Eldridge, 2000). On the basis of these promising initial results, 134 married couples were randomly assigned to either TBCT or IBCT in the largest randomized trial of marital therapy ever conducted (Christensen et al., 2004). Notably, the sample consisted of seriously distressed couples who reported chronic distress; couples low in distress and/or those couples who were acutely distressed were excluded and referred for treatment elsewhere. Couples received an average of 23 sessions, with a maximum of 26 sessions.

Results immediately post-treatment indicated that IBCT was as effective as TBCT (Christensen et al., 2004). Analysis of clinically significant change showed that 59 percent of couples receiving TBCT showed reliable improvement or recovery compared to 71 percent of couples receiving IBCT; these results did not differ statistically. Marital satisfaction increased in both treatments. Couples in both treatments reported decreasing numbers of steps toward dissolution, particularly early in treatment, and indicated improvements in their self-reported communication behavior.

Further analysis of the results lends support to the idea that the two treatments have different mechanisms of change. First, although marital satisfaction increased in both treatments, the patterns of change were different: the marital satisfaction of couples receiving TBCT improved more quickly and then plateaued, whereas IBCT couples showed slow and steady improvement (Christensen et al., 2004). Second, couples' in-session behaviors showed distinct patterns of change (Sevier, Atkins, Doss, & Christensen, 2013). Couples who received traditional behavioral couple therapy showed an initial increase in positive behaviors that peaked and then gradually declined over time, along with a corresponding decrease in negative behaviors that gradually increased over time. Couples participating in IBCT showed a mirror of this pattern, such that positive behavior initially decreased and then increased, and negative behavior initially increased and then decreased. Taken together, these patterns are consistent with TBCT's focus on increasing positive behaviors and resolving minor problems early in treatment, thus providing a short-term boost. In contrast, IBCT focuses on couples' core themes from the start of treatment, leading to steady improvement as couples are increasingly able to use acceptance and change strategies.

Extensive follow-up data were then gathered to determine the lasting effectiveness of the treatments. Over the first 2-year post-treatment, couples completed assessments of marital and individual functioning every 6 months and participated in problem discussions in the lab at 2-year follow-up. The trajectory of satisfaction over the 2 years showed a "hockey-stick" pattern of initial rapid deterioration followed by increases in marital satisfaction (Christensen, Atkins, Yi, Baucom, & George, 2006). At the time of 2-year follow-up, 74 percent of IBCT couples and 70 percent of TBCT couples had maintained their gains post-treatment, such that 47 percent of IBCT couples were categorized as recovered and 37 percent of TBCT couples were categorized as recovered. Accordingly, both treatments produced lasting effects on marital satisfaction. Lasting treatment effects for both interventions were also found when examining couples' observed communication during problem discussions at 2-year follow-up (K. W. Baucom, Sevier, Eldridge, Doss, & Christensen, 2011). Although positivity worsened, husbands' and wives' withdrawal and negativity showed significant declines from post-treatment to 2-year follow-up, and problem-solving skills remained stable. These effects show the lasting benefit of these behavioral approaches on couples' communication.

There was also some indication that couples participating in IBCT fared better than couples participating in TBCT at 2-year follow-up. Although couples in both treatment modalities showed the hockey stick pattern of satisfaction described above, the initial period of deterioration was shorter for couples receiving IBCT (Christensen et al., 2006). Among couples who remained married, those who received IBCT were significantly more satisfied with their relationships at 22-week post-treatment and remained so throughout the 2-year follow-up period. Behaviorally, wives who received IBCT showed significant declines in negativity but wives who received TBCT did not, and husbands who received IBCT were able to maintain stable levels of positivity, whereas husbands who received TBCT showed significant declines in positivity (K. W. Baucom et al., 2011). Taken together, results from the 2-year follow-up support the effectiveness of both behavioral approaches, with somewhat stronger effects for IBCT.

Finally, couples' outcomes were assessed again 5-year post-treatment (Christensen, Atkins, Baucom, & Yi, 2010). Couples in both treatments showed maintenance and gains from years 3–5, with no parallel drop in satisfaction as was shown immediately following treatment. Effect sizes were strong for both treatments from pre-treatment to 5-year follow-up, with *d*'s of 1.03 and 0.92 for IBCT and TBCT, respectively. Approximately 50 percent of couples showed clinically significant improvement, whereas another 25 percent had separated or divorced. Unlike the previous assessment, no statistically significant differences were found in couples' outcomes between IBCT and TBCT.

Overall, the results from this well-designed, rigorous study provide convincing support of the efficacy of IBCT and TBCT in the amelioration of couple distress among a sample of chronically distressed couples. Although the treatments are conceptually distinct and showed somewhat different mechanisms of change, both were effective. Indeed, large treatment effects were found not only at post-treatment, but were maintained over 2- and 5-year follow-up. The strength of these results is especially striking in comparison to the only two previous studies with similar follow-up periods. In one, 43.6 percent of couples who had received conjoint therapy and 70.2 percent of couples who had received non-conjoint therapy had divorced by 5 years (Cookerly, 1980); in the second, 38 percent of couples receiving behavioral marital therapy had divorced by 4 years (Snyder et al., 1991). Couples in both treatments in this study had significantly better outcomes (25 percent divorce) than in these previous studies (Christensen et al., 2010). Together, these results add to the large body of evidence cited above supporting the use of traditional behavioral couple therapy approaches to treat couple distress, and indicate that IBCT functions at least as well as this well-supported approach.

Emotion-focused treatments

Emotion-focused couple therapy (EFT) has also been shown to be an effective treatment for distressed couples. Compared to the behavioral therapies, EFT is a more humanistic intervention that draws on attachment theory to conceptualize relationship distress as the result of an insecure attachment bond (Greenman & Johnson, 2013; S. M. Johnson, 2004). Emotion is primary and is the agent of change. Treatment takes an intrapersonal focus as partners access their attachment-related emotional responses, with a particular emphasis on translating secondary emotions such as anger into more primary emotions such as fear or grief, as well as an interpersonal focus on couples' interactional cycles (S. M. Johnson, 2004, p. 9). Throughout, the aim is on creating a more secure bond and increasing the couple's sense of connection. The treatment is designed to be implemented in 8–20 sessions.

In the review of empirically supported couple interventions described earlier (Baucom et al., 1998), EFT was classified as an "efficacious and possibly specific" treatment for distressed couples (p. 62). Support comes from a meta-analysis of four randomized clinical trials comparing EFT to a no-treatment condition showing a large treatment effect (mean effect size = 1.30) following treatment and a 70 percent recovery rate for relationship distress at short-term follow-up (S. M. Johnson, Hunsley, Greenberg, & Schindler, 1999). Couples participating in EFT were able to maintain their gains through 2-year follow-up (Cloutier, Manoin, Walker, & Johnson, 2002), though this study lacked follow-up data on control group couples for comparison. More recently, EFT has been shown to be effective in the treatment of attachment injuries (Makinen & Johnson, 2006), with 3-year follow-up data on a subset of these couples indicating that these effects were maintained over time (Halchuk, Makinen, & Johnson, 2010). Process research indicates that deeper emotional experiencing, blamer softening, intimate self-disclosure, and resolving attachment injuries are all associated with positive outcomes (e.g., S. M. Johnson & Greenberg, 1988; see Greenman & Johnson, 2013, for review).

In sum, like Behavioral Couples Therapy and Integrative Behavioral Couples Therapy, EFT is an effective intervention for distressed couples. We note, however, that the strongest results have generally been found with relatively less distressed couples, leading some authors to question "whether EFT is appropriate for highly distressed couples or whether it should be used primarily with less distressed couples who have maintained some sense of attachment to each other" (Baucom et al., 1998, p. 62). Going forward, further research with more distressed couples is needed to support the validity of using EFT with this population. In addition, with the exception of the early treatment studies (S. M. Johnson & Greenberg, 1985; Goldman & Greenberg, 1992), much of the research on EFT has not compared it to other effective treatments. Such research is needed to make claims about the relative effectiveness of the intervention as well as to better understand for whom EFT is particularly effective.

FUTURE DIRECTIONS

Taken together, we have learned much over the last several decades about what types of interventions are effective for optimizing relationship development. In the context of helping couples maintain their functioning and prevent declines in satisfaction and other positive processes, educational interventions such as skills training have short-term effectiveness, but benefits for satisfaction and dissolution prove to be more limited longer term. Emerging evidence also indicates that skills training may not be necessary to promote relationship quality, as interventions without a skills component prove effective, as do interventions that are very brief in duration. These findings are promising in indicating that intensive prevention may not be necessary for all couples hoping to maintain their relationship, thus providing opportunities for more expansive reach and access to a range of couples. For couples needing more intensive therapeutic intervention to ameliorate distress, behavioral and emotion-focused therapies have proven to be effective in many clinical trials. The recent work on traditional and integrative behavioral therapy models is particularly noteworthy for its methodological rigor, and highlights the long-lasting benefits of these interventions on couples' relationships.

Considering this body of work in its entirety, it is noteworthy that therapeutic interventions to ameliorate distress have more consistently been shown to be effective compared to no-treatment controls than have educational interventions to prevent distress. This discrepancy begs the question of why helping low-distress couples prevent adverse outcomes has proven to be so difficult. One explanation is that effective prevention requires a deeper understanding of how relationships change and develop, as we have argued previously (Bradbury & Lavner, 2012). Yet another explanation, however, is that the tasks and aims of preventive programs have in large part not mapped onto the goals of these programs. That is, prevention programs are primarily being delivered to couples who are satisfied with their relationships and who are hoping to maintain that satisfaction. The focus of prevention programs has historically not been on maintenance, however, but rather on equipping couples with skills such as problem-solving and social support that have been shown to be associated with declines in satisfaction. In this manner these programs have adapted the focus of therapeutic intervention (particularly behavioral interventions) to serve a prevention-seeking population. What we learn from the results of these programs, however, is that it is not a perfect parallel: the types of approaches needed to help couples maintain their functioning are not necessarily the approaches needed to help couples regain their functioning.

We look forward to the next generation of research on interventions for low distress couples. First and foremost, we argue that models of prevention are more likely to be successful to the extent that they emphasize general relationship principles (e.g., be mindful of the impact of your behaviors on your partner) rather than prescribe specific behaviors (Bradbury & Lavner, 2012). General relationship principles allow couples to tailor the general idea to their own relationship, rather than giving them specific rules and standards that may be difficult to meet (see Rogge et al., 2013, for evidence of paradoxical effects of psychoeducational interventions). This focus on general principles is consistent with an emphasis on relationship maintenance by encouraging couples to use their existing skills to promote positive relationships. Even so, there continues to be a need for research into new specific targets of intervention that more fully embrace this "relationship maintenance" focus in a variety of forms. As one example, interventions that encourage prayer have been shown to benefit some couples (e.g., Beach et al., 2011; Fincham, Lambert, & Beach, 2010). These findings are consistent with those from the studies of brief interventions indicating that couples benefit from interventions that build on their existing strengths and encourage self-change. Third, new methods of program delivery that are more consistent with relationship maintenance may prove effective. Traditional psychoeducational programs have adapted the therapeutic model of intensive intervention (e.g., many hours of instruction in a relatively short period of time). Although this approach may be beneficial for couples in distress, it may not be necessary for couples aiming to maintain their current level of satisfaction. These couples may benefit more from less intensive interventions spaced out over longer periods of time (e.g., Doss, Cicila, Hsueh, Morrison, & Carhart, 2014), as was the case in the brief interventions discussed here. In this manner, the focus on relationship maintenance can guide program content and program delivery. Finally, more research is needed regarding whether models of brief intervention can prove similarly effective for high-risk (but low distress) couples. Initial evidence indicates that high-risk couples participating in the relationship awareness intervention described earlier fare as well as low-risk couples (Williamson et al., 2015); future research must test these types of brief programs specifically among larger samples of high-risk populations.

The data on therapeutic interventions for couples high in distress paint a more optimistic picture going forward, and raise new questions about what types of services prove most effective for what types of people (e.g., B. R. Baucom, Atkins, Rowe, Doss, & Christensen, 2014). It would be valuable, for example, to compare the behavioral interventions with the emotion-focused interventions, both to determine relative efficacy as well as to have a better understanding of who benefits most from what type of treatment. This information would be useful for the field and for the general public as they consider what type of therapy to pursue. At the same time, we recognize that there remains room to improve, as only 50 percent of couples were able to achieve and maintain clinically significant change over time and another 25 percent divorced. Although these statistics may improve with a better understanding of treatment-couple match, continued refinement of these therapeutic models may also improve outcomes. Process research can be used to identify the mechanisms of change in these treatments and to determine which components drive treatment effectiveness. Adaptations to program delivery may also prove beneficial. For example, booster sessions were not included in the randomized trial of behavioral treatments, although these are common in behavioral interventions for other clinical concerns and have shown some benefit (e.g., Clarke, Rohde, Lewinsohn, Hops, & Seeley, 1999). Indeed, data from the Marriage Checkup highlight the utility of booster sessions in the prevention context, suggesting that incorporating booster sessions post-treatment may promote further gains and/or prevent declines following couple therapy.

We are also hopeful that the coming years will include an increased emphasis on increasing the accessibility of therapeutic services. Given that a minority of couples actually receives couple therapy (e.g., Karney et al., 2003), identifying ways to increase reach and encourage distressed couples to access services before their distress becomes too severe and intractable is needed. Recent work indicates that one pathway to increased therapy utilization begins with preventive interventions: couples who received pre-marital education were more likely to receive couples counseling, and this was particularly true among high-risk populations (e.g., individuals with lower incomes, African-American couples, and those with less formal education; Williamson, Trail, Bradbury, & Karney, 2014). Thus, even if educational interventions are not consistently effective in stabilizing satisfaction, they may serve as a gateway to subsequent therapeutic services. We also note the recent adaptation of IBCT into an Internet-based self-help program (www.ourrelationship.com) designed as a secondary intervention to help couples with existing relationship problems before they warrant couple therapy (Doss, Benson, Georgia, & Christensen, 2013). Although this program does not serve as a perfect parallel to couple therapy (e.g., creating empathic joining proved to be more difficult in an Internet context, though unified detachment and behavior change were still possible), it nonetheless provides access to an evidence-based program to a much broader segment of the population than would receive it otherwise. We eagerly await the effectiveness results of this and other creative interventions over the upcoming years.

More generally, it will be important to evaluate the strengths and limitations of preventive and therapeutic models as they move from the lab to the community. The few studies that have done so underscore the challenges of this shift. As we described earlier, findings from the federal prevention programs with low-income couples generally showed smaller effects than would be expected from previous experimental studies. In the context of interventions for distressed couples, a study of behavioral couple therapy within Veteran Administration Medical Centers indicates that average gains were higher than would be expected from natural remission but lower than in the efficacy trials described earlier, with higher rates of premature termination (Doss et al., 2012). Going forward, research examining ways to enhance the efficacy of interventions and to improve the effectiveness of these interventions under real-world conditions will do much to advance understanding of the factors that promote optimal relationships and the best methods of doing so.

REFERENCES

Baucom, B. R., Atkins, D. C., Rowe, L. S., Doss, B. D., & Christensen, A. (2014). Prediction of treatment response at 5-year follow-up in a randomized clinical trial of behaviorally based couple therapies. *Journal of Consulting and Clinical Psychology.* doi:10.1037/ a0038005

Baucom, D. H., Epstein, N. B., LaTaillade, J. J., & Kirby, J. S. (2008). Cognitive-behavioral couple therapy. In A. S. Gurman (Ed.), *Clinical handbook of couple therapy* (pp. 31–72). New York: Guilford Press.

Baucom, D. H., Shoham, V., Mueser, K. T., Daituo, A. D., & Stickle, T. R. (1998). Empirically supported couple and family interventions for marital distress and adult mental health problems. *Journal of Consulting and Clinical Psychology,* 66, 53–88. doi:10.1037/0022-006X.66.1.53

Baucom, K. W., Sevier, M., Eldridge, K. A., Doss, B. D., & Christensen, A. (2011). Observed communication in couples two years after integrative and traditional behavioral couple therapy: Outcome and link with five-year follow-up. *Journal of Consulting and Clinical Psychology,* 79, 565–576. doi:10.1037/a0025121

Beach, S. H., Fincham, F. D., Amir, N., & Leonard, K. E. (2005). The taxometrics of marriage: Is marital discord categorical? *Journal of Family Psychology,* 19, 276–285. doi:10.1037/0893-3200.19.2.276

Beach, S. H., Hurt, T. R., Fincham, F. D., Franklin, K. J., McNair, L. M., & Stanley, S. M. (2011). Enhancing marital enrichment through spirituality: Efficacy data for prayer focused relationship enhancement. *Psychology of Religion and Spirituality,* 3, 201–216. doi:10.1037/a0022207

Beaton, J., Dienhart, A., Schmidt, J., & Turner, J. (2009). Clinical practice patterns of Canadian couple/marital/family therapists. *Journal of Marital and Family Therapy,* 35, 193–203. doi:10.1111/j.1752-0606.2009.00116.x

Blanchard, V. L., Hawkins, A. J., Baldwin, S. A., & Fawcett, E. B. (2009). Investigating the effects of marriage and relationship education on couples' communication skills: A meta-analytic study. *Journal of Family Psychology,* 23, 203–214. doi:10.1037/a0015211

Bradbury, T. N., & Fincham, F. D. (1990). Attributions in marriage: Review and critique. *Psychology Bulletin,* 107, 3–33. doi:10.1037/0033-2909.107.1.3

Bradbury, T. N., & Fincham, F. D. (1992). Attributions and behavior in marital interaction. *Journal of Personality and Social Psychology,* 63, 613–628. doi:10.1037/ 0022-3514.63.4.613

Bradbury, T. N., & Lavner, J. A. (2012). How can we improve preventive and educational interventions for intimate relationships? *Behavior Therapy,* 43, 113–122. doi:10.1016/j.beth.2011.02.008

Christensen, A., Atkins, D. C., Baucom, B., & Yi, J. (2010). Marital status and satisfaction five years following a randomized clinical trial comparing traditional versus integrative behavioral couple therapy. *Journal of Consulting and Clinical Psychology,* 78, 225–235. doi:10.1037/a0018132

Christensen, A., Atkins, D. C., Berns, S., Wheeler, J., Baucom, D. H., & Simpson, L. E. (2004). Traditional versus integrative behavioral couple therapy for significantly and chronically distressed married couples. *Journal of Consulting and Clinical Psychology, 72,* 176–191. doi:10.1037/0022-006X.72.2.176

Christensen, A., Atkins, D. C., Yi, J., Baucom, D. H., & George, W. H. (2006). Couple and individual adjustment for 2 years following a randomized clinical trial comparing traditional versus integrative behavioral couple therapy. *Journal of Consulting and Clinical Psychology, 74,* 1180–1191. doi:10.1037/0022-006X.74.6.1180

Clarke, G. N., Rohde, P., Lewinsohn, P. M., Hops, H., & Seeley, J. R. (1999). Cognitive-behavioral treatment of adolescent depression: Efficacy of acute group treatment and booster sessions. *Journal of the American Academy of Child & Adolescent Psychiatry, 38,* 272–279. doi:10.1097/00004583-199903000-00014

Cloutier, P. F., Manion, I. G., Walker, J. G., & Johnson, S. M. (2002). Emotionally focused interventions for couples with chronically ill children: A 2-year follow-up. *Journal of Marital and Family Therapy, 28,* 391–398. doi:10.1111/j.1752-0606.2002.tb00364.x

Cohen, J. (1988). *Statistical power analysis for the behavioral sciences* (2nd ed.). Hillsdale, NJ: Lawrence Erlbaum.

Cookerly, J. R. (1980). Does marital therapy do any lasting good? *Journal of Marital and Family Therapy, 6,* 393–397. doi:10.1111/j.1752-0606.1980.tb01331.x

Cordova, J. V., Fleming, C., Morrill, M., Hawrilenko, M., Sollenberger, J. W., Harp, A. G., Gray, T. D., Darling, E. V., Blair, J. M., Meade, A. E., & Wachs, K. (2014). The Marriage Checkup: A randomized controlled trial of annual relationship health checkups. *Journal of Consulting and Clinical Psychology, 82,* 592–604. doi:10.1037/a0037097

Cordova, J. V., Scott, R. L., Dorian, M., Mirgain, S., Yaeger, D., & Groot, A. (2005). The Marriage Checkup: An indicated preventive intervention for treatment-avoid couples at risk for marital deterioration. *Behavior Therapy, 36,* 301–309. doi:10.1016/S0005-7894(05)80112-1

Cordova, J. V., Warren, L. Z., & Gee, C. B. (2001). Motivational interviewing as an intervention for at-risk couples. *Journal of Marital and Family Therapy, 27,* 315–326. doi:10.1111/j.1752-0606.2001.tb00327.x

Doss, B. D., Benson, L. A., Georgia, E. J., & Christensen, A. (2013). Translation of Integrative Behavioral Couple Therapy to a web-based intervention. *Family Process, 52,* 139–153. doi:10.1111/famp.12020

Doss, B. D., Cicila, L. N., Hsueh, A. C., Morrison, K. R., & Carhart, K. (2014). A randomized controlled trial of brief coparenting and relationship interventions during the transition to parenthood. *Journal of Family Psychology, 28,* 483–494. doi:10.1037/a0037311

Doss, B. D., Rhoades, G. K., Stanley, S. M., & Markman, H. J. (2009a). Marital therapy, retreats, and books: The who, what, when, and why of relationship help-seeking. *Journal of Marital and Family Therapy, 35,* 18–29. doi:10.1111/j.1752-0606.2008.00093.x

Doss, B. D., Rhoades, G. K., Stanley, S. M., & Markman, H. J. (2009b). The effect of the transition to parenthood on relationship quality: An 8-year prospective study. *Journal of Personality and Social Psychology, 96,* 601–619. doi:10.1037/a0013969

Doss, B. D., Rowe, L. S., Morrison, K. R., Libet, J., Birchler, G. R., Madsen, J. W., & McQuaid, J. R. (2012). Couple therapy for military veterans: Overall effectiveness and predictors of response. *Behavior Therapy, 43,* 216–227. doi:10.1016/j.beth.2011.06.006

Epstein, N. B., & Baucom, D. H. (2002). *Enhanced cognitive-behavioral therapy for couples: A contextual approach.* Washington, DC: American Psychological Association.

Feinberg, M. E., Jones, D. E., Kan, M. L., & Goslin, M. C. (2010). Effects of family foundations on parents and children: 3.5 years after baseline. *Journal of Family Psychology*, 24, 532–542. doi:10.1037/a0020837

Fincham, F. D., Lambert, N. M., & Beach, S. H. (2010). Faith and unfaithfulness: Can praying for your partner reduce infidelity? *Journal of Personality and Social Psychology*, 99, 649–659. doi:10.1037/a0019628

Finkel, E. J., Slotter, E. B., Luchies, L. B., Walton, G. M., & Gross, J. J. (2013). A brief intervention to promote conflict reappraisal preserves marital quality over time. *Psychological Science*, 24, 1595–1601. doi:10.1177/0956797612474938

Goldman, A., & Greenberg, L. (1992). Comparison of integrated systemic and emotionally focused approaches to couples therapy. *Journal of Consulting and Clinical Psychology*, 60, 962–969. doi:10.1037/0022-006X.60.6.962

Greenman, P. S., & Johnson, S. M. (2013). Process research on emotionally focused therapy (EFT) for couples: Linking theory to practice. *Family Process*, 52, 46–61. doi:10.1111/famp.12015

Grossman, I., & Kross, E. (2014). Exploring Solomon's Paradox: Self-distancing eliminates the self-other asymmetry in wise reasoning about close relationships in younger and older adults. *Psychological Science*, 25, 1571–1580. doi:10.1177/0956797614535400

Halchuk, R. E., Makinen, J. A., & Johnson, S. M. (2010). Resolving attachment injuries in couples using emotionally focused therapy: A three-year follow-up. *Journal of Couple & Relationship Therapy: Innovations in Clinical and Educational Interventions*, 9, 31–47. doi:10.1080/15332690903473069

Halford, W. K. (2011). *Marriage and relationship education: What works and how to provide it.* New York: Guilford.

Halford, W. K., Markman, H. J., & Stanley, S. (2008). Strengthening couples' relationships with education: Social policy and public health perspectives. *Journal of Family Psychology*, 22, 497–505. doi:10.1037/a0012789

Halford, W. K., Petch, J., & Creedy, D. K. (2010). Promoting a positive transition to parenthood: A randomized clinical trial of couple relationship education. *Prevention Science*, 11, 89–100. doi:10.1007/s11121-009-0152-y

Hawkins, A. J., Blanchard, V. L., Baldwin, S. A., & Fawcett, E. B. (2008). Does marriage and relationship education work? A meta-analytic study. *Journal of Consulting and Clinical Psychology*, 76, 723–734. doi:10.1037/a0012584

Hawkins, A. J., Fawcett, E. B., Carroll, J. S., & Gilliland, T. T. (2006). The marriage moments program for couples transitioning to parenthood: Divergent conclusions from formative and outcome evaluation data. *Journal of Family Psychology*, 20, 561–570. doi:10.1037/ 0893-3200.20.4.561

Hawkins, A. J., Stanley, S. M., Blanchard, V. L., & Albright, M. (2012). Exploring programmatic moderators of the effectiveness of marriage and relationship education programs: A meta-analytic study. *Behavior Therapy*, 43, 77–87. doi:10.1016/ j. beth.2010.12.006

Hsueh, J., Alderson, D. P., Lundquist, E., Michalopoulos, C., Gubits, D., Fein, D., & Knox, V. (2012). *The Supporting Healthy Marriage Evaluation: Early impacts on low-income families.* OPRE Report 2012–11. Washington, DC: Office of Planning, Research and Evaluation, Administration for Children and Families, U.S. Department of Health and Human Services.

Jacobson, N. S., & Christensen, A. (1998). *Acceptance and change in couple therapy: A therapist's guide to transforming relationships.* New York: Norton.

Jacobson, N. S., Christensen, A., Prince, S. E., Cordova, J., & Eldridge, K. (2000). Integrative behavioral couple therapy: An acceptance-based, promising new treatment for couple discord. *Journal of Consulting and Clinical Psychology*, 68, 351–355. doi:10.1037/0022-006X.68.2.351

Jacobson, N. S., Follette, W. C., Revenstorf, D., Hahlweg, K., Baucom, D. H., & Margolin, G. (1984). Variability in outcome and clinical significance of behavioral marital therapy: A reanalysis of outcome data. *Journal of Consulting and Clinical Psychology*, 52, 497–504. doi:10.1037/0022-006X.52.4.497

Jacobson, N. S., & Margolin, G. (1979). *Marital therapy: Strategies based on social learning and behavior exchange principles*. New York: Brunner/Mazel.

Johnson, C. A., Stanley, S. M., Glenn, N. D., Amato, P. R., Nock, S. L., Markman, H. J., & Dion, M. R. (2002). *Marriage in Oklahoma: 2001 baseline statewide survey on marriage and divorce (S02096 OKDHS)*. Oklahoma City: Oklahoma Department of Human Services.

Johnson, M. D. (2012). Healthy marriage initiatives: On the need for empiricism in policy implementation. *American Psychologist*, 67, 296–308. doi:10.1037/a0027743

Johnson, M. D. (2013). Optimistic or quixotic? More data on marriage and relationship education programs for lower income couples. *American Psychologist*, 68, 111–112. doi:10.1037/a0031793

Johnson, S. M. (2004). *The practice of emotionally focused couple therapy* (Second Edition). New York: Brunner-Routledge.

Johnson, S. M., & Greenberg, L. S. (1985). Differential effects of experiential and problem-solving interventions in resolving marital conflict. *Journal of Consulting and Clinical Psychology*, 53, 175–184. doi:10.1037/0022-006X.53.2.175

Johnson, S. M., & Greenberg, L. S. (1988). Relating process to outcome in marital therapy. *Journal of Marital and Family Therapy*, 14, 175–183. doi:10.1111/j.1752-0606.1988.tb00733.x

Johnson, S. M., Hunsley, J., Greenberg, L., & Schindler, D. (1999). Emotionally focused couples therapy: Status and challenges. *Clinical Psychology: Science and Practice*, 6, 67–79. doi:10.1093/clipsy.6.1.67

Karney, B. R., Garvan, C. W., & Thomas, M. S. (2003). *Family formation in Florida: 2003 baseline survey of attitudes, beliefs, and demographics relating to marriage and family formation*. Gainesville, FL: University of Florida.

Kreider, R. M., & Ellis, R. (2011). *Number, timing, and duration of marriages and divorce: 2009. Current Populations Reports*. Washington, DC: U.S. Census Bureau.

Lavner, J. A., & Bradbury, T. N. (2010). Patterns of change in marital satisfaction over the newlywed years. *Journal of Marriage and Family*, 72, 1171–1187. doi:10.1111/j.1741-3737.2010.00757.x

Lavner, J. A., Bradbury, T. N., & Karney, B. R. (2012). Incremental change or initial differences? Testing two models of marital deterioration. *Journal of Family Psychology*, 26, 606–616. doi:10.1037/a0029052

Lavner, J. A., Karney, B. R., & Bradbury, T. N. (2013). Newlyweds' optimistic forecasts of their marriage: For better or for worse? *Journal of Family Psychology*, 27, 531–540. doi:10.1037/a0033423

Lebow, J. L., Chambers, A. L., Christensen, A., & Johnson, S. M. (2012). Research on the treatment of couple distress. *Journal of Marital and Family Therapy*, 38, 145–168. doi:10.1111/j.1752-0606.2011.00249.x

Lundquist, E., Hsueh, J., Lowenstein, A. E. Faucetta, K., Gubits, D., Michalopoulos, C., & Knox, V. (2014). *A family-strengthening program for low-income families: Final impacts from the Supporting Healthy Marriage Evaluation*. OPRE Report 2014–09A. Washington, DC: Office of Planning, Research and Evaluation, Administration for Children and Families, U.S. Department of Health and Human Services.

Makinen, J. A., & Johnson, S. M. (2006). Resolving attachment injuries in couples using emotionally focused therapy: Steps toward forgiveness and reconciliation. *Journal of Consulting and Clinical Psychology*, 74, 1055–1064. doi:10.1037/0022-006X.74.6.1055

Markman, H. J., Rhoades, G. K., Stanley, S. M., Ragan, E. P., & Whitton, S. W. (2010). The premarital communication roots of marital distress and divorce: The first five years of marriage. *Journal of Family Psychology*, 24, 289–298. doi:10.1037/a0019481

Markman, H. J., Stanley, S. M., & Blumberg, S. L. (2010). *Fighting for your marriage* (3rd Edition). San Francisco, CA: Jossey-Bass, Inc.

Miller, W. R., & Rollnick, S. (1991). *Motivational interviewing: Preparing people to change addictive behavior*. New York: Guilford.

Mitnick, D. M., Heyman, R. E., & Smith Slep, A. M. (2009). Changes in relationship satisfaction across the transition to parenthood: A meta-analysis. *Journal of Family Psychology*, 23, 848–852. doi:10.1037/a0017004

Morrill, M. I., Eubanks-Fleming, C., Harp, A. G., Sollenberger, J. W., Darling, E. V., & Cordova, J. V. (2011). The Marriage Checkup: *Increasing access to marital health care*. *Family Process*, 50, 471–485. doi:10.1111/j.1545-5300.2011.01372.x

Petch, J. F., Halford, W., Creedy, D. K., & Gamble, J. (2012). A randomized controlled trial of a couple relationship and coparenting program (Couple CARE for Parents) for high- and low-risk new parents. *Journal of Consulting and Clinical Psychology*, 80, 662–673. doi:10.1037/a0028781

Pinquart, M., & Teubert, D. (2010). A meta-analytic study of couple interventions during the transition to parenthood. *Family Relations*, 59, 221–231. doi:10.1111/j.1741-3729.2010.00597.x

Rogge, R. D., Cobb, R. J., Lawrence, E., Johnson, M. D., & Bradbury, T. N. (2013). Is skills training necessary for the primary prevention of marital distress and dissolution? A 3-year experimental study of three interventions. *Journal of Consulting and Clinical Psychology*, 81, 949–961. doi:10.1037/a0034209

Schulz, M. S., Cowan, C., & Cowan, P. A. (2006). Promoting healthy beginnings: A randomized controlled trial of a preventive intervention to preserve marital quality during the transition to parenthood. *Journal of Consulting and Clinical Psychology*, 74, 20–31. doi:10.1037/0022-006X.74.1.20

Sevier, M., Atkins, D. C., Doss, B. D., & Christensen, A. (2013). Up and down or down and up? The process of change in constructive couple behavior during traditional and integrative Behavioral Couple Therapy. *Journal of Marital and Family Therapy*. doi:10.1111/jmft.12059

Shadish, W. R., & Baldwin, S. A. (2005). Effects of behavioral marital therapy: A meta-analysis of randomized controlled trials. *Journal of Consulting and Clinical Psychology*, 73, 6–14. doi:10.1037/0022-006X.73.1.6

Snyder, D. K., Wills, R. M., & Grady-Fletcher, A. (1991). Long-term effectiveness of behavioural versus insight-oriented marital therapy: A 4-year follow-up study. *Journal of Consulting and Clinical Psychology*, 59, 138–141. doi:10.1037/0022-006X.59.1.138

Stanley, S. M., Rhoades, G. K., Loew, B. A., Allen, E. S., Carter, S., Osborne, L. J., Prentice, D., & Markman, H. J. (2014). A randomized controlled trial of relationship education in the U.S. Army: 2-Year outcomes. *Family Relations*, 63, 482–495. doi:10.1111/fare.12083

Stuart, R. B. (1969). Operant interpersonal treatment for marital discord. *Journal of Consulting and Clinical Psychology*, 33, 675–682. doi:10.1037/h0028475

Swindle, R., Heller, K., Pescosolido, B., & Kikuzawa, S. (2000). Responses to nervous-breakdowns in America over a 40-year period: Mental health policy implications. *American Psychologist*, 55, 740–749. doi:10.1037/0003-066X.55.7.740

Trillingsgaard, T., Baucom, K. J. W., Heyman, R. E., & Elklit, A. (2012). Relationship interventions during the transition to parenthood: Issues of timing and efficacy. *Family Relations*, 61, 770–783. doi:10.1111/j.1741-3729.2012.00730.x

Walton, G. M., & Cohen, G. L. (2011). A brief social-belonging intervention improves academic and health outcomes of minority students. *Science*, 331, 1447–1451. doi:10.1126/ science.1198364

Weiss, R. L. (1980). Strategic behavioral marital therapy: Toward a model for assessment and intervention, Volume 1. In J. P. Vincent (Ed.), *Advances in family intervention, assessment and theory* (pp. 229–271). Greenwich, CN: JAI Press.

Whisman, M. A., Beach, S. H., & Snyder, D. K. (2008). Is marital discord taxonic and can taxonic status be assessed reliably? Results from a national, representative sample of married couples. *Journal of Consulting and Clinical Psychology*, 76, 745–755. doi:10.1037/0022-006X.76.5.745

Williamson, H. C., Rogge, R. D., Cobb, R. J., Lawrence, E., Johnson, M. D., & Bradbury, T. N. (2015). Risk moderates the outcome of relationship education: A randomized controlled trial. *Journal of Consulting and Clinical Psychology*, 83, 617–629. doi: 10.1037/a0038621

Williamson, H. C., Trail, T. E., Bradbury, T. N., & Karney, B. R. (2014). Does premarital education decrease or increase couples' later help-seeking? *Journal of Family Psychology*, 28, 112–117. doi:10.1037/a0034984

Wood, R. G., McConnell, S., Moore, Q., Clarkwest, A., & Hsueh, J. (2010). *Strengthening unmarried parents' relationships: The early impacts of Building Strong Families, Executive Summary*. Princeton, NJ: Mathematica Policy Research, Inc.

Wood, R. G., Moore, Q., Clarkwest, A., & Killewald, A. (2014). The long-term effects of Building Strong Families: A program for unmarried parents. *Journal of Marriage and Family*, 76, 446–463. doi:10.1111/jomf.12094

Wood, R. G., Moore, Q., Clarkwest, A., Killewald, A., & Monahan, S. (2012). *The long-term effects of Building Strong Families: A relationship skills education program for unmarried parents, Executive Summary*, OPRE Report # 2012–28B, Washington, DC: Office of Planning, Research and Evaluation, Administration for Children and Families, U.S. Department of Health and Human Services (OPRE).

14

Forgiveness interventions for optimal close relationships: problems and prospects

FRANK D. FINCHAM, ROSS MAY,
AND STEVEN R.H. BEACH

> It takes a strong person to say sorry, and an even stronger person to forgive.
> – Anonymous

Forgiveness, optimal functioning, and close relationships are the subject matter of this chapter, although scholarly writings have seldom integrated these three core aspects of human existence. Because the present chapter is among the first to do so, it begins by providing some necessary historical context for this exercise. This historical analysis makes clear the need for conceptual clarity, a task that is addressed before moving on to consider forgiveness in close relationships. The efficacy of forgiveness interventions and specifically the possibility of using them to improve relationships are considered next. In the penultimate section of the chapter, several issues are highlighted to advance understanding of forgiveness and optimal relationship development. The chapter concludes with a summary of the main points.

HISTORICAL CONTEXT

Forgiveness is a "goal commonly advocated by all of the world's longstanding religions" (Thoreson, Luskin, & Harris, 1998, p. 164), and it is these religious roots that have led philosophers and social scientists to shy away from the construct until relatively recently. For example, less than 25 years ago, pioneering publications on forgiveness did not contain reference to any published empirical research. But with the infusion of $10 million in grant money in 1998 by the John Templeton Foundation to stimulate research on this topic, scientific studies of forgiveness have since mushroomed (for reviews, see Fehr, Gelfand, & Nag, 2010; Riek & Mania, 2012).

Concomitant with the rise of research on forgiveness has been the emergence of interest in human strengths and virtues among psychologists. Indeed, the formal naming of a field of positive psychology occurred in 1998 by the then APA (American Psychological Association) President Martin Seligman. Like forgiveness, this area has since undergone tremendous growth. Attention has focused on the three pillars of positive psychology – positive experiences, positive individual traits, and positive institutions – as captured in the definition of the field: "Positive psychology is the scientific study of positive experiences and positive individual traits, and the institutions that facilitate their development" (Duckworth, Steen, & Seligman, 2005, p. 630).

Both of these developments took place in the context of steadily growing interest in research on close relationships. In fact, their emergence occurred almost simultaneously with the coming of age of what Berscheid (1999) called, the "greening of relationship science." But neither the forgiveness nor positive psychology literatures emphasized relationships per se. However, in forgiveness research a small body of work has begun to emerge on forgiveness in close relationships based on the view that forgiveness might function differently in this context (see Fincham, 2010). At first glance it may appear that the study of close relationships was integral to positive psychology as positive psychologists openly acknowledged that "close personal relationships are essential to well-being" (Diener & Oishi, 2005, p. 164) and even stated that there is a "three-word summary of positive psychology: *Other people matter*" (Peterson, p. 249, italics in original). Notwithstanding such observations, in their research "positive psychologists have paid relatively little attention to how strengths, well-being, and human flourishing may be embedded in relational contexts" (Maniaci & Reis, 2010, p. 47).

The upshot has been that each of the three domains mentioned above has developed in relative isolation from the two others. An unfortunate consequence is that constructs central to this chapter, such as the nature of optimal relationship functioning, have not been well articulated. As science is advanced more by error than by confusion, we turn to offer a brief analysis of the constructs addressed.

CONCEPTUAL HYGIENE

Forgiveness. Because it is a complex construct, considerable effort has been expended on defining forgiveness. Central to various approaches to forgiveness is the idea of a freely chosen motivational change in which the desire to seek revenge and/or to avoid contact with the transgressor is overcome. This reduction in negativity toward the transgressor has been accepted as the operational definition of forgiveness in the research literature. Researchers also agree that forgiveness is distinct from pardoning, condoning, excusing, forgetting, and denying. Finally, forgiveness is viewed as inherently interpersonal in that it is "outward-looking and other-directed" (North, 1998, p. 19). However, forgiveness (an intrapersonal process) should not be confused with relationship reconciliation (a dyadic process).

Forgiveness can also be conceptualized at different levels of specificity: as a trait, as a tendency toward a specific relationship partner, and as an offense-specific response. Trait forgiveness, or forgivingness, occurs across relationships, offenses, and situations, whereas the tendency to forgive a particular relationship partner, sometimes referred to as dyadic forgiveness (Fincham et al., 2005), is the tendency to forgive him or her across multiple offenses. Finally, offense-specific forgiveness, or episodic forgiveness, is defined as a single act of forgiveness for a specific offense within a particular interpersonal context. Associations among these levels of forgiveness are modest at best (e.g., Allemand et al., 2007; Eaton, Struthers, & Santelli, 2006). In many studies of forgiveness, trait level forgiveness is studied and thus these studies tend to ignore the importance of relationship context for understanding forgiveness.

Optimal relationship functioning. In light of the historical context offered earlier, it is perhaps not surprising that analysis of optimal relationship functioning is nowhere to be found in positive psychology. Even relationship scientists have expended little effort on this task. For example, the definitive *Encyclopedia of Human Relationships* has no entries pertaining to flourishing or optimal relationships. However, there are discussions of positive affectivity in relationships, a defining characteristic of a recent attempt to conceptualize relationship flourishing.

Fincham and Beach (2010) argue that a flourishing relationship

> is emotionally vital; is characterized by intimacy, growth, and resilience (e.g., rising to challenges and making the most of adversities or setbacks); and allows a dynamic balance between relationship focus, focus on other family subsystems, focus on other social network involvement, and engagement in the broader community within which the relationship exists (p. 7).

These authors go on to suggest that a science of relationship flourishing would examine how various processes in relationships (e.g., positive affect, forgiveness, love, trust, spirituality) combine to give partners "a sense of meaning and purpose in life, a sense that their life as a couple is a life well lived" (p. 7). Although this conceptualization is helpful in drawing attention to optimal relationship functioning, it is not without problems (for critiques, see, Caughlin & Huston, 2010; Karney, 2010; Maniaci & Reis, 2010; Walker & Hirayama, 2010). Clearly there is much work to be done in order to characterize fully optimal or flourishing relationships but this is beyond the scope of the present chapter.

Close relationships. Kelley et al.'s (1983) landmark text offered a functional definition of close relationships as those that involve high interdependence as evidenced by frequency, intensity, and diversity of impacts over an extended period of time. Although Berscheid, Snyder, and

Omoto (1989) operationalized this definition in developing the Relationship Closeness Inventory, the field did not adopt this measure as a gold standard for identifying close relationships. Rather it adopted legal (e.g., marriage), biological (e.g., family relationship), subjective (e.g., "close friend"), or temporal (e.g., dating for at least 3 months) definitions of close relationships. Despite being less than ideal, these approaches have, for the most part, served the field adequately.

FORGIVENESS IN CLOSE RELATIONSHIPS

Although most forgiveness research has studied overcoming the desire to seek revenge and/or to withdraw, legitimate questions arise as to whether this decrease in unforgiveness is adequate for understanding forgiveness in the context of ongoing relationships? It is a logical error to infer the presence of the positive (e.g., health, forgiveness) from the absence of the negative (e.g., illness, unforgiveness). Therefore, it bears noting that equally fundamental to forgiveness is "an attitude of real goodwill towards the offender as a person" (Holmgren, 1993, p. 342), and this is especially relevant to ongoing relationships. However, measurement of forgiveness has primarily focused on unforgiveness (avoidance, retaliation), and hence most of what has been learned about forgiveness rests on inferences made from the absence of the negative (dysfunction). Forgiveness research has therefore (unwittingly) focused on human dysfunction in opposition to which positive psychology was born. Although the benevolence dimension of forgiveness is not entirely absent from general research on forgiveness (e.g., McCullough, Root, & Cohen, 2006), concerns about measuring forgiveness adequately in close relationships have led to the development of relationship specific measures (e.g., The Marital Offence Forgiveness Scale; Paleari, Regalia, & Fincham, 2009).

There is some evidence to show that positive and negative dimensions of forgiveness have different correlates in relationships. For example, unforgiveness predicts partner reported acts of psychological aggression in marriage whereas forgiveness predicts partner reports of constructive communication (Fincham & Beach, 2002). Moreover, wives' forgiveness predicts husbands' reports of conflict resolution 12 months later whereas neither spouse's unforgiveness predicts later partner reports (Fincham, Beach, & Davila, 2007).[1] In the first few weeks following a transgression, avoidance and revenge motivation decrease whereas benevolence motivation does not change (McCullough, Fincham, & Tsang, 2003). Finally, Worthington et al.

---

[1] Many studies do not use separate measures of forgiveness and unforgiveness. Instead, they use a single unidimensional measure that comprises both types of items. For ease of presentation the word forgiveness is used in describing results from these studies.

(2007) marshal evidence to show that some peripheral and central nervous system changes do not occur because of reduced unforgiveness but are unique to forgiveness.

Because it is a major component of a popular current approach to couple therapy (Christensen, Atkins, Baucom, & Yi, 2010), acceptance needs to be distinguished from forgiveness. Whereas acceptance implies that the victim changes his/her view of the offense, forgiveness does not require the transgression to be seen as anything less than unacceptable. This is one reason why Gandhi (2000) stated that "the weak can never forgive. Forgiveness is an attribute of the strong" (p. 301). Rather, an individual forgives despite the wrongful nature of the offense and the fact that the offender is not entitled to forgiveness.

Is forgiveness associated with relationship well-being?

From a theoretical perspective, McCullough, Kurzban, and Tabak (2010) argue that "forgiveness systems evolved in response to selection pressures for restoring relationships that, on average, boosted lifetime reproductive fitness" (p. 231). This evolutionary perspective comports well with interdependence theory where relationship maintenance has been integral to forgiveness (Finkel, Rusbult, Kumashiro, & Hannon, 2002). Not surprisingly, then, forgiveness tends to promote prosocial motivational processes that can lead to relationship repair and the re-emergence of a healthy relationship. In fact, it has been argued that the main function of forgiveness is to help "individuals preserve their valuable relationships" (McCullough, 2008, p. 116).

At an empirical level, researchers have investigated the association between forgiveness and relationship quality possibility because relationship quality is widely accepted as the common pathway that leads couples to seek help. An association has been documented between both forgiveness and unforgiveness and marital quality (see Fincham, 2010; Fincham et al., 2005), with some indication of a more robust relationship for unforgiveness (Coop Gordon, Hughes, Tomcizk, Dixon, & Litzinger, 2009; Paleari et al., 2009). Longitudinal evidence suggests that marital quality predicts later forgiveness and that forgiveness also predicts later marital satisfaction (Fincham & Beach, 2007; Paleari et al., 2005).

Turning to mechanisms that might account for the association, Fincham et al. (2004) suggested that unresolved transgressions may spill over into future conflicts and, in turn, impede their resolution, thereby putting the couple at risk for developing the negative cycle of interaction that characterizes distressed marriages. This is further supported by the finding that forgiveness predicts behavioral responses to partner transgressions (Fincham, 2000). However, Braithwaite, Selby, and Fincham (2011) provided concurrent and longitudinal data for two mechanisms linking forgiveness to relationship satisfaction that parallel the positive and negative dimensions of motivational change posited to underlie forgiveness in intimate relationships. The mechanisms involved the relative absence of negative conflict tactics and the presence of increased positive behavior (behavioral regulation), respectively. Each mechanism was found to operate in the presence of the other showing that both are important, nonredundant means by which forgiveness may influence relationship satisfaction. There is also some evidence that trust mediates the forgiveness-marital satisfaction association in the case of both positive and negative forgiveness dimensions (Gordon et al., 2009). Finally, Schumann (2012) provides evidence to suggest that partners with higher relationship satisfaction are more forgiving as they tend to view apologies offered by the transgressor as more sincere.

It is possible to continue in this vein and document further aspects of relationships (e.g., commitment, trust, gratitude) associated with forgiveness but there is no need to do so as it is readily apparent that forgiveness likely influences relationship health and vice versa. Given the link between relationship quality and numerous psychological disorders (Beach & Whisman, 2012), it comes as no surprise that forgiveness is also related to indices of mental health. Across 22 studies involving 4,510 participants a statistically significant inverse relationship emerged between forgiveness and depression ($r = -.26$, Riek & Mania, 2011). As might be expected, higher levels of forgiveness are related to greater life satisfaction ($r = .25$, 11 studies, 2,984 participants) and reported positive affect ($r = .32$, 9 studies, 1,502 participants, Riek & Mania, 2011). In a similar vein negative associations exist between forgiveness and anxiety ($r = -.18$), perceived stress ($r = -.23$), and negative affect ($r = -.47$, Riek & Mania, 2011). These links with relationship health and mental health raise the question of whether it is possible to implement interventions that will increase forgiveness.

Do interventions for forgiveness work?

Various models of forgiving have emerged in the intervention literature (Enright, 2001; Luskin, 2007). However, model builders in this literature have skipped the task of validating their models and proceeded directly to intervention outcome research. Perhaps more importantly, the intervention literature has far outstripped empirical data on forgiveness, leaving us in the awkward position of attempting to induce forgiveness without knowing how it operates in everyday life. Finally, it is important to note that the vast majority of invention studies have not been conducted with clinical populations but instead with community samples.

Several meta-analyses have emerged on intervention research beginning with Worthington, Sandage, and Berry's (2000) summary of 14 available

studies (delivered to 393 participants) that showed a linear dose-effect relationship for the effect sizes they yielded. Specifically, clinically relevant interventions (defined as those of six or more hours' duration) produced a change
in forgiveness (effect size, ES = 0.76) that was reliably different from zero,
with non-clinically relevant interventions (defined as 1- or 2-hour duration)
yielding a small but measurable change in forgiveness (ES = 0.24). These
authors tentatively concluded, "amount of time thinking about forgiveness
is important in the amount of forgiveness a person can experience" (p. 234).

In a subsequent meta-analysis of 27 studies, Wade, Worthington, and
Meyer (2005) showed that although amount of time spent in the intervention
predicted efficacy, intervention status (full vs. partial vs. no intervention)
predicted outcome over and beyond intervention duration. However, the
outcome investigated was limited to forgiveness, making these efforts analogous to a manipulation check. A further limitation is that only group interventions were examined.

Focusing on 16 studies of "process" models of forgiveness, where forgiveness is achieved only after going through several different phases or steps,
Lundahl, Taylor, Stevenson, and Roberts (2008) found large effect sizes for
increasing forgiveness (ES = 0.82) and positive affect (ES = 0.81). Negative
affect was also decreased (ES = 0.54). Participants with elevated levels of
distress benefitted more than those with lower distress levels and participants
who received the intervention individually showed greater improvement
than those who experienced group interventions. In contrast to individual
outcomes, no improvement in the relationship with the perpetrator of the
transgression was found. This led to the suggestion that intervention programs designed to enhance forgiveness may "not be consistently better than
no treatment in improving relationships" (p. 474).

In the most recent meta-analysis using 53 post-treatment effect sizes
involving 2,323 participants who had received a forgiveness intervention for
a specific hurt, Wade, Hoyt, Kidwell, and Worthington (2014) showed not
only that participants displayed greater forgiveness than non-participants or
those who received an alternative intervention but that they also displayed
fewer depressive and anxiety symptoms and greater hope. Importantly, the
effect size obtained for depressive symptoms (ES = .34, studies = 10), anxiety
symptoms (ES = .63, studies = 7), and hope (ES = 1.00, studies = 6) did not
differ significantly from those obtained for forgiveness in these studies.
However, the effects of the intervention for reducing depression and anxiety
were 40–50 percent lower than for forgiveness. Overall, greater change in
forgiveness was achieved in individual as compared to group interventions
and in interventions of longer duration[2] but the small number of studies
involved did not allow testing of moderators for mental health indices.

---

[2] These moderator effects were not significant in comparisons with alternative interventions.

Do forgiveness interventions improve relationships? Notwithstanding Lundhal, et al.'s (2008) conclusion that general forgiveness interventions do not improve the relationship with the transgressor, it is worth asking whether couple-based forgiveness interventions improve relationships. Before doing so, it is noteworthy that the association between relationship health and mental health documented in the above findings provides indirect evidence to answer the question posed in the affirmative. Even though marital therapists note that forgiveness is a critical part of the healing process for major relationship transgressions such as infidelity (Gordon et al., 2005), and survey data support this view (Heintzelman et al., 2014), direct evidence is quite limited.

In reviewing the literature Worthington, Jennings, and DiBlasio (2010) identified 11 couple intervention studies, several of which showed improvements on relationship (e.g., intimacy, satisfaction, communication) and individual mental health outcomes (e.g., anger, anxiety, depression, and global symptoms). They conclude that "interventions to help couples have been found to be consistently effective" (p. 242). Unfortunately, the literature from which this conclusion is drawn includes numerous studies that use small sample sizes (4 of the 11 studies comprise samples of 10 or fewer couples) and are therefore underpowered. Nonetheless, consistent with the basic research findings reviewed earlier, the results of the three recent and adequately powered intervention studies in Wade et al.'s (2014) meta-analysis are worthy of note. For example, Baskin et al. (2011) found that their intervention improved forgiveness (ES = .51) and marital satisfaction (ES = .45) and decreased depressive symptoms (ES = .34); improvements that were maintained at 3.5-month follow-up. Importantly, Greenberg et al. (2010) showed that changes in forgiveness correlated significantly with improved marital satisfaction and trust in their study.

Summary There is compelling evidence that interventions can improve forgiveness and promising data that they also improve individual mental health outcomes, particularly depressive symptoms. Evidence regarding forgiveness interventions in relationships is more rudimentary but suggests that forgiveness, and likely some relationship outcomes, can be changed by these interventions.

Critique Because intervention studies are often experimental in design, they are an important test of the hypothesis that facilitating forgiveness may cause benefits in romantic relationships rather than merely being associated with beneficial relationship outcomes due to third variables. However, interventions are a relatively blunt experimental manipulation that comprises many components and may influence a number of variables. It is therefore imperative that a component analysis is conducted to determine what actually causes change in forgiveness interventions. Such an analysis has yet to be conducted for forgiveness interventions in general or in relation to couples. Its importance is emphasized by findings such as (a) improvements in observed couple communication following a forgiveness intervention unaccompanied by changes in forgiveness or (b) changes in forgiveness without changes in relationship outcomes (see Worthington et al. 2010).

The most important question in intervention research, however, was long ago articulated by Paul (1967) when he asked "*What* treatment, by *whom*, is most effective for *this* individual with *that* specific problem, and under *which* set of circumstances?" (p. 111). The diversity of problems addressed in forgiveness interventions relating to couples (from relatively minor hurts, through men hurt by partners' abortion decision, to extramarital affairs) as well as diversity of samples studied (from community samples engaging in marital enrichment to clinical samples engaging in intensive psychotherapy), do not readily address this question, which requires greater homogeneity in problems addressed, greater specificity of treatment populations, and so on.

Perhaps most troubling in regard to the question posed above is the failure to investigate possible iatrogenic effects of forgiveness interventions. For example, facilitating forgiveness for someone who has a strong social network that encourages a hostile response may deprive the person of social support and, at worst, set him or her in conflict with support providers. In a similar vein, there are some data to show that women in domestic violence shelters who forgive their abusive partner intend to return to the partner, thereby placing themselves at risk of re-experiencing domestic violence (Gordon, Shacunda, & Porter, 2004). What such examples highlight is the danger of decontextualizing the study of forgiveness and its facilitation, an issue that is addressed in considering how to best facilitate forgiveness in the service of improving relationships.

THE WAY FORWARD FOR IMPROVING RELATIONSHIPS THROUGH FORGIVENESS

In considering the way forward, it is worth noting that because hurt in relationships is so ubiquitous, the need for intervention far outstrips available resources as interventions are typically delivered by a professional to an individual or a small group of individuals. It therefore behooves us to conceive of forgiveness interventions more broadly than is typically done. Forgiveness interventions can potentially range from universal preventive intervention (e.g., a forgiveness awareness media campaign), through selective prevention (psychoeducation for those at risk) and indicated prevention (psychoeducation that includes instruction on how to forgive for those who have suffered a transgression), to forgiveness-focused individual psychotherapy. Elsewhere the first author has outlined various interventions using breadth of delivery (reach) and depth of delivery (intensity) as an organizational framework (Fincham, 2015) and has offered a forgiveness intervention approach to relationship transgressions conceptualized as a public health concern (Fincham & Beach, 2002).

In moving forward it is also useful to look for existing interventions in the community that might include forgiveness as well as those that might be enhanced by including a focus on forgiveness. The first author has identified the legal system as a promising starting point because forgiveness is gaining attention in new problem solving courts as well as restorative justice programs, such as victim–offender mediation (see Fincham, 2009). Although ripe with opportunity, such possibilities are also fraught with potential danger if we do not more fully embrace the view that anything that has the potential to help also has the potential to harm. Informed by this observation, the remainder of this section highlights issues that need to be addressed to better ensure that forgiveness facilitates optimal relationship functioning.

Context matters

McNulty has emphasized the importance of contextual factors in understanding forgiveness (see McNulty & Fincham, 2012, for discussion). His research shows that the isolated study of forgiveness may be counterproductive for its facilitation in relationships. For example, McNulty (2010) demonstrated that less-forgiving spouses experienced declines in the psychological and physical aggression their partners directed toward them over the first 4 years of marriage, whereas more-forgiving spouses actually experienced stable or growing levels of psychological and physical aggression over those years. Similarly, among newlyweds forgiveness helped maintain marital satisfaction among spouses married to infrequently hostile partners, but was associated with steeper declines in satisfaction among spouses married to partners who more frequently engaged in hostile behaviors (McNulty, 2008). Finally, McNulty and Russell (2010) demonstrated that spouses' tendencies to forgive their partners lead to decreases in partners' use of psychological aggression over time for agreeable partners but was associated with increases in partners' use of psychological aggression over time when partners were disagreeable.

McNulty (2008) suggests that by removing aversive stimuli experienced by the transgressor (e.g., feelings of guilt, remorse), forgiveness may sometimes increase the likelihood of future hurtful behavior. This perspective is consistent with others in which negative reinforcement maintains aversive relationship behaviors that are difficult to extinguish (Patterson, 1982). McNulty (2008) may be correct in viewing the withholding of forgiveness as a means of regulating partner behavior but his findings could reflect something about the way people communicate forgiveness rather than forgiveness per se.

How forgiveness occurs matters

Forgiving is an intra-individual process even though the referent is interpersonal. As a consequence, a person might forgive a relationship hurt without verbally communicating such forgiveness to the partner or indeed even saying anything about the hurt to the partner. In such cases it is quite possible that the partner infers that his/her hurtful behavior is acceptable. This would be consistent with the view of forgiveness as a negative reinforcer and is likely to have the adverse relationship consequences outlined earlier. Theoretically, such consequences could be avoided by a clear and unequivocal statement from the victim that the hurtful behavior is unacceptable and will not be tolerated in the future. This is fully compatible with also silently forgiving the partner and resuming loving behavior toward them. It therefore may not be necessary to withhold forgiveness in order to regulate partner behavior.

It is also possible to verbally communicate forgiveness to the partner. How this happens is critical. It follows from the above analysis that communication should include a clear statement about the wrongfulness of the hurt and its unacceptability in the future. Beyond this, however, communicating about forgiveness is fraught with danger. This is because talking about forgiveness may lead to harm when it is unskillfully done. For example, forgiveness may be conveyed in a manner that puts down the transgressor or explicitly elevates the forgiver as morally superior to the transgressor. Even forgiveness that is offered in a genuine manner, when done poorly, can come across to the partner as a form of retaliation, or a humiliation. Likewise, if there is disagreement about whether a transgression has occurred, statements of forgiveness may be seen as accusatory. In addition, statements of forgiveness may be intentionally abused. They can be used strategically to convey contempt, engage in one-upmanship, and the like. Likewise, verbal statements of forgiveness may not reflect true feelings. Such statements of forgiveness, without accompanying internal changes, have been labeled hollow forgiveness (Baumeister et al., 1998), should not be confused with genuine forgiveness, and could result in different outcomes.

It is also easy to confuse forgiveness with a specific statement of forgiveness (e.g., Hargrave & Sells, 1997; Baumeister et al. 1998). However, the statement "I forgive you" is not performative. That is why the statement "I will try to forgive you" makes sense. Compare this to the statement "I promise." Because the utterance of the promise statement completes the action (i.e., it is performative) it does not make sense to say, "I will try to promise." Thus because the words "I forgive you" are not performative they really signal the beginning of a process for the speaker (of trying to forgive the transgression), but tend to be seen as the end of the matter by the offending partner – who is also likely to be only too willing to put the transgression in the past and act as if it never happened. This brings us to our next issue concerning time.

Time matters

As noted, forgiveness is not instantaneous but occurs over time, a circumstance that can lead to problems when the offending spouse takes a partner's statement of forgiveness literally rather than as a promissory note ("I am trying to forgive you"). The temptation to equate forgiveness with a specific act at a specific point in time (usually now) is strong. Thus, when hurt feelings regarding a transgression arise after a statement of forgiveness, the offending partner may experience confusion or anger if they believe that the matter had been previously resolved; in the normal course of events, the statement "I forgive you" is more likely to occur than the statement "I want to try and forgive you."

It is also the case that the rate at which forgiveness occurs is a function of the perceived value of the relationship (McCullough, Root, & Cohen, 2006) and is independent of relationship closeness. The issue of relationship value therefore might need to be addressed in facilitating forgiveness. Regardless of perceived value, however, there are data to show that some level of unforgiveness will continue to be experienced. Even those reporting "complete forgiveness" displayed some degree of unforgiveness although the magnitude and range was smaller than for those who endorsed lower degrees of forgiveness (Wade & Worthington, 2003). Attempts to facilitate forgiveness that explicitly or implicitly focus on the complete eradication of unforgiveness are likely to be unrealistic and potentially harmful.

Type of forgiveness matters

A distinction that may be useful to make is that between "decisional" and "emotional" forgiveness (Worthington et al., 2007). Decisional forgiveness is defined as a behavioral intention to control one's negative behavior toward the offender whereas "emotional forgiveness is the replacement of negative unforgiving emotions with positive other-oriented emotions" (Worthington et al., 2007, p. 291). Although it can be argued that this definition is tantamount to relabeling the negative and positive dimensions of forgiveness, it serves a useful function. By using the language of emotion, the temporal dimension becomes salient as control of emotions is not easily achieved and usually takes time. Also, because emotions may be re-experienced long after the event that triggered them it may be easier to cast experiences of unforgiveness as normative even in the face of "complete" forgiveness.

Adding to the distinction noted between hollow and genuine forgiveness, Fincham, Hall and Beach (2005) distinguished between different forms of forgiveness, drawing upon the positive and negative dimensions of forgiveness. Ambivalent forgiveness exists when the forgiver experiences high levels of both positive and negative sentiment toward the offender. In contrast, low levels of positive and negative sentiment characterize detached forgiveness. Complete or genuine forgiveness involves low levels of negative sentiment and high levels of positive sentiment toward the offender. It is unlikely that these different forms of forgiveness follow the same temporal course or function in the same manner. The need to document these differences to ensure that forgiveness leads to optimal relationships is apparent.

Relationship history matters

Each transgression in a close relationship is embedded in a complex relational history and that history will matter. For example, one cannot help a person move toward forgiveness of a partner's one-time infidelity in the same manner that one would treat a couple where the partner had a history of multiple transgressions of this kind. Thus, transgression history influences the forgiveness of subsequent offenses within that relationship, particularly because the avoidance and retaliation that characterize unforgiveness of one transgression may spill over into subsequent interactions. Moreover, chronic transgressions, such as long-standing emotional neglect, do not constitute an event and how partners forgive one another for hurts that are endured day after day is not known. Addressing such issues necessarily entails considering patterns of wrongdoing in the relationship, and in some cases the referent for forgiveness may change to become forgiveness of a hurtful relationship.

Because partners in a close relationship can be both transgressors and victims an important dimension of relationship history is the balance between forgiving the partner and being forgiven by the partner. However, there is only weak evidence of reciprocity in marital forgiveness (Hoyt et al., 2005), suggesting that, at least within these relationships, perceiving imbalance in forgiveness may be a more common experience than perceiving equity. Equity theory suggests that such imbalance would predict negative psychological and relational outcomes. Paleari, Regalia, and Fincham (2011) provide some longitudinal data to support this view in that the effects of forgiveness in married couples depended more on the experienced imbalance between giving and receiving forgiveness than the total amount of forgiveness given or forgiveness received in the relationship, especially for wives. Thus to ensure that forgiveness facilitates optimal relationship functioning it will be important to pay attention not only to partners' propensity to grant forgiveness or to accept it, but also to their perceptions of fairness and equity of forgiveness in the relationship.

The focus and beneficiary of forgiveness matters

A partner's view of who is the primary beneficiary of forgiveness is likely to have important implications for how they, among other things, interpret attempts to encourage forgiveness. Although analyses of lay beliefs about forgiveness identify self-healing as a primary reason for forgiving a transgressor, researchers have tended to overlook the issue of who benefits from forgiveness.

Addressing this lacuna, Strelan, McKee, Dragana, Cook, and Shaw (2013) offer a functional analysis of forgiveness, arguing that transgressor, victim, and relationship can all be (non-exclusive) foci of forgiveness. They go on to suggest that transgressor and relationship foci will be related to both unforgiveness and forgiveness whereas a victim (self) focus will only be related to the avoidance component of unforgiveness. Strelan et al. (2013) provide data that are largely consistent with this perspective. Interestingly, however, concern for the transgressor was associated only with reduced vengefulness and not relationship satisfaction, whereas self-focus was associated with avoidance in the immediate aftermath of a transgression and may therefore ultimately not be beneficial for the relationship. Relationship focus seems to be important for promoting optimal relationships as it was related to benevolent responding, less unforgiveness, and greater closeness and relationship satisfaction.

Self-forgiveness matters

Forgiveness research has tended to focus on victims of transgressions, leading self-forgiveness by transgressors to be labeled "the stepchild of forgiveness research" (Hall & Fincham, 2005). But what is self-forgiveness and why might it be important for relationships? Briefly stated, self-forgiveness is the process whereby a transgressor who acknowledges responsibility for the offence, overcomes negative emotions directed toward the self (e.g., self-resentment, shame) and is more benevolent toward the self (e.g., shows greater self-compassion, and restores self-respect and a positive image of the self; Holmgren, 1993). As long as offenders do not forgive themselves, they are more likely to dwell on the wrongdoing and be troubled by intrusive feelings and thoughts that are likely to impact adversely their motivation to apologize and to seek forgiveness and conciliation toward the victimized partner. So, just as forgiveness may be the victim's relationship-oriented coping strategy that serves as a relationship maintenance mechanism (Rusbult, Hannon, Stocker, & Finkel, 2005), self-forgiveness might be considered the offender's relationship-oriented coping strategy. If this is the case, then one might expect transgressor self-forgiveness to have interpersonal consequences and impact the victim's relationship satisfaction.

Examining such possibilities, Pelucci et al. (2013) found that assessment of self-forgiveness for perpetrating a relationship hurt also yielded two distinct dimensions: a positive dimension reflective of benevolence and compassion toward the self, as well as self-growth (forgiveness of self), and a negative dimension that captured lack of benevolence and compassion toward the self as well as the presence of self-resentment and a negative self-view (unforgiveness of self). For men and women in romantic relationships, both self-forgiveness dimensions were related to their own self-reported relationship satisfaction, whereas only unforgiveness of self was related to partner-reported relationship satisfaction: less negative (but not more positive) thoughts and feelings toward themselves were associated with greater relationship satisfaction in their victimized partners. For the victim, it may be particularly dissatisfying to live with a partner who is prone to negative thoughts and feelings, such as remorse, rumination, guilt, distrust, and depression, fostered by a lack of self-forgiveness (Hill & Allemand, 2010; Mauger et al., 1992). It is also known that offenders who ruminate about the transgression are less motivated to apologize and to ask for forgiveness and conciliation with the victim (Witvliet, DeYoung, Hofelich, & DeYoung, 2011).

The relatively greater importance of unforgiveness of self is one instantiation of research showing that "bad is stronger than good" (Baumeister et al., 2001, p. 362), both generally and specifically in marital relationships (Fincham & Beach, 2010), in that negative events tend to influence emotion, cognition, and behavior more strongly than positive ones (Rozin & Royzman, 2001). This is consistent with interpersonal forgiveness research where, as noted earlier, the negative dimension of forgiveness is a better predictor of both self-reported and partner-reported dyadic satisfaction than the positive dimension (e.g., Gordon et al., 2009). It is also consistent with an evolutionary perspective; being able to recognize and control negative emotions and/or situations is more adaptive than being able to recognize and control positive ones.

In sum, facilitating optimal relationship functioning is likely to require us to pay attention to self-forgiveness as it may help address both personal and relational distress resulting from hurts committed in close relationships such as marriage.

Working toward wise forgiveness interventions

Walton (2014) has identified a new class of brief, focused, and precise interventions analogous to everyday experiences, which he labels "wise interventions" or interventions that "alter a specific way in which people think or feel in the normal course of their lives to help them flourish" (p. 73). They are "*wise* to specific underlying psychological processes" that "contribute to recursive dynamics that compound with time" (p. 76), thereby having the potential to alter consequences downstream.

An example is provided by Finkel et al.'s (2013) study. This study sought to prevent the negativity that develops around conflicts using a simple task.

In the context of a 2-year study in which spouses were surveyed every 4 months, some couples received a perspective taking intervention in their survey where they wrote about how a "neutral third party who wants the best for all" would view a conflict in their marriage and how they could apply this perspective to future conflicts (Finkel et al., 2013, p. 1597). Whereas marital satisfaction, love, intimacy, and trust decreased among those in the control group, they did not decrease for those who received the intervention.

Although not a forgiveness intervention per se, the Finkel et al. (2013) study is relevant as it addressed conditions, conflict in this case, that often give rise to transgressions and hence potential forgiveness. Its success likely reflects the fact that it addressed a critical process that often gives rise to conflict, namely, the failure to see the partner's perspective. Fincham and Beach (2009) have conceptualized this process that gives rise to conflict as a change in goal orientation. They argue that when conflicts of interest arise, couples switch from the cooperative goals they profess and believe most of the time to emergent goals that are adversarial in nature. For example, rather than focusing on generating a couple-level solution to the problem at hand (taking into account the other's perspective), partners find themselves focused on getting their way – or at least focused on not losing the argument to the other partner. Fincham and Beach have used this conceptualization to inform their intervention research on forgiveness.

In several studies, Fincham and colleagues have argued that an everyday activity that is common to most of the world's population, prayer, can be used to facilitate the transition from emergent goals back to cooperative goals. These studies show that prayer has an impact on relationships, including forgiveness in relationships (e.g., Fincham et al., 2010). The focus of this work is prayer for the partner's well-being. They have shown experimentally that such prayer, unlike prayer as usual and several other control conditions, leads to greater forgiveness both in laboratory studies as well as in everyday life (e.g., Lambert et al., 2010; Lambert et al., 2013).

This work draws attention to a way in which forgiveness might be related to optimal functioning that goes beyond the identification of a dynamic psychological process for intervention. Specifically, the exercise of forgiveness facilitates gratification in one of the main realms of life (the interpersonal) and thus contributes to the good life (Seligman, 2002). But forgiveness may also promote a meaningful life. All three of the major monotheistic religions emphasize forgiveness, and the practice of forgiveness in Judaism, Christianity, and Islam can easily be seen as serving something much larger than the forgiver and, therefore, contributing to the meaningful life. However, two very important caveats must be added. First, forgiveness does not necessarily contribute to a meaningful life among the faithful; it will do so only when exercised freely and not as the mindless exercise of a religious obligation (cf. Huang & Enright, 2000). Second, the exercise of forgiveness can also contribute to the meaningful life for non-religious forgivers. However, to do so, it is likely to require the forgiver to be consciously motivated by a desire to contribute to something larger than the self (e.g., create a better community or society) and to view his or her action as contributing to the realization of this goal. At an applied level, the implication is that, where appropriate, efforts should be made to show the link between the individual's action and the service of something greater than the individual, such as God's will for the faithful, or for the secular, the betterment of a social unit (e.g., family, neighborhood, school) or the community as a whole (e.g., through the establishment of more humane norms). In short, attention to an important, but relatively unexplored, issue pertaining to forgiveness is its meaning for the forgiver which may have important implications for how it relates to optimal functioning.

CONCLUSION

Many researchers and clinicians believe that forgiveness is the cornerstone of a successful close relationship such as marriage (e.g., Worthington, 1994), a view that is often shared by spouses in that they cite the capacity to seek and grant forgiveness as one of the most significant factors contributing to marital longevity and marital satisfaction (Fenell, 1993). As this chapter shows, there is some evidence to support the value placed on forgiveness in close relationships, and attempts to facilitate it have been shown to have both individual and relationship benefits. At the same time, however, research is increasingly showing the boundary conditions under which forgiveness is beneficial rather than harmful.

Despite the progress made to date, however, it is not clear how best to facilitate forgiveness in such a way that it optimizes relationship development. The second half of the chapter was therefore devoted to identifying numerous issues to advance understanding of forgiveness in relationships. Such understanding will allow the development of wise interventions that can be implemented as part of everyday life. Given the ubiquity of transgressions in close relationships, easily implemented, large-scale interventions are needed if forgiveness is to be used to facilitate optimal relationship functioning.

REFERENCES

Allemand, M., Amberg, I., Zimprich, D., & Fincham, F. D. (2007). The role of trait forgiveness and relationship satisfaction in episodic forgiveness. *Journal of Social and Clinical Psychology*, 26, 199–217.

Baskin, T. W., Rhody, M., Schoolmeesters, S., & Ellingson, C. (2011). Supporting special-needs adoptive couples: Assessing an intervention to enhance forgiveness, increase marital satisfaction, and prevent depression. *The Counseling Psychologist*, 39, 933–955.

Baumeister, R. F., Bratslavsky, E., Finkenauer, C., & Vohs, K. D. (2001). Bad is stronger than good. *Review of General Psychology*, 5, 323–370.

Baumeister, R. F., Exline, J. J., & Sommer, K. L. (1998). The victim role, grudge theory, and two dimensions of forgiveness. In E. L. Worthington (Ed.), *Dimensions of forgiveness: Psychological research and theological perspectives* (pp. 79–106). Philadelphia: Templeton Press.

Beach, S. R. H., & Whisman, M. (2012). Relationship distress: Impact on mental illness, physical health, children, and family economics. In S. R. H. Beach, R. Heyman, A. Smith Slep, & H. Foran (Eds.), *Family problems and family violence* (pp. 91–100). New York, NY: Springer

Berscheid, E. (1999). The greening of relationship science. *American Psychologist*, 54, 260–266.

Berscheid, E., Snyder, M., & Omoto, A. M. (1989). The Relationship Closeness Inventory: Assessing the closeness of interpersonal relationships. *Journal of Personality and Social Psychology*, 57, 792–807.

Braithwaite, S., Selby, E., & Fincham, F. D. (2011). Forgiveness and relationship satisfaction: Mediating mechanisms. *Journal of Family Psychology*, 25, 551–559.

Caughlin, J. P., & Huston, T. L. (2010). The flourishing literature on flourishing relationships. *Journal of Family Theory & Review*, 2, 25–35.

Christensen, A., Atkins, D. C., Baucom, B., & Yi, J. (2010). Marital status and satisfaction five years following a randomized clinical trial comparing traditional versus Integrative Behavioral Couple Therapy. *Journal of Consulting and Clinical Psychology*, 78, 225–235.

Diener, E., & Oishi, S. (2005). The nonobvious social psychology of happiness. *Psychological Inquiry*, 16, 162–167.

Duckworth, A. L., Steen, T. A., & Seligman, M. E. P. (2005). Positive psychology in clinical practice. *Annual Review of Clinical Psychology*, 1, 629–651.

Eaton, J., Struthers, C. W., & Santelli, A. G. (2006). Dispositional and state forgiveness: The role of self-esteem, need for structure, and narcissism. *Personality and Individual Differences*, 41, 371–380.

Enright, R. D. (2001). *Forgiveness is a choice: A step-by-step process for resolving anger and restoring hope*. Washington, DC: American Psychological Association.

Fehr, R., Gelfand, M. J., & Nag, M. (2010). The road to forgiveness: A meta-analytic synthesis of its situational and dispositional correlates. *Psychological Bulletin*, 136, 894–914.

Fenell, D. L. (1993). Characteristics of long-term first marriages. *Journal of Mental Health Counseling*, 15, 446–460.

Fincham, F. D. (2000). The kiss of the porcupines: From attributing responsibility to forgiving. *Personal Relationships*, 7, 1–23.

Fincham, F. D. (2015). Facilitating forgiveness using group and community interventions. In S. Joseph (Ed.), *Positive Psychology in Practice* (pp. 659–680). Hoboken, NJ: Wiley.

Fincham, F. D., & Beach, S. R. (1999). Marital conflict: Implications for working with couples. *Annual Review of Psychology*, 50, 47–77.

Fincham, F. D. & Beach, S. R. H. (2002). Forgiveness in marriage: Implications for psychological aggression and constructive communication. *Personal Relationships*, 9, 239–251.

Fincham, F. D., & Beach, S. R. H. (2007). Forgiveness and marital quality: Precursor or consequence in well-established relationships. *Journal of Positive Psychology*, 2, 260–268.

Fincham, F. D., & Beach, S. R. H. (2010). Of memes and marriage: Towards a positive relationship science. *Journal of Family Theory and Review*, 2, 4–24.

Fincham, F. D., Beach, S. R. H., & Davila, J. (2004). Forgiveness and conflict resolution in marriage. *Journal of Family Psychology*, 18, 72–81.

Fincham, F. D., Beach, S. R. H., & Davila, J. (2007). Longitudinal relations between forgiveness and conflict resolution in marriage. *Journal of Family Psychology*, 21, 542–545.

Fincham, F. D., Lambert, N. M., & Beach, S. R. H. (2010). Faith and unfaithfulness: Can praying for your partner reduce infidelity? *Journal of Personality and Social Psychology*, 99, 649–659.

Finkel, E. J., Rusbult, C. E., Kumashiro, M., & Hannon, P. A. (2002). Dealing with betrayal in close relationships: Does commitment promote forgiveness? *Journal of Personality and Social Psychology*, 82, 956–974.

Finkel, E. J., Slotter, E. B., Luchies, L. B., Walton, G. M., & Gross, J. J. (2013). A brief intervention to promote conflict reappraisal preserves marital quality over time. *Psychological Science*, 24, 1595–1601.

Gandhi, M. (2000). *The collected works of Mahatma Gandhi* (2nd Rev. ed.). New Delhi, India: Veena Jain Publications.

Gordon, K., Baucom, D., & Snyder, D. (2005). Treating couples recovering from infidelity: An integrative approach. *Journal of Clinical Psychology*, 61, 1393–1405.

Gordon, K. C., Burton, S., Porter, L. (2004). Predicting the intentions of women in domestic violence shelters to return to partners: Does forgiveness play a role? *Journal of Family Psychology*, 18, 331–338.

Gordon, K. C., Hughes, F. M., Tomcik, N. B., Dixon, L. J., & Litzinger, S. (2009). Widening circles of impact: The effects of forgiveness on family functioning. *Journal of Family Psychology*, 23, 1–13.

Greenberg, L. S., Warwar, S. H., & Malcolm, W. M. (2010). Emotion-focused couples therapy and the facilitation of forgiveness. *Journal of Marital and Family Therapy*, 36, 28–42.

Hall, J. H., & Fincham, F. D. (2005). Self-forgiveness: The stepchild of forgiveness research. *Journal of Social and Clinical Psychology*, 24, 621–637.

Hargrave, T.D., & Sells, J.N. (1997). The development of a forgiveness scale. *Journal of Marital and Family Therapy*, 23, 41–62.

Heintzelman, A., Murdock, N. L., Krycak, R. C., & Seay, L. (2014). Recovery from infidelity: Differentiation of self, trauma, forgiveness, and posttraumatic growth among couples in continuing relationships. *Couple and Family Psychology: Research and Practice*, 3(1), 13–29.

Hill, P. L., & Allemand, M. (2010). Forgivingness and adult patterns of individual differences in environmental mastery and personal growth. *Journal of Research in Personality*, 44, 245–250.

Holmgren, M.R. (1993). Forgiveness and the intrinsic value of persons. *American Philosophical Quarterly*, 30, 342–352.

Hoyt, W. T., Fincham, F., McCullough, M. E., Maio, G. & Davila, J. (2005). Responses to interpersonal transgressions in families: Forgivingness, forgivability, and relationship-specific effects. *Journal of Personality and Social Psychology*, 89, 375–394.

Huang, S. T., & Enright, R. D. (2000). Forgiveness and anger-related emotions in Taiwan: Implications for therapy. *Psychotherapy*, 37, 71–79.

Karney, B. R. (2010). A science of healthy relationships is not a healthy relationship science. *Journal of Family Theory & Review*, 2, 42–46.

Kelley, H. H., Berscheid, E., Christensen, A., Harvey, J. H., Huston, T. L., Levinger, G., McClintock, E., Peplau, L. A., & Peterson, D. R. (1983). *Close relationships*. San Francisco, CA: Freeman.

Lambert, N. M., Fincham, F. D., DeWall, C. N., Pond, R. S., & Beach, S. R. H. (2013). Shifting toward cooperative goals: How partner-focused prayer facilitates forgiveness. *Personal Relationships*, 20, 184–197.

Lambert, N. M., Fincham, F. D., Stillman, T. F., Graham, S. M., & Beach, S. R. M. (2010). Motivating change in relationships: Can prayer increase forgiveness? *Psychological Science*, 21, 126–132.

Lundahl., B. W., Taylor, J., Stevenson, R., & Roberts, K. D. (2008). Process-based forgiveness interventions: A meta-analytic review. *Research on Social Work Practice*, 18, 465–478.

Luskin, F. (2007). *Forgive for love: The missing ingredient for a healthy and lasting relationship*. San Francisco, CA: HarperOne/HarperCollins.

Maniaci, M. R., & Reis, H. T. (2010). The marriage of positive psychology and relationship science: A reply to Fincham and Beach. *Journal of Family Theory and Review*, 2, 47–53.

Mauger, P. A., Perry, J. E., Freeman, T., Grove, D. C., McBride, A. G., & McKinney, K. E. (1992). The measurement of forgiveness: Preliminary research. *Journal of Psychology and Christianity*, 11, 170–180.

McCullough, M. E. (2008). *Beyond revenge: The evolution of the forgiveness instinct*. San Francisco, CA: Jossey-Bass.

McCullough, M.E., Fincham, F.D., & Tsang, J. (2003). Forgiveness, forbearance, and time: The temporal unfolding of transgression-related interpersonal motivations. *Journal of Personality and Social Psychology*, 84, 540–557

McCullough, M. E., Kurzban, R., & Tabak, B. A. (2010). Evolved mechanisms for revenge and forgiveness. In P. R. Shaver & M. Mikulincer (eds.), *Human aggression and violence* (pp. 221–239). Washington, DC: American Psychological Association.

McCullough, M. E., Root, L. M., & Cohen, A. D. (2006). Writing about the benefits of an interpersonal transgression facilitates forgiveness. *Journal of Consulting and Clinical Psychology*, 74, 887–897.

McNulty, J. K. (2008). When positive processes hurt relationships. *Current Direction in Psychological Science*, 19, 161–171.

McNulty, J. K. (2010). Forgiveness increases the likelihood of subsequent partner transgressions in marriage. *Journal of Family Psychology*, 24, 787–790.

McNulty, J. K. (2008). Forgiveness in marriage: Putting the benefits into context. *Journal of Family Psychology*, 22, 171–175.

McNulty, J. K., & Fincham, F. D. (2012). Beyond Positive Psychology? Toward a contextual view of psychological processes and well-being. *American Psychologist*, 67, 101–110.

McNulty, J. K. & Russell, V. M. (2010). When "negative" behaviors are positive: a contextual analysis of the long-term effects of problem-solving behaviors on changes in relationship satisfaction. *Journal of Personality and Social Psychology*, 98, 587-60

North, J. (1998). The "ideal" of forgiveness: A philosopher's exploration. In R.D. Enright & J. North (Eds.), *Exploring forgiveness* (pp. 15–45). Madison: University of Wisconsin Press.

Paleari, G., Regalia, C., & Fincham, F. D. (2005). Marital quality, forgiveness, empathy, and rumination: A longitudinal analysis. *Personality and Social Psychology Bulletin*, 31, 368–378.

Paleari, F. G., Regalia, C., & Fincham, F. D. (2009). Measuring offence-specific forgiveness in marriage: The Marital Offence-Specific Forgiveness Scale (MOFS). *Psychological Assessment*, 21, 194–209.

Paleari, F. G, Regalia, C., & Fincham, F. D. (2011). Inequity in forgiveness: Implications for personal and relational well-being. *Journal of Social and Clinical Psychology*, 30, 297–324.

Patterson, G. (1982). *Coercive family process*. Eugene, OR: Castalia.

Paul, G. L. (1967). Strategy of outcome research in psychotherapy. *Journal of Consulting Psychology*, 31, 109–118.

Pelucci, S., Regalia, C., Paleari, F. G., & Fincham, F. D. (2013). Self-forgiveness in romantic relationships: It matters to both of us. *Journal of Family Psychology*, 27, 541–549

Riek, B.M., & Mania, E.W. (2012). The antecedents and consequences of interpersonal forgiveness: A meta-analytic review. *Personal Relationships*, 19, 304–325.

Rozin, P., & Royzman, E. B. (2001). Negativity bias, negativity dominance, and contagion. *Personality and Social Psychology Review*, 5, 296–320.

Rusbult, C. E., Hannon, P. A., Stocker, S. L., & Finkel, E. J. (2005). Forgiveness and relational repair. In E. L. Worthington, Jr. (Ed.), *Handbook of forgiveness* (pp. 185–206). New York: Brunner-Routledge.

Schumann, K. (2012). Does love mean never having to say sorry? Associations between relationship satisfaction, perceived apology sincerity, and forgiveness. *Journal of Social and Personal Relationships*, 29, 997–1010.

Seligman, M. E. P. (2002). *Authentic happiness: Using the new positive psychology to realize your potential for lasting fulfillment*. New York: Free Press.

Strelan, P., McKee, I., Dragana, C., Cook, L., & Shaw, S. (2013). For whom do we forgive? A functional analysis of forgiveness. *Personal Relationships*, 20, 124–139.

Thoresen, C. E., Luskin, F., & Harris, A. H. S. (1998). Science and forgiveness interventions: Reflections and recommendations. In E. L. Worthington (Ed.), *Dimensions of forgiveness* (pp. 321–340). Philadelphia, PA: Templeton Foundation Press.

Wade, N. G., Hoyt, W. T., Kidwell, J. E., & Worthington, E. L. (2014). Efficacy of psychotherapeutic interventions to promote forgiveness: A meta-analysis. *Journal of Consulting and Clinical Psychology*, 82, 154–170.

Wade, N. G., & Worthington, Jr., E. L. (2003). Overcoming interpersonal offenses: Is forgiveness the only way to deal with unforgiveness?, *Journal of Counseling and Development*, 81, 343–353.

Wade, N. G., Worthington, Jr., E. L., & Meyer, J. E. (2005). But do they work? A meta-analysis of group interventions to promote forgiveness. In E. L., Jr., Worthington (Ed.), *Handbook of forgiveness* (pp. 423–440). New York, NY: Brunner/Routledge.

Walker, A. J., & Hirayama, R. (2010), Missing pieces of a positive relationship science: Comment on Fincham and Beach. *Journal of Family Theory & Review*, 2, 36–41.

Walton, G. M. (2014). The new science of wise psychological interventions. *Perspectives in Psychological Science*, 23, 73–82.

Witvliet, C. V. O., DeYoung, N. J., Hofelich, A. J., & DeYoung, P. A. (2011). Compassionate reappraisal and emotion suppression as alternatives to offense-focused rumination: Implications for forgiveness and psychophysiological well-being. *The Journal of Positive Psychology*, 6, 286–299.

Worthington, Jr., E. L. (1994). Marriage counseling: A Christian approach. *Journal of Psychology and Christianity*, 13, 166–173.

Worthington, E. L., Jennings, D. J., & DiBlasio, W. (2010). Interventions to promote forgiveness in couple and family context: Conceptualization, review, and analysis. *Journal of Psychology and Theology*, 38, 231–245.

Worthington, E. L., Sandage, S. J., & Berry, J. W. (2000). Group interventions to promote forgiveness. In M. E. McCullough, K. I. Pargament, & C. E. Thoresen (Eds.), *Forgiveness: Theory, research, and practice* (pp. 228–253). New York: Guilford Press.

Worthington, Jr., E. L., Witvliet, C. V. O., Pietrini, P., & Miller, A. J. (2007). Forgiveness, health and wellbeing: A review of evidence for emotional versus decisional forgiveness, dispositional forgivingness, and reduced unforgiveness. *Journal of Behavioral Medicine*, 30, 291–302.

15

Brief interventions to strengthen relationships and prevent dissolution

JACI L. ROLFFS AND RONALD D. ROGGE

Couples counseling, although effective (see Dunn & Schwebel, 1995 for a review), has long been observed to yield only modest benefits over time with roughly 66 percent of couples showing pre-post treatment improvements in relationship quality, and only 66 percent of those couples maintaining those gains over the first year following treatment (e.g., Hahlweg & Markman, 1988; Jacobson et al., 1984). Although this suggests lasting gains for roughly half of the couples engaging in marital therapy, these results (combined with clinical observations of couples therapists) would suggest that marital therapy often comes too late (or not at all) to help couples (e.g., see Veroff, Kulka, & Douvan, 1976, p. 190). Although many couples (roughly 40 percent) do engage in some form of premarital preparation (Sullivan & Bradbury, 1997), most of the studies that have examined the effectiveness of naturally occurring preparation in the United States have found only small to negligible effects (e.g., Sullivan & Bradbury, 1997), and so the divorce rate in the United States continues to hover just shy of 50 percent and a large proportion of those divorces (roughly 40 percent) occur in the first 4–5 years of marriage (National Center for Health Statistics, 1990). Taken together, these findings suggest a clear need for empirically validated interventions for strengthening romantic relationships as the marital preparation currently being offered does not seem to be stemming the tide of early divorce. They further suggest that the early years of marriage represent a unique window of opportunity to help couples achieve rewarding and stable marriages.

The current chapter will review the array of relationship-strengthening interventions that have been developed and evaluated in the literature to address this issue. These programs typically target couples satisfied in their relationships (screening out couples for extreme levels of relationship discord and distress), with the hope of preventing relationship discord and dissolution before it has truly taken hold within relationships. We will conclude by presenting some new directions involving an intervention that couples can engage on their own in the comfort of their own homes.

ASSESSMENT-BASED INTERVENTIONS

A number of relationship-enhancing interventions have focused on using some sort of standardized assessment to help couples strengthen their relationships and prepare for marriage. This typically involves having partners complete a battery of questionnaires separately, and then bringing them together with a facilitator (e.g., priest, pastor, therapist) to discuss the areas of similarity and difference across their answers. These interventions primarily seek to ensure that couples are going into marriage with similar expectations and beliefs (e.g., PREPARE/ENRICH, FOCCUS, RELATE), but more involved programs also address potentially problematic patterns of conflict and ineffective support through direct behavioral observation and clinical feedback (e.g., the Marriage Checkup).

PREPARE/ENRICH

The format and content of PREPARE/ENRICH   The PREPARE/ENRICH program was initially developed to assist clergy in their work with premarital and married couples (Knutson & Olson, 2003; Olson, Fournier, & Druckman, 1986). PREPARE is specifically designed to assist premarital couples in their preparation for marriage, whereas ENRICH is specifically aimed at strengthening married relationships. PREPARE/ENRICH consists of roughly 200 items with 12 relationship scales (e.g., communication, conflict resolution, finances, and sexuality), 5 personality scales (e.g., assertiveness, self-confidence, and avoidance), 4 couple and family scales, 4 relationship dynamics scales, and an additional 30 customized scales. Counselors working with premarital couples receive a 15-page report based on the couples' PREPARE results and are then recommended to meet with the couple for at least four sessions. The report serves as a guide for the premarital sessions and provides a classification of the couples' typology (see below). Furthermore, counselors receive a *Counselor Feedback Guide* that outlines the six exercises of the PREPARE program which are designed to strengthen couple communication (e.g., active listening, assertiveness, conflict resolution). Couples can also be given the *Building a Strong Marriage Workbook* that includes the material for completing the PREPARE couples exercises (Knutson & Olson, 2003; Larson, Newell, Topham, & Nichols, 2002).

The research on PREPARE/ENRICH   PREPARE was initially disseminated within Christian churches in the early 1980s. To examine its potential for identifying problems that could lead to divorce, Fowers and Olson (1986) called upon the clergy from churches using PREPARE to each identify two to five highly satisfied and two to five divorced, separated, or dissatisfied couples in their congregations that had completed PREPARE 3 years prior. This retrospective sampling technique (selecting couples based on their outcomes and then using archival data to predict between those extreme outcome groups) yielded a sample of 164 couples. Analyses suggested that eight of the PREPARE subscales were effective at distinguishing between those extreme outcome groups. In a highly similar study that retrospectively sampled 179 couples based on their outcomes, premarital scores on PREPARE subscales were able to accurately classify roughly 80 percent of the couples into their 3-year outcome groups (e.g., satisfied vs. dissatisfied/divorced; Larsen & Olsen, 1989). Thus, these analyses would suggest that PREPARE is assessing critical information to the success of marriage.

Cross-sectional cluster analyses in 5,030 individuals completing PREPARE identified four basic types of engaged couples (Fowers & Olson, 1992). These included (1) *vitalized* – the most satisfied couples with high levels of relationship functioning on all dimensions, (2) *harmonious* – couples who were moderately happy with good communication, (3) *traditional* – couples with moderately lower satisfaction who were more realistic about marriage and generally more religious, and (4) *conflicted* – couples with the lowest levels of current relationship satisfaction and relationship functioning across all dimensions. Although these clusters do not necessarily offer any validation for PREPARE itself, they provided researchers with a method of using PREPARE to examine the risk of adverse outcomes across these four groups. Secondary analyses in the same retrospective samples from Fowers and Olson (1986) and Fowers and Olson (1989) suggested that *conflicted* couples were three times as likely to have canceled their marriages, *traditional* couples were least likely to have separated or divorced, and *harmonious* couples were more likely than *traditional* couples to have separated or divorced over the following 3 years (Fowers, Motel, & Olson, 1996), again suggesting predictive validity for PREPARE.

A study of 153 premarital couples examined three conditions: (1) PREPARE program group in which couples received an average of four 1-hour feedback sessions ($N = 59$), (2) PREPARE no feedback group in which couples did not receive feedback until after the conclusion of the study ($N = 46$), and (3) a wait list control group where couples completed the PREPARE program at the conclusion of the study ($N = 48$). Only couples in the PREPARE program group demonstrated increases in relationship satisfaction from pre-test to post-test (2 months later). These results suggest that PREPARE is most effective when couples are able to receive feedback from a professional. PREPARE feedback has also been examined as a 1-day group workshop (Futris, Barton, Aholou, & Seponski, 2011), demonstrating comparable improvements to relationship quality to those obtained when conducted with individual couples as six separate weekly sessions.

The ENRICH inventory is highly similar in content to PREPARE but was designed to be used with married couples. Cross-sectional analyses in a large national sample of married couples who had completed the ENRICH inventory (N = 7261) suggested that ENRICH was able to discriminate between happily married (n = 2664) and unhappily married (n = 2375) couples with 85–95 percent accuracy (Fowers & Olson, 1989). Olson and Fowers (1993) used cluster analysis to identify five types of married couples in a large national sample of couples completing ENRICH (N = 6942): (1) *devitalized* – couples with the lowest scores on all of the ENRICH scales, (2) *conflicted* – couples with a mixture of low scores (e.g., conflict management) and higher scores (e.g., leisure activities), (3) *traditional* – couples with moderate scores on interpersonal satisfaction and higher scores on religion and parenting scales, (4) *harmonious* – couples with higher scores on the marital relationship scales, and (5) *vitalized* – couples with high levels of satisfaction across all the ENRICH scales. As would be expected, these couple types significantly differed in their current overall relationship satisfaction and how often they had considered divorce. Allen and Olson (2001) replicated these typologies in a sample of 415 African-American married couples. Taken together, these results suggest convergent validity of ENRICH to the cross-sectional cluster analytic results of PREPARE, indicating that ENRICH might also be tapping key aspects of relationship functioning. However, no longitudinal studies have examined the prospective utility/validity of ENRICH, nor has the utility of ENRICH feedback been evaluated in the context of a randomized clinical trial (RCT).

RELATE

The format and content of RELATE   The RELATionship Evaluation Questionnaire (RELATE; Holman, Busby, Doxey, Klein, & Loyer-Carlson, 1997) is a 271-item assessment-based prevention questionnaire where the couple rates both themselves and their partners on perceptions of their relationship, individual traits, and relationship satisfaction. RELATE measures four contexts within the couple's relationship: Individual, Family, Culture, and Couple. The individual context is comprised of personality traits (e.g., kindness, calmness, and sociability), beliefs and attitudes (e.g., gender roles, spirituality), and individual characteristics (e.g., age, gender). The Family context assesses family of origin such as the style of the parent's relationship (e.g., validating, avoidant, hostile), the quality of the parent–child relationship, and the family environment (e.g., family stress, trauma, and family tone). Aspects of the Culture context include race, religion, occupation, education, and income. Finally the Couple context assesses relationship traits such as the length of the relationship and cohabitation, interactional patterns between the couples (e.g., criticism, empathy, and defensiveness), consensus between partners on values and attitudes, and relationship satisfaction.

Upon completing the inventory, couples receive a report that organizes similarities and differences that the couple may benefit from addressing. Self-ratings and partner ratings are presented side by side in graphic format. Graphs are divided into three zones to help highlight each couples' strengths, challenges, and areas that need improvement. A unique feature of the RELATE instrument is that couples can interpret and discuss their results entirely on their own with the aid of provided discussion questions or they can seek out a therapist to facilitate their discussion.

Research on RELATE   The RELATE instrument was first examined in an RCT in 79 dating couples (76 percent undergrads). Specifically, couples were randomized to either complete: (1) RELATE (in which couples received the feedback report and then spent six sessions with a facilitator to discuss their results), (2) a therapist-directed condition (in which couples met with a therapist for six 1-hour sessions of traditional talk therapy), or (3) a premarital workbook condition with approximately 6 hours of exercises (Busby, Ivey, Harris, & Ates, 2007). Results demonstrated that only couples in the RELATE condition showed improvements in relationship satisfaction across the 2- and 6-month follow-up assessments, whereas the workbook condition showed stability in relationship satisfaction across time, and the therapist-directed condition showed stability from pre to post treatment and then a decline at the 6-month follow-up.

In a separate RCT, Larson and colleagues (2007) compared three treatment conditions in a sample of engaged or dating couples ($N = 39$): (1) Self-interpretation RELATE condition ($n = 13$), (2) Therapist-assisted RELATE condition ($n = 13$), and (3) a wait list control ($n = 13$). Results demonstrated improvements in relationship satisfaction and readiness for marriage 60 days following discussion for both interpretation groups. However, the use of a therapist to guide discussion of RELATE results yielded stronger benefits than seen in the other two groups. In a more recent RCT of 39 married or cohabiting couples, Halford and colleagues (2012) also explored the potential benefits of having a therapist help couples discuss RELATE results by randomizing couples to discuss their RELATE results on their own or with therapist assistance (via a 1-hour telephone call 1 week later). Comparisons failed to uncover any differences in relationship satisfaction across 6 months between these two groups (Halford et al., 2012), suggesting that couples might be able to make good use of RELATE on their own. Overall, RELATE has demonstrated its usefulness in assisting couples in discussion of their relationship strengths, challenges, similarities, and differences, with evidence that RELATE may be used without professional assistance.

FOCCUS

The format and content of FOCCUS   In addition to the PREPARE/ENRICH program, FOCCUS (Facilitating Open Couple Communication, Understanding, and Study) has been primarily used within Christian churches and is most commonly used by the Roman Catholic Church (Williams & Jurich, 1995). FOCCUS is a 156-item inventory intended to assist premarital couples in exploring their relationship (e.g., personality match, communication, friends, problem solving, parenting, religion, personal issues, finances, and sexuality). FOCCUS has four versions available for premarital couples: (1) A General Edition with no Christian language, (2) a Christian Nondenomination Edition, (3) a Catholic Edition, and (4) an Alternate Edition for those with limited ability to read or have English as a second language. Furthermore, FOCCUS is available in several languages such as Spanish, Polish, Italian, Vietnamese, and Braille, as well as an audiotape version for nonreaders. After completing FOCCUS, couples are provided with a computer report for all the scales, which shows where the couples agree and disagree. Responses are also compared to "preferred" responses, which are responses the authors believe to be the most beneficial to couples (Larson et al., 2002).

Research on FOCCUS   FOCCUS was first evaluated in a sample of 207 Roman Catholic married couples who were retrospectively sampled (based on their notably positive or negative marital outcomes) from a larger pool of couples that had completed FOCCUS 5 years prior during their engagements (Williams & Jurich, 1995). When the various scales of FOCCUS were entered as predictors of 5-year outcomes, all but one of the scales (marriage covenant, a scale specific to the Roman Catholic Edition) helped to discriminate between high-quality and low-quality couples. Consistent with the work on PREPARE/ENRICH and RELATE, these retrospective prediction findings suggest that FOCCUS is assessing important areas of relationship functioning for the early years of marriage.

More recently, the use of FOCCUS has been examined as a tool to promote marriage commitment (Burgoyne, Reibstein, Edmunds, & Routh, 2010). Couples ($N = 42$) were interviewed before their wedding and then randomly assigned to either a marriage preparation group where they could complete FOCCUS and a single feedback session or a non-marriage preparation group. They were then interviewed again 1 year later. The 13 couples actually completing FOCCUS and providing 1-year follow-up data demonstrated stronger increases in commitment when compared to the 16 no-preparation couples. These results suggest that the FOCCUS inventory with a single feedback session may foster a deeper understanding of commitment to marriage. Taken as a set, the limited and preliminary research on FOCCUS has begun to demonstrate its potential utility in strengthening marriages.

Marriage Checkup

The format and content of the Marriage Checkup   The Marriage Checkup
(MC) is an assessment-based intervention that synthesizes both self-reported
and direct observational data into a comprehensive report that offers couples
very concrete advice on how to improve their dyadic functioning within the
context of a motivational interview. The MC was specifically designed to
attract at-risk couples for relationship deterioration who are unlikely to seek
traditional relationship treatment (Cordova, Warren, & Gee, 2001). Thus, the
MC is meant to be a "safe and routine procedure for relationship health
maintenance, early problem detection, and early intervention" (Cordova
et al., 2014, p. 593), and represents one of the first programs in the current
review that does not shy away from more distressed couples but instead
targets them. The MC is composed of two sessions, an assessment session
where couples complete tasks to provide information about their relationship,
and a feedback session where couples receive individualized feedback to
promote change within their relationship (Cordova et al., 2001).

   In the assessment session, couples fill out questionnaires and complete two
video-recorded social support interactions and one problem-solving interaction. Furthermore, couples participate in a therapeutic interview where they
discuss the strengths and areas of concern within their relationship as well as
their relationship history. The 2-hour feedback session occurs approximately
2–4 weeks after the assessment session. Couples receive feedback reports that
are tailored to their specific strengths and areas of concern. Feedback sessions
begin with an overview of the couple's history, followed by a review of their
relationship strengths, and a summary of their questionnaire scores. The
session concludes with a discussion of the couple's concerns as well as options
for how the couple might address these areas. Therapists use motivational
interviewing techniques (Miller & Rollnick, 2002) and acceptance-promotion
strategies of Integrative Behavioral Couples Therapy (Jacobson & Christensen,
1998) to foster increased acceptance, intimacy, and satisfaction as well as to
activate couples in service of their own marital health (Cordova et al., 2014).
Thus, feedback reports strive to (1) provide structured feedback on current
relationship status, (2) highlight personal responsibility of both partners for
change, (3) provide clear advice, (4) offer a variety of alternative choices, (5)
demonstrate appropriate empathy, and (6) emphasize and promote the client's
self-efficacy or ability to pursue change on their own (Cordova et al., 2001).

Research on the Marriage Checkup   The MC program was successfully
piloted in a sample of 29 couples at risk for further marital deterioration
(Cordova et al., 2001), showing consistent pre-post intervention gains in
relationship quality. Thus, although the MC is fairly brief in format, those
results suggest that it would still be appropriate for use in dissatisfied couples.
Additional longitudinal analyses in that same sample suggested that those

pre-post gains were maintained 2 years after the feedback session and promoted treatment seeking in wives over the following 2 years (Gee, Scott, Castellani, & Cordova, 2002). Although these results are somewhat limited by the single group design (lacking a control group), they suggested that a two-session intervention could have benefits over as many as 2 years. In the first randomized clinical trial of the MC, the 39 couples participating in the MC demonstrated significant pre-post improvement on relationship quality in comparison to the 35 no-treatment control couples (Cordova et al., 2005). More recently, the MC program (including a new 1-year booster session) was evaluated in a large scale randomized controlled trial of 209 heterosexual couples (Cordova et al., 2014). Analyses suggested that couples that completed the Marriage Checkup demonstrated significantly greater gains in relationship satisfaction, intimacy, and acceptance (that were maintained for up to 2 years) in comparison to non-treatment control couples (Cordova et al., 2014). Thus, a growing body of work suggests that the Marriage Checkup can offer both immediate and long-term benefits to romantic relationships.

SKILLS-TRAINING INTERVENTIONS

A separate set of relationship enhancing programs have built on the research supporting the efficacy of behavioral marital therapy (e.g., Dunn & Schwebel, 1995) by taking a skill building approach. Thus, these programs begin with the premise, adapted from social learning theory, that relationship quality is directly linked to the patterns of rewarding and punishing behaviors that partners exchange (e.g., Jacobson & Margolin, 1979) and that ongoing negative interactions could easily spiral into coercive cycles of conflict, rapidly eroding relationships (Koerner & Jacobson, 1994, p. 208). These programs are most typically given in a group format where 4–6 couples are brought together for a number of sessions in which they are taught specific skills to more effectively handle central relationship processes like managing conflict, problem solving, and providing effective support, as such processes have been linked to marital outcomes over time (see Karney & Bradbury, 1995 for a review). Such interventions typically include lectures, exercises, and group demonstrations during the workshop sessions as well as homework exercises to be completed between workshop sessions to reinforce the skills being taught.

PREVENTION AND RELATIONSHIP ENHANCEMENT PROGRAM (PREP)

The format and content of PREP

The Prevention and Relationship Enhancement Program (PREP; Markman, Stanley, & Blumberg, 1994) is a 14–16-hour psychoeducational skills-training workshop, typically given over four to six sessions that provides couples with training in communication and problem-solving skills. Much of the skill training in PREP is organized around the speaker-listener technique. This technique was designed to slow the pace of communication by encouraging active listening, helping to ensure that each point an individual is trying to make gets accurately understood and reflected by their partner before that partner responds with a new point. Thus, in the speaker-listener technique couples identify an object as "the floor" and partners are only allowed to share their own point of view when holding the floor. While the partner with the floor is sharing, the other partner is encouraged to actively listen. When the partner with the floor has finished explaining a point, the other partner is asked to reflect that point back, paraphrasing in their own words what they heard their partner saying. This not only helps to ensure a higher level of understanding, but it also helps to prevent a natural tendency for individuals to spend most of their attention on constructing counter arguments while their partner is talking rather than listening. The speaker-listener technique therefore seeks to slow down the pace of communication, keeping it focused on understanding each other rather than sparring in hopes of preventing escalations into negative conflict behaviors like shouting, yelling, and name calling. In a series of 14 psychoeducational lectures, eight exercises, and several homework assignments, couples are taught to use the speaker-listener technique with additional behavioral communication skills (e.g., problem solving, XYZ statements, uncovering hidden issues) to effectively manage conflict in their relationships. Thus, each module in PREP contains a brief psychoeducational lecture given by the workshop leader (typically a mental health professional or para-professional), some skills training time where couples are encouraged to practice using the speaker-listener technique to talk about a specific area of their relationship (e.g., problem solving, expectations, support, friendship, commitment, teamwork, fun, sensuality), and homework exercises.

Research on PREP

In the first RCT of PREP, 42 couples planning marriage were matched on baseline relationship quality and randomly assigned to PREP or a no-treatment control condition (Markman, Floyd, Stanley, & Storaasli, 1988). Couples participating in PREP demonstrated higher relationship satisfaction 1.5 and 3 years after the intervention than couples in the control group, suggesting fairly long-term benefits for such a brief intervention. A non-randomized follow-up study of 114 couples planning marriage demonstrated that the 25 couples completing PREP had lower levels of negative communication behaviors, higher levels of positive communication behaviors, and lower relationship dissolution 4 years after the intervention when compared to the 47 couples in the control group (Markman, Renick, Floyd, Stanley, & Clements, 1993). Similarly, a non-randomized trial of PREP in 96 engaged couples from Germany suggested that the 64 couples participating in PREP had higher levels of satisfaction, higher positive communication behaviors, lower negative communication behaviors, and lower rates of dissolution after 3 years than the 32 control couples that elected a different form of marital preparation.

Building on this work, Halhlford, Sanders, and Behrens (2001) added self-regulatory skills into PREP in an effort to bolster the maintenance of PREP's benefits by engaging spouses more directly in the process of maintaining the new skills. Thus, their modified PREP program (termed self-PREP) taught partners to actively appraise their own skill use, encouraged partners to select their own goals surrounding the integration of the skills into their lives, and encouraged them to evaluate their own efforts at effecting change. Couples were stratified by risk for divorce (with high risk being identified as any couple where the female partner reported parental divorce or where the male partner reported parental male to female physical aggression), and were then randomly assigned to either self-PREP or a no-treatment control group. Analyses in the 61 couples providing 4-year follow-up data suggested that participating in PREP yielded higher levels of relationship satisfaction over 4 years for the high-risk couples. However, participating in PREP predicted lower levels of 4-year satisfaction than observed in the control couples for couples identified as low risk at baseline. Thus, this study was the first to highlight the importance of examining possible moderators of treatment response as its results suggested that not all couples might equally benefit from PREP.

In what grew to be an RCT of 217 couples planning marriage, PREP offered by university research staff (U-PREP) was compared to PREP offered by religious organizations (RO-PREP) and to the naturally occurring marital preparation (NO) offered by a subset of the 57 religious organizations participating the study. Analyses in the first 138 couples recruited for the study suggested that couples participating in PREP demonstrated pre-post intervention increases in positive communication behaviors and decreases in negative communication behaviors (Stanley et al., 2001). Analyses in the 217 couples providing 1-year follow-up data further suggested that RO-PREP couples demonstrated greater drops in negative communication behaviors and greater maintenance of positive communication behaviors (Laurenceau et al., 2004). Finally, analyses in the 193 couples providing follow-up data over the first 8 years of marriage from this sample identified baseline negative conflict behavior as a moderator of treatment effects (Markman, Rhoades, Stanley, & Peterson 2013). Specifically, PREP yielded lower divorce in couples with low levels of observed negative conflict behavior at baseline whereas PREP yielded higher divorce rates in couples with higher levels of negative conflict behavior. As with the findings of Halhlford, Sanders, and Behrens (2001), these results begin to suggest that not all couples respond well to PREP, and some couples might find that it ultimately weakens their relationships.

Shilling and colleagues (2003) examined the potential benefits of a version of PREP modified to be given on a single weekend (termed PREP-WK) in a single group study of 65 premarital couples. The intervention demonstrated immediate pre-post improvement in both male and female communication and better relationship outcomes over the next 5 years. Unexpectedly, pre-post increases in positive communication observed in female partners predicted more adverse relationship outcomes. Although these results began to test shifts in communication behavior as a possible mechanism of change, they also continued to highlight the possibility that some couples might have adverse reactions to PREP.

More recently, PREP has been examined in an RCT of 662 married couples in which one partner is an active duty service member in the United States Army. Given the population, PREP was modified for this study to include examples, videos, and references relevant to military families (termed PREP for strong bonds), and was offered in a weekend format often by the active duty Army chaplain attached to the service member's unit. The study was primarily conducted at a base with a fairly high level of deployment activity, drawing 476 of the couples from that base. Analyses in those 476 couples suggested that PREP was effective at improving pre-post relationship quality and communication skills (Allen, Stanley, Rhoades, Markman, & Loew, 2011) and was also effective at reducing divorce over 1 year (2 percent vs. the 6.2 percent observed in the control couples; Stanley, Allen, Markman, Rhoades, & Prentice, 2010) and 2 years (8 percent vs. 15 percent; Stanley et al., 2014). The analyses further suggested that PREP might have been particularly effective at preventing divorce over 2 years in minority couples (Stanley et al., 2014).

In summary, longitudinal data from a number of randomized and non-randomized trials has suggested that PREP can help to improve couples' communication as well as their relationship quality and stability over a number of years when compared to either no treatment or to naturally occurring marital preparation.

COMPASSIONATE AND ACCEPTING RELATIONSHIPS THROUGH EMPATHY (CARE)

Background

Whereas PREP was derived from traditional behavioral marital therapy (TBMT), the CARE program (Rogge, Cobb, Johnson, Lawrence, &

Bradbury, 2002) sought to build upon PREP by developing a psychoeducational skill-based couples workshop based on an acceptance-based marital therapy. Responding to limitations of TBMT for treating relationship distress, Jacobson and Christensen (1998) developed an acceptance-oriented treatment (Integrative Behavioral Couples Therapy; IBCT; Jacobson & Christensen, 1996). Whereas TBMT employs strategies specifically focused on enacting change (e.g., problem-solving, behavioral exchange), IBCT takes a more emotion-focused approach, targeting ways that partners can empathize with and understand each other's perspectives and building acceptance between partners rather than effecting change. In an RCT of 134 distressed couples, IBCT was shown to be as effective as TBMT in improving relationship quality when assessed immediately after treatment (Christensen et al., 2004) and 2 years later (Christensen, Atkins, Yi, Baucom, & George, 2006), and IBCT was shown to promote greater relationship stability over 2 years than TBMT (Christensen et al., 2006).

Shifting from therapy to prevention

The CARE program sought to build on the innovative work of IBCT by translating many of the interventions used in IBCT into skills that non-distressed couples could be trained to use on their own. The CARE program involves roughly 14–16 hours of training spread out over five sessions and consists of three modules: social support, conflict management, and forgiveness. The core concepts of each of the three modules are described in a series of 16 lectures (15–40 minutes each), and followed up with group discussions, the use of role-plays, transcripts of actual couples' discussions, practice exercises, and homework assignments. CARE shares common goals with PREP in seeking to prevent hostile and attacking interactions between spouses. However, CARE takes a markedly different approach toward these goals by teaching couples skills to approach discussions with greater empathy and compassion, shifting the emotional tone of the discussion toward empathy and understanding rather than using an imposed structure like the speaker-listener technique. The CARE program also differs from the PREP program in that the CARE skills are applied to the domains of social support and forgiveness in addition to conflict resolution, with five of the nine exercises devoted to developing empathy-based skills in these domains.

The CARE program also shares strong similarities to the Relationship Enhancement (RE) Program developed by Guerney (1977). RE is a psychoeducational program offered in a group format in which couples are taught empathy-based communication skills. In the Empathic Responder Mode taught within RE, couples are instructed to go beyond paraphrasing and communicate an empathic understanding of their partner's perspective in a manner highly similar to the amplification technique central to the CARE program (described below). However, in contrast to CARE, the RE program (1) focuses primarily on conflict resolution, (2) does not formally extend the practice of this skill into the domains of social support and forgiveness, and (3) retains a more structured set of rules for switching between empathic listening and expressing modes (the Mode Switching skills) more comparable to the structure provided in the PREP program.

Building empathy through the language of acceptance

The main focus of CARE is to teach couples ways to introduce empathy and compassion into their interactions. The core skill used to promote greater levels of empathy in all three domains is *amplification*. This involves a spouse setting aside his or her own point of view as much as possible and actively taking up their partners' position and arguing it emphatically, going beyond simple paraphrasing, filling in "soft" feelings (e.g., sadness, hurt, loneliness) that their partner might not have mentioned, and validating those feelings. Spouses are asked to "play detective" and explain not only *what* their partner felt, but also *why* it makes sense that their partner might have felt that way.

The use of amplification shifts the focus of discussion away from blaming attacks toward dialog focused on understanding each other, building an environment of Emotional Acceptance (EA) similar to that described in IBCT (Jacobson & Christensen, 1996). By amplifying, spouses are no longer trying to change or blame each other but instead are using empathy to understand and accept one another. In addition, the use of amplification in discussions serves as a powerful form of validation, reducing defensive barriers and creating a safe environment for spouses to open up and be emotionally intimate.

Once again drawing from IBCT, couples are also taught the distinction between hard feelings (e.g., anger, resentment) and the soft feelings that lie underneath them (e.g., sadness, hurt, disappointment). Couples are taught that although hard disclosures are easier to make as they assert control and mask vulnerability, they often come across as attacking and tend to elicit hard disclosures and defensiveness in response. Couples are encouraged to focus on their soft feelings, as these tend to elicit compassion and vulnerability from both sides in a discussion. The use of amplification with a primary focus on the soft feelings involved is called the *Language of Acceptance*, after the equivalent IBCT technique. Given the central nature of this empathic skill, all of the CARE exercises incorporate the Language of Acceptance as an integral component.

Research on CARE

The potential benefits of the CARE program were directly compared to three other treatment conditions in a sample of 174 engaged couples followed over the first 3 years of marriage (Rogge, Cobb, Lawrence, Johnson, & Bradbury, 2013): (1) PREP, (2) a no treatment control group, and (3) a novel self-directed program in which couples sought to strengthen their own relationships by using movies to stimulate semi-structured discussions of their own relationships (PAIR, see below). Couples were initially randomly assigned to the treatment conditions. However, couples were allowed to self-select into the PAIR or No-Treatment groups if logistic limitations interfered with their participation in CARE or PREP (e.g., childcare issues, prohibitively long commutes to UCLA campus, schedule conflicts). Despite being a non-randomized study, the four groups of couples failed to differ from one another on demographics or on over a dozen baseline measures of relationship functioning, suggesting that the groups were roughly equivalent at baseline. Analyses suggested that CARE was as effective as PREP at reducing divorce over the first 3 years of marriage, as both programs yielded divorce rates of 11 percent in couples completing the programs compared to 24 percent in the no-treatment couples. Additional analyses exploring moderators of treatment response over 3 years suggested that PREP had stronger benefits for couples reporting higher childhood family discord and for couples reporting lower levels of empathy in their relationships (Williamson et al., 2015). Similarly, CARE demonstrated stronger benefits in couples reporting lower levels of empathy. These results suggest that CARE might offer similar benefits to those seen with PREP.

COUPLE COMMITMENT AND RELATIONSHIP ENHANCEMENT (COUPLE CARE)

The format and content of Couple CARE

In an effort to increase the flexibility of skill-based training programs – particularly for couples living in remote areas – Halford and colleagues (2004) developed the Couple CARE program. Building on the content of PREP and adding in self-regulation skills comparable to those in self-PREP, Couple CARE is a psychoeducational skill-based training program made up of six modules covering a number of topics: (1) committing to self-change and making change happen in relationships, (2) effective couple communication, (3) intimacy and caring, (4) managing differences, (5) sexuality, and (6) adapting to change. Each module is designed to be completed within a week and begins with the couple watching a 12–15-minute instructional video that introduces the module's key concepts and examples of the relevant skills. The couples are then asked to complete individual and joint tasks from the corresponding section of a companion guidebook. In each module, spouses are also asked to develop and implement individual self-change plans in each area of relationship functioning covered (a central element of the self-regulatory component). After watching the video and completing the guidebook exercises, couples conclude each module by having a 45-minute phone call with a licensed clinical psychologist trained in Couple CARE. This allows a therapist to review the couples' progress with them and help troubleshoot any problems or difficulties that might have arisen. By making the video clips and guidebook available in either hard copy or online formats, Couple CARE can be delivered anywhere from one centralized location.

Research on Couple CARE

Couple CARE was first evaluated in an RCT within 59 couples who were either married, planning marriage, or had been living together between 1 and 5 years (Halford et al., 2004). Couples were randomly assigned to either Couple CARE or a waitlist control group, and analyses suggested that Couple CARE yielded significant pre-post treatment gains in relationship satisfaction and perceived relationship stability. Analyses further suggested that the benefits of Couple CARE might have been stronger for couples with lower relationship satisfaction at baseline. A single-group study of 66 couples completing Couple CARE (including 47 of the couples from Halford et al., 2004) extended these results by demonstrating that lower levels of male negative communication behaviors and higher levels of relationship self-regulation post-treatment predicted sustained levels of relationship satisfaction over the following 4 years (Hahlford & Wilson, 2009). This suggests that Couple CARE was successful at strengthening some relationships by improving communication and relationship self-regulation. Couple CARE was also evaluated in an RCT of 59 newlywed couples followed over 1 year (Halford et al., 2010). Couples in this study were either assigned to complete an online version of RELATE or to complete online RELATE followed by the Couple CARE program. The results suggested that the combination of RELATE and Couple CARE yielded greater improvement in communication behaviors and higher levels of female satisfaction over the following 12 months. Thus, this study provides some of the first evidence to suggest that skills training might offer benefits beyond what can be achieved through simple assessment-based interventions like RELATE. Couple CARE has also been modified as an intervention for first-time parents to help smooth the transition to parenthood (see Halford, Petch, & Creedy, 2010).

SELF-DIRECTED INTERVENTIONS

Self-help books are a multi-million dollar industry, suggesting that individuals have an interest in self-directed approaches to tackling their own problems. Despite this, most relationship enhancement programs have stopped short of developing and validating fully self-directed programs that couples can engage entirely on their own. Arguably, the Couples CARE program (and possibly RELATE) has taken the greatest strides toward developing a program that can be easily disseminated, and yet even the Couples CARE program requires contact with a licensed clinical psychologist, thereby limiting its widespread dissemination. Spouses and couples less comfortable with mental health professionals or attending some form of couple or group therapy might not be willing to even try most of the programs reviewed thus far. However, many of those couples might be willing to try a self-guided intervention in the comfort of their own homes. The following section will review work on a recent self-guided intervention for couples that might meet this need, offering couples a method of strengthening their relationships that is not tethered to a trained clinical provider. As a result, this program offers the possibility of massively broad dissemination with only nominal associated costs.

PROMOTING AWARENESS, IMPROVING RELATIONSHIPS (PAIR)

The format and content of the PAIR program

PAIR encourages couples to use popular movies portraying dynamics in long-term romantic relationships (e.g., "American Beauty") as a method of easing into discussions of their own relationship, thereby facilitating communication and raising partners' awareness of their own behavior. PAIR combines a positive activity (watching popular movies with a partner) with a set of straightforward semi-structured questions touching on various couple processes (e.g., acceptance/empathy, friendship/support, conflict management, negative and positive communication, handling hurt feelings/forgiveness, relationship expectations) to facilitate relationship discussions. The discussion questions were developed to cover comparable content to that in the CARE and PREP programs, asking couples to discuss and critique their own behavior rather than trying to teach them specific skills. Each pair of semi-structured questions specifically asks the couples to first talk about how the on-screen couple handled a specific area of relationship functioning (e.g., "Did the couple have a strong friendship with each other? Were they able to support each other through bad moods, stressful days, and hard times? Did the couple in the movie do considerate or affectionate things for each other?") Couples then compare and contrast that to their own behavior (e.g., "In what way was this relationship similar to or different from your own relationship in this area?"). Feedback from couples trying the PAIR program suggests that they find this an easier and less threatening method of talking about their own relationships as the discussion of the on-screen couple helps to provide some emotional distance and helps to normalize (and even diffuse with humor) maladaptive behaviors about which spouses might otherwise be defensive. PAIR offers couples a list of over 100 pre-screened movies, chosen to ensure that each movie will portray enough relationship dynamics to prompt useful comparative discussions. The PAIR program is currently presented as a set of interactive online tools (www.couples-research.com). Couples are encouraged to watch five movies together over the course of a month, with a 30–45-minute discussion following each movie. The interactive PAIR tools send couples weekly automated email reminders with links to the movie lists and discussion questions. For interested couples, the online tools also offer pre and post PAIR assessments that provide individualized feedback on the health of their relationship, comparing their responses to those of thousands of respondents across a number of dimensions (e.g., support, conflict, forgivingness). It should be noted that those pre and post assessments are not conceptualized as integral parts of the CARE program, but as incentives for couples to engage the online tools.

Research on PAIR

The PAIR program was first tested by Rogge and colleagues (2013) in their non-randomized clinical trial of the CARE and PREP programs. PAIR was a separate treatment condition in that study (termed Relational Awareness in that manuscript) and was included primarily as a control to help determine how much couples could strengthen their own relationships without any formal skill training. As mentioned above, the 33 newlywed couples completing the PAIR program appeared to be equivalent to the couples in the CARE, PREP, and No-Treatment groups at baseline across demographic and relationship factors. The longitudinal results of the study suggested that PAIR was as effective as the CARE and PREP programs, yielding 11 percent divorce/separation over the first 3 years of marriage in comparison to the 11, 11, and 24 percent seen in the CARE, PREP, and No-Treatment conditions respectively (Rogge et al., 2013). These unexpected results suggested that for at least some newlywed couples, it might not be necessary to go through formal skill training to strengthen their relationships. More recently, the PAIR program was evaluated in a single group study of 74 couples of various relationship stages (61 percent married an average of 16 years, 10 percent engaged, 39 percent dating an average of 4 years) engaging the PAIR online tools (Rogge, Crasta, Maniaci, Funk, & Lee, under review). These couples were not only more diverse than the couples in the Rogge and colleagues (2013) sample in the relationship stages represented, but also in the range of relationship satisfaction within the sample. As couples were not screened out of the online tools for being too dissatisfied or distressed (in sharp contrast to a majority of the studies reviewed above), 36 percent of the married participants, 14 percent of the engaged participants, and 27 percent of the dating participants fell below commonly accepted thresholds of dissatisfaction on relationship satisfactions measures. Within the 74 couples providing pre and post (1 month) data, 54 of the couples had engaged in at least one movie-based discussion. Although those 54 couples participating in PAIR failed to demonstrate any differences from the remaining 20 no-treatment couples on baseline measures of relationship satisfaction, the longitudinal analyses suggested that PAIR demonstrated significant gains in relationship satisfaction in comparison to the no-treatment condition (Rogge et al., under review). This result suggests that PAIR might be effective at strengthening relationships across a wide range of relationship stages and across a wide range of relationship functioning.

SUMMARY/FUTURE DIRECTIONS

The body of work reviewed in this chapter has demonstrated that fairly brief and focused interventions can be effective at strengthening relationships over as long as 8 years. Although the individual programs can be notably distinct from one another in form and focus, when taken as a set they also seem to be narrowing in on a key set of processes critical for relationship success like managing conflict, sustaining friendship, and handling stressors as a team. Despite the convergence of findings within this literature, this review of the relationship enhancement literature has also highlighted some of the next critical steps in this area.

Need for dissemination

Although the programs reviewed hold the promise of helping individuals achieve and maintain more rewarding and satisfying relationships, we would argue that that promise is far from realized. Although roughly 30–40 percent of couples in the United States receive some sort of preparation prior to marriage (e.g., Sullivan & Bradbury, 1997), longitudinal results suggest that the naturally occurring preparation most couples receive either offers fairly weak benefits (e.g., Schumm, Resnick, Silliman, & Bell, 1998; Stanley, Amato, Johnson, & Markman, 2006) or possibly no consistent benefits (e.g., Sullivan & Bradbury, 1997; Fawcett Hawkins, Blanchard, & Carroll, 2010). This might be due to the fact that 90 percent of the marital preparation offered to couples is offered informally through religious organizations (Glenn, 2005) and does not involve one of the empirically supported programs reviewed in this chapter. In fact, a recent poll of religious leaders from the United States suggested that religious preparation often simply involves meetings with a priest or pastor (Wilmoth & Smyser, 2012). Thus, there is a clear need to disseminate these research-based programs at a broader scale. Although the creators of PREP have invested over 20 years of tremendous effort into dissemination they still have likely tapped into a very small fraction of the possible market for their program. Similarly, the creators of Couple CARE have developed and begun to validate a more portable form of relationship enhancement, but have yet to truly disseminate it across entire countries. Given the promising findings for the PAIR program, we would suggest that research and development of self-directed programs like PAIR might offer researchers a method of truly reaching a broad spectrum of couples. For example, a few weeks of (no-cost) media coverage following the initial paper on PAIR was successful in drawing over 40,000 interested individuals to the PAIR online materials. More targeted efforts with even a modest budget could potentially reach millions of couples who might be willing to give such a program a try.

Need for comparison and deconstruction

Following a similar trend in the larger treatment literature, we would argue that when taken as a set, the empirically developed relationship enhancement programs reviewed here have more than demonstrated their ability to benefit romantic relationships compared to no-treatment or treatment as usual conditions. We would argue that it is now time to push the control conditions used in RCTs of such programs further. As exemplified by the findings with PAIR (Rogge et al., 2013), including a minimal treatment control that takes specific sub-elements of a more elaborate intervention and evaluates them separately can lead to ground breaking insights. In the case of PAIR, including that control condition has led to a very promising intervention in its own right. Similarly, the results contrasting RELATE to RELATE with Couples CARE (Halford et al., 2010) helped to highlight the advantages of Couples CARE beyond what could be obtained from a comprehensive assessment approach. We would argue that our understanding of strengthening relationships will be most markedly advanced by RCTs contrasting active treatments and RCTs that deconstruct interventions into their component parts across intervention conditions. For example, even a fairly simply intervention like PAIR could be deconstructed by using control conditions to determine if it is simply increased time together that is the true active agent or if relationship discussions are necessary to obtain the observed benefits. Such studies would allow us to not only identify the critical components of any intervention, but subsequent moderation analyses would also allow us to identify which components might be most effective for specific types of couples. Thus, by shifting toward RCTs that focus on uncovering the critical elements of couples interventions, we might ultimately be able to tailor interventions to the specific needs of individual couples.

Need for diversity

Despite the robust set of findings reviewed in the current chapter, the majority of the samples were predominantly white and fairly well educated. It is not reasonable to assume that the efficacy of interventions developed in middle class samples will generalize to more diverse samples. It will be important for future studies to seek out diverse samples. Several recent studies have begun to address this issue. The sample in the recent study contrasting CARE, PREP, and PAIR (Rogge et al., 2013) was notably diverse (55 percent Caucasian, 21 percent Latino/Hispanic, 11 percent Asian, 13 percent other/biracial) and the study examining PREP in a military sample (Allen et al., 2011) included a high proportion of couples with a minority spouse (40 percent) and lower levels of SES (e.g., a majority of husbands and wives reported no more than a high school education). Despite the promising results in these studies, future work needs to examine relationship enhancing interventions across a wide range of sociocultural groups, as recent results also suggest that such groups might yield significantly different findings (e.g., Stanley et al., 2014).

CONCLUSION

The research reviewed in this chapter identifies a number of promising interventions for strengthening relationships and preventing divorce. By targeting relationship processes shown to be important for relationship outcomes over time (e.g., negative conflict, social support, forgiveness; see Karney & Bradbury, 1995 for a review), these interventions help couples have more rewarding and fulfilling relationships. Although each intervention might not be without its own faults, when taken as a set, the results across these interventions offer couples tangible methods of enhancing their relationships over several years with as little as 4–16 hours of investment.

REFERENCES

Allen, E. S., Stanley, S. M., Rhoades, G. K., Markman, H. J., & Loew, B. A. (2011). Marriage education in the Army: Results of a randomized clinical trial. *Journal of Couple and Relationship Therapy*, 10, 309–326. doi:10.1080/15332691.2011.613309

Allen, W. D., & Olson, D. H. (2001). Five types of African-American marriages. *Journal of Marital and Family Therapy*, 27, 301–314.

Burgoyne, C. B., Reibstein, J., Edmunds, A. M., & Routh, D. A. (2010). Marital commitment, money and marriage preparation: What changes after the wedding?

Journal of Community & Applied Social Psychology, 20, 390–403. doi:10.1002/casp.1045

Busby, D. M., Ivey, D. C., Harris, S. M., & Ates, C. (2007). Self-directed, therapist-directed, and assessment-based interventions for premarital couples. *Family Relations, 56*, 279–290. doi:10.1111/j.1741-3729-2007.00459.x

Christensen, A., Atkins, D. C., Berns, S., Wheeler, J., Baucom, D. H., & Simpson, L. E. (2004). Traditional versus integrative behavioral couple therapy for significantly and chronically distressed marital couples. *Journal of Consulting and Clinical Psychology, 72*, 176–191. doi:10.1037/0022-006X.72.2.176

Christensen, A., Atkins, D. C., Yi, J., Baucom, D. H., & George, W. H. (2006). Couple and individual adjustment for 2 years following a randomized clinical trial comparing traditional versus integrative behavioral couple therapy. *Journal of Consulting and Clinical Psychology, 74*, 1180–1191. doi:10.1037/0022-006X.74.6.1180

Cordova, J. V., Fleming, E., Morrill, M. I., Hawrilenko, M., Sollenberg, J. W., Harp, A. G., Gray, T. D., Darling, E. V., Blair, J. M., Meade, A. E., & Wachs, K. (2014). The marriage checkup: A randomized controlled trial of annual relationship health checkups. *Journal of Consulting and Clinical Psychology, 82*, 592–604. doi:10.1037/a0037097

Cordova, J. V., Scott, R. L., Dorian, M., Mirgain, S., Yeager, D., & Groot, A. (2005). The marriage checkup: An indicated preventive intervention for treatment-avoidant couples at risk for marital deterioration. *Behavior Therapy, 36*, 301–309. doi:10.1016/S0005-7894(05)80112-1

Cordova, J. V., Warren, L. Z., & Gee, C. B. (2001). Motivational interviewing as an intervention for at-risk couples. *Journal of Marital and Family Therapy, 27*, 315–326. doi:10.1111/j.1752-0606.2001.tb00327.x

Dunn, R. L., & Schwebel, A. I. (1995). Meta-analytic review of marital therapy outcome research. *Journal of Family Psychology, 9*, 58–68. doi:10.1037/0893-3200.9.1.58

Fawcett, E. B., Hawkins, A. J., Blanchard, V. L., & Carroll, J. S. (2010). Do premarital education programs really work? A meta-analytic study. *Family Relations, 59*, 232–239.

Fowers, B. J., Montel, K. H., & Olson, D. H. (1996). Predicting marital success for premarital couples types based on PREPARE. *Journal of Marital and Family Therapy, 22*, 103–119. doi:10.1111/j.1752-0606.1996.tb00190.x

Fowers, B. J., & Olson, D. H. (1986). Predicting marital success with PREPARE: A predictive validity study. *Journal of Marital and Family Therapy, 12*, 403–413. doi:10.1111/j.1752-0606.1986.tb00673.x

Fowers, B. J., & Olson, D. H. (1989). ENRICH martial inventory: A discriminant validity and cross-validity assessment. *Journal of Marital and Family Therapy, 15*, 65–79.

Fowers, B. J., & Olson, D. H. (1992). Four types of premarital couples: An empirical typology based on PREPARE. *Journal of Family Psychology, 6*, 10–21.

Futris, T. G., Barton, A. W., Aholou, T. M., & Seponski, D. M. (2011). The impact of PREPARE on engaged couples: Variations by delivery format. *Journal of Couple & Relationship Therapy, 10*, 69–86. doi:10.1080/15332691.2011.539175

Gee, C. B., Scott, R. L., Castellani, A. M., & Cordova, J. V. (2002). Predicting 2-year marital satisfaction from partners' discussion of their marriage checkup. *Journal of Marital and Family Therapy, 28*, 399–407. doi:10.1111/j.1752-0606.2002.tb00365.x

Glen, N. D. (2005). *With this ring: A national survey on marriage in America.* Washington, DC: National Fatherhood Initiative.

Guerney, B. (1977). *Relationship enhancement.* San Francisco, CA: Jossey-Bass, Inc.

Hahlweg, K., & Markman, H. J. (1988). Effectiveness of behavioral marital therapy: Empirical status of behavioral techniques in preventing and alleviating marital distress. *Journal of Consulting and Clinical Psychology*, 56, 440–477.

Halford, W. K., Chen, R., Wilson, K. L., Larson, J., Busby, D., & Holman, T. (2012). Does therapist guidance enhance assessment-based feedback as couple relationship education? *Behaviour Change*, 29, 199–212. doi:10.1017/bec.2012.20

Halford, W. K., Moore, E., Wilson, K. L., Farrugia, C., & Dyer, C. (2004). Benefits of flexible delivery relationship education: An evaluation of the Couple CARE program. *Family Relations*, 53, 469–476.

Halford, W. K., Petch, J., & Creedy, D. K. (2010). Promoting a positive transition to parenthood: A randomized clinical trial of couple relationship education. *Prevention Science*, 11, 89–100. doi:10.1007/s11121-009-0152-y

Halford, W. K., Sanders, M. R., & Behrens, B. C. (2001). Can skills training prevent relationship problems in at-risk couples? Four-year effects of a behavioral relationship education program. *Journal of Family Psychology*, 15, 750–768. doi:10.1111/j.1741-3729.2001.00067.x

Halford, W. K., & Wilson, K. L. (2009). Predictors of relationship satisfaction four years after completing flexible delivery couple relationship education. *Journal of Couple & Relationship Therapy: Innovations in Clinical and Educational Interventions*, 8, 143–161, doi:10.1080/15332690902813828

Halford, W. K., Wilson, K., Watson, B., Verner, T., Larson, J., Busby, D., & Holman, T. (2010). Couple relationship education at home: Does skill training enhance relationship assessment and feedback? *Journal of Family Psychology*, 24, 188–196.

Holman, T. B., Busby, D. M., Doxey, C., Klein, D. M., & Loyer-Carlson, V. (1997). *The Relationship Evaluation (RELATE)*. Provo, UT: RELATE Institute.

Jacobson, N. S., & Christensen, A. (1996). *Integrative couple therapy: Promoting acceptance and change*. New York: WW Norton & Co.

Jacobson, N. S., & Christensen, A. (1998). *Acceptance and change in couple therapy: A therapist's guide to transforming relationships*. New York, NY: Norton.

Jacobson, N. S., Follette, W. C., Revenstorf, D., Baucom, D. H., Hahlweg, K., & Margolin, G. (1984). Variability in outcome and clinical significance of behavioral marital therapy: A reanalysis of outcome data. *Journal of Consulting and Clinical Psychology*, 52, 497–504.

Jacobson, N. S., & Margolin, G. (1979). *Marital therapy: Strategies based on social learning and behavior exchange principles*. New York: Brunner/Mazel.

Karney, B. R., & Bradbury, T. N. (1995). The longitudinal course of marital quality and stability: A review of theory, method, and research. *Psychological Bulletin*, 118, 3–34.

Knutson, L., & Olson, D. H. (2003). Effectiveness of PREPARE program with premarital couples in community settings. *Marriage & Family*, 6, 529–546.

Koerner, K., & Jacobson, N. S. (1994). Emotion and behavioral couple therapy. In S. M. Johnson & L. S. Greenberg (Eds.), *The heart of the matter: Perspectives on emotion in marital therapy* (pp. 207–226). New York: Brunner/Mazel.

Larsen, A. S., & Olson, D. H. (1989). Predicting marital satisfaction using PREPARE: A replication study. *Journal of Marital and Family Therapy*, 15, 311–322. doi:10.1111/j.1752-0606.1989.tb00812.x

Larson, J. H., Newell, K., Topham, G., & Nichols, S. (2002). A review of three comprehensive premarital assessment questionnaires. *Journal of Marital and Family Therapy*, 28, 233–239. doi:10.1111/j.1752-0606.2002.tb00360.x

Laurenceau, J. P., Stanley, S. M., Olmos-Gallo, A., Baucom, B., & Markman, H. J. (2004). Community-based prevention of marital dysfunction: Multilevel modeling of a randomized effectiveness study. *Journal of Consulting and Clinical Psychology*, 72, 933–943. doi:10.1037/0022-006X.72.6.933

Markman, H. J., Floyd, F. J., Stanley, S. M., & Storaasli, R. D. (1988). Prevention of marital distress: A longitudinal investigation. *Journal of Consulting and Clinical Psychology*, 56, 210–217. doi:10.1037/0022-006X.56.2.210

Markman, H. J., Renick, M. J., Floyd, F. J., Stanley, S. M., & Clements, M. (1993). Preventing marital distress through communication and conflict management training: A 4- and 5-year follow-up. *Journal of Consulting and Clinical Psychology*, 61, 70–77. doi:10.1037/0022-006X.61.1.70

Markman, H. J., Rhoades, G. K., Stanley, S. M., & Peterson, K. M. (2013). A randomized clinical trial of the effectiveness of premarital intervention: Moderators of divorce outcomes. *Journal of Family Psychology*, 27, 165–172. doi:10.1037/a0031134

Markman, H. J., Stanley, S., & Blumberg, S. L. (1994). *Fighting for your marriage*. San Francisco, CA: Jossey-Bass.

Miller, W. R., & Rollnick, S. (2002). *Motivational interviewing: Preparing people for change* (2nd ed.). New York, NY: Guilford Press.

National Center for Health Statistics (1990). Advance Report of Final Marriage Statistics, Monthly Vital Statistics Report, 38, Supplement.

Olson, D. H., Fournier, D. G., & Druckman, J. M. (1986) *Counselor's Manual for PREPARE-ENRICH*. (rev. ed.), Minneapolis, MN: PREPARE-ENRICH, Inc.

Olson, D. H., & Fowers, B. J. (1993). Five types of marriage: An empirical typology based on ENRICH. *The Family Journal*, 3, 196–207.

Rogge, R. D., Cobb, R. M., Johnson, M. D., Lawrence, E. E., & Bradbury, T. N. (2002). The CARE Program: A Preventive Approach to Marital Intervention. In A. Gurman & N. Jacobson (Eds.), *Clinical Handbook of Couple Therapy* (pp. 420–435). New York: Guilford.

Rogge, R. D., Cobb, R. M., Lawrence, E., Johnson, M. D., & Bradbury, T. N. (2013). Is skills training necessary for the primary prevention of marital distress and dissolution? A 3-year experimental study of three interventions. *Journal of Consulting and Clinical Psychology*, 81, 949–961. doi:10.1037/a0034209

Rogge, R. D., Crasta, D, Maniaci, M. R., Funk, J. L., Lee, S. (under review). *How well can we detect shifts in relationship satisfaction over time? Evaluating responsiveness to change in relationship satisfaction scales.*

Schilling, E. A., Baucom, D. H., Burnett, C. K., Allen, E. S., & Ragland, L. (2003). Altering the course of marriage: The effect of PREP communication skills acquisition on couples' risk of becoming martially distressed. *Journal of Family Psychology*, 17, 41–53. doi:10.1037/0893-3200.17.1.41

Schumm, W. R., Resnick, G., Silliman, B., & Bell, D. B. (1998). Premarital counseling and marital satisfaction among civilian wives of military service members. *Journal of Sex and Marital Therapy*, 24(1), 21–28.

Stanley, S. M., Allen, E. S., Markman, H. J., Rhoades, G. K., & Prentice, D. (2010). Decreasing divorce in Army couples: Results from a randomized controlled trial of PREP for Strong Bonds. *Journal of Couple and Relationship Therapy*, 9, 149–160. doi:10.1080/15332691003694901

Stanley, S. M., Amato, P. R., Johnson, C. A., & Markman, H. J. (2006). Premarital education, marital quality, and marital stability: Findings from a large, random household survey. *Journal of Family Psychology*, 20(1), 117–126.

Stanley, S. M., Markman, H. J., Prado, L. M., Olmos-Gallo, P. A., Tonelli, L., St. Peters, M., Leber, B. D., Bobulinski, M., Cordova, A., & Whitton, S. W. (2001). Community-based premarital prevention: Clergy and lay leaders on the front lines. *Family Relations*, 50, 67–76. doi:10.1111/j.1741-3729.2001.00067.x

Stanley, S. M., Rhoades, G. K., Loew, B. A., Allen, E. S., Carter, S., Osborne, L. J., Prentice, D., & Markman, H. J. (2014). A randomized controlled trial of relationship education in the U.S. Army: 2-year outcomes. *Family Relations*, 63, 482–495. doi:10.1111/fare.12083

Sullivan, K. T., & Bradbury, T. N. (1997). Are premarital prevention programs reaching couples at risk for marital dysfunction? *Journal of Consulting and Clinical Psychology*, 65, 24–30. doi:10.1037/0022-006X.65.1.24

Veroff, J., Kulka, R. A., & Douvan, E. (1976). *Mental health in America*. New York: Basic Books.

Williams, L., & Jurich, J. (1995). Predicting marital success after five years: Assessing the predictive validity of FOCCUS. *Journal of Marital and Family Therapy*, 21, 141–153. doi:10.1111/j.1752-0606.1995.tb00149.

Williamson, H. C., Rogge, R. D., Cobb, R. J., Johnson, M. D., Lawrence, E., & Bradbury, T. N. (2015). Risk moderates the outcome of relationship education: A randomized controlled trial. *Journal of Consulting and Clinical Psychology*. Advance online publication. doi:10.1037/a0038621

Wilmonth, J. D., & Smyser, S. (2012). A national survey of marriage preparation provided by clergy. *Journal of Couple & Relationship Therapy*, 11, 69–85.

INDEX

CPSIA information can be obtained
at www.ICGtesting.com
Printed in the USA
LVOW05*1445020616
490957LV00013B/150/P